Thinking in the Light of Time

Heidegger's Encounter with Hegel

Karin de Boer

State University of New York Press

Published by
State University of New York Press, Albany

Printed in the United States of America

First published in Dutch in 1997 by Van Gorcum as *Denken in het licht van de tijd. Heideggers tweestrijd met Hegel*.

The translation was made possible by a grant from the Netherlands Organization for Scientific Research (NWO).

For information, address State University of New York Press,
State University Plaza, Albany, N.Y. 12246

Production by Diane Ganeles
Marketing by Patrick Durocher

Library of Congress Cataloging-in-Publication Data

Boer, Karin de.
[Denken in het licht van de tijd. English]
Thinking in the light of time : Heidegger's encounter with Hegel / Karin de Boer.
p. cm. — (SUNY series in contemporary continental philosophy)
Includes bibliographical references and index.
ISBN 0-7914-4505-4 (hardcover : alk. paper). — ISBN 0-7914-4506-2 (pbk. : alk. paper)
1. Heidegger, Martin, 1889–1976—Contributions in concept of the finite. 2. Finite, the—History—20th century. 3. Hegel, Georg Wilhelm Friedrich, 1770–1831. I. Title.
II. Series.
B3279.H49B 2000
193–dc21 99-38489
CIP

10 9 8 7 6 5 4 3 2 1

Contents

Thinking in the Light of Time

SUNY series in Contemporary Continental Philosophy
Dennis J. Schmidt, editor

Preface

This translation is the result of close cooperation between myself and Janet Taylor. As I am responsible for the choices concerning the translation of Heidegger's and Hegel's idioms, it seems appropriate to briefly account for these choices here. The translations of those texts by Heidegger that have not yet been translated are my own. Quotations from the other texts are taken from the available translations. In quite a few cases, however, I have slightly modified these translations (this is indicated by "tr. m."). Heidegger's use of the German language is so particular that any translation of his texts must more than in other cases rely on a preceding interpretation of them. Any interpretation that attempts to cast new light on at least some aspects of Heidegger's work will therefore inevitably have to reconsider the existing translations and modify them so as to accord with the interpretation.

As is well known, Heidegger very often attempts to formalize or recoin common German words in such a way that they no longer refer to their usual meaning, but should lead the reader to an ontological structure which underlies concrete phenomena. Thus, a formally indicating concept—as the early Heidegger calls it—is primarily supposed to enact a movement that departs from the common meaning in order to intend a basic ontological structure. I take the view that in translating such concepts, one should try to follow this movement and not focus too much on the common or literal meaning of the concepts. Those who read the German text will usually be aware of the different meanings suggested by one term and will not cling to its common meaning; a plain translation, however, entails the risk of preventing those who read only the English text from following the direction indicated by a concept.

Aware that all translations are tentative and provisional, I have sometimes translated concepts in a way that differs from the existing translations. Even if they are far from satisfying, they may direct attention to aspects which remain in the background in other translations. It is, perhaps, primarily the difference between the possible translations that may contribute to a fuller and more nuanced understanding of Heidegger's work. On the other hand, I realize that new translations of certain terms may make it difficult to correlate the passages with the cited primary texts. Consequently, although in some cases my interpretation specifically demands a different translation of certain expressions, I have modified the structure of the quoted passages as little as possible.

Heidegger sometimes recoins concepts by emphasizing the roots of different parts of common words. The term *Entschlossenheit*, for instance, no longer primarily refers to the capacity to decide and act, but rather to a specific mode of openness—that is, to a modification of the primordial openness of Dasein that Heidegger calls *Erschlossenheit*. To preserve the relation between these two existential concepts, I have translated *Erschlossenheit* as "primordial openness" and *Entschlossenheit* as "resolute openness," while Stambaugh in her translation of *Being and Time*—which I consider a great achievement—chooses "disclosedness" and "resoluteness" respectively. Also in some other cases I have used an adjective and a noun to better cover the different meanings of a German noun. Thus, *Entwurf* has become "projective preconception" instead of "project," and, staying closer to the translation of Macquarrie and Robinson, I have translated *Augenblick* as "momentary vision."

Because it seems slightly awkward to use "constitution of being of Dasein" and related expressions, I have translated *Seinsverfassung* as "ontological structure." While Stambaugh translates *Verfallenheit* with "falling-prey-to," which is certainly better than "fallenness" insofar as the meaning is concerned, I have nevertheless chosen the latter, traditional translation because it makes the sentences flow better. The term *Destruktion* I have translated as "deconstruction." Various translators have rendered *sich zeitigen* with "to temporalize." Although Heidegger here plays with the root *zeit* and uses this verb exclusively with respect to the temporal ecstases, the verb normally means something like "to ripen" or "bring into being." I have therefore rendered *sich zeitigen* with "to accomplish."

Some minor changes in the existing translations have been made without noting that I modified them. This is the case with the term "Dasein": while Stambaugh in *Being and Time* follows Heidegger's own wish to have it hyphenated, I leave it as "Dasein." The fact that this word remains untranslated indicates well enough, I think, that it refers to something other than the mere existence of something. To emphasize the fundamental-ontological meaning of the temporal ecstases and to distinguish them from their usual meaning, I have capitalized them. Thus, *Gewesenheit*, *Gegenwart*, and *Zukunft* are translated as Past, Present, and Future.

In line with existing translations, the two modes of primordial time that Heidegger calls *Zeitlichkeit* and *Temporalität* will be translated as temporality and Temporality, respectively. I agree with Stambaugh's decision to no longer capitalize "being"; in most cases the context of the sentence makes clear enough that Heidegger does not mean a specific being, but being as such. This translation also has an additional advantage. Since I consider it important to maintain the difference between *Sein* and *Seyn*—which occurs in some of Heidegger's later texts—I render *Seyn* with Being. One of the words that are most difficult to translate is doubtlessly *Ereignis*. Because "event," "appropriation," and "properizing event" do not seem satisfactory, I have translated it tentatively as "the occurrence of own-ing," meaning the movement of turning toward one's innermost possibilities or of coming into one's own. This movement primarily pertains not so much to something that is enacted by Dasein, but rather to the dynamic of being itself. *Ereignis* necessarily entails its own countermovement; what Heidegger calls *Ent-eignis* I have translated as "the occurrence of dis-owning."

I changed rather less the quotations taken from the works of Hegel. The term *Begriff* I have translated as "concept," and not, as is done in Miller's translation of *The Science of Logic* and in some other texts, as "notion." In line with recent developments, I have not capitalized Hegelian concepts such as idea, spirit, and so on. I have tacitly altered the translations on these points. While some translators render *Verstand* with "intellect," I have translated this term as "understanding" or "discursive understanding."

When a text from which I quote has been translated, I refer to the original pagination and that of the translation respectively. When translations contain the pagination of the German texts, such as *Being and Time* and the volumes published by Indiana Press, I generally only give the German page number. For the abbreviations used, I refer to the bibliography. With respect to those works by Heidegger in which the original page numbers are given in the margin, like *Holzwege* and *Wegmarken*, I refer to these page numbers.

I wish to thank Dennis Schmidt for his support and advice. Above all, I am grateful to Janet Taylor for her endless patience and accuracy. Moses needed his brother Aaron to put his thoughts into words. She has been the best possible Aaron for me.

Karin de Boer

Introduction

A text or an oeuvre can be read in many ways. The meaning of a text can appear in just as many ways. One possible manner of reading is to search for a simple principle that underlies the text but does not itself appear at first sight. Such a principle might be, for instance, the method that guides the various analyses. It is also possible to understand the various texts as attempts to answer one single, simple question, which motivates the way of thinking and gives it direction again and again. Such a motive might even be found to determine the method that structures the various answers. The question that drives the thinking and the way in which that thinking moves toward a possible answer would then turn out to be the same event viewed from different angles.

While realizing the problematic nature of the category "unity"—inseparably bound up with the distinction between the essential and its accidents—I consider that a reading, as an act of gathering, in one way or another always presupposes unity. If unity is to be found anywhere, it should be in the work of great philosophers. Philosophical texts therefore especially lend themselves to an interpretation which traces that unity. The fact that such a principle itself only gradually takes shape during the process of thinking should not hinder this interpretation. It could even be that what a thinker is really concerned about can only appear as itself in later interpretations. Even then, however, the principle should in no way be seen as independent of the texts in which it shows forth and out of which it withdraws. What is the least complex can perhaps scarcely, if at all, be articulated. It is precisely for this reason that the interpretation of texts must start from the beginning time after time—and to a certain extent must fail.

I take Heidegger to be a thinker for whom it was, from the outset, of utmost importance to inquire whether that which at first sight withdraws from the eye might possibly be brought to light. My intention is to show that Heidegger's project is solely motivated by this very question; it is, among other things, the question concerning the possibility and the incapacity of philosophy itself.

From the first lectures in the early 1920s, Heidegger's thought focuses explicitly on the question concerning philosophy. The question as to how the radically finite dynamic of human life might appropriately be thematized thus leads him to critically question traditional philosophy. Where that philosophy turns out to be largely or entirely incapable of letting life appear as itself, it will be necessary to search for the grounds of that incapacity. Heidegger argues that traditional philosophy, despite its concern with the essence of things, has not been sufficiently capable of freeing itself from the perspective that guides the everyday and the scientific involvement with beings. The essential could therefore only appear as that which persists in the midst of all changes, which remains identical, and thus, as that which is constantly present, is above all accessible to pure beholding. He maintains that this interpretation of the essential as such makes it impossible for modern philosophy to understand human life otherwise than as a self-identical subject.

The question concerning the possibility of a thematization which either avoids or overcomes all reification or objectification is not new, however: it motivates the history of thinking just as much as the question concerning the being of beings. Two thinkers who, each in his own way, critically question traditional metaphysics on the grounds of its incapacity to do justice to the essential dynamic of life are Hegel and Nietzsche. Both were extremely important for Heidegger's thinking. At a very early stage, Heidegger proposes that philosophy can only stay alive if it is capable of not so much reacting against Hegel—as was done by Kierkegaard, Nietzsche, and Dilthey, among others—but facing Hegel at his own level. In 1915 he writes:

> Philosophy . . . now faces the huge task of fundamentally confronting the system of a historical worldview which is most powerful with regard to its fullness, its depth, its conceptuality, and the richness of its experiences, and which as such has removed and surpassed all preceding fundamental philosophical problems; that is, it has to confront Hegel. (GA 1:410–11)

Heidegger will have to show that Hegel also ultimately fails to free himself from the traditional perspective of metaphysics. He will therefore make every effort to develop a concept of metaphysics that even allows the limitation of Hegel's all-encompassing system to emerge. Such a radical deconstruction of metaphysics should prepare the ground for a thinking that might do justice to the insurmountable finitude of life and of the thinking which tries to understand that life.

In the early 1920s Heidegger turns to Aristotle with the intention of revealing the confinement of the entire history of philosophy by deconstructing the basic principles of his ontology. Hegel, who is the first to understand this history as a unity and thus bring it to its completion, is a thinker with whom Heidegger relentlessly and to the end is engaged in strife. This is indeed most appropriate: the very attempt to understand the history of thought as a unity already brings Heidegger dangerously close to Hegel.

In the period prior to *Being and Time,* during which Heidegger intensively studies Aristotle, he develops a concept of time that he considers capable of grounding his critique of metaphysics. He understands the reach within which metaphysics lets beings appear as beings to be solely delimited by time as present. While this limited temporal space allows beings to show forth and be grasped, it does so in such a way that their being and being itself can only be understood as that which is permanently and preeminently present. Metaphysics, including Hegel, he considers to have always been incapable of acknowledging that every understanding of being is made possible by such a temporal background. In order to understand how Heidegger, starting out from a close affinity with Hegel, attempts to break free of his philosophy, I think it is necessary to examine Heidegger's specific concept of temporality. Although in *Being and Time* and *The Basic Problems of Phenomenology* Heidegger did not succeed in truly thematizing this mode of time, I consider that the analyses that Heidegger did actually elaborate provide a sufficient basis for elucidating the meaning of this temporality.

Heidegger's thinking may be characterized as an attempt to reveal the unstable ground that both makes possible and tends to make impossible every ontology. This attempt does not start from an external position but rather, as it were, from within metaphysics itself. His relation to Hegel is particularly appropriate for gaining a better understanding of how his thinking arises out of metaphysics in order to radically distance itself from it. This "position" makes

Heidegger one of the thinkers who opened the way for the work of Derrida and other postmodernists. My investigation therefore consists not so much in comparing certain themes in the thought of Heidegger and Hegel, but in clarifying the basic structure and dynamic of Heidegger's thinking insofar as it enacts a movement that also determines our present cultural and philosophical situation: the attempt to overcome Hegelian thinking from within. In this study Heidegger's interpretation of Hegel on the one hand serves to elucidate what Heidegger intended by his deconstruction of metaphysics; on the other hand, Heidegger's work will be interpreted from the outset against the background of Hegel. From this perspective, the aspects of Heidegger's work relating to phenomenology, hermeneutics, and the philosophy of existence will not be emphasized.

Any attempt to thematize a movement entails the necessity of distinguishing the various aspects of that movement and describing them one by one. In this study, chronology will not be the most important criterion for ordering the various aspects of Heidegger's thinking. Thus Heidegger's interpretation of Hegel, first expressed in the period around *Being and Time*, is only examined in part III. With regard to the distinction between the early and the later Heidegger, I take the view that the different phases of Heidegger's thinking constitute different moments in one single line of thought. As I see it, the unity of this thinking lies in the ultimately simple question of how one may articulate the essential without transforming it into something that is constantly present and gradually actualizes itself. By modifying what is normally understood by "essence," Heidegger attempts to understand both human life and history as fundamentally determined by a continuous and irresolvable conflict between the predominance of present on the one hand and the effort to resist this predominance on the other.

However, the abstract outline given above says, in itself, very little. Its fulfillment demands concretization and differentiation—at the risk of getting lost in details. I will attempt, in the various parts of my study, to start out from Heidegger's simple question, and to return to it in the many analyses—at the risk of tiresome repetition.

I will start by investigating how Heidegger in the 1920s tries to understand the inadequacy of the entire metaphysical tradition, while also keeping open the possibility of a thinking that might be able to do justice to that to which it relates. This is what Heidegger was to have particularly elaborated in the third division of *Being and Time*, which was never published. In part I, I attempt to pursue the line of thought developed in *Being and Time* beyond the published part of this work. Thus, the content of the third division can—as far as possible—be reconstructed. The relation between Heidegger's concept of temporality and his own method will play an important part here. This sketch of the third division may then be used to demonstrate the unity of Heidegger's earlier and later work: I will show that this division constitutes the missing link connecting the different phases of Heidegger's thinking. In part II, I emphasize that Heidegger's later work, despite a fundamental change of perspective, continues to be guided by the idea of a temporality that grounds every thinking and every occurrence of being.

Finally, Part III examines Heidegger's interpretation of Hegel. I here try to clarify how Heidegger's methodical principle is akin to the basic structure of Hegel's thinking, yet differs from it in a fundamental way. In order to bring out, more than Heidegger himself often does, the affinity between Heidegger and Hegel, I examine in some detail Hegel's *Science of Logic*. In his texts on Hegel, Heidegger tries to show that the structure of the concept, which serves as Hegel's methodical principle, remains dominated by a temporal horizon that is delimited by present. Since Heidegger primarily seeks to achieve a modification of this same horizon, his deconstruction of Hegel's philosophy, although often not really elaborated, can serve as an example of his attempt to overcome the narrow perspective of metaphysics. Thus, the first two parts of this study do not simply form the basis for the third part. While parts I and II take a detour that is necessary for understanding Heidegger's relation to Hegel, part III can in turn be seen as a detour that enables a better understanding of what is at stake in Heidegger's work.

I am aware that this study is wide-ranging and entails risks. In fact, I give a systematic interpretation of Heidegger's entire thinking. As the number of available texts has increased greatly since the publication of Heidegger's courses began in 1975, such an interpretation can only succeed if attention is focused on the internal logic that underlies these texts. One of the restrictions I have imposed is to minimize any consideration as to how far Heidegger's interpretations of his predecessors' texts are *correct*. With the exception of Hegel, I will examine other philosophers only insofar as this is necessary for understanding Heidegger's interpretations.

Regarding the choice of texts, I take the view that the courses and other recently published texts in most cases have more to offer than the texts—apart from *Being and Time*—which were published in Heidegger's lifetime. This study therefore devotes considerable attention to texts that have only been available for a few years, such as the early Freiburg lecture courses and the *Contributions to Philosophy* from 1936 to 1938.

I

Time and Method

Introduction

> *[A]ls es gerade die Absicht dieser Exposition ist, vor das ontologische Rätsel der Bewegtheit des Geschehens überhaupt zu führen.*[1]

When thinking turns to the essential, it will always determine the essence of something as that which persists amidst all change. Throughout his work, Heidegger raises the question as to how the essential structure of human beings can be disclosed against this background, when this structure is nothing other than the movement of turning toward and turning against its most proper possibilities. Does philosophy itself, as a mode of life, have the tendency to turn away from what it could possibly be? And if so, why?

In this first part, Heidegger's early work will be interpreted in such a way that the question concerning the essence, the incapacity, and the possibility of philosophy itself appears as the question that motivates Heidegger's thinking.

Being and Time will in this part be read as an investigation which attempts to show that every understanding of being and hence every mode of thinking is grounded in a temporal horizon that tends to confine itself to a realm of mere presence. This perspective will deprive the analytic of Dasein of its independence—acquired in many interpretations—in order to embed it within the development from which it emerges and to which it is on the way.

Being and Time was originally meant to consist of two parts. Starting from an interpretation of the basic temporal structure of Dasein, the first part was to have revealed time as the transcendental horizon that determines every question concerning being (BT 41). With this concept of temporality as the guideline, Heidegger intended in the second part to thematize the confinement of metaphysics, concentrating on a critical analysis of Kant, Descartes, and Aristotle (39–40). Of these two main parts, only the first two divisions of the first part were published, namely, the analytic of Dasein and its repetition with regard to time. The third division of this part—entitled *Time and Being*—was to have elaborated how the understanding of being that underlies metaphysics is also guided by temporality. Heidegger argues that it is only possible to understand what metaphysics is if the temporal structure of the understanding of being as such, which grounds both every involvement with beings and every ontology, has been revealed. Hence, *Being and Time* thematizes the being of Dasein only in order to gain insight into the understanding of being that underlies all the ways in which human beings relate to innerworldly beings, to others, and to themselves (BT 1).[2]

In his published work and courses Heidegger therefore emphasizes many times that the analytic of Dasein may not be read as an investigation concerning the human being in the sense of a philosophical anthropology or a philosophy of existence, but must be understood as preparing an answer to the question concerning the meaning of being as such. However, as long as we do not know what precisely he intended with the third division of the first part of *Being and Time*, the assertion that the analytic of Dasein is of minor importance in Heidegger's thinking cannot truly be supported, and this division will continue to be read mistakenly as an independent text.[3]

Insofar as this is possible, I will try in this first part to reconstruct *Time and Being*. The course *The Basic Problems of Phenomenology* (GA 24) will have a central role here; Heidegger himself considered this text from 1927 to be "a new elaboration of division 3 of part 1 of *Being and Time*."[4] Starting out from a different point, GA 24 does indeed bring us further into the area of *Time and Being*, but it only partially realizes the program outlined in its introduction. To clarify what is at stake in *Time and Being*, I will therefore use not only GA 24 and other courses, but also dispersed remarks in *Being and Time* itself and in other texts that refer to the third division. These texts and extracts are in themselves not sufficient, but they may help us to understand the proper movement of *Being and Time* in such a way that Heidegger's thinking can be followed further than the published part of this work.

It is quite understandable that Heidegger in one of his courses describes *Time and Being* as the most important division of *Being and Time* (GA 49:40): it is the aim of the "systematic" part of *Being and Time* and forms the bridge between the "systematic" part and the "historical" part, which also remained unelaborated.[5] *Time and Being* thus constitutes the basis for Heidegger's deconstruction of metaphysics, as it took shape time and again in his later work.

To shift the emphasis from the analytic of Dasein to *Time and Being*, I will start by examining the general structure of *Being and Time*. First, in chapter 1, I will introduce the analyses out of which *Being and Time* emerges. Then in chapter 2 the analytic of Dasein itself will be interpreted with regard to its significance for the general question of *Being and Time*. Chapters 3 to 5 will offer a schematic reconstruction of *Time and Being*. This division was to have explicitly elaborated the issues from which *Being and Time* first starts out. Both the starting point and the return to that starting point are beyond the scope of the text, but belong essentially to the meaning of the text itself—like Dasein, a text is more than it actually is.

The different possible modes of ontology itself would undoubtedly have been thematized in *Time and Being*. The structures and modes of being of Dasein on the one hand, and of ontology as a specific possibility of Dasein on the other, will be understood in chapter 3 as *analogous*; this will allow the analyses in the published part of *Being and Time* to be read as foreshadowings of *Time and Being*.[6] This chapter is mainly concerned with Heidegger's attempt to develop a fundamental concept of the confinement of traditional metaphysics: he argues that metaphysics, from within a limited temporal horizon, has unduly understood being as constant presence.

Heidegger will have to develop a method that does not permit such a presentification of being to occur. The nature of this method and the way in which it is grounded in temporality—as metaphysics is, but in a different mode—were also to have been elaborated in *Time and Being*. Chapter 4 therefore concentrates on the problem of method. The question concerning Heidegger's method essentially belongs to the question concerning the meaning of being, which is at issue in chapter 1, and thus equally precedes the elaboration of *Being and Time*. However, since it is obviously impossible to say everything at once, I initially defer the problem of method and elaborate it only at the point where Heidegger himself would have explicitly turned to his own method.

When Heidegger poses the question concerning the understanding of being that grounds both Dasein and ontology, he concurs with transcendental philosophy in taking the human being as his provisional starting point. However, the analysis of temporality (which Heidegger intends from the outset) was to have allowed *Being and Time* to leave behind this starting point, in order to attain a perspective which reveals the occurrence of time and being as an event that takes place in human beings, but does not have its ultimate ground therein. In line with *Being and Time*, GA 24 makes a first attempt to accomplish this turn to the occurrence of time and being. With this turning, which will be thematized in chapter 5, Heidegger comes back to the question concerning the meaning of being, although without explicitly answering this question. At the end of chapter 5, I will consider the reason for this reticence. This simultaneously prepares the transition to Part II, in which I will show how Heidegger in his later work enacts the turning to the occurrence of being itself, which is only prepared in *Being and Time* and GA 24.

1

The Development of *Being and Time*

This chapter briefly interprets some of the themes in Heidegger's early work that played a decisive part in the development of *Being and Time*, themes that have all left traces within that text. I make no attempt to start at the beginning, nor to achieve completeness. Neither do I describe the precise course of the thinking that resulted in *Being and Time*: my interpretation assigns no great importance to the time within which events actually take place.

1.1 Husserl and Dilthey

Husserl's *Logical Investigations* are known to have considerably influenced the first phase of Heidegger's thinking (cf. BT 38). His attempt to shake off the dogmatic, academic tradition and to turn to "the things themselves" is something that Heidegger takes up and sustains throughout his life, though not without changing its direction. In *Being and Time* he rightly names Husserl as the thinker who taught him to use the tools that are needed for concrete philosophical investigation (50n). The courses that he gives from 1919/20 onward, however, reveal how his own questioning begins to differ from that of Husserl; the method of Husserl's phenomenology itself is called into question.

Influenced particularly by Dilthey's philosophy of life, Heidegger begins to realize that philosophy—as one of the possibilities of life itself—should reveal life in its concreteness and its own dynamic.[1] As time goes by, he increasingly considers Husserl's focus on the intentionality of consciousness to be insufficient. A thinking that tries to reveal human life in its essential historicity and finitude will have to free itself from an epistemological perspective that takes sensory perception as its point of departure. If the human sciences wish to do justice to the way in which human beings relate to themselves and to their world, they will have to develop a method appropriate for the nonobjectifying way in which human beings understand themselves. This is the hermeneutic approach.

For Heidegger, however, the task of philosophy consists not only in investigating the foundation of the human sciences: since philosophy also itself thematizes the human being, it must likewise scrutinize its *own* basic principles. Heidegger will have to show that although philosophical thematization in some respects resembles hermeneutics, it is essentially different from it. Philosophy, in contrast to all other forms of knowledge, consists in revealing that which is essential and as such constitutes the condition of possibility of that which is actually the case. As the investigation of the a priori, philosophy relates to essential structures *without* following the prevailing path of reasoning and abstraction. This is something that Heidegger learned from Husserl's doctrine of the beholding of essences.[2] Heidegger's question thus becomes how human life can explain itself with respect to the essential structures that underlie its facticity and historicity. This "hermeneutics of facticity" can no longer take (objectifying) perception as its starting point.[3] Since it focuses on essential structures, however, this hermeneutical approach is also different from the method of the human sciences.

Now one of the tasks of the inquiry into the basic principles of philosophy itself, as Heidegger intends it, is to understand the shortcoming of philosophy *as* an essential—if not the only—tendency of life itself. This tendency will itself have to be thematized. In a course from 1921/22 Heidegger remarks:

> Philosophy is a fundamental "how" of life itself, in which life is retrieved, withdrawn from its lapsing (*Abfall*). This withdrawal, as radical inquiry, belongs to life itself. (GA 61:80)

I consider this early explanation of what Heidegger understands by retrieving repetition to be very illuminating. The repetition of life that occurs in philosophy aims at bringing life back out of its lapse into inauthenticity from within, thus turning it to the proper possibilities that it has to assume. One may recognize this retrieval, later mainly applied to the history of metaphysics, as a first formulation of what Heidegger will later call *Kehre*. Factic life *can* be repeated in a proper or authentic mode in philosophy, certainly, but at the same time it is itself that which fundamentally thwarts this movement:

> [T]he factic experience of life must not only serve as a starting point for philosophy, but is precisely that which essentially thwarts philosophizing itself. (GA 60:16)

This is because the way in which life conceives itself "has a tendency to lapse . . . into significance" (16); it is inclined to abandon itself to the world. Like factic life itself, philosophy—as a specific mode of life—is determined by both an inauthentic tendency and the possibility of resisting it. According to Heidegger, Husserl's phenomenology does not fulfill its proper possibilities. Since Husserl remains committed to the understanding of being that underlies the natural attitude of consciousness, Heidegger always considers phenomenology to be a *possibility* and not as yet an actual discipline; it still needs, we could say, to be retrieved from its lapse.[4] As one might expect, then, Heidegger considers his own thinking to be an authentic mode of phenomenology: when Husserl's distinction between consciousness and that which transcends consciousness is no longer ultimate, and the question concerning the meaning of being as such is posed,

> phenomenology is not driven beyond itself, but is precisely brought back to itself, to its most proper and purest possibility.[5]

The way in which this might be done in a radical way only becomes clear to Heidegger around 1923. It leads him to search in the history of philosophy for the presuppositions that from the outset determined the direction of its questions and which it was itself unable to thematize.

1.2 Back to Aristotle

The Book on Aristotle

With the question as to how life in its facticity and historicity can be thematized, Heidegger turns in 1921—immediately after his courses on the religious life—to the texts of Aristotle, Brentano's dissertation having already acquainted him with these during his school days. In October 1922, this results in a text presenting the introduction and an outline of a book on Aristotle that Heidegger was hoping to write; he had to produce a publication for a possible post in Marburg. He obtained the post, but the book was never written. Or more accurately: the plan of the book changed so much in the subsequent years, that it was eventually published in 1927 as the first division of *Being and Time*.[6] This book was also produced under external pressure: in order to take over Husserl's chair in Freiburg, Heidegger—having meanwhile become famous for his courses—finally had to publish a book.

The text from 1922 is entitled *Phenomenological Interpretations with Respect to Aristotle* and is based on the courses that Heidegger gave on Aristotle in 1921 and 1922.[7] The deconstruction of metaphysics first elaborated here in a fragmentary way was crucial for the development of Heidegger's thinking, and consequently deserves considerable attention. Because of its sketchy character, however, it is almost impossible to give a satisfactory interpretation of this text. I will therefore include later elaborations of the same themes implicitly or explicitly in my interpretation, although these in turn have the disadvantage that they scarcely develop the proper deconstruction. This is particularly the case with his detailed interpretation of Aristotle in the course *Plato's Sophist* from 1924/25 (GA 19).

In the long introduction (A 1–28), Heidegger presents a global analysis of the basic structures of human life and of philosophy as one of the possibilities of that life to interpret its own being.[8] The analysis mainly relates to the primary tendency of life to lapse from itself and the possibility of accomplishing a countermovement from within this tendency; these elements underlie the facticity of human life (9–11). Life's tendency to turn away from itself is understood as a mode of life that even then is still concerned with its own being (13). This being can only be reached through the "detour" of a movement that runs counter to the lapsing (13). This analysis, which also starts to take shape in the courses from this period, leads ultimately to the analytic of Dasein in *Being and Time*.

The text on Aristotle starts out from the analysis of factic life in order to critically question the basic principles of ontology and logic (1), which Heidegger takes to be incapable of doing justice to the proper dynamic of the human mode of being. Life that explains itself—that is to say, philosophy—"receives its perspective and mode of speaking from worldly objects" (19, tr. m.). Traditional philosophy, his main concern, he considers to be dominated by Greek concepts which have lost their primordial function during the course of history (19). Heidegger sees this tendency of philosophy to lapse or fall prey to the world (*Verfallenstendenz*) as defining the situation in which the hermeneutics of facticity encounters itself (18–19). To make philosophy aware not only of its inauthentic tendency but also of its proper possibility, this hermeneutics sees its task as

> to loosen up the hidden motives of the traditional and dominant explanation . . . and, in a dismantling return (*abbauender Rückgang*), obtain access to the primordial motivating sources of this explanation. (20, cf. 1, tr. m.)

Heidegger maintains that the inadequate basic principles of traditional philosophical anthropology can ultimately be traced back, via late scholasticism, to Aristotle. Hence, any phenomenological deconstruction of that tradition must offer an interpretation of Aristotle's philosophy (22–24). In his view, Aristotle's interpretation of beings insofar as they are in motion—in the *Physics*—was especially crucial for his ontology and logic; and the entire philosophical tradition subsequently remained under the spell of Aristotle's position (24). The analysis of moving beings must therefore be capable of giving access to the motivating source of Aristotle's ontology (27). An interpretation of what Aristotle understands by movement will therefore allow an explication of the preontological understanding of being (*Seinsvorhabe*), which underlies his characterization of the being of human beings.[9]

In the outline of the planned book on Aristotle, which follows the introduction, Heidegger begins by thematizing the nature of Aristotle's own investigation (29–43). He shows how philosophical knowledge forms a specific modification of the way in which we relate to beings in daily life. The relation between *phronēsis* and *sophia* is the most important theme in this part—as it is two years later in the part of GA 19 on Aristotle. Heidegger then sketches the basic outline of his interpretation of the *Physics* (43–48), and finally, with equal brevity, indicates how Aristotle is always guided in his investigation by a meaning of being as "being-produced" (48–51). This is the result the deconstruction is aiming for. The structure is broadly similar to that of *Being and Time*, although there the question concerning the nature of philosophy itself was to follow the analytic of Dasein. In the 1922 text Heidegger makes a distinction between his own analysis of facticity and his interpretation of Aristotle, though it is already clear that these follow naturally from each other. In *Being and Time* this distinction is no longer evident, but the work on Aristotle continues to play an extremely important background role. I will now thematize the various parts of Heidegger's interpretation in more detail.

Phronēsis *and* Sophia

Heidegger places great emphasis on book VI of the *Ethica Nicomacheia*. In this, Aristotle distinguishes five different ways of bringing beings to unconcealment—namely, *techne*, *epistēme*, *phronēsis*, *sophia*, and *nous* (29–30). Heidegger here gives an initial interpretation of *alētheia* as unconcealment; however, I will defer consideration of this theme to 5.4. At the moment I am largely concerned with Heidegger's interpretation of *nous*, *phronēsis*, and *sophia*. In *Being and Time* these concepts return as respectively the understanding of being, the way in which Dasein relates to its own factic situation, and the contemplation of last causes in philosophy.

Heidegger interprets *nous* as the faculty of beholding as such, that provides access to the beings to which we relate in a practical or a theoretical manner. This primordial beholding is directed toward the being or the "what" of beings and does not involve any articulation of (categorial) determinations (33–34). The *nous* is directed to the *archai* of beings, and as such underlies every concrete form of uncovering. Usually, however, the *archai* of beings are not explicitly brought to light: in speaking of beings, the understanding of being (to use the term from *Being and Time*) itself remains implicit. The highest and most proper accomplishment of *nous* consists in "entrusting to truth the *archai* that belong to a certain ontological area." This "authentic entrusting" is concretely accomplished as *sophia* and *phronēsis* (34, tr. m.). The *difference* between these two forms of beholding of *archai* is extremely important for Heidegger.

In *phronēsis*, human life uncovers that to which it ultimately relates when it is practically involved with itself (its own being, that is). In this way *phronēsis* gives direction to every practical acting (35). *Phronēsis* gives human beings who are acting access to their own situation by elucidating the purpose of the action, its appropriate moment and its appropriate way. That which the action must achieve (and which *phronēsis* thus explains) on the one hand does not yet exist, but on the other hand already exists as revealed possibility (35–36). Heidegger remarks that this distinction between a "not yet" and an "already" can be traced back to a specific concept of movement (namely, I assume, the increasing actualization of an already given possibility). This concept of movement, in which—as Heidegger notes in passing—Hegel's dialectic has its roots, he radically questions in the next part. But first I will indicate more specifically what Heidegger is seeking in—or attempting to do with—Aristotle's concept of *phronēsis*.

Phronēsis allows factic life to gain access to its own being with regard to what has to be done. Heidegger somewhat implicitly distinguishes two moments of *phronēsis*—namely, the insight into that which has to be done as far as innerworldly beings are concerned, and the insight into one's own being (35–36). These moments return in *Being and Time* as circumspection (*Umsicht*) and momentary vision (*Augenblick*). Heidegger is mainly concerned with the second moment. This *phronēsis*, which Heidegger here still calls *Umsicht* in the proper meaning of the word, uncovers the *archē* and the *telos* of practical acting, that is to say, that for the sake of which the acting takes place. This "for the sake of" is ultimately the rightful acting itself (35–36; cf. GA 19:148).

Thus, *phronēsis* consists not only in the capacity to come to a rightful decision in a process of deliberation; such a prudential insight must always already be guided by an understanding of what life is ultimately all about. This understanding, which underlies all concrete deliberations and gives human beings an insight into what they themselves essentially are, is the noetic moment of *phronēsis.* However, this mode of immediate beholding is different from the *nous* accomplished in *sophia*, because it always intends a very concrete *archē*, that is, an *agathon* that could have been otherwise. In the text on Aristotle from 1922 Heidegger comments only that, according to Aristotle, *phronēsis* relates to an ultimate or extreme (*eschaton*) (A 35). On the basis of the concrete analysis of Aristotle, GA 19 makes further attempts to reveal this transcendental or existential moment of *phronēsis*.

What Aristotle himself understands by the *eschaton* may be summarized as follows.[10] A doctor has set himself the goal of bringing about health. He does not have to know explicitly what health as such is, but in treating a patient he has to know what must concretely be done. In his deliberations about the right treatment of a certain patient, he can conclude that in view of (1) the general goal, namely "health" and (2) the actual situation of the patient, this person needs "warmth." This concrete *agathon* is the outcome of the deliberations and subsequently constitutes *archē* and *telos* of the actual treatment: it is that which actually brings about health. "Warmth" is thus the "ultimate" limit that practical orientation can reach, and at the same time is that which must be actualized in the treatment. Both in the professional work of the doctor and in the way the decision is made on the basis of *phronēsis* about how to act, there is a "noetic" relation to a concrete *eschaton* (cf. GA 19:158). In the second case, however, this is the rightful acting (*praxis*) itself, which orients all the concrete decisions about what has to be done.

Thus, Heidegger already in his interpretation of Aristotle detaches *phronēsis* from the context of an analysis of the virtues that determine a rightful way of living together in society, and relates the concept to an essential structure of human life as such. In *Being and Time* he will even go a step further: the extreme possibility to which the phronetic view is directed is understood here as a possibility that is not subject to causality and therefore cannot be actualized by means of a number of actions. This "existential" *phronēsis* gives Dasein access to its own being—that is to say, to its factic situation and its essential possibilities, and does so in the light of an extreme possibility which can in no way be actualized: one's own death.[11] This exceeds all Aristotelian limits.

Heidegger's rigorous modification of the meaning of *phronēsis* in *Being and Time* takes place against the background of a concept of movement that no longer concerns the increasing actualization of a given possibility. This is still so implicit in the 1922 text on Aristotle, however, that it can only be read by anticipating the later developments. In any case, it is important that Heidegger goes along with Aristotle's conception of *phronēsis* in order to show that there is a form of *alētheuein* which is explicitly directed to *archai,* but at the same time manages to grasp them in their concreteness. The problem is naturally that this noetic moment of *phronēsis* very often remains implicit, as Heidegger indeed recognizes:

> In *phronēsis* the *ou heneka* is given and, along with it, also the *archē* and the *telos,* the *eupraxia*—for the *archē* is the *telos* itself—, yet here too they are not considered thematically. (GA 19:57, tr. m.)

Nevertheless:

> [T]o *phronēsis* [belongs] the possibility of a sheer grasp of the *archē* as such, i.e., a mode of uncovering transcending the *logos*. . . . That corresponds precisely to the position in which we left *sophia*. *Sophia* is directed toward the *archai* as such; thus, something like a pure *noein* is alive in it. . . . The question arises whether, in analogy with the way *sophia* is *nous kai epistēme*, *phronēsis* could just as well be able . . . to uncover and retain the *archē* as such, whether there is something like a pure *noein*, a pure beholding in it. (145, tr. m.)

The explicit thematization of that which is ultimately disclosed by the *phronēsis* qua *noein* (the being of the human being in its facticity and essential possibilities) to which Heidegger refers, calls for a thinking that cannot show forth from Aristotle's perspective: it is the hermeneutics of facticity itself.

We can now go back to the text from 1922. Heidegger states here that what *phronēsis* discloses—namely, factic life itself in its essential possibilities—is not explicitly characterized by Aristotle from within this primordial openness itself. He understands the *archai* of concrete human life only as the variable, that which could also be otherwise, in contrast to the *archai* to which *sophia* is directed (A 37). According to Aristotle, the highest mode of being is not susceptible of any change or movement, because it has come to its end in the movement itself. This determination of being serves him as the criterion for his characterization of human life as an "unrolling movement," which to a lesser extent fulfills this criterion (38). The determination of being as that in which the movement has accomplished itself is understood by Heidegger to itself spring from an idea of movement that belongs to the realm of manual production.[12] In order to clarify this, he first thematizes the nature of *sophia* and then indicates wherein the concept of movement that guides Aristotle's determination of *sophia* is grounded.

The mode of knowledge that Aristotle calls *sophia* is not directed to human life in its facticity, nor to human life as such: after all, this is a being that can be otherwise (38). *Sophia* is, by contrast, a pure beholding of unchangeable principles. This beholding is the highest form of knowledge and hence also the completion and highest mode of the movement of human life as such. This proper movement of *nous* is a movement that has come to rest and has overcome the difference between being underway and having reached that characterizes ordinary forms of movement (38–39). This beholding totally withdraws from the normal involvement with beings.

What is gained and what is lost with this? Every form of knowledge—also medical science, for instance—aims to "see" more than can actually be seen: it turns to the "why" of phenomena (40). According to Aristotle, this tendency culminates in that form of knowledge which is directed only to the *archai* that determine beings as such. However, as Heidegger remarks, this beholding is no longer able to gain a view of life itself, to which it belongs. Heidegger seems to be saying that Aristotle understands this tendency of knowledge as a linear, progressive development, while he himself understands theoretical beholding as a mode of being "in which life establishes itself with regard to *one* of its fundamental tendencies" (41–42, italics mine, tr. m.). If that is the case, then it has not yet been decided whether the beholding of unchangeable principles belongs to the authentic or to the lapsing tendency of life. We can gather from the beginning of the text that Heidegger undoubtedly takes it to belong to the improper tendency of life, as it loses sight of its own facticity. On the other hand, *phronēsis*, which *is* involved with life in its facticity and does not complete or sublate its own movement, seems in itself unable to explicitly interpret the facticity intended by Heidegger. Should philosophy then be capable of combining that which characterizes *phronēsis* with the *explicit* orientation on essential structures of *sophia*? Heidegger does not raise this question in this text. Apart from in the above-mentioned passage of GA 19, he does raise it—although again not really in so many words—at the beginning of a course given in 1923/24:

> It is my conviction that philosophy has come to an end. We are faced with completely new tasks, which have nothing to do with traditional philosophy.
>
> To think that one has no prejudice, is itself the greatest prejudice. . . . Not to be free of prejudices, but to be free for the possibility of abandoning a prejudice at the decisive moment, if the confrontation with the matter itself demands it. Such is the mode of existence of the scientific human being.

Thus, one has

> to renounce any premature answer. That requires liberation from a tradition that was genuine in Greek philosophy: scientific comportment as theory.[13]

Heidegger suggests here that, in contrast to the prevailing theoretical philosophy, it should be possible for thinking to accord with the *phronēsis* that guides acting and yet, unlike *phronēsis* but like the prevailing philosophy, to explicitly focus on the *archai* of being as such. This thinking, which withdraws itself from metaphysics, will be guided from within its factic situation by an ultimate possibility that is not to be actualized, but rather to be kept open. It will be concerned with principles and ends on which causality and chronology have no hold, but which nevertheless, as "already" and "not yet," underlie everything that happens within this domain. In Heidegger's interpretation the meaning of *phronēsis* thus appears to undergo a change that makes it fit both his own idea of resolute openness (*Entschlossenheit*) and his interpretation of authentic thinking. First, Heidegger emphasizes the moment of understanding of being in *phronēsis* much more than

Aristotle, and second, he indicates the possibility of a thinking that explicitly thematizes this understanding of being without losing the dynamic of *phronēsis.*

The Principles of Movement

From where, then, does Aristotle derive the idea of movement that guides his conception of human life and the various modes of knowledge? As I said, Heidegger looks for the answer to this question in Aristotle's analysis of moving beings in his *Physics.*[14] His evaluation of Aristotle is positive at least with regard to his critique of predecessors, whose unifold concept of being did not allow them to understand the phenomenon of movement (A 43–45). Aristotle is the first to succeed in this—albeit only to a certain degree. He uncovers three principles that he considers to permit an understanding of movement: *dunamis*, *energeia*, and *entelecheia* (48). Heidegger considers these principles to be derived from the "region" of manual production, which is concerned with a pregiven possibility that increasingly realizes itself and comes to its truth in the thing that is produced. When Aristotle subsequently understands the distinction between *dunamis* and *energeia* as that which underlies the being of beings as such, it is then only a small step to also start out from this distinction to explain the dynamic of human life (48–49). Heidegger regards this preconception as inadequate, yet does not mention a possible alternative.

The text ends with the observation that the other essential distinctions that Aristotle takes to determine being as being, the categories, also originate in the way we address the things we are involved with in daily life. This means that Aristotle starts out from a very specific concept of being:

> For the original meaning of being is "being-produced" (*Hergestellt-sein*). . . . The meaning of being is thus a very specific one, not just the vague and indifferent meaning of reality as such. (50, tr. m.)

What makes a house a house in the first place is the fact that it is *produced*—that is to say, it is the result of the movement that consists in the realization of a specific possibility. According to Heidegger, this concept of being already loses its original regional meaning in the thinking of Aristotle himself, only to become even more diluted in the further course of ontology to an "undetermined, average meaning of reality or actuality" (51, tr. m.). This brings to a close the outline of the book on Aristotle.

With the conclusion that "being" in the sense of "being-produced" constitutes the motivating source of Aristotle's ontology, Heidegger has returned to the question that he says already engaged him during his school years.[15] During this time Heidegger read Brentano's dissertation *On the Manifold Sense of Being in Aristotle*, concerning the different ways in which, according to Aristotle, being is articulated. It is articulated with regard to (1) the different categories, or ways of addressing things, of which *ousia* is the first and most important, (2) being possible or being real, (3) the being true of beings, and (4) being's accidental properties. The motto of Brentano's book, derived from Aristotle, *to on legetai pollachōs*, leads Heidegger already at this first acquaintance to the question concerning the basic meaning of being itself, on the basis of which the many modes of addressing can be distinguished.

Thus, Heidegger can now provisionally answer this question: for Aristotle, "being" ultimately means "being-produced" as the completion and sublation of a certain kind of movement. The highest mode of being then becomes the being of the *archai*, which no longer take part in any movement, while human life for its part is only capable in its highest form—its beholding of the *archai*—of sublating the lively movement of life itself into the proper movement, that is to say, the movement that has come to rest.

A thinking that is guided by this meaning of being, Heidegger argues, will not be able to adequately understand life in its facticity—including the authentic possibility of philosophy itself as the hermeneutics of that facticity. It is not always clear that Heidegger's reading of Aristotle is in fact characterized by a double deconstruction: first, the meaning of Aristotle's thinking is "freed" from prevailing, concealing interpretations; second, the meaning that emerges in this way is itself revealed in its confinement. Only this second step prepares the way for the proper, displacing retrieval of metaphysics, such as Heidegger begins to perform in *Being and Time*. The fundamental pattern of Heidegger's deconstruction of metaphysics is developed in principle in the interpretation of Aristotle from 1922, and it will not essentially change in the later texts.

However, one final link is still missing from the line of thinking: if being-produced is inappropriately understood as the fundamental meaning of being as such, it should be possible to reveal a (manifold) meaning of being that underlies the four meanings of the being of beings distinguished by Aristotle. In a course from 1931 on the concepts *dunamis* and *energeia* Heidegger elaborates a part of what was only planned in the 1922 text. He here establishes that being itself, which according to Aristotle has many meanings, itself remains obscure:

> [T]hus the first meaning for the *pollachōs* in the broad sense is obscure. . . . So we neither know how the *on* as *dunamis* and *energeia* relates to the other meanings nor how it is, together with them, contained in the unity of being. . . . It is necessary to leave everything open and questionable; only thus will we really be capable of setting free and keeping alive Aristotle's unresolved innermost questioning . . . and accordingly our own. What are beings as such? What is being, that it unfolds itself in a fourfold way? *Is the fourfoldness intended by Aristotle's treatment of the question of being the most original manifold of being anyway?* If not, then why not? . . . How is being understood in all ancient questioning such that it extended itself into the realms of questioning which we find here? (GA 33:47/38–39, italics mine, tr. m.)

In 1931 Heidegger has long since found an answer to these questions, which first arose as real questions in his reading of Brentano and developed more clearly in a certain direction in the 1922 text on Aristotle.[16] However, the answer that is given in this latter text—being is being-produced, or being-completed-movement—must nevertheless have been unsatisfactory for Heidegger. The distinction between *dunamis* and *energeia* is crucially important for Aristotle, certainly, but it does not constitute the most fundamental determination of beings as such. Heidegger therefore investigates whether Aristotle's concept of *ousia* is equally guided by the one-sided understanding of being that oriented his concept of movement. This happens around 1923. The texts from this period have not (yet) been published. However, later texts allow a general indication to be given of how Heidegger's thinking must have developed in 1922 to 1923. I will begin with a very brief outline of Aristotle's question concerning beings as beings.

Ousia *as Constant Presence*

For Aristotle, the question concerning beings as such becomes the question concerning the *ousia* or being-ness of beings. That which determines beings as what they are comes about insofar as the beings actualize themselves, and thus take shape. What beings themselves are, can be delimited by a concept. On the basis of this first delimitation, the beings concerned can then be further determined and thus appear; they can be articulated with respect to the question: to what extent has that which they possibly are, actually come into force or reached its accomplishment; with respect to the question: what accidental properties do they have; and with respect to the question: is that which is being said about them true or untrue. All these questions are directed to beings insofar as they are actually present and do not change; without taking account of what could also have been otherwise. For instance, the concept "house" delimits a being in its "what," without regard to such aspects as size, color, or degree of habitability.

On the basis of the meaning that *ousia* has in daily life, Aristotle recoins the term in such a way that it comes to refer to the being of beings. The word *ousia* primarily refers to one's goods and chattels. We can rely on our belongings because they are, like immovable goods, to some extent permanently present.[17] This character of unchangeable presence can therefore come to relate to separate beings insofar as they have actually come about and are (to a certain degree) permanently present. However, unchangeable presence is preeminently applicable to, for example, the firmament and the stars; these are *parousia*. Aristotle takes over this meaning of unchangeable presence for his philosophical concept of that which determines beings as beings. Only on the basis of this constantly present "moment" of being can it be conceptually determined.

This meaning of *ousia* as constant presence leads Heidegger to a more fundamental concept of the meaning of being than that in which his interpretation of the *Physics* resulted: genuine being means being unchangeable, not being in movement (any more), being enacted in such a way that there is no longer any distinction between a possibility and its actualization.

That which belongs to beings as such cannot be seen at first sight. In its involvement with beings, human understanding focuses primarily on the changeable, but even then it is always already directed to causes and ends that are not observable through the senses. Philosophy is the kind of knowledge that distances itself in such a way from involvement with beings that it is free to direct itself to the principles of beings as such. Only insofar as beings are unchangeable can they actually be present for pure beholding.

Aristotle's ontology is thus not only guided by an understanding of being as completion or actualization; this meaning itself turns out to be grounded in the meaning of being as constant presence. According to Heidegger, this fundamental meaning makes it impossible to reveal the being of human beings in its facticity and to understand the possible, phronetic character of philosophy itself. He maintains that this meaning of being is also derived from the region of innerworldly beings; more than anything that can be said about them, these beings lend themselves to being understood as being constantly present.

1.3 The Temporal Meaning of *Ousia*

This is where Heidegger has arrived around 1923. He dwells on the meaning of *ousia* in various texts, including an unpublished course from 1924, entitled *Basic Concepts of Aristotle's Philosophy* (GA 18).[18] In July of that year he gives a lecture for theologians entitled *The Concept of Time*, followed in November by a long article with the same title. The article has not yet been published.

In the lecture, which contains a part of the article's line of thought, Heidegger radically questions the theological presupposition that the meaning of time must be understood from the perspective of eternity. He tries to develop a concept of time that might allow an understanding of the distinction between the finite and the infinite as a derived distinction. He does this by searching for a primordial temporal structure in Dasein itself. This lecture is the first prototype of the analytic of Dasein in which temporality has an important role.

What happened, somewhere around 1923, to shift Heidegger's attention from Aristotle's *ousia* to the concept of time? Nothing less than—as Heidegger himself seems to have said—a "flash of genius" (*Geistesblitz*), which would prove to be of crucial importance for all his further thinking.[19] This inspiration provides a ground for all his previous attempts not only to deconstruct metaphysics in its entirety but also to develop a hermeneutics of facticity, such that both moments of thinking can henceforth be understood in their unity. It is this inspiration—obviously not coming out of the blue—that really clears the path for *Being and Time*, that is to say, for the revealing of time as the transcendental horizon of every understanding of being.

In fact, the idea is simple: following Plato, Aristotle's question concerning beings as beings—that is to say, concerning that which essentially belongs to beings—is guided by a specific concept of being as such: that which of beings is constantly present for a theoretical beholding is above all that which is. From this perspective, "being" in the most proper sense of the word means remaining identical to itself, not being subject to change. According to Heidegger, this meaning of being or essence as constant presence could not be explicitly thematized from within the perspective of ontology itself.

Because the concept "present" has a temporal meaning, the preceding, implicit understanding of being that underlies ontology does indeed seem to be guided by some kind of temporality. This time seems to function as a sort of ultimate presupposition or horizon that could not appear as such from within ontology itself, because it was only directed to the being of beings *from within* this horizon. The presentification of being that occurs in ontology must therefore somehow result from time as present. Present, however, is only one moment or dimension of time. This brings Heidegger to understand the confined, presence-oriented perspective of metaphysics to be based on a self-confinement of the temporal horizon to present. He can thus trace back Aristotle's fourfold distinction within the being of beings to a unifold meaning of being—namely, constant presence—and subsequently show that this meaning is nonprimordial and derived.

What Heidegger now understands by primordial temporality bears very little relation to the prevailing concept of time. This "time" constitutes a means—and nothing more—to show that every mode of experience or knowledge is only possible when a perspective has opened up within which beings can appear as beings, while this perspective at the same time also tends to confine itself in such a way that being itself can *initially and mostly* only appear as that aspect of beings which remains identical to itself in the midst of every change, and is therefore above all present. That this concept of being is not primordial can be understood on the basis of a temporality that primarily modifies itself in such a way that the temporal dimension Present (*Gegenwart*) increasingly determines the horizon of the understanding of being. An appropriate thinking would have to attempt, counter to the predominant tendency of metaphysics, to acquire a temporal horizon in which Present no longer has the upper hand. The other temporal dimensions, which extend themselves to a fundamental and insurmountable absence, might then be given their due. On the basis of a different, "wider" and manifold temporal horizon of this kind, it would also be possible to do justice to the being of Dasein in its facticity. The essential structures of Dasein could then be revealed without losing the proper and irreducible movement of this being.

When being itself owes its meaning to the different possible modifications of the temporal horizon, it cannot be reduced to the way in which it appears in Greek metaphysics—as constant presence—and to Aristotle's fourfoldness, which is grounded in this. When Heidegger in *Being and Time* thematizes care (*Sorge*) as Dasein's fundamental threefold structure, he remarks that at the end it will become clear

> that the idea of being as such is no more "simple" [*einfach* also suggests "undivided" here] than the being of Dasein. (BT 196)

However, that end—the third division—turned out not to be simple to reach.

The relation between being, understanding of being, and temporality gives Heidegger a means to understand the confinement of metaphysics as such.[20] He will repeat in many texts that the history of metaphysics has always in some way been guided in its understanding of being by time as Present. This means that metaphysics is not all-encompassing, even though it relates to all beings, but is marked by an insurmountable confinement and dependence. By indicating a mode of time that even underlies the order of the infinite and unchangeable, Heidegger undermines the distinction between the temporal and the supratemporal. Metaphysics, which has derived its certainty and complacency from this distinction, is thus confronted not only with the fundamental limits of its situation, but also with the possibilities that it is given *as* possibilities on the basis of this temporal situation.

One of the first (published) texts in which this thinking is explicitly accomplished is the series of lectures on Dilthey from 1925:

> What I really take being to mean . . . is the central question. This question also concerns the way in which it becomes possible to experience the meaning of being. When we pose this kind of questions, the otherwise so confused aspect of the history of philosophy becomes very simple. It is remarkable that the Greeks interpreted being with regard to time: *ousia* means presence (*Anwesenheit*), present (*Gegenwart*). Because that is what being means, being in the proper sense is that which is never not present, which is always present: *aei on*. . . . Thus it becomes clear that the Greek doctrine of being, when uncritically taken as absolute, blocks the possibilities of scientific research to understand a reality such as historical existence.[21]

Very simple. Everything falls into place. It means that *Being and Time* can now really begin to reveal the confinement of the history of thinking from Plato to Hegel, and indeed to Husserl. The book everyone has been waiting for can at last be written. Now it is just a matter of writing it, this passage suggests. The beginning is there—but that does not entail that its ending is also guaranteed. Several questions arise.

On the one hand, Heidegger will have to reveal the insufficiency of the traditional concept of time and make clear what he himself understands by primordial time. In the lecture *The Concept of Time* he makes his first attempt at this, although probably realizing that his own conception of time might only attain meaning in the context of the question concerning the horizon of ontology as such.

There is another way. In line with Dilthey, Heidegger has argued from his very first courses that philosophy is a specific possibility of human life and hence should also be understood on the basis of the facticity of life as such. If every mode of philosophy is grounded in a temporality that brings about the openness within which beings can be encountered, then factic existence as such will have to be grounded in this same temporality. Therefore, on the other hand, Heidegger will now have to resume his early analyses of facticity, in order to show how the various essential tendencies and possibilities of concrete human existence result from various modifications of the same basic temporal structure. He does this in the analytic of Dasein in *Being and Time*.[22] That Heidegger repeats and deepens his first analyses of human facticity on the basis of his new understanding of temporality is evident from the twofold structure of the published part of *Being and Time*. As we will see, the analyses in the first division of *Being and Time*—all of which have already to some extent taken shape in the courses from the early 1920s—are resumed in the second division with respect to their basic temporal structure.

Since the early 1920s, Heidegger has been searching for a possibility of understanding metaphysics as a mode of the lapsing or fallenness (*Verfallenheit*) that characterizes human life as such. This tendency to flee from oneself can now be understood as grounded in a mode of temporality in which Present increasingly detaches itself from the other temporal dimensions so as to gain absolute dominance over them. The possibility of resisting this predominant tendency can now be understood as based on a temporality in which this absolute predominance of Present is not allowed to take place. In *Being and Time* this dynamic only emerges with regard to the factic existence of Dasein. Fallenness and resolute, forerunning openness (*vorlaufende Entschlossenheit*) are thus understood to be ultimately grounded, as inauthentic and authentic modification respectively, in a basic temporal structure within which Present constantly threatens to gain the upper hand.

The third division of *Being and Time* was to have elaborated how this dynamic no less threatens the mode of "life" that attempts to thematize the being of beings—that is to say, ontology. Only then would Heidegger have returned explicitly to the flash of insight that both constitutes the starting point of *Being and Time* and orients its actual elaboration.

The analytic of Dasein itself can be understood as an attempt to interpret the being of human beings from within the ontology and anthropology of Aristotle, while at the same turning against them.[23] However, this largely implicit deconstruction is directed not only to Aristotle, but to the entire history of philosophy. This entails that the various modes of that philosophy still remain very much in the background in the analytic of Dasein itself: Heidegger first has to show how the preontological, implicit understanding of being is grounded in temporality.

1.4 Beyond Husserl and Dilthey

I will now briefly go back to 1924 and 1925. On the basis of the deconstructive reading of Aristotle and the new concept of time resulting from this, Heidegger can now formulate his critique of Husserl more clearly. He argues that even Husserl, despite his radical innovations, bases his thinking on a concept of being that does not do justice to the distinction between the being of consciousness on the one hand and the being of that to which it relates on the other. Although Husserl tries as far as possible to avoid reifying the subject, transcendental subjectivity is still conceived as an ultimate, self-identical ground for everything that appears for the subject. This concept of subjectivity is no less grounded, according to Heidegger, in an understanding of being as constant presence. This daring critique of Husserl—after all, Heidegger was hoping to take over his chair at Freiburg—we find for the first time in a course from 1924 (GA 17). Here it is closely connected to a deconstructive interpretation of Descartes. This interpretation recurs in *Being and Time,* but without reference to Husserl. It seems that Heidegger's critique of Descartes was also—or even primarily—directed against Husserl's subject-philosophy, but that he did not consider it opportune to elaborate this in his book.[24]

Again in the introductory part of GA 20 from 1925, a course that is beginning to closely resemble *Being and Time*, Heidegger comments extensively on Husserl. The question concerning being itself is raised here against the background of Husserl's "forgetting" of that question in his phenomenology of transcendental consciousness.[25] The answer to the question of being—time—entails that the subject can no longer be regarded as the ultimate foundation. While from Husserl's perspective only the different modes of intentionality can actually come into view, Heidegger tries to show that this intentionality itself is grounded in a primordial horizon, opened by temporality, which Dasein has not itself brought about.

Heidegger's concept of temporality also allows him to formulate more clearly his critique of Husserl's idea of pure intuition, which serves as the phenomenological way to gain access to the intentional structures of consciousness. He argues that Husserl cannot do justice to the situated and projecting character of philosophy, and that his method therefore remains no less bound to a temporal horizon dominated by Present. Heidegger understands his own *hermeneutic* phenomenology, by contrast, to be guided by a temporality in which Present does not become predominant. I will return to this in chapter 4.

Even Dilthey's questions concerning the proper nature of human life and its historicity are now no longer sufficiently radical for Heidegger. At the end of 1923 Heidegger resolves to review the letters between Dilthey and Yorck which were published in that year.[26] This results in a text in which Heidegger mainly develops his own ideas about the temporal structure of the being of human beings, with the intention of using this analysis to situate Dilthey's thinking. When this text is considered unsuitable to serve as a review, Heidegger elaborates it further in November 1924 and conducts the analysis back to its original context: the deconstruction of Greek ontology and logic.[27] This results in the aforesaid article *The Concept of Time.* Part of his commentary on the letters between Dilthey and Yorck is included in the definitive version of *Being and Time* itself (§77). Heidegger's view is basically that Yorck correctly emphasized the fundamental difference between nature and the historicity of human life, but that neither Dilthey nor Yorck could adequately ground this difference (BT 399–403). The question concerning the historicity (*Geschichtlichkeit*) of human beings and the way in which they relate (scientifically) to history must, he argues, be conducted back to the more fundamental question concerning the being of Dasein as such; only when this being has been understood with respect to its temporality is it possible to also investigate how the historicity of Dasein is grounded in this temporal structure (cf. 403, 404). He asserts that Dilthey, while questioning the proper nature of human beings and the sciences concerned with human beings, has not been able to radically question the traditional meaning of being either.

In spring 1925 Heidegger elaborates this critique into the aforementioned lectures on Dilthey.[28] These may be seen as his farewell to the philosophy of life and hermeneutics in the narrower sense. He does, however, take over the term "hermeneutics" for his own purposes in *Being and Time*. Here it no longer relates to the method of the human sciences, but primarily to the way in which philosophy explicates the basic structures of Dasein (37–38). Hermeneutic philosophy will try to do justice to the proper, irreducible dynamic of human existence.

1.5 The Meaning of Being in *Being and Time*

The most important results of Heidegger's investigations between about 1920 and 1926 are all included in some way in *Being and Time*. In the published part, however, he gives very little attention to the temporal character of the understanding of being of traditional metaphysics; this was only to be thematized in the third division. Apart from a few brief remarks, only in §5 and §6—which in the context of the introduction give an outline of the entire book—do we find anticipatory indications of the relation between time and the understanding of being. Heidegger states here that the concrete answer to the question concerning the meaning of being as such can only be given when the problem of Temporality (*Temporalität*) has been elaborated.[29] However, he continues, this answer is only *sufficiently* given if the specific mode of being of traditional ontology—that is to say, "the questioning, findings and failures destined to it"—is understood from within the same problem of Temporality (BT 19, tr. m.). In the subsequent outline of the deconstruction of ontology that he intended to develop in part II of *Being and Time*, he argues that the ancient interpretation of the being of beings is oriented toward "world" or "nature" in the widest sense of the word. That ancient ontology understood this being against the background of time is also evidenced by:

> the determination of the meaning of being as *parousia* or *ousia*, which ontologically and temporally means "presence" (*Anwesen-*

> *heit*). Beings are grasped in their being as "presence," that is to say, they are understood with regard to a specific mode of time, namely Present (*Gegenwart*).[30]

Thinking, however, is not aware of the preontological determination of being that it accomplishes (26). Heidegger will clearly have to show first in what (confined) way ontology has always been guided by time, and second how thinking might let itself knowingly and properly be guided by this same time. The first aspect he calls fundamental ontology. This thinking is no longer concerned with beings as beings, but takes a step back from this questioning and turns to the understanding of being which underlies every kind of ontology. The analytic of Dasein, which aims to thematize the temporality of the understanding of being, constitutes the first part of this fundamental-ontological investigation (13–14). At the same time the investigation into the being of Dasein itself is already guided by a temporal understanding that does not confine being to constant presence; thus, it is itself also a first *example* of an ontology that tries to break free from the perspective of traditional ontology. The analytic of the being of Dasein is hence ontological insofar as it relates to the being of a certain being, but fundamental-ontological insofar as this is done *for the sake of* elucidating the condition of possibility of ontology as such. I will now further indicate the character of this fundamental-ontological perspective.

Uncovering the temporal meaning of *ousia* allows Heidegger to understand time as the horizon within which being is understood. This answer entails that the question concerning the *meaning* of being, which Heidegger has taken up from Brentano's interpretation of Aristotle, itself acquires a different meaning. What Heidegger in *Being and Time* intends by the meaning of being (*Sinn von Sein*) no longer pertains only to the meaning of being in the sense of, for instance, being-produced or presence, but also—and even primarily—to the horizon within which being as such receives meaning in the first place, that is to say, becomes understandable at all.[31]

The concepts meaning (*Sinn*) and significance (*Bedeutung*) are thus distinguished in such a way that "meaning" comes to pertain to the condition of possibility of every (ontic and ontological) significance. Thus the question concerning the meaning of being henceforth bears upon being "insofar as it has entered the realm of human understandability" (BT 152, tr. m.), that is to say—I add—insofar as it is understood from within a temporal horizon. Time itself, as that which guides every understanding of being, *is* thus the meaning of being (*Sinn von Sein*)—even though that answer to the question of being required that the meaning of the question itself be modified.

In various courses after *Being and Time* Heidegger tries to further specify the horizonal character of time. GA 24, for instance, describes time as the light that makes it possible to understand being and hence to be concerned with beings. Heidegger thus regards his own thinking as an attempt to go "beyond being to the light from which and in which it itself comes into the brightness of an understanding."[32] Being itself has to be illuminated in order to become in one way or another understandable by human beings. Time, as the source of light, opens as it were the realm within which being can have meaning for Dasein, and thus makes possible every unconcealment of beings. However, time is not only the source of light, but is also the open space or clearing delimited by that light (*Entwurfsbereich*). Heidegger calls this "moment" the transcendental horizon.[33] These two "moments" of time, which cannot be separated from one another, will be encountered in the analytic of Dasein as respectively the ecstatic and the horizonal aspect of time. What Heidegger understands by primordial time clearly bears only a slight relation to the time that we have or do not have, the time that we measure or the time within which all events occur and beyond which something supratemporal might be found.[34]

But when Heidegger attempts to "go beyond being" in order to gain insight into primordial time he does not claim that time is even more primordial or fundamental than being itself. We must not lose sight of the fact that Heidegger (at least for the time being) is only concerned with being *insofar as* it is understood in the light of time. He does, however, consider his *question* concerning time to be more primordial than the question concerning being (as the question concerning the being of beings) that has always been posed by metaphysics. The expression "question of being" thus acquires an essential and intentional ambiguity. With this one expression, philosophy is summarized in its different moments: on the one hand as the thinking that implicitly answers the question of being by directing itself to the being of beings and understanding this being as the foundation of everything that appears; and on the other as the thinking that radically criticizes that answer (in its various modifications) and thus for the first time makes that question really a question.[35]

While the history of metaphysics could only understand being as the foundation of beings that remains identical to itself—for example as substance, essence, subject, mind, or will to power—Heidegger traces back the totality of these meanings to the meaning of being as constant presence and then deprives this one meaning of its exclusive right. The idea of a primordial temporality thus allows Heidegger to uncover a common characteristic in the most varied forms of Western metaphysics and to reveal "the fundamental occurrence of occidental metaphysics" (GA 31:115). As we saw, this common characteristic consists in the confinement of its horizon:

> The meaning of "being" is confined to the realm of presentness (*Gegenwärtigkeit*), presence (*Anwesenheit*), existence (*Bestehen*), permanence, abiding and happening. (EM 69/92, tr. m.)
>
> *Hence the hitherto existing concept of being fails to name everything that "is."* Therefore, being must be experienced in a radically new way and with regard to the whole reach of the possible occurring of its essence (*seines möglichen Wesens*).[36]

According to Heidegger, this different reach can be experienced by a thinking that is not so much guided by Present, but rather by the "ecstatic unity of time" (GA 49:52)—that is to say, by the primordial unity of Future, Past, and Present. What this means will be elucidated in the following chapters.

In *Being and Time* itself we find only a few passages that explicitly mention the confinement of the traditional meaning of being. In the section *Dasein, Worldliness and Reality,* Heidegger maintains that both the ontic experience of innerworldly beings and the ontological understanding of being are *initially* oriented toward being as reality or substantiality. Not only the being of innerworldly beings, but also the being of Dasein is understood from within this (insufficient) understanding of being. Therefore,

> not only the analytic of Dasein, but the elaboration of the question concerning the meaning of being as such must be wrested from the one-sided orientation toward being in the sense of reality. (BT 201, tr. m.)

This different, broader orientation should allow for a more appropriate insight into the being of Dasein, which will thus no longer be conceived as a constantly present subject relating to present objects. From this perspective, innerworldly beings themselves will appear not only as present things with certain properties, but primarily as "utensils" (*Zeug*) that always already have a practical significance and are part of a coherent whole. Before turning to the analytic of Dasein, I will first briefly describe Heidegger's specific use of the term "being" in *Being and Time.*

1.6 Being and Essence

Partly because of Heidegger's own vagueness, the word "being" has become surrounded by a kind of ethereal cloud. It is conceived as an ultimate signified that withstands all conceptual grasping, somehow serves to replace God and can only be experienced in an instant of mystical surrender. My interpretation turns against such *Schwärmerei*. I will indicate here how Heidegger recoins the term "being" in such a way that it comes to pertain to what is traditionally understood—albeit insufficiently—by "essence."

When Heidegger analyzes the being of Dasein or the being of innerworldly beings, he is clearly *not* referring to "being" in the sense of reality. Thus the term "handiness" (*Zuhandenheit*) pertains to the being of innerworldly beings, and says more about beings than the fact that they exist or have been produced. This handiness, which makes it possible for something to appear as "at hand" and ready for use, refers to that which constitutes the hammer *as* a hammer—in other words, to that which is "essential" for the hammer. When someone is using a hammer, he or she understands the hammer in its "being-a-hammer"—that is to say, as "in order to hammer." This does not mean, however, that this "in order to" can be conceived as the "what" or essence of the hammer; what is essential for the hammer lies rather *in* the way it is used and is thus found to be fit or unfit.[37]

Even more than other beings, Dasein has no fixed or stable essence. Dasein is nothing other than the way it concretely accomplishes its existence (as openness): "the 'essence' of Dasein lies in its existence" (BT 42). In this well-known formulation, Heidegger puts "essence" in quotation marks to prevent it from being conceived as an essence that somehow exists independently. He tries to trace back the distinction between essence and existence, which the philosophical tradition would take to be self-evident, to an original meaning of *ousia*.[38] Thus, the expression "the being of beings" does indeed pertain to the "essential," but not to what the tradition calls "essence." When Heidegger translates *ousia* not as "essence" but as "being," this concept in a certain sense *encompasses* both the "what" and the possible ways in which this "what" may enact or accomplish itself. The ontological difference thus comes to pertain to the distinction between "being" as primordial unity of essence and mode of being on the one hand, and beings, which can only appear against the "background" of this unity, on the other. "Essential" for beings is precisely the way in which a certain "what" actually accomplishes itself and could possibly accomplish itself. In a course on Aristotle from 1931, Heidegger says:

> We should learn to understand that the full essence of a being, however, pertains as much to the "what" of a being as to the "how" of its possible or actual reality.[39]

That is the first step. Aristotle would say that of a being whose "what" has been delimited, it is then possible to determine whether it is still constructing this "what" or has actualized it. Making a table from wood can serve as an example of this. Heidegger, by contrast, will no longer wish to understand the dynamic of a "what" accomplishing itself as a process of increasing actualization. From his perspective, the being of beings—that is to say, what they essentially are—becomes delimited by (1) a possibility that (2) usually does not and (3) possibly does accomplish itself as itself. The twofold distinction between essence and existence thus changes into an at least threefold structure: the "actualization" enacts itself essentially in two different directions—namely, as turning toward and turning against its proper possibilities. In this threefold structure the moment of turning against or inauthenticity is no longer a subordinate moment that can be overcome in the process of increasing self-actualization.

With this new interpretation of the concept of "being," Heidegger—while "retaining" the forged unity of essence and mode of being—no longer understands the *ousia* as that which is constantly present and remains identical to itself, but as a dynamic that is divided in and against itself and therefore radically finite. Thus, the essential is nothing but the movement of a possibility turning toward and against itself, in which both the preceding possibility and the proper realization of this possibility withdraw from the realm of presence.[40] What this means in concrete terms will be elucidated in the course of this study. For now, I would like to draw attention to the characteristic way in which Heidegger deals with the meaning of *ousia*: from the concealing "translations" (which have arisen during the course of history) Heidegger goes back to the (presumed) original meaning of a Greek term, in order to then modify—or repeat in an appropriate way—this meaning on the basis of a preconception that is not guided by constant presence. This is the movement of retrieving repetition (*Wiederholung*).

Finally, one last remark. If Heidegger's formulation "the being of beings" refers to the "essential" of those beings, then "being itself"—which our understanding of the being of beings ultimately intends—should be understood as the "essential" as such.[41] It may not, however, be conceived as the eternal essence, or the foundation that remains identical to itself, of everything that is. Rather, the "essential" is in itself a finite and unstable dynamic which not only makes possible the appearing of beings, but also constantly threatens it. This other meaning of "being" will therefore also allow the being of Dasein to appear in its finitude and internal dividedness. Which is precisely what Heidegger attempts to achieve in the published part of *Being and Time*.

2

The Analytic of Dasein

We have seen how Heidegger in the early 1920s realizes that traditional philosophy fails to adequately thematize the dynamic of human life itself. The question concerning human beings thus leads him back to the question concerning the incapacity and possibilities of philosophy itself. However, philosophy is itself a possible mode of existence. Heidegger will therefore have to understand how the inadequacy of philosophy is grounded in the essential structure of life itself, that is, in the understanding of being which underlies every mode of human life. From this perspective the analysis of human life itself also takes on a more fundamental character. If it can be shown that every understanding of being is grounded in temporality, it should also become possible to answer the question concerning the meaning of being as such—which only shows forth in this understanding of being. This line of thought not only *precedes* the analytic of Dasein but also outlines the content of *Time and Being*, which was to have *followed* the analytic of Dasein. Here, however, I will first elucidate the "detour" of the analytic of Dasein itself. Since *Being and Time* draws together and deepens the various analyses from the early courses, we will encounter once again the themes discussed in chapter 1.

2.1 The Aim of the Analytic of Dasein

If Heidegger's ultimate concern is not the human being but being itself,[1] why does he make this detour at all? In later texts Heidegger repeatedly emphasizes that his insight into time as the horizon for the understanding of being led him to search in Dasein itself for the primordial and grounding structure of time. If ontology consists in explicating the usually implicit, preontological understanding of being, and if every ontological understanding of being is guided by time, then time must also ground this preontological understanding of being itself.[2] Thus, *Being and Time* is not concerned with humans as beings among other beings, but purely with the human being *as* the primordial openness—*Erschlossenheit*—within which the fundamental question concerning being takes place. This openness of Dasein consists in the movement in which it transcends beings toward their being; this movement has always already begun to take place.[3]

Although *Being and Time* itself does not give a comprehensive analysis of human existence in the sense of a philosophical anthropology, Heidegger in no way denies the (relative) importance of the investigation concerning the human being as a being.[4] Once "the horizon for the most primordial interpretation of being" has been exposed, he writes, the analytic of Dasein must be repeated "on a higher, genuinely ontological basis" (BT 17). Hence, in order to adequately comprehend the being of Dasein, thinking must first obtain a horizon from within which being as such can be adequately understood. We may deduce from the courses soon after *Being and Time* that in this period Heidegger was indeed intending to only defer the investigation concerning human beings as beings.

In a course on Leibniz given in 1928 (GA 26) Heidegger explicitly distinguishes between the analytic of Dasein and a metaphysics of Dasein; he asserts that only this metaphysics can deal with ethical and anthropological problems.[5] From what is implicitly or explicitly excluded from *Being and Time,* we can gain an impression of some new themes that the metaphysical repetition of the analytic of Dasein was to have contained: corporeality, passions, and desires, the entire spectrum of sentiments, the difference between humans and animals, and the sexual difference, for instance.[6] Heidegger seems to hold the view that these and other all too human phenomena can only really be understood on the basis of a fundamental analysis of the essential structure of human life, which he calls "care" (*Sorge*). One may question, however, whether this is indeed the case.

In GA 26 Heidegger proposes that the "metaphysics of existence" should constitute a part of what he here terms "metontology" (*Metontologie*) or "metaphysical ontics" (*metaphysische Ontik*). This does not refer to a mode of positive science, but to the investigation, grounded on the outcome of fundamental ontology, that attempts to understand the totality of beings, that is to say, nature as well (GA

26:199–201). In this way, after taking the initially necessary "step back" from metaphysics, Heidegger would have reentered the ontological perspective and again turned to beings as beings, though now with different eyes. Fundamental ontology would thus lose its abstract character, and serve as a basis for more concrete questions concerning human existence.[7]

This investigation concerning beings as beings therefore differs from traditional ontology in that it is guided by the outcome of fundamental ontology. The investigation concerning the condition of possibility of every understanding of being on the one hand, and the concrete investigation based thereon concerning beings as beings on the other, constitute a unity that Heidegger in GA 26 calls "the concept of metaphysics" (202). This "authentic" or "appropriate" metaphysics thus contains first, fundamental ontology, consisting of the analytic of Dasein and the "analytic of the Temporality (*Temporalität*) of being" (the published and unpublished divisions respectively of part I of *Being and Time*) and second, "metontology."[8]

The question remains whether Heidegger was really planning to elaborate such a "metontology," and if so, in what context. A remark from 1962 indicates that he did indeed regard such a repetition as a serious task.[9] One can easily imagine that at the end of *Being and Time* he saw himself faced with a branching of possible roads, and decided then to elaborate the deconstruction of the history of metaphysics. This road would still allow him to reveal temporality as that which both opens and limits every understanding of being. He had not, after all, been able to do this on the basis of the analytic of Dasein in *Being and Time*. It may be that Heidegger, when he no longer had to take Dasein as his starting point, chose this "turning" (*Kehre*) in preference to the overturning of fundamental ontology into metontology, which in GA 26 he also calls a "turning" (GA 26:201). It is also possible that his increasing turning away from philosophy as a comprehensive system may have played a part in this.

Heidegger's "choice" after *Being and Time* to more or less ignore the way back to the issue of concrete human existence, and to take a path that seems only to lead away from it, has not always been favorably regarded. While the question concerning facticity and the question concerning the thinking that tries to thematize this facticity still have a certain equality in Heidegger's first courses, the latter receives the greater emphasis after *Being and Time*, although it in turn becomes subordinated to the question concerning the occurrence of being itself. Thus, the line of fundamental ontology as developed from 1922 onward is extended, albeit no longer to prepare the ground for a possible hermeneutics of facticity.

The analytic of Dasein has now been distinguished from a possible metaphysical investigation concerning human beings. Having gained a clearer view of what *Being and Time* did not intend, we may proceed to further thematize the analytic of Dasein itself.

2.2 Dasein and Ontology

It has been repeatedly emphasized that Heidegger intended to use the analytic of Dasein to thematize the way in which ontology understands being as such: being occurs only insofar as it is understood by human beings (BT 183). Because of his phenomenological method, however, Heidegger does not start the first division of *Being and Time* by unfolding the question of being itself, but with the factic being-in-the-world of Dasein. This method is not in fact greatly different from that of Hegel in the *Phenomenology of Spirit*.

To ensure that the being of human beings does not appear in the light of metaphysical preconceptions that conceal the matter itself, Heidegger (like a theater director or puppeteer) lets Dasein itself have experiences that gradually bring it to greater insight into its own being. *Going along with* the ways in which Dasein relates to innerworldly beings, to other human beings, and to its own being, Heidegger only has to conceptually articulate these experiences of Dasein:

> The phenomenological interpretation must give to Dasein itself the possibility of primordial disclosure and let it, *as it were*, interpret itself. It goes along with this disclosure only in order to raise the phenomenal content of that which is disclosed to an existential-conceptual level.[10]

The experiences of Dasein are arranged in such a way that Dasein is first observed in its simplest and most immediate involvement with innerworldly beings. Then, after analyzing the way in which Dasein encounters other people from within its world, Heidegger lets Dasein retrieve itself, via anxiety and conscience, from its one-sided involvement with things, that is to say, from the meaningful world to which it initially abandons itself.

Heidegger does not, however, only want to show how Dasein can gain insight into its own factic existence. The next step, which in the published part of *Being and Time* is only prepared, consists in showing that Dasein itself has the possibility of explicitly elucidating the implicit preontological understanding of being that guides all its doings. Dasein itself must be able to interrupt its ontic involvement with beings in such a way that the being of beings and the meaning of being as such can be explicitly brought to light. Because the understanding of being essentially belongs to Dasein, Heidegger seems to conceive an authentic modification of this understanding as the most authentic human possibility as such. However, Dasein initially and mostly does not accomplish this change of perspective (*Einstellungsänderung*)—and when it does, then not radically enough. Perhaps it is especially at the level of ontology that the tendency of fallenness remains predominant.

Heidegger thus intended in *Being and Time* to let Dasein develop itself in such a way that it would ultimately coincide with the standpoint of the phenomenologist himself. Since the published part of *Being and Time* presents this development only up to resolute openness (*vorlaufende Entschlossenheit*) as the authentic possibility that pertains merely to Dasein's own factic existence, the movement in which Dasein turns to its most proper possibility does not become entirely visible here.

The introduction of *Being and Time* distinguishes between the *existentiell* self-understanding of factically existing Dasein and the *existential* understanding that guides the philosophical analysis of the fundamental structures of existence (BT 12). Because this existential-ontological understanding is a specific modification of the existentiell understanding, the two modes of understanding must not only be essentially different, but must also in a certain respect show similarities. Heidegger indeed regards the ways in which Dasein relates to its own being and to being as such, as *analogous*. At both levels his analysis is structured by the distinction between an inauthentic possibility that Dasein initially and mostly accomplishes (fallenness or metaphysics in the narrower sense) and an authentic possibility (resolute openness or phenomenological ontology) that always remains preserved as a possibility.[11]

I consider the distinction between the analysis of factically existing Dasein on the one hand and the analysis of ontology itself as a specific modification of that existence on the other to be of crucial importance for understanding Heidegger's project. The two levels are characterized by the same dynamic because they are both grounded in the understanding of being that precedes every ontic and ontological thematization. The nature of this understanding of being remains implicit not only in the everyday involvement with beings but also in traditional metaphysics; only Heidegger's own thinking can be said to both explicate and modify this preontological understanding. I will now first elucidate the various tendencies which, according to Heidegger, determine the being of factically existing Dasein.

2.3 Inauthenticity and Authenticity

Heidegger tries in *Being and Time* to reveal the being of Dasein without objectifying it and without anchoring the analysis in a transcendental subject. Fictively going along with the ways in which Dasein understands itself does not in itself guarantee success, however. Neither is it sufficient to start out from Dasein's involvement with utensils instead of its theoretical relation to the world. Above all, the analysis will have to keep in mind that Dasein is characterized by a specific dynamic that cannot be traced back to the increasing actualization of a pregiven possibility. From Heidegger's perspective, it is essential that Dasein initially and mostly turns away from its most proper possibilities, while *in* that turning it nevertheless retains the possibility of turning toward itself.

As Heidegger wants to bring this finite dynamic into view, he has to articulate its various moments separately. This means that the analysis must on the one hand reveal the (formal) ontological structure of Dasein and on the other must indicate how this structure initially and mostly occurs and could possibly occur. The inauthentic and the authentic tendency together delimit the entire reach of human possibilities; that reach forms as it were the space within which each tendency tries to become predominant. Heidegger reveals this realm by thematizing its extremities. At the same time, however, he has to show how the counterstriving tendencies that constitute the being of Dasein are both grounded in the facticity of everyday life and generally do not evolve into their extremes. He therefore stresses that both tendencies are embedded in everydayness (*Alltäglichkeit*). Starting out from this indifferent modification of the formal fundamental structure of Dasein, both the inauthentic and the authentic tendency can be shown to constitute specific existentiell modifications of this everydayness.[12]

Heidegger considers it crucial to thematize the dynamic character of these various modifications; he explicitly calls fallenness an ontologically dynamic concept (BT 180). The fall (*Absturz*) or downward whirling (*Wirbel*) is not a movement whose beginning and end can be established. The indifferent everydayness entails *of itself* that Dasein tends to abandon itself entirely to its involvement with beings and thus lose sight of its most proper possibilities:

> The kind of movement of plunging into and within the groundlessness of inauthentic being in the "they" constantly tears understanding away from projectively preconceiving authentic possibilities. (BT 178, tr. m.)

The double "into and within" (*in die und in der*) clearly expresses that the alienation (178) has always already begun, but may not be understood as a static situation. Neither can the retrieval from fallenness ever be fully accomplished; that is to say, it can only occur as the finite attempt of Dasein not to be determined by what it is not itself.

2.4 Temporality

Heidegger strives to make clear how the various tendencies of human existence constitute different modifications of one and the same fundamental structure. Near the end of the first division of *Being and Time* he characterizes the formal structure of the being of Dasein as care (*Sorge*) (192). This term, a translation of what Heidegger formally understands by *phronēsis*, merely indicates that every relation to something (being-with) is only possible on the basis of a familiarity with a pregiven whole that is already there (being-already-in). Against this background, Dasein understands what is to be done and projectively preconceives certain possibilities (ahead-of-itself). This applies for the practical involvement with innerworldly beings (*Besorgen*), for the way in which Dasein relates to other human beings (*Fürsorge*), and for Dasein's involvement with itself. The phronetic movement in which Dasein comes toward itself while returning to its own thrownness, is the condition of possibility that grounds every actual expectation or remembering. This analysis of care is not, however, Heidegger's ultimate aim:

> When we have found "care" to be the primordial ontological structure of Dasein, then it will also become possible to conceptually grasp on this basis the understanding of being which lies in care, that is, to delineate the meaning of being. (230, tr. m.)

In order to do this Heidegger will first have to show that the structure of care is a structure determined by *time,* and that time grounds all the ways in which Dasein concretely exists. This first repetition of the analytic of Dasein takes up most of the second division of *Being and Time*.

Heidegger chooses to call the phenomenon that grounds the structure of care itself "temporality" (*Zeitlichkeit*). This primordial time contains the moments Future (*Zukunft*), Past (*Gewesenheit*), and Present (*Gegenwart*).[13] Future is the moment that makes possible every kind of being-ahead-of-itself—that is to say, every understanding or projective preconception. Past grounds every being-already-in or factic situation. Finally, Present is that which makes possible every relation to something *as* something (327). This temporality allows Dasein to stretch itself in one single movement into the directions Future, Past, and Present. Since in everyday life Dasein usually turns away from the way in which it is determined by its thrownness and from its most proper possibilities, this primordial temporal dynamic is not readily visible when we look at how human beings usually exist. Nevertheless, the threefold temporality always underlies the primordial openness that Dasein is itself.

If this openness, being-in-the-world or being-outside-oneself of Dasein is at all levels grounded in temporality, this temporality must itself also be characterized as "outside-itself":

> What is essential for Future is the *coming-toward-oneself*, what is essential for Past is the *back-to*, and what is essential for Present is the *dwelling-with*, that is, the being-with. . . . As determined by this "toward," "back-to," and "with," temporality is *outside itself*. . . . Temporality . . . is itself the *primordial outside-itself*, the *ekstatikon*. (GA 24:377, tr. m.)

The ecstatic character of time leads Heidegger to now term the three "directions" in which temporality stretches itself the temporal ecstases (BT 329). This may sound at first somewhat abstract. The important point is, in any case, that the concept of temporality allows Heidegger to trace back the indifferent, inauthentic and authentic modifications of the basic structures of Dasein to a common "root."[14] And not only that: ultimately Heidegger wishes to show how temporality's own dynamic entails that inauthenticity constantly and at all levels threatens to become predominant at the expense of Dasein's own possibilities.

I will now briefly discuss how Heidegger understands the primordial openness of Dasein (*Erschlossenheit*) and its inauthentic and authentic modifications to be grounded in different modifications of primordial temporality. From this perspective I will clarify his analyses of the everyday involvement with innerworldly beings and with other human beings. Finally, I will thematize fallenness (*Verfallenheit*) and resolute openness (*vorlaufende Entschlossenheit*) as modifications of the way in which Dasein relates to itself. These will turn out to determine the way in which Dasein encounters innerworldly beings and other human beings. I will therefore take the first and second divisions of *Being and Time* together. It will sometimes not be possible to avoid a certain over-simplification.

2.5 A Sketch of the Analytic of Dasein

Dasein's Primordial Openness

As mentioned earlier, Heidegger considers that every intentional relation to objects is grounded in a primordial openness. This openness, which Heidegger also designates the *Da* of Dasein (BT 132), makes it possible to understand something, to take and to thematize it *as* something. Because this fundamental structure of Dasein plays a part in *all* its doings, its analysis in *Being and Time* occupies a somewhat different place than the analyses of Dasein's involvement with innerworldly beings, other human beings, and itself. Dasein's primordial openness is always enacted as it were in these different directions, for example as the "seeing" that guides the involvement with innerworldly beings or as the understanding that guides existing as such.[15] Since the analysis of primordial openness is concerned with Dasein's *access* to that with which it is involved, this analysis seems to take the place of an epistemology. However, Heidegger attempts to trace back the different modes of "seeing" to an understanding that precedes, for example, the distinction between practical, phronetic, and theoretical insight; in these and other modes, "truth" always takes place in one way or another.[16] With his analysis of the primordial disclosure of world, which Dasein is itself, Heidegger also undermines the traditional interpretation of the relationship between subject and object.

Heidegger distinguishes different constitutive moments within the primordial openness of Dasein. First, every mode of perception can only take place from within a situatedness that cannot be reduced to the receptivity of sensory perception. Dasein has itself a pretheoretical access to its own thrownness because it is always already in a certain mood: a certain mood always already "colors" my experiences and cannot itself be understood on the basis of these actual experiences. Dasein always already relates to itself through its moods; this is what Heidegger calls the disposition (*Befindlichkeit*) of Dasein. Second, every experience is guided by a movement that opens up a realm of possibilities. This projective preconception (*Entwurf*) entails that one possibility comes to the forefront, while another does not. Heidegger calls this movement "understanding" (*Verstehen*). The encounter of beings is always supported by these two moments, but also requires a "capacity" of interpretation or explicit articulation. As soon as I, for instance, understand in the handling of tools the hammer *as* a hammer, a mode of explanation is enacted that can possibly result in a linguistic mode of articulation. The condition of possibility of any articulation or meaningfulness is called "discourse" (*Rede*).[17] This concept, Heidegger's translation of *logos,* takes the place of traditional concepts like reason or spirit. Discourse is distinguished from these concepts in that it is primordially embedded within dispositional understanding.

Like the formal moments of care, the three structural moments of primordial openness are understood in the second division of *Being and Time* as grounded in temporality. Thus, understanding is primarily made possible by the temporal ecstasis Future and disposition by Past.[18] Primordial discourse underlies every (linguistic) articulation. Contrary to what one might expect, Heidegger indicates that discourse is not grounded in a specific temporal ecstasis. But insofar as discourse mostly accomplishes itself as speaking about innerworldly beings, which thus become present, "*making present* has, however, a *privileged* constitutive function" (349, tr. m.). The second division of *Being and Time* understands the dynamic of fallenness, in which Dasein abandons itself more and more to its world, as also an essential moment of primordial openness, and as equally grounded in the temporal ecstasis Present (335, 346). Discourse and fallenness thus both seem to be grounded in Present, albeit in a different manner.

Behind Heidegger's vagueness lurks the crucial problem that two modes of making something present must be distinguished: an objectifying and a nonobjectifying mode, both grounded in an implicit understanding. It may be inferred from the above quotation that a nonobjectifying mode of thematization would not be grounded in a mode of temporality dominated by Present. Discourse and fallenness, then, must pertain respectively to the possibility of bringing something to presence and the tendency to completely abandon oneself to the presence of beings. Both possibilities are grounded in Present, and in such a way, one could say, that discourse entails in itself the tendency toward fallenness. However, this subtle relation is not clearly elaborated in *Being and Time*, and therefore easily leads to misunderstandings.[19]

Since this question is especially important with respect to Heidegger's effort to distinguish his own thematization of the being of beings from that of metaphysics, I will return to it in that context. It can be noted here, however, that Heidegger also distinguishes between two modes of making present with regard to the way in which Dasein relates to itself. The authentic mode of being-present-at is characterized by an insight into one's own situation that guides every concrete decision. This phronetic view, which Heidegger calls "momentary vision" (*Augenblick*), is distinguished from a mode of making present in which Dasein is not aware of its own thrownness and its own possibilities, but loses itself in what at that moment presents itself from within the world.[20] In *Being and Time* Heidegger leaves undecided whether the way in which ontology brings to light the being of beings also necessarily entails a certain presentification:

> Whether every science and whether indeed philosophical knowledge aims at a making present, is as yet to remain undecided here. (363n, tr. m.)

This issue was to have been broached in the third division of *Being and Time*.[21] We will see that Heidegger already in the second division of this work tries to show how *every* objectification is grounded in a mode of temporality in which Present has become predominant. This is even the case with Dasein's relation to innerworldly beings, which is elaborated at the beginning of *Being and Time*. Heidegger here starts by turning to everydayness, which means that the extreme modifications of fallenness and resolute openness are for the time being deferred. However, even within this limited scope, he already tries to distinguish between an objectifying and a nonobjectifying tendency of the involvement with innerworldly beings.

The Involvement with Utensils and the Relation to Objects

In his analysis of Dasein's everyday involvement with tools and utensils, Heidegger shows that the perception of things is not a suitable starting point for understanding the way in which Dasein relates to innerworldly beings. The traditional epistemological standpoint makes it impossible to gain a view of how Dasein is always already familiar with the coherent whole from which those beings derive their meaning. The carpenter, for example, does not so much pay attention to the hammer, the nails, and the planks as things, but is always already familiar with their interrelations and proper possibilities. The workshop constitutes a meaningful environment in which all elements refer to each other. The carpenter can only do his work—that is to say, be present at the beings—because he is aware of this coherent whole and of what is still to be done. Heidegger thus distinguishes three moments in the mode of seeing that guides every practical involvement with beings: the anticipatory understanding of possibilities, the retaining of an already existing coherent whole, and the being present at something.

The second division of *Being and Time* interprets this dynamic as "a making present that awaits and retains" (354). In this structure can be recognized the formal moments of care; these are accomplished—in a still limited way—in the involvement with innerworldly beings. Being a mode of care, this involvement is ultimately grounded in temporality. As primordial time stretches itself into its three directions, it brings about the horizon within which beings can appear as meaningful. Heidegger asserts that in the practical involvement with beings, making present remains embedded within the other two temporal moments:

> The way Present is rooted in Future and Past constitutes the existential-temporal condition of the possibility that what is projectively preconceived in circumspect understanding can be brought nearer in a making present. (360, tr. m.)

The embedment of Present in the other ecstases disappears when the familiar involvement with beings at hand overturns into the objectifying beholding of present things. The specific dynamic of awaiting and retaining stops at the instant that we start to objectify beings: the hammer is then detached from the workshop and from its practical possibilities, only to appear again as a thing with quantifiable properties. Heidegger takes the temporal precondition of this overturning to lie in the movement in which the temporal ecstasis Present breaks away from its juncture with Future and Past to become independent and overshadow the other temporal moments.[22] This new mode of making present causes both the anticipatory understanding of the "what-for" and the familiarity with a given coherent whole to disappear into the background. The meaningfulness that constitutes the structure of world makes way for a homogeneous space within which something has certain properties and obeys certain laws.[23] This temporal modification grounds the positive sciences (cf. 356f).

With his interpretation of the practical involvement with beings and the theoretical perspective that is a modification of this, Heidegger shows that a certain "narrowing of vision" occurs "as soon as" Dasein explicitly makes something present. The first division of *Being and Time* indicates that, apart from this mode of thematization, a mode of seeing is also possible whereby the referring character of beings does *not* disappear, but can in fact be explicitly experienced *as* such. In my view, the analysis of the sign (§17) is meant to show *already at an ontic level* that it is possible to make something present without objectifying it; this mode rather elucidates the primordial structure of the being of beings. The structural moment of making present here remains rooted in awaiting and retaining. I will return to the significance of the analysis of the sign in 4.3.

Dasein's Relation to Other Human Beings

Heidegger's somewhat sketchy analysis of Dasein's ways of relating to other human beings (*Mitsein*) and of the different modes of concern (*Fürsorge*) has often been criticized. Here, I will only implicitly refer to this critique and briefly try to show what Heidegger in my view intends with his analysis of the ways in which Dasein initially and mostly encounters other human beings. Because this analysis is set within the context of everydayness, it has a limited reach.

First of all, Heidegger—clearly with Husserl in mind—criticizes every philosophy that starts out from the perception of the other. Empathy is not a primordial phenomenon, because it already presupposes a natural familiarity with the other.[24] With regard to the way in which we encounter other human beings, which is essentially different from the involvement with innerworldly beings, Heidegger is likewise looking for modes of involvement that precede every objectification.[25]

Heidegger finds an example of a nonobjectifying, everyday involvement with other human beings insofar as they share our world (*Mitdasein*) in the way Dasein is involved with other people when working with them (120). In working together with someone, the other appears only indirectly—namely, as the one together with whom I am focusing on the work that is to be done. Next, Heidegger shows Dasein's attention already moving rather more toward the other human being itself, yet without the practical context being abandoned and without objectification taking place. All modes of caring for somebody are formally indicated by the term "concern" (*Fürsorge*). Within this involvement with other human beings, Heidegger distinguishes different modes; the way in which he does this clearly shows the different moments that he always distinguishes in his analyses.

First, concern is often accomplished in an indifferent way: we pass the other by, he or she does not matter to us (121). Besides various indifferent modes, Heidegger distinguishes two crystalized possibilities—namely, an inauthentic and an authentic mode.[26] When I take over my colleague's work—Heidegger continues to use the workshop as his starting point—I am focusing on the work that must be completed, and I thus prevent the person from freely accomplishing his or her own possibilities. In this way the other is made dependent. An authentic mode of concern, by contrast, consists in acting in such a way that the person with whom I am involved is allowed to carry out the work in his or her own way. This is a form of giving due to the other in which Dasein tries to restrain itself, and does not try to take the place of the other. In this case the innerwordly being (the work) no longer determines the way in which Dasein encounters other human beings. Usually, according to Heidegger, concern will accomplish itself in an indifferent or inauthentic way, but it may possibly do this in an authentic way.[27] The latter is only possible if Dasein is free in relation to itself—that is, if it no longer understands its *own* possibilities against the background of innerworldly beings.

Although the second division of *Being and Time* does not elaborate the temporal meaning of the different modes of concern, it is clear that the analysis of these modes is also guided by the idea of a temporality in which Present again and again tends to get the upper hand. This dynamic entails that the freeing restraint which characterizes authentic concern can hardly—if at all—resist the predominant mode of concern.

It should be noted here that Heidegger's analysis of concern at least partly pertains to the ways in which *ontology* can relate to Dasein: either using categories that are intended for the analysis of innerworldly beings, or with respect to Dasein itself.[28] This latter approach is said to free Dasein for its most proper possibility:

> Thus the development of resolute openness . . . becomes the interpreting liberation of Dasein *for* its most extreme possibility of existence. (303, tr. m.)

Read against the background of the analysis of concern, this passage suggests that the thinker has a certain concern for the human being as such. Keeping well away from metaphysical interventions, this thinker does not take away the actual "work" of Dasein—and perhaps especially that of fellow philosophers—but rather indicates the possibilities that usually remain hidden for Dasein itself. Thus, for example, the proper meaning of Aristotle's work is "freed" from its concealing interpretations by Heidegger's reading of it (cf. 22–23).

Within the context of his analysis of everydayness, Heidegger can strictly speaking only thematize the way in which we *initially and mostly* encounter other human beings.[29] The second division of *Being and Time* indicates that the authentic mode of concern only becomes possible when Dasein retrieves itself from fallenness (298). The question is, however, whether the experience of the other *as* other—who then no longer appears as a human being with whom I share a world—can indeed be sufficiently understood from such an authentic mode of concern.[30]

Heidegger's idea of a Present which always tends to dominate the other ecstases does, however, make it possible to comprehend how Dasein tends to understand the other human being as part of a relational whole or as a being with certain properties, that is to say, from within the environing world and not as itself. Because the concept world pertains to the horizon within which beings can appear as present, this concept can also be used to clarify what *cannot* be thematized from within this confined horizon.

In his later work, Heidegger in fact only elaborates this in relation to the way in which *being itself* shows itself and recedes; only when Dasein is guided by a temporal horizon that is no longer dominated by the temporal ecstasis Present, can it do justice to the radical difference between being and beings. Initially, however, being can only be understood by starting out from beings—that is, from within world. Following from this, we could say that human beings too *can* only be encountered from within a meaningful world. It is this very world, however, which constantly threatens to make it impossible to encounter the other *as* other—that is to say, to do justice to that which withdraws itself from this world. From Heidegger's perspective, this counterstriving dynamic does not have its ultimate ground in Dasein itself, although Dasein does have to bear the full responsibility for what it does and fails to do.

I think Heidegger would have dealt with this issue in his proposed repetition of the analytic of Dasein. In any case, he would only have elaborated an ethics after the question concerning the meaning of being as such had been answered. Because he wished to show that every human capacity and incapacity is ultimately grounded in a temporal dynamic that is not itself brought about by human beings, a primordial ethics cannot start out from the human being. This does not mean, however, that such an ethics would be a later addition to an ethically neutral ontology: fundamental ontology understands the relation between being and temporality in such a way that an ethical moment is always already involved.[31] It is not my intention to fit the thinking of Levinas, for example, into Heidegger's framework. Heidegger's specific perspective simply entails that certain matters can appear, while others can scarcely, if at all. I do however think that Heidegger's analysis of everyday encounters with other human beings is of minor importance. It is true that a real ethics indeed cannot yet be found in this analysis.

I will now return to the analyses that Heidegger did actually elaborate in *Being and Time.* We have seen how the different modes of involvement with innerworldly beings and other human beings are grounded in the predominance or nonpredominance of the temporal ecstasis Present. This is also the case for the ways in which Dasein—*in* its involvement with innerworldly beings and other human beings—relates to itself. Fallenness and resolute openness should now be more closely considered. With this, we accomplish, as it were, the transition from the level of "consciousness" to that of "self-consciousness." Dasein, at home in a world that it shares with others, is thus again brought closer to itself.

Fallenness and Resolute Openness

The various moments of the primordial openness of Dasein—namely, understanding, disposition, and discourse—bear witness to the dynamic temporal structure that Heidegger calls care. The temporal ecstasis Present opens up the horizon within which beings appear as meaningful. This same Present allows Dasein to be concerned with beings. However, this temporal ecstasis also entails that Dasein tends to abandon itself entirely to its world. This means that everydayness, as the indifferent mode in which Dasein does not yet clearly move away from or toward itself, in itself entails the tendency toward fallenness; the "natural" direction to innerworldly beings in itself leads Dasein to be carried away by these beings, and also to understand itself and other human beings in the light of what it is not itself. Although Heidegger thus distinguishes between Dasein's "indifferent" and "inauthentic" modes of being, these modes must be understood as two moments of the same movement of making present, the former always tending to lead up to the latter.[32] Everything in *Being and Time* is intended, I think, to reveal this dynamic.

The second division of *Being and Time* tries to do this on the basis of, among other things, the phenomenon of curiosity, which was introduced in the first division as one aspect of fallenness. Heidegger here states that the dynamic of fallenness is grounded in a mode of making present in which Present increasingly frees itself from the other temporal ecstases—as it were, breaking away from them:

> Present "breaks away" from (*entspringt*) the awaiting that belongs to it in the emphasized sense of a running away. . . . When the awaiting leaps behind, making present is left more and more to itself. It makes present for the sake of Present. . . . This mode of Present constitutes the most extreme opposite phenomenon to *momentary vision*. (BT 347, tr. m.)

The more Present gains independence and thus overshadows the proper nature of the other temporal ecstases, the more Dasein flees from its proper possibilities, and the less it can come back to itself as thrownness.[33] Heidegger is clearly not so much concerned here with a phenomenological description of curiosity as with a fundamental dynamic of Dasein, or better still, of temporality itself. Thus, like the modification of handiness into objective presence, the mode in which Dasein turns away from its situatedness and proper possibilities is grounded in the movement in which Present breaks away from its juncture with the other temporal ecstases in order to gain absolute dominance over them. In everyday life, this movement has always already been enacted—otherwise there could be no openness whatsoever; in fallenness, Present, which has always already begun to predominate, absolutely overshadows the other ecstases.

The way in which Present accomplishes itself as "breaking away" (348) is indeed the predominant, but not the only basic movement of Dasein. Heidegger suggests that Dasein can only turn to itself through the alienation of its most proper possibilities:

> Present breaks away from its authentic Future and Past, so as to let Dasein come to authentic existence only insofar as it takes a detour through this Present. (348, tr. m.)

This quotation makes clear that temporality may not be understood as a faculty that can be found in Dasein. Dasein is in a certain sense abandoned to the dynamic of time, yet does have the possibility of resisting its predominant modification. Resolutely it can retrieve itself from its being at a loss, gain insight into its most proper possibilities, and take responsibility for its own thrownness. Only in this authentic modification of care can the structure of temporality itself show forth as itself—that is, as the primordial, dynamic unity of the three ecstases. When Dasein has modified its primordial openness into a resolute and anticipatory one, it is no longer exclusively absorbed in making present, but explicitly accomplishes the movement of the "toward-itself" (Future) and the "back-to" (Past), in order to be present at something in an authentic way (Present).

Heidegger calls these three moments of the authentic mode of being respectively anticipation (*Vorlaufen*), repetition (*Wiederholung*) and momentary vision (*Augenblick*). In this modification, Dasein will relate to its own possibilities (with as the most extreme possibility its own death) in a projective, forerunning manner, taking responsibility for its thrownness by means of a renewing repetition of what is always already given, and being attentive to whatever the situation of a specific moment demands (325, 328). This threefold temporality thus constitutes the ground of the specific dynamic of human life for which Heidegger has been searching since the early 1920s. This life is such, however, that it initially and mostly does not allow this structure to come into its own.

This, then, is Heidegger's provisional analysis of Dasein in the light of temporality. In the next chapter various aspects of this analysis will be further elucidated. If we now leave aside the chapters on the historicity of Dasein and on the way in which temporality grounds the everyday and scientific interpretations of time, we have reached the end of the published part of *Being and Time*.[34] Heidegger has shown that the being of Dasein is characterized by a threefold temporal structure that grounds all the ways in which Dasein can encounter or avoid innerworldly beings, other human beings and itself. He has also shown that every ontic relation to beings is made possible by a pretheoretical understanding of the being of beings—that is to say, by a familiarity with the "essential."

However, the fact that this primordial understanding of being itself is also structured by temporality has not yet been explicitly thematized. On the last pages of *Being and Time,* Heidegger says about this:

> However, the explanation of the ontological structure (*Seinsverfassung*) which constitutes Dasein is nothing but *a passage* (*nur ein Weg*). Our *goal* is to work out the question concerning being as such. (436, tr. m.)

> The existential-ontological structure which constitutes the whole of Dasein is grounded in temporality. Accordingly, a primordial way in which ecstatic temporality accomplishes itself must itself allow for the realm of being itself to be opened up ecstatically. . . . Is there a way leading from primordial *time* to the meaning of *being*? Does *time* itself reveal itself as the horizon of *being*? (437, tr. m.)

These questions close the second division of *Being and Time* and prepare the third division. What remains to be elaborated is the temporal structure of the preontological understanding of being itself and its different modifications. In the most proper modification of that understanding of being, Dasein will no longer gain insight into its proper being—that is to say, into its own thrownness and its proper possibilities—but rather into the being of beings and the meaning of being as such. What that means is partially elaborated in the course entitled *The Basic Problems of Phenomenology*.

3

The Initial Attempt to Elaborate *Time and Being*

The book has reached its end, but not its goal. In the following chapters I will try to elucidate what Heidegger was to have elaborated in the third division of *Being and Time.* My interpretation will therefore depart more from the content of *Being and Time* than hitherto, turning to that which underlies the various analyses and at first sight does not show itself. As I noted at the end of the last chapter, I will mainly draw on *The Basic Problems of Phenomenology* from 1927 (GA 24). Following the movement of the published part of *Being and Time*, I will first consider Heidegger's attempt to comprehend both the understanding of being itself and its explication in ontology on the basis of temporality.

Starting out from the analogy between the being of Dasein and the being of ontology, I will examine the latter's character, incapacity, and possibility. From this perspective I will also take a closer look at the analytic of Dasein. After considering the implications of Heidegger's method in chapter 4, I will turn in chapter 5 to the temporal meaning of being itself, as understood in the various modifications of ontology.[1] This analysis would have grounded Heidegger's deconstruction of the history of metaphysics in the second part of *Being and Time.* I will try to show how the seeds of this deconstruction are already present in GA 24.

3.1 Primordial Temporality

The course *The Basic Problems of Phenomenology* consists of an introduction and two parts. In the first part, Heidegger elucidates the concepts of being of Kant, Aristotle, Scholasticism, and modern logic. In preparation for the second part, he attempts to show why these traditional conceptions of being are inadequate.[2]

The second part is entitled *The Fundamental-Ontological Question of the Meaning of Being as Such. The Basic Structures and Basic Modes of Being* (GA 24:321, tr. m.). As this part follows on from the published part of *Being and Time*, it is extremely important for my study. We read in the introduction of the course that four problems are to be considered.[3] Of these four basic problems, however, only the first is worked out: the title of the first and indeed only chapter of the second part is *The Problem of the Ontological Difference.* Here, before commencing on the understanding of being, Heidegger repeats some of the analyses from *Being and Time* for the benefit of his students. He examines in detail the difference between his own concept of time and traditional views of time (§19) and shows how temporality founds both ontic and existentiell understanding (§20). In consequence of this repetition, Heidegger again does not get around to what the introduction indicates he was planning. Of course this external reason may not have been the only one.

Whereas the second part of GA 24 is only partially elaborated, the third part promised in the introduction is entirely absent. Its title was to have been *The Scientific Method of Ontology and the Idea of Phenomenology* (32). It is clear from *Being and Time* that Heidegger wanted to thematize the method of his own thinking: §7 of *Being and Time* offers a "Preliminary Concept of Phenomenology," distinguished from the "Idea of Phenomenology" (BT 357), which remained to be developed. This self-understanding of phenomenology, which in my view was also to have concluded the systematic part of *Being and Time*, will be elucidated in the next chapter. First, I will look at the passages in the second part of GA 24 that try to extend the line of thought of *Being and Time*.

This part begins where the published part of *Being and Time* ends:

> *The ontological structure of Dasein is grounded in temporality* (Zeitlichkeit). . . . *But then, if indeed the understanding of being belongs to the existence of Dasein, this understanding too must be based in temporality. . . . Temporality* takes over the enabling of the understanding of being and thus *the enabling of the thematic interpretation of being, of its articulation and* of its *manifold modes*; it thus makes ontology possible. (GA 24:323, tr. m., cf. 388)

The specific mode of temporality that grounds the understanding of being as such Heidegger now calls Temporality:

> The term "Temporality" (*Temporalität*) . . . means temporality (*Zeitlichkeit*) insofar as temporality itself is explicitly understood as the condition of the possibility of the understanding of being and of ontology as such.[4]

Heidegger thus uses the term Temporality to refer to temporality insofar as it underlies the understanding of being itself and its different modifications. He considers this mode of temporality to be the most primordial.[5] Just as the understanding of being underlies every ontic way of relating to beings, Temporality grounds the modes of temporality which manifest themselves in the ontic and existentiell modifications of Dasein's primordial openness.

If this mode of temporality grounds the understanding of being, then it also constitutes the condition of possibility of Dasein's primordial transcendence. Being in the world, Dasein has always already "transcended" beings (both innerworldly beings and itself as a being) toward the being of beings; only from a prior, projective understanding of what essentially belongs to beings can Dasein explicitly come back to them.[6] Insofar as the distinction between being and beings only comes about *in* this transcending movement of the understanding of being, this distinction is also grounded in Temporality (454). This distinction usually remains implicit, but it can be explicitly elucidated *as* the ontological difference. Thus, Heidegger now understands primordial ecstatic time as the differencing dynamic that grounds the ontological difference between being and beings. Time therefore first gives rise to the openness within which beings can be encountered. This occurrence of openness "begins" as soon as Dasein exists—that is to say, understands being, exceeds itself, is in the world. It has always already begun.

The characterization of time as the "light" that makes possible the primordial openness, disclosure or "truth" of Dasein is only one side of the story. As we saw, the "realm" that is delimited by the light of time also belongs to time itself. When Heidegger states that temporality has an "ecstatic-horizonal structure," he is referring to the horizon that constitutes the *reach* of the realm within which beings can present themselves as beings. Both *Being and Time* and GA 24 call this reach the "whither of the ecstasis" or the "horizonal scheme of the ecstasis."[7]

Just as transcendence and world constitute two moments of the same movement—namely, the "subjective" and the "objective" moment of the understanding of being—the temporal ecstases that cast the light and the horizons that delimit the enlightening open space also constitute an inseparable unity. It now emerges that world, as the "realm" within which beings can have meaning, is ultimately made possible by the unity of these temporal horizons:

> *The existential-temporal condition of the possibility of world lies in the fact that temporality, as ecstatic unity, has something like a horizon*. (BT 365, tr. m.)

This transcendental horizon allows Dasein to understand the being of beings and on the basis of that understanding to use, perceive, or comprehend them. The investigation of the condition of possibility of the way in which Dasein encounters beings has now reached its most fundamental level (GA 24:437). It is still necessary, however, to further elucidate the *character* of this temporal horizon itself—that is to say, of its different possible modifications.

In this respect, the section *Temporality and Being* starts again from the beginning, namely, with an analysis of the horizon from within which Dasein understands the *being* of innerworldly beings in its practical involvement with them. Thus, we find here once again a radicalizing repetition of Dasein's practical involvement with beings. This temporal interpretation, intended as an example (431), is the only one that is really worked out in GA 24. We have seen that *Being and Time* and GA 24 interpret this involvement with beings as an "awaiting and retaining way of making present." This means that the innerworldly beings are initially brought to light by the ecstasis Present, though in such a way that the other two ecstases also play a part.

Now that he has revealed not only the ecstatic but also the horizonal character of time, Heidegger can designate the horizon that is opened up by Present as the horizon of Praesens (*Praesenz*).[8] From the horizon of Praesens, being as such can be understood as presence, and the being of innerworldly beings as handiness or objective presence. Only on the basis of this understanding can Dasein encounter beings as beings. Praesens is thus the temporal precondition of what *Being and Time* calls "world." Heidegger subsequently remarks that the ecstases Future and Past also have their own horizon, but that for the sake of clarity he will restrict himself to interpreting the ecstasis Present and its horizon. This simplification makes it difficult to gain insight into the possible modifications of temporality as such, which was in fact what Heidegger was attempting to reach.

In summary, Heidegger now states:

> Everything that is encountered in making present, is understood as present . . . on the basis of the horizon which springs from the ecstasis itself, that is, on the basis of Praesens. . . . [T]he being of beings encountered within the world is projectively preconceived in a praesential way and hence in a fundamentally temporal way. *Accordingly, we understand being on the basis of the primordial horizonal schema of the ecstases of temporality.* (436, tr. m.)

I would point out that with this last sentence Heidegger departs for a moment from his "practical" example of the involvement with innerworldly beings. That *this* involvement relates to "Presence with regard to Praesens" does not mean that this is *always* the case:

> According to the ways in which temporality accomplishes itself . . . the ways in which the horizonal schemata of time are temporally interrelated vary as well. (436, tr. m.)

Being and Time has shown that this variation in fact consists in the alternative between a Present that breaks away from its juncture with the other ecstases to become predominant, and a Present that accomplishes itself in accordance with the original threefold of Temporality. GA 24 leaves this issue undecided; it mentions only the priority that the one ecstasis can have over the others.

Returning to his example, Heidegger does however indicate what happens when Dasein relates to something that is no longer there: a tool that is missing, for instance. Such a change he considers to be made possible by a modification of Praesens into Absence:

> To the ecstasis of absencing (*des Ungegenwärtigens*), which makes it possible for something to be missing, belongs the horizonal scheme of Absence (*Absenz*). This modification of Praesens into Absence, in which Praesens maintains itself in a modified way, cannot be interpreted more precisely without . . . clarifying the way in which it is related to time. (442, tr. m.)

It seems that Heidegger, well aware of the inadequacy of this tentative interpretation, wishes to make clear that Praesens is not the only horizon from which the being of beings is understood, but that a modification of this horizon is possible whereby Dasein in an absencing movement relates to something that is not present. If, as Heidegger says, this movement underlies the ontic absence of something, we may infer that an even more far-reaching absencing movement should constitute the condition of possibility of *every* experience of absence or lack.

I am almost sure that this modification of Praesens into Absence (443), in which Praesens does not disappear but rather modifies itself, is related to the horizons of Future and Past. Heidegger's simple example was intended to indicate how primordial time *already at the level of Dasein's involvement with innerworldly beings* may give rise to an openness that does not exclude the absential from its realm. This is only possible if Praesens remains even more firmly embedded within the horizons of Future and Past than in the everyday involvement with utensils (that is to say, in the awaiting and retaining mode of making present). But Heidegger does not say this: "We are not well enough prepared to penetrate into this obscurity" (443, tr. m.).

3.2 Inauthentic and Authentic Thinking

At the end of GA 24 Heidegger argues that metaphysics has always based itself, albeit unknowingly, on the same horizon that has guided the usual ontic involvement, that is to say, Praesens. This is evidenced by the meaning of *ousia* as *Anwesenheit*, but equally by Kant's concept of being (449). With this Heidegger has arrived at (that is to say, returned to) his own starting point:

> Reference to the fact that the Greeks understood being on the basis of Present, that is, of Praesens, is a confirmation not to be overestimated of our interpretation of time as that which makes possible the understanding of being, yet it is not its foundation. At the same time, however, it bears witness to the fact that in our own interpretation of being we are attempting nothing other than to repeat the problems of ancient philosophy, so as to let them radicalize themselves in this repeating movement. (449, tr. m.)

It is striking that Heidegger here tones down his great inspiration of 1923, which motivated the entire interpretation, into a *confirmation* of the same interpretation. However, he does not make clear what he means by the "radicalization" of philosophy.

Only near the end of the text does he indicate the essential difference between the thematization of beings that occurs in the positive sciences and the thematization of beings in ontology, although both possibilities are grounded in temporality:

> Thus, with the factic existence of Dasein two essential and fundamental ways of thematization (*Vergegenständlichung*) are given, both of which are . . . despite their fundamental difference, apparently interrelated. (456, tr. m.)
>
> Our question aims at the thematization of being as such, that is, at the second essential way of thematization, in which philosophy is to constitute itself as science. (458, tr. m.)

We see that Heidegger here still takes the term "thematization" in a neutral, formal sense: it is a thematization of the being of beings that may or may not be objectifying.[9] Insofar as the positive sciences explicitly thematize beings, they share a common ground with the straightforward direction of everyday apprehension (456) and hence (although Heidegger does not say this here) their understanding is as much guided by Praesens as is the everyday involvement with beings. However, the *being* of beings, which the positive sciences must always implicitly intend, can *not* be encountered from this prevailing perspective (457). How, then, can the being of beings itself be thematized? On this Heidegger remarks only that the perspective from which "being" can be thematized is *opposite* to the prevailing direction:

> *[T]he projective preconception of being onto the horizon of its understandability* . . . is delivered up to uncertainty and stands continually in danger of being reversed. For this thematization of being must necessarily move in the direction of a projective preconception that runs counter to the everyday comportment to beings. (459, tr. m.)

If Dasein is guided by Praesens both in its involvement with beings and in the positive sciences, and if ontology unknowingly takes on this perspective, the projective preconception that enacts a countering movement should consist in drawing back from this narrow, one-sided perspective. This would allow it to do justice to the proper character of ecstatic Future and Past.[10]

Heidegger does not consider this further in GA 24—the movement stops, and only the temporal significance of the a priori for the phenomenological method is briefly mentioned again (461f). On the basis of the above, and in preparation for the coming chapters, I would like to present Heidegger's line of thought as follows.

Only when Praesens has been disclosed can anything appear as meaningful within that openness. Beings can only be encountered once the being of beings has been understood, but itself remains in the background. To allow beings to be encountered, ecstatic Present opens up a realm within which being can be understood as presence. This is also the case when thinking, from within the given horizon of Praesens, turns explicitly to the being of beings. In the way philosophy understands being, Praesens becomes so predominant that being—the essential as such—can merely be understood as final cause, ultimate ground, or in any case as that which cannot be affected by accidental and concomitant changes.[11] This means that being not only shows forth, but also withdraws from the way in which it presents itself. Heidegger considers this withdrawing movement to first enact the history of thinking.

If thinking is to modify itself so as to accord with its authentic possibilities, it should attempt to turn from beings to their being in a more radical way than metaphysics ever could. This thinking will have to modify the horizon of Praesens in such a way that the primordial threefoldness of Future, Past, and Present is given its due. We have seen how this occurs at the *existentiell* level in Dasein's authentic modification of its primordial openness, in which Dasein outstretches itself toward its thrownness (opened up by Past) and proper possibilities (opened up by Future). This means at the level of ontology that Past and Future open up a realm within which the absential as such is allowed to occur. In the light of this threefold Temporality, being itself will no longer appear as constant presence but as a presence which is pervaded to the core by absence—just as Dasein may permit the imminent possibility of death in its life.

To put it more concretely, Heidegger will no longer answer the question of "what something is" in terms of a prior ground or essence that also constitutes the ideal of all actual realizations. Heidegger tries to allow the "what" or the essential to show forth as the whole of the counter-striving ways in which a certain formal structure or possibility usually enacts itself and possibly might enact itself. Thus, for instance, the movement of human life can be understood against the background of a prior *archē* and a future *telos* that withdraw from life as it enacts itself, but, as absent, still play a part in it. The *telos* will then no longer appear as a possibility that is given at the outset and increasingly realizes itself. The very idea of a possible complete realization of the essential rests in a predominance of Present, which Heidegger sees as the ground for every fallenness.

The fact that thinking is finite and situated thus ultimately means not so much (or not only) that it is actually part of a concrete history, but primarily that it is guided by a temporal horizon that it has not itself brought about. Only on the ground of "forgetting" this horizon can something like the history of Western philosophy occur. Insofar as Temporality has in itself the tendency to increasingly confine itself to Present, philosophy has no power over the course of its own history. On the other hand, Heidegger will always emphasize that thinking has the possibility of freeing itself from the confined temporal perspective of the tradition. This does not, however, deny the finitude of that thinking. Freedom, whether it concerns the thematization of beings or of being, is always a thrown freedom.[12]

Now that is clarified how the threefold ecstatic-horizonal time constitutes the final condition of possibility of the understanding of being, the answer to the question concerning the meaning of being has in fact also been given. After all, meaning means nothing other than the toward-which or upon-which (*Woraufhin*) of the projective preconception (BT 151)—that is, the horizon from within which something is understandable. The unity of the horizonal schemes of time constitutes the meaning of being. This meaning turns out to consist not only of Praesens: if ecstatic Future and Past can extend themselves in such a way that they open up the absential that essentially belongs to being, they shed a different light on being.

Heidegger's remark that the idea of being is not simple or unifold (*einfach*) (196) refers to the primordial temporal horizon within which the being of beings can be understood and explicated in a variable manner. The primordial temporal meaning of being, which constantly threatens to confine itself to mere presence, grounds distinctions such as those between essence and existence or a priori and a posteriori. Hence, the different meanings of being thematized by Aristotle can only arise from within a projective preconception in which Present already decisively dominates the temporal horizon.

3.3 The Analogous Structures of Dasein and Ontology

The above account has elucidated how Heidegger traces every inauthenticity back to the self-increasing predominance of Present. Only a movement that runs counter to the dynamic of fallenness might allow primordial time to accomplish itself in an authentic way. The inauthentic and the authentic modification take different shapes in the involvement with innerworldly beings, in the concrete existence of Dasein and in ontology. The preontological understanding of being—guided by Praesens—always underlies these different possibilities. We have seen how Heidegger from his very first courses emphasizes that the philosophy which interprets factic life is marked by the same dynamic as life itself (cf. also 13). Up to now we have not considered the question of how the inauthentic and the authentic mode of being of philosophy itself should be understood. Apart from the question of *what* is brought to light in philosophy, it must also be possible to show *how* ontology—as a mode of human life—may enact itself and how these modes of enactment are grounded in temporality. It should be noted, however, that the mode of temporality which structures these possibilities is still different from the Temporality which delimits the reach of the understanding of being as such.

In any case, Heidegger will no longer understand the theoretical beholding of unchangeable principles as the authentic mode of thinking. A thinking that turns against metaphysics will have to do justice to the phronetic dynamic that belongs to human existence as such. This means on the one hand that it will no longer turn away from the ecstatic-horizonal temporality into which it has always already been thrown. On the other hand, when thinking assumes the confinements of the ontological realm that has been imparted to it, it will also be able to projectively widen the given boundaries of its horizon in such a way that "being" will no longer appear as constant presence. Thus it accomplishes a retrieving repetition at a most fundamental level. I will come back to this in 4.6.

I will now elucidate in more detail the parallels between the being of Dasein and the being of ontology. I take the view that Heidegger would have done this in *Time and Being*.[13] Passages from the early courses will confirm that Heidegger from the outset attuned his analytic of Dasein to the specific modification of human life that philosophy itself is. For this second repetition of the analytic of Dasein I will again start out from Dasein's primordial openness and its different modifications.

Understanding

When Heidegger in *Being and Time* characterizes understanding as a moment of primordial openness, his starting point is the implicit and nontheoretical understanding of innerworldly beings (148). This analysis of understanding, however, seeks to clarify the process of articulation or thematization *as such*. In this process—within which Heidegger distinguishes the "phases" understanding, interpretation, and assertion (§32–33)—the hermeneutical "as" is overturned into the apophantical "as" (158): the understanding of the hammer *as* hammer turns into a statement about the hammer *as* a thing with certain properties. In this way Heidegger indicates how the explicit elucidation of something tends to conceal the primordial character of that which is brought to light.

This clearly applies equally, if not even more, to the thematization of the being of beings: Heidegger considers the metaphysical thematization to have always concealed the phenomena as they are in themselves. An adequate interpretation first has to dismantle these concealments. This is only possible when thinking is aware of the assumptions and preliminary choices that already inhere in understanding as such.

Now Heidegger distinguishes three types of "choices" that precede every mode of thematization (150). Every interpretation consists in an appropriation of that which is understood and can only take place when Dasein is from the outset familiar with a given relevant whole. Heidegger calls this implicit familiarity the preliminary having (*Vorhabe*) of understanding. At the same time this appropriation is always guided by a certain perspective—the preliminary view (*Vorsicht*)—which "broaches" what has been given in the preliminary having with respect to a specific kind of interpretation. In the preliminary having and view one can recognize the two moments of retaining and awaiting. Heidegger calls the third moment the preliminary grasping (*Vorgriff*). This third moment pertains to the process of conceptualization and especially shows that Heidegger's analysis of understanding is not so much concerned with the way we interpret innerworldly beings, but with the understanding and thematization of being:

> That which is understood is held in the preliminary having and caught sight of in the "pre-view," and becomes comprehensible through the interpretation. The interpretation can draw the conceptuality belonging to the beings which are to be interpreted from these themselves, or else force them into concepts to which they, according to their own way of being, are opposed. Whatever the case—the interpretation has always already decided . . . upon a specific conceptuality; it is grounded in a *preliminary grasping*. (150, tr. m.)

We can imagine that a utensil will be interpreted on the basis of an appropriate preliminary grasping in its "in-order-to" character, and on the basis of an inappropriate one as a thing with certain properties. Yet Heidegger's formulation unmistakably refers to the way in which metaphysics "chooses" its concepts and to his own attempt to choose concepts in such a way that they disclose the matter itself. In this respect, the difference between the concepts of subject and Dasein is self-evident.[14]

Discourse, Idle Talk and Fallenness

A second moment of primordial openness, discourse, is explicated in the introduction of *Being and Time* as the *logos* which together with the word *phainomenon* makes up the concept of phenomenology. Heidegger uses this concept to summarize his own method, which consists in revealing that which shows itself as it is in itself (34). The *logos* is the condition of possibility of every disclosing or thematization of something, and hence grounds both the statements about beings and the beholding of the being of beings (33). Although *logos* or discourse is at work in every process of articulation, to say that the *logos* makes it possible to reveal beings and being is not to tell the full story. Heidegger's analysis of Aristotle's concept of *logos* from this period—to which I will return in the following chapters—shows that Heidegger considers this phenomenon to be that which also *thwarts* the disclosure of the being of beings. The apophantical *logos* allows the thematization of beings and is also indispensable in the disclosure of the being of beings. In the latter case, however, this *logos* has to draw back:

> [T]his discernment, insofar as it is to grasp the *archē*, must leave the *logos* behind. . . . That the *logos* can recede here has its ground in the *logos* itself. . . . Speaking as such does not primarily have the meaning of *apophainesthai*, letting beings be seen. On the contrary, only a quite specific *logos* is *logos apophantikos*. (GA 19:180; tr. m., cf. GA 17:25)

Although this questioning of the apophantical *logos* is scarcely visible in *Being and Time*, we have seen that Heidegger here refers briefly to a mode of thematization in which discourse does not become predominant at the expense of the other moments. As far as ontology itself is concerned, only such a retreating *logos* might do justice to the proper character of that which it discloses, that is to say, prevent the presentification of being. However, the *noein* as *human* faculty always needs the *logos*, which, once enacted, always threatens to take its own course.

While the introduction of *Being and Time* is concerned with the method of ontology—that is, with the way in which the being of beings can be revealed—when Heidegger reaches the thematic elucidation of discourse he starts out from the way in which *beings* are disclosed. His elucidation of the relation between discourse and language particularly attempts to understand the phenomenon of language on a more primordial level than the whole of spoken words. He understands language insofar as it is explicitly spoken to be grounded in a primordial capacity to articulate and constitute meaning.[15] What Heidegger says here about discourse, however, can also be applied to ontology:

> Discourse is the articulation of what is understandable. Thus it already underlies interpretation and statement. We called what can be articulated in interpretation, and thus more primordially already in discourse, meaning. (BT 161, tr. m.)

In *Being and Time* "meaning" especially pertains to the "meaning of being." In this context, "meaning" refers to the temporal horizon that is always already understood and which should be brought to light as such (151–52). In everydayness, that is, initially and mostly, discourse modifies itself in an inauthentic way:

> Discourse . . . has the possibility of becoming idle talk, and as such of not really keeping being-in-the-world open in an articulated understanding, but of closing it off (*verschließen*) and covering over (*verdecken*) innerworldly beings. (169)

"Closing off" and "covering over" are words that Heidegger also uses with respect to the concealing tendency of traditional ontology. Dasein is initially, and to a certain extent always, delivered over to veiling interpretations.[16] The existing language "decides" which matters can show forth and how this happens. This applies equally to the interpretation of beings and to the thematization of being:

> The understanding already stored in spoken language *not only* pertains to the . . . traditional uncovering of beings, *but also* to the way in which being is understood in a certain period (*das jeweilige Verständnis von Sein*) and to the possibilities and horizons available for new interpretation and conceptual articulation.[17]

Heidegger knows that he belongs to a metaphysical tradition that through its concepts has already decided how the being of beings can be thematized. The "they" of metaphysics, which suppresses and postpones every new questioning and discussion (169), is inconspicuously present throughout *Being and Time*. Heidegger often contrasts his own analyses with what "they" think—that is, are accustomed to thinking. No more than Dasein can fully withdraw from the power of the societal "they," can thinking fully discard the metaphysical idle talk that claims to have understood everything.[18] Thinking can, however, decide to open a way for itself from within traditional metaphysics to a different and more authentic mode of interpretation:

> Dasein can never escape the whole of everyday interpretations into which it has grown initially. All genuine understanding, interpretation and linguistic expression, rediscovery and new appropriation take place within it, out of it and against it. (169, tr. m.)

It seems hardly possible to express Heidegger's relation to traditional metaphysics more concisely than with the three prepositions "within," "out of," and "against."

Anxiety and Resolute Openness

As yet we have not considered the question as to how thinking can actually retrieve itself from fallenness. We have seen, however, that Heidegger distinguishes two moments in this countering movement. First, the usual relation to beings must be interrupted in order to explicitly gain insight into the essential, the being of beings or the conditions of possibility of what appears. One might say that philosophy from Plato to Husserl accomplishes only this first change of perspective. Second, the character of the ontological perspective must become radically different from the perspective guided by presence or Praesens that characterizes both the ontic and the traditional ontological mode of thematization. This is what Heidegger still has to do.

The analysis of anxiety shows that the possibility of accomplishing the first change of perspective already inheres in factically existing Dasein itself (§40). This brings us to the third moment of primordial openness, namely, disposition (*Befindlichkeit*). This moment pertains to the way in which Dasein primarily discloses its own thrownness. Dasein usually evades anxiety, the mood that confronts it with its thrownness and nothingness. However, anxiety can overtake Dasein; when this happens the beings to which Dasein has always clung lose their meaning. Not only is Dasein then thrown back on itself, but it also, according to Heidegger, gains insight into "world" itself as the horizon that allows beings to appear as meaningful (187). However, this worldliness can only really be understood in the phenomenological analysis itself (187). This analysis goes along with what is revealed to Dasein through anxiety, in order to conceptually articulate what Dasein only implicitly understands.

Because anxiety radically interrupts Dasein's everyday involvement with beings, Heidegger considers this mood to have a "*fundamental* methodical function" (190): this break with the world constitutes the condition for Dasein's turning to its own being and to being as such.[19] When Heidegger tries to trace back the possibility of the "reduction" of beings to their being at a *theoretical* level to a possible *existentiell* experience of Dasein, this in no way has to mean that phenomenologists must have experienced anxiety themselves. At issue here is primarily the *structural* analogy between human existence and philosophy. It is necessary, however, that the phenomenologist be able to suspend the self-evidence of the world in his or her own way.

In later texts—to anticipate matters—Heidegger indicates that the different phases of the history of philosophy are characterized by different basic moods, each of which in its own way interrupts the immediate involvement with beings and thus makes possible the turning toward being. The basic mood in which Greek thinking could take place was—also according to Plato and Aristotle themselves—wonder or amazement. In modern thinking this mood makes way for a doubt that is merely the obverse of an unshakable certainty. Heidegger finally designates the—plural—basic mood of authentic thinking in the *Contributions* with words like dread, reticence, and timidity.[20] We could say that these three basic moods are respectively characterized by an experience of negativity which is permitted to a certain extent in Greek thinking, not at all in modern thinking, and to the full extent in an authentic thinking. The degree to which the understanding of being admits the "not" will therefore determine the way being itself appears: either it does not yet appear as constant presence, or it does, or it no longer does. The basic moods of thinking can thus be understood as different modes of what Heidegger at the level of the analytic of Dasein denotes with the phenomenon of anxiety. Even in *Being and Time*, however, the analysis of anxiety is already guided by the question as to how Dasein can turn away from beings and toward their being—that is to say, accomplish the possibility of ontology.

With regard to the second "reduction," which constitutes the difference between traditional ontology and his own thinking, Heidegger in *Being and Time* likewise searches for an authentic possibility of Dasein's factic existence. Being overtaken by anxiety does not in itself lead to authenticity, but as the first moment of the movement in which the openness of Dasein accomplishes itself in a resolute and anticipating way it must be accompanied by an explicit turning toward itself. Now Heidegger takes the structure of conscience to confirm that Dasein in its factic existence is indeed able to come into its own, that is, to face itself *as* a thrown and finite openness (cf. 267–68). By formalizing the movement in which Dasein answers the call of conscience, Heidegger can interpret this turning as a proper or authentic modification of Dasein's primordial openness (296–97). Going along with Dasein's understanding of its own conscience, his analysis of Dasein's relation to its own death (as extreme possibility) and to its own thrownness (as radical being-guilty) reveals the radical finitude of the movement in which Dasein opens itself to its "future" and "past."[21]

If Dasein attempts to no longer evade this finitude, it is not only involved in that which is present (to which past and anticipated events also belong), but extends itself to that which essentially withdraws from its reach. While ecstatic Future allows Dasein to open itself to that which is futural or possible as such, ecstatic Past throws light on its irretrievable and abysmal ground (325–26). In thus resisting the tendency of fallenness, Dasein in no way withdraws from the world: an authentic modification of "being with" only means that things, other human beings and one's own being are brought to light in a new way (298).

The analysis of Dasein's being-guilty can now also be read with respect to its meaning for the way in which ontology relates to its own temporal "ground." On this Heidegger says:

> [D]asein . . . which as such has to lay the ground of itself, can *never* gain power over that ground, and yet it has, in its existence, to take upon itself the ground that it is. Being the ground into which it has been thrown, is the possibility of existence about which care is concerned. (284, tr. m.)

Analogously, Heidegger's own thinking is concerned with a primordial grounding of metaphysics (KM 204), that is, a way in which philosophy might ground itself (GA 26:275). It is Temporality that ultimately grounds every thinking and can be explicitly revealed by thinking *as* ground. However, the "foundation" given in fundamental ontology no less *undermines* the possibility of ontology. Temporality is an abyss that makes possible the openness of Dasein yet also essentially threatens it: "'Ground' [is] only accessible as meaning, even if that meaning itself is an abyss of meaninglessness" (BT 152). A thinking which faces that abyss and somehow bears the unbearable ground by which it is borne, will on this "basis" allow itself to be guided by a temporal projective preconception that gives the radical finitude of human life its due. However, such a turn is not simply to be achieved from within Dasein or from within thinking itself. This seems to be something else that Heidegger wants to indicate in his analysis of conscience. With the call of conscience—"it calls"—something emerges which is neither within nor outside of Dasein, and by which it is overtaken (275). As a mode of primordial openness, conscience is grounded in temporality, which is equally neither within nor outside Dasein (419). In a certain sense, this final condition of possibility of every form of right or wrong deprives Dasein of its autonomy, but not of its ethical obligation to attempt to resist the constantly lurking dominance of Present.

In this chapter I have tried to put the analytic of Dasein into perspective and to focus attention on the meaning of this analysis for the being of ontology itself in its inauthentic and authentic possibilities. This first focus on *Time and Being* entails that the distinction between an early and a later Heidegger is moderated. A second aspect of this proposed focus consists in a thematization of Heidegger's own method. This will allow a closer determination of what Heidegger considers to be the possibility most proper to thinking.

4

The Temporality of Thinking: Heidegger's Method

In the third part of GA 24, *The Scientific Method of Ontology and the Idea of Phenomenology,* Heidegger was to have elucidated the temporal structure of his own method. Here he could have clarified how the difference between his method and that of metaphysics has its ground in different modifications of Temporality. However, as mentioned earlier, this part was not written. At the end of GA 24 Heidegger makes some brief remarks on deconstruction, reduction, and construction as moments of the phenomenological method, remarks which clearly do not belong in the chapter about the ontological difference. Evidently he wishes to indicate where he had been intending to go:

> We cannot now enter any further into the essential and fundamental constituent parts of this method. In fact, we have applied them all the time. All we would have to do now would be to follow again the ways we already took, yet now explicitly reflecting on them. (GA 24:467, tr. m.)

This repetition of the ways already taken, explicitly considering the method, will be undertaken in this chapter. I will initially examine Heidegger's first courses and show how deeply these are already concerned with the problem of method. Thus, starting again at the "beginning," but now explicitly with regard to the problem of method, this interpretation supplements the discussion of Heidegger's early interpretation of Aristotle in chapter 1; in the early 1920s Heidegger tries to answer the question of how philosophy can do justice to Dasein's facticity by reflecting on both Aristotle's distinction between *phronēsis* and *sophia* and Husserl's phenomenology.

One might say that Heidegger's early texts are all devoted to the question as to whether—and if so, how—thinking can thematize the being of beings in such a way that it may appear as itself. I will try to show that this question concerning philosophy's own possibility, and that also means its own method, continues to play an important role in *Being and Time*. Heidegger was also to have thematized the character of his own method in *Time and Being*.[1] I take the concept of temporality, which underlies his method, to be an important key to the meaning of all his work.

Although Heidegger never explicitly elucidated the temporality of his method, it seems to me that all his analyses point in this direction. In order to cast light on the themes Heidegger planned to elaborate in the last part of GA 24 and in a part of *Time and Being*, I will proceed in two different ways. First, I will examine what Heidegger himself says about the phenomenological method in the texts before, around, and in *Being and Time*. Second, I will try to clarify the character of Heidegger's methodical principle by analyzing what he actually does, using the analytic of Dasein as the main example. More historical aspects of Heidegger's relation to his predecessors and contemporaries will remain in the background.[2]

4.1 Phenomenology as a Basic Problem for Itself

> "Basic problems of phenomenology"—the most urgent and never eradicable, the most primordial and most definitive basic problem of phenomenology is phenomenology *itself* for itself. (GA 58:1)

Not without pathos Heidegger thus begins one of his first courses, which has the same title as GA 24. Here I will use Heidegger's very first course to show how in this period he begins to radically question phenomenology itself. The title of this course is *The Idea of Philosophy and the Problem of Worldview*.[3] In the introduction Heidegger follows Husserl in distinguishing philosophy from the idea of worldview. As a mode of positive involvement with beings, worldview can itself become one of the problems for philosophy, but it is not the main issue: "The cardinal question concerns the essence, the concept of philosophy" (GA 56/57:12). The philosophy that tries to remain free from every ontic involvement, Heidegger here calls primal science (*Urwissenschaft*). The meaning of this science is to be elucidated as the course proceeds, and by means of the method of primal science itself. The problem is, however, that this method still has to be developed. Philosophy must drag itself out of the "swamp" of the natural attitude and give itself its ground; this is the very "Münchhausen-problem of spirit" (16). Heidegger's first approach to extracting philosophy from the swamp of traditional conceptions is a negative one: various standard "ways out" are critically discussed and then rejected as possible solutions. In particular—following in Husserl's footsteps—he "deconstructs" the attempt to ground philosophy in (empirical) psychology.[4] Further, he argues that current value-philosophy uncritically assumes that all modes of experience are grounded in a theoretical relation to reality. This primacy of theory must be rejected, since the theoretical itself refers back to pretheoretical experiences.[5] But he criticizes not only the neo-Kantians. Viewed from the perspective of primal science:

> the idea of a *system*, which according to its essence entails that the theoretical gains absolute dominance, becomes as such illusory. We then find ourselves face to face with Hegel, that is, we face one of the most difficult confrontations. (97)

The confrontation with Hegel is not pursued in this course—things are already difficult enough. In any case, all the neo-Kantian theoretical terms will have to be left behind in order to make way for a more primordial thinking. Poor in concepts, this thinking must try to thematize as purely as possible the structure of lived experiences (63).

In the second and final part, Heidegger uses a few examples to gain insight into the structure of experiencing a utensil (a lectern) and its modification into a perception of a thing. Having taken these first steps toward the analysis of innerworldly beings, he returns in the last chapter to the problem of the method of primal science. This chapter is concerned with the question whether lived experiences (*Erlebnisse*) can be thematized at all (98). When someone actually perceives something that belongs to the environing world, like a lectern, and is fully immersed in that perception, it is possible to subsequently behold this perception itself. Heidegger then takes a further step and asks how this beholding is itself accomplished.[6] It may be, he suggests, that the phenomenological beholding of the lived experience is itself a mode of theory that does not do justice to the proper mode of being of that which it beholds:

> Knowledge has objects, issues. It fixates things (*sie stellt fest*), and does so objectively. Thus, a science of experiences (*Erlebnisse*)

> would have to thematize and objectify these experiences anyway. Thereby it would precisely deprive them of their character of being lived through, of occurring (*ihr Er-lebnis- und Ereignischarakter*), that is, deprive them of their nonobjectifiable character.
>
> But all such difficulties are perhaps surmountable. (76–77)

The course—and not only this one—is largely taken up by the attempt to surmount these difficulties. This also leads Heidegger to discuss Natorp's criticism of phenomenology. Natorp stated that phenomenological thematization and description inevitably bring the stream of experiences to a halt.[7] Heidegger takes seriously this criticism of Husserl, although the solution he seeks is different from Natorp's. He considers Natorp's effort to reconstruct the subjective sphere by and through unavoidable, disrupting objectifications at the expense of everything else to show a radical predominance of the theoretical, "like had not been proclaimed since Hegel" (108).

But how might one proceed otherwise? Is a nonobjectifying science at all possible? Heidegger argues that Natorp's arguments may be based on a prejudice: it is not certain that all language is necessarily objectifying, and neither is it certain that phenomenological beholding is necessarily descriptive. It could be that this way of seeing—if the term "seeing" is not misleading in itself—has "a totally different character" (111). If Heidegger wishes to retain the possibility of a primal science, he will have to defend against Natorp that not every thematization necessarily entails objectification. He does this by searching at the level of the lived experiences themselves for a phenomenon that confirms the possibility of a nonobjectifying mode of thematization. He thus returns to the analysis of experiences, without however explicitly pursuing the issue of method again.

In this course Heidegger investigates three types of experiences. First, the formal question as to whether there is something at all (*gibt es etwas*), second the nonobjectifying experience of something that is meaningful, and finally the objectification of something.

If we look carefully at what happens when we ask if there is something at all, then we do not encounter anything like a psychic process, let alone an "ego": the question is *directed* toward something, and thus has the character of an occurring movement in which I am involved myself (*Ereignis*). This is not just a mere existing event (*ein bloßes seiendes Geschehen*) (69, cf. 75). This specific question pertains to the "something" as such (*das Etwas*) or the sheer fact that "there is" (*es gibt*) something. Although the content of this "something" is not determined at all, it may not be equated with that which all things have in common.[8]

Heidegger next contrasts the question concerning the formal "something" with a lived experience of a concrete being: seeing the lectern when entering the lecture hall in the morning. The experience of the lectern is not based on the perception of brown surfaces, but the lectern is immediately given as meaningful—for example, as too high or too low—that is to say, as "worldly" (*welthaft*).[9] This is not the case when we ask whether there is something at all:

> [T]he "something" as such, which is questioned with regard to the way it "is given," is not worlding (*weltet nicht*). . . . This grasping, fixating thematization of something can only take place thanks to a repression of my own self. . . . The experience which consists in such a fixation is no more than a residue of a lived experience (*Erlebnis*); it is a de-living experience (*ein Ent-leben*).[10]

Heidegger here suggests—deliberately, I think—that the ultimate objectification consists in the formal inquiry into the "something" as such, but only to later retract this "presupposition." First, however, he introduces the objectifying, de-living experience of a thing. In the series "lectern—box—brown—wood—thing," the increasing objectification of the lectern infringes more and more upon its worldly, meaningful character.[11] When epistemology, for instance, regards the mere givenness or reality of something as the most primordial characteristic of beings, it mistakes the nonprimordial for the primordial, and does not do justice to the way things are initially experienced.

Heidegger, using various examples, thus tries to let the character of a lived experience appear as itself. He does this on the one hand by keeping traditional philosophical theories at a distance, and on the other by contrasting a lived experience of what belongs to the environing world (*Umwelterlebnis*) with the de-living experience, which constitutes its objectifying modification. These two "moments" are so closely related that it is sometimes difficult to distinguish them. After all, the traditional philosophical reflection on lived experiences is itself a form of de-living:

> [I]n reflection we have taken up a theoretical position. As we said before, every theoretical relation consists in a de-living experience (*ist ein entlebendes*). (100)

That is indeed what Heidegger said. But was it true? We are moving toward the denouement.

Up to now Heidegger has presented the process of theorization as a linear process in which experiences are increasingly deprived of their lived character, culminating in the empty, formal "something" as such, which is absolutely deprived of world (*Weltlos*). This argument is revealed at the end of the course to be untenable (112). According to Heidegger, a fundamental distinction must be made between the different degrees of theorization, which pertain to—and remain bound to—a certain region on the one hand, and a purely formal way of theorizing on the other. The latter possibility is not in fact the final link in the chain of de-living experiences, but, on the contrary, is not in any way part of it. Because the fact that something is, the "something" as such, can be said not only of a lectern, a color, and a thing, but also of an experience:

> *The formal thematization is free*, that is, it is not bound to a certain level (*hat keine Stufengebundenheit*). *Every* level has in itself the possibility of being seen in a formal way. (114)
>
> Accordingly, one would have to distinguish between two fundamentally different modes of the theoretical, whose essential connection initially poses a huge problem.[12]

If the formal theorization is qualitatively different from the objectifying theorization, philosophy does not necessarily have to be objectifying. Here, we might say, Heidegger draws a breath of relief, in spite of the advent of a new problem. Natorp's criticism of phenomenology does not mean that scientific philosophy *as such* is impossible.

However, in order to reach this point Heidegger has had to implicitly take a final step, which is difficult to trace in the text. He has established that at the level of ontic experiences a relation to beings is possible which does not pertain to the meaningful, environing world, but is not objectifying either: the purely formal question "is there something." This question does not encroach, has no influence on the character of that about which it is posed. Viewed rightly, the experience of the "something" as such does not focus on something specific, but on that which can be experienced as such. This means that the involvement with the "something" as such precedes *every* concrete experience; the something

> does not constitute . . . a theoretical and stiffening fixation of that which can be experienced. It is rather the index of the highest potentiality of life. . . . It is the "*not-yet*," that is, that which has not yet burst into a genuine life, it is essentially *preworldly*. (115)

This passage evidences that Heidegger no longer regards the question concerning the "something" as one of the many lived experiences, but as an approach which precedes every experience. That which as "not-yet" precedes the ontic experiences of something specific can only be adequately revealed at a *theoretical* level by means of a formal theorization. This theorization is intended to thematize the primordial understanding of "something" as such, preceding any actual experience of something. In later years this understanding will develop (partly on the basis of Aristotle) into the preontological understanding of being.[13] That there is a difference between the "something" that grounds every possible ontic experience and the "something" that is a correlate of a formal theorization, is briefly indicated in the following passage:

> The formally thematized "something" that can become an object of knowledge is rooted in the pre-worldly "something" of life itself (*diesem vorweltlichen Lebens-etwas*). . . . The tendency into a world can be theoretically deflected *before* it has actually accomplished itself. (116)

In the words of *Being and Time*: starting from the understanding of being that grounds every ontic involvement with beings, the being (of Dasein or innerworldly beings) can be explicitly thematized, and in such a way (formally) that no objectification occurs. This means that the possibility of phenomenology as primal science is grounded in or motivated by an essential moment of human experience as such, in other words, of life itself (116). It also means that in contrast to Natorp, Heidegger does not try to turn back to life itself through a series of objectifications. That leads only to a dead end.

Starting out from what will later be called the understanding of being, Heidegger maintains that a formal, nonobjectifying perspective is able to preserve the relation with the preworldly something. This formal approach allows the living, dynamic character of lived experiences to proceed undisturbed, while these experiences are nevertheless understood in their essential structure.

Here we see Heidegger distancing himself from Husserl with regard to the analogy between the natural and the phenomenological attitude, though still accepting the idea of such an analogy. First, after tracing back these two possibilities to the preworldly understanding of the "something" as such, Heidegger distinguishes between an objectifying and a nonobjectifying mode of both lived experiences and the phenomenological thematization of these experiences. Second, Heidegger no longer understands the *character* of phenomenological thematization as analogous to perception. However, he remains somewhat vague as to the specific character of this theorization. At the end he briefly refers in this regard to hermeneutical intuition, which goes along with the proper dynamic of experiencing (117). This understanding, contrasted with the fixating gaze of phenomenology, is to become the methodical basis for Heidegger's primal science.

The course ends by summarizing the distinction between the "preworldly 'something' of life in itself," with which every experience is always already implicitly involved, and two theoretical spheres that spring from this: the sphere of formal thematization and the sphere of objectifying thematization.[14] These spheres constitute the correlates of primal science and the traditional modes of science, respectively. Heidegger appears not to distinguish between the traditional modes of philosophy and the positive sciences.[15] The formal "object" of primal science springs directly from the preworldly sphere, while the correlate of the objectifying sciences arises from secondary, generalizing acts that deprive lived experiences of their lived character.

In other words: the objectifying, theoretical thematization tries to gain access to life as such—that is to say, to the structure of the lived experiences—*via* the positive involvement with beings. The formal thematization that occurs in primal science, on the other hand, turns itself, from within the implicit involvement with the "something" proper to human life as such, directly to the preworldliness itself, that is to say, to the not-yet, to that which precedes the plurality of possible experiences. This mode of science thus has nothing in common with natural ontic involvement, as the positive sciences and traditional philosophy do.

I must say, however, that in GA 56/57 Heidegger is still struggling with these issues and that his analysis is far from clear. The terminology he uses is also difficult and at times unfathomable. However, it is clear that here for the first time the decisive questions are raised.

At the end of his first course, Heidegger further remarks that language does not necessarily have an objectifying character. Normal speech is also capable of expressing the dynamic character of occurring lived experiences (*Ereignischaraktere*)—that is to say, of going with the flow of life itself (117). It is clear that formal theorization will have to develop a mode of speaking that is different from objectifying theorization. The concepts of primal science will have to refer to the "preceding" without presentifying it. This function of theoretical concepts will be called "formal indication" fairly soon after GA 56/57. A formal indicative concept does not presentify something, does not fixate, but indicates a *direction*. The reader follows this direction and thus gains insight into that which cannot be objectified, but may show itself by using (existing) language in a different way.

We have seen that GA 56/57 tries to answer the question concerning the possibility of philosophy as nonobjectifying science via a negative and a positive way. The negative way will in later texts develop into the deconstruction of the history of philosophy. The positive way is exemplified in the early courses when Heidegger, starting out from the analysis of how something is experienced and thematized in daily life, tries to indicate the different possible modes of philosophical thematization. This analysis develops into the analytic of Dasein. The phenomena that are thematized in the early courses are unmistakably chosen because of their significance for the question concerning the character of philosophy itself.

While in GA 56/57 the analysis of the different lived experiences still plays a subordinate role and remains embedded within the deconstruction of philosophy on the one hand and the question concerning the possibility of Heidegger's own thinking on the other, this analysis becomes increasingly dominant in the subsequent courses. The increasing elaboration of the analysis of Dasein does not, however, entail a real change of perspective. In the courses up to *Being and Time,* the question concerning the possibility of philosophy itself remains extremely important for the analyses of the structures that ground the ways in which Dasein encounters beings. I tried to show in chapter 3 that this is also the case in *Being and Time* itself and in GA 24, but that there it is less clearly evident, as both texts are incomplete.

4.2 The Formal Indication

The early courses will only be discussed further here insofar as they add anything to GA 56/57 with respect to the question of method.

This mostly concerns the remarks—generally quite rare—about the meaning of the formal indication. That which is seen in phenomenology will have to be adequately explained to others. The question is thus how phenomena can be articulated in such a way that they can appear as themselves.

The term formal indication is used for the first time in the course *Basic Problems of Phenomenology* given in 1919/1920. From Heidegger's few remarks on the issue, we may infer that the formal indicative use of a concept is no more than a first step.[16] Only in the next course, *Phenomenology of Intuition and Expression*, does Heidegger state in so many words that the formal indication is indeed indispensable, but also entails a danger: the formal indication might be understood as a purely formal concept, relating only to the general and saying nothing more about the phenomena that are gathered together in such a concept (GA 59:62–63). Heidegger emphasizes that the formal indication, despite its formal character, must intimate something about the concrete possibilities that inhere in the concept. A first formal indication of, for example, the phenomenon of facticity can therefore never be the goal of the analysis, but is

> a non prejudicing, delimiting way of touching the factic (*Antastung des Faktischen*), by which, however, no decisive results are produced.[17]

Thus, the formal indication, unlike the generalizing concept, appears not to break the relation with meaningful facticity. It does not encroach, does not infringe upon facticity. But if the formal indication is not brought about by universalizing the factic, what then is its relation to facticity? While both GA 59 and GA 58 mainly describe what the formal indication is not, this question is explicitly thematized in the next course.

The course *Introduction to the Phenomenology of Religion* from 1920/21 consists of two parts, the first of which deals with the method of philosophy.[18] Heidegger argues here that philosophy, which springs from factic life, should turn back to this life in order to understand itself (GA 60:8). Thus, one will first have to understand the proper character of this life. According to Heidegger, life can be formally characterized as "historical" (55). The question is, however, what this means precisely. Is human life historical because, like all kinds of other things, it occurs in time, because it is a kind of process? In that case we start from the apparently most general meaning of "historical," which is then applied to factic life

(56). However, the proper character of human temporality can never come to light in this way (cf. 65). The formal indication must therefore have a different meaning. As the first moment of phenomenological thematization (65), its aim is to keep off (any) obtruding objectifications:

> [T]he formal indication *keeps off* something, it is a preliminary way of *securing* that preserves the enacting character (*Vollzugscharakter*). The necessity of this precautionary measure ensues from the lapsing tendency of factic life experience, which is again and again inclined to slide down into what is object-like. Nevertheless, it is from out of this tendency that we must bring the phenomena to the fore. (64, cf. 141)

Heidegger proposes that three moments must be distinguished when an experience is thematized in phenomenology. One should ask first *what* is intended in that experience, second *how* this "what" is experienced, and third how this experience actually *enacts* itself.[19] Here we may think of the lectern, the initially pretheoretical relation to this "what," and the different ways in which this relation can modify itself.

Since a formal-ontological determination—in the sense of Husserl's formal ontology—merely starts from the theoretical involvement with the "what," this determination conceals the dynamic, occurring character of the experience (63). The formal indication, on the other hand, should be able to prevent this theoretical preconception. Not because it already specifies the content of the different ways in which a relation to something enacts itself, but because it still keeps these possibilities open:

> The relation (*Bezug*) and enactment (*Vollzug*) of the phenomenon is *not* determined in advance, but is left in the air (*wird in der Schwebe gehalten*). (64)

This remark can be clarified with an example from *Being and Time*. When Heidegger characterizes the being of Dasein as "being-in-the-world," this formal indication on the one hand keeps away traditional presuppositions concerning the relation between subject and object. On the other hand this formal indication is such that it still leaves enough space to further determine the different possible modifications of this "being-in-the-world."[20] Heidegger was to have elucidated this in GA 60 by starting out from the formal indication of factic life as "historical."[21]

The explanation of this methodical principle was meant to prepare the analysis of the "historical" and the way in which it becomes accessible in the religious experience of life. However, Heidegger does not get the chance to complete his preparatory reflections on method. Students had complained to the dean of the faculty about the abstract, methodological character of the course, when they had been promised phenomenology of religion. During the course they also seem to have protested against Heidegger's abstract explanation. Heidegger therefore switches abruptly to an interpretation of Paul's epistles, knowing that the students will not understand his real intentions.[22]

But he doesn't give up. A year later he comes back to the problem of the formal indication, now in connection with the question concerning the "what" of philosophy itself. The course *Phenomenological Interpretations to Aristotle. Introduction to Phenomenological Research* (GA 61) deals not so much with Aristotle, but mainly with the question as to how philosophy itself should be defined. The two main parts focus on the question concerning philosophy and factic life as fundamental phenomenon respectively. In the latter part we find important steps toward the analytic of Dasein, especially with regard to fallenness and the possibility of resisting this ruining tendency. Insofar as philosophy frees itself from its one-sided involvement with world and objectivity, it constitutes one of the possible ways of enacting a "counter-ruining movement."[23]

What philosophy is, can be denoted with a formal indication as a cognitive relation which "grasps" and determines its subject of inquiry (GA 61:54). This can be said of all sciences—so as yet it says nothing about the proper meaning of science or about the different modes of science, including philosophy (55). The first formal indication may therefore not be considered independently, but must guide the understanding to the full meaning of philosophy. Even when philosophy is more closely determined as a mode of knowledge that is concerned with fundamental principles, it has not yet been decided what "principle" means in this connection (57). It is possible, however, to indicate what belongs to beings in principle:

> It is important to explicitly keep in mind that being, the meaning of being, is that which belongs to all beings as their philosophical principle. However, this principle is not what is "general" to all beings, it is not a highest species under which beings are subsumed as particular cases. (58)

We can see that in the meantime Heidegger has reread Aristotle. He can now formally define philosophy as

> *a cognitive relation to beings as being.* It still remains to be seen whether to all beings and to every particular being. . . . Further, we do not specify the meaning of the "as," how it is to be understood. (58)

Thus, even this formal characteristic still leaves open different possibilities. It remains as yet undecided how philosophy actually relates to beings as being. We know that in this regard Heidegger will always distinguish between a ruining and a counter-ruining possibility. If the philosophical definition of philosophy relates to that which essentially belongs to philosophy—that is to say, to the *being* of this mode of knowledge—then this definition will have to be such that it allows for a further specification of the different possible ways in which philosophy can enact itself. In GA 61 Heidegger tries to develop such a definition via the detour of analyzing the ontological meaning of factic life as such (cf. 88, 117).

We may infer from the example of the formal indication of philosophy that this indication pertains to the "what" or the "being" of philosophy, but in such a way that the denoted "what" is not posited as an independent essence. If the formal indication is understood in the right way, one does not intend the content of the formal indication itself, but that to which it refers (32). Thus, by pointing in an initial direction, the formal-indicative definition should lead to the fulfillment (*Erfüllung*) or confirmation (*Ausweisung*) of what initially was only indicated:

> The empty content (*das leer Gehaltliche*), viewed with respect to the structure of its meaning, is at the same time that which indicates the direction of its enactment (*die Vollzugsrichtung*). (33)

> The indicating definition is . . . characterized as a definition by which the theme that is to be determined (*der zu bestimmende Gegenstand*) is not fully and appropriately given, but only indicated. As a genuine indication however, this definition first brings its theme to the fore in a fundamental way. The indication itself implies that the concretization cannot be had right away, but constitutes a task . . . for a specifically structured accomplishment. (32)

Far from being meaningless or random, the formal indication guides the understanding toward the full concreteness of the phenomenon (34, 35). The formal indication demands as it were of itself a specification of the various ways in which the "what" might enact itself.[24] In the early courses, however, the methodical significance of this deformalization is not really thematized.[25] We will therefore now move on from these courses.

Heidegger's attempt to break through to the proper dynamic of factic life can only succeed if its actual content remains undetermined. In chapter 2 in particular I showed how Heidegger's analysis of the being of Dasein always starts out from the distinction between a formal structure on the one hand and the indifferent, inauthentic and authentic modifications of this structure on the other. Formal concepts such as existence, discourse, care, and primordial openness reveal different aspects of the formal fundamental structure of Dasein (cf. BT 53). Since the different modifications of such formal structures essentially belong to the being of Dasein, these are also denoted by formal-indicative concepts. They are indeed less "empty," but nevertheless delimit a realm of concrete possibilities. This means that the existential analysis does not decide on the question as to how individual human beings can realize specific possibilities from within their own factic situation (cf. BT 12, 298). According to Heidegger, it is not the task of philosophy to give direction to the factic mode of existence of human beings, but that of for instance religion, ethics, or science. This distinction between philosophy and worldview is to be found in the introductions of almost all the early courses.

4.3 The Analytic of Dasein from a Methodical Perspective

What has been said up to now about Heidegger's method will have to be confirmed by the way he actually proceeds. Taking the analytic of Dasein as an *example* of that procedure can now serve to elucidate the specific character of Heidegger's method.[26] In doing this, I will not so much focus on the formal-indicative concepts that Heidegger uses, but rather on that which these concepts bring to light. This perspective will also allow the analysis of the being of innerworldly beings to appear in a different way. Precisely because this analysis seems rather contrived, it can be used to show how much Heidegger forces the phenomena to conform to his methodical preconception.

The Being of Dasein

Evidently, Heidegger cannot be satisfied with merely revealing the being of Dasein by means of a formal structure that modifies itself in either an inauthentic or an authentic manner. Although these three moments allow life to be revealed in its dynamic, they do not account for the radical finitude of that life. The Greek-Christian perspective—which culminates in Hegel's philosophy—also interprets human life by means of such a threefold structure. From that perspective, however, every mode of inauthenticity or lapsing can at best be understood as a subordinate moment in the movement in which a principle that is given at the outset increasingly realizes itself.[27] Such a concept of movement, Heidegger argues, cannot do justice to the radical finitude of Dasein. But how, then, can that be done from within the given threefoldness? Does it allow itself to be modified?

First of all, I should add something here about the meaning of the structure which indicates that Dasein is, one way or another, always its own being (*Jemeinigkeit*) (BT 42). This concept can easily be misunderstood; one tends not to take it as a formal indication, but as a determination of a content. By this concept, however, Heidegger solely means that Dasein itself always in some way has to accomplish its own being, and that it does this in an indifferent, inauthentic or authentic way:

> [Dasein] can only have lost itself and it can only have not yet gained itself because it is, according to its essence, possibly *authentic*, that is, belongs to itself. Both the ontological modes *authenticity* and inauthenticity . . . are grounded in the fact that Dasein as such is determined by always-being-mine (*Jemeinigkeit*). (BT 42–43, tr. m., cf. 53)

When Dasein frees itself from the grasp of the "they," this is an existentiell modification of the "they" in which the formal structure of the always-being-mine is first explicitly given its due (cf. 130). Dasein then opens itself for its own being—that is to say, for the essential possibilities it has in itself. The concept always-being-mine does not itself give any concretization to this "being," but pertains only to the distinction between the different modes of existence as such. It thus structures the further determinations of the being of Dasein as being-in-the-world, openness, and care, which are all revealed in their different modifications.

The always-being-mine hence expresses that Dasein initially and mostly turns away from itself, but can possibly turn toward itself. In order to do more justice to the movement in which Dasein turns away from itself than is possible from the traditional metaphysical perspective, *Being and Time* starts out from the indifferent modification of the being of Dasein. This everydayness or averageness can hardly be articulated conceptually, precisely because it is a mode in which Dasein does not specifically move itself in a certain direction:

> Mostly, and that is important, Dasein indwells neither the mode of authenticity nor that of a sheer being at a loss, but . . . indwells a particular indifference that, again, is not nothing, but something positive: the averageness of Dasein, which we call everydayness and of which it is very difficult to categorically grasp the ontological meaning (*Seinssinn*). (GA 21:229–30, cf. BT 43–44)

However, Heidegger understands this modification in such a way that of itself—due to the presentifying dynamic of temporality—it tends more toward inauthenticity than toward authenticity. The term "initially and mostly" therefore pertains to the whole of the indifferent and the inauthentic modification—that is to say, to the movement in which Dasein tends to increasingly turn away from its proper possibilities.[28]

Since Heidegger understands everydayness as a privative modification of the formal structure of Dasein, this analysis can also give an insight into that formal structure itself. Heidegger does this, for example, when he formally characterizes the being of Dasein as care. This structure is the condition of possibility that grounds the different possible modifications of human existence. The indifferent-inauthentic mode of being of Dasein is thus thematized by moving back and forth between the formal structure of Dasein and the deformalization in which this structure is not given its due. In this way the analysis corresponds to the predominant movement of existence itself.

But we have not yet reached the end. Because it essentially belongs to Dasein to be more than it actually is, an analysis of this indifferent-inauthentic mode of existence does not reveal the whole of the being of Dasein (BT 230, 232). Heidegger therefore tries in a third step to delimit the structure of the authentic or proper mode of existence. He does this by forging a mode of existence which explicitly does justice to the given formal fundamental structure of Dasein. This second deformalization thus reveals the proper possibilities of Dasein. Since the threefold temporality that grounds the different modifications initially and mostly modifies itself into Present, this authenticity can only occur as a possible countermovement to fallenness. The Present, which allows that which is essential to occur in the world, is at the same time that which unremittingly thwarts this movement. Precisely for this reason, the authentic modification of the being of Dasein can only be delimited as a possibility, and not as a *telos* that increasingly actualizes itself. The "initially and mostly" is thus complemented with the "possibly." Heidegger understands these two modes to delimit the entire realm of existentiell possibilities.[29]

The structure of the analytic of Dasein as sketched above is not yet complete, however. As I pointed out earlier, Heidegger also wished to fulfill the phenomenological requirement to keep off any metaphysical constructions. Heidegger owes it to his phenomenological origins to bring his analyses into line with concrete human experiences, albeit perhaps only to conceal the constructed character of his own analyses. The attempt to also bring the authentic modification of the being of Dasein into line with possible experiences of Dasein itself thus leads him to take the phenomena of anxiety and conscience to be affirmations of a possible existentiell overturning from inauthenticity to authenticity.[30] This constructed overturning, despite various precautionary measures, makes it hardly possible for Heidegger to prevent Dasein's "itinerary" from closely resembling a movement that comes from and through inauthenticity to authenticity. Such a traditional approach to human life does not allow the being of Dasein to show forth as an essential and insurmountable strife between the movement in which it turns away from itself and the movement in which it tries to resist that turning.

If *Being and Time* fails anywhere, I would say that it is on this point. In the attempt to indicate the authentic possibility of Dasein, this possibility always threatens to be brought within the reach of the attainable. I can imagine that Heidegger began to realize how *Being and Time,* against his wishes, still remained tied to the projective preconception from which he was trying to free himself.[31] Precisely that failure indicates how inevitably Present prevails whenever thinking tries to find words to articulate the essential. Before you know it, a work in progress turns itself against its initial intentions.

The Being of Innerworldly Beings

The analysis in *Being and Time* of the way in which we use utensils has the purpose of revealing the phenomenon of world. The formal indication "world" pertains to the horizon within which beings can appear as meaningful. This horizon is characterized as significance (*Bedeutsamkeit*) (87). The different ways in which innerworldly beings appear to Dasein will each in their own way have to show something of this significance. As I said, involvement with utensils takes place from within a horizon of Praesens, which is kept open by the awaiting-retaining mode of making present:

> *Significance is first of all a mode of presence*, with respect to which all beings that belong to the world are discovered. (GA 20:287, tr. m.; cf. BT 354)

This is no longer the case when a being is objectified: it completely loses its practical meaning. A third possible mode of the being of innerworldly beings has not yet been considered; this is the sign. Here I would like to show how Heidegger's analysis of the sign attempts to indicate already at the level of innerworldly beings that a being can explicitly draw attention to itself *without* the significance (*Bedeutsamkeit)* being lost. That is what happens in an authentic modification.

Heidegger calls the sign a specific kind of utensil; it has the same ontological structure as the utensil, which consists in referring. The hammer is not independent, but refers to the rest of the gear, the materials, and the work that is to be done. Things at hand serve a certain purpose and derive their meaning from their interrelatedness, which Heidegger calls a "relevant whole" (*Bewandtnisganzheit*) (84). Like utensils and unlike present objects, signs also serve a purpose, namely, to refer.[32] On the other hand, however, the sign must also be distinguished from other utensils: it not only has the ontological structure of referring, but it also *actually* refers.

Hence, that which is proper to the utensil as such shows forth explicitly in the sign. Heidegger therefore considers the sign to be a privileged mode: it allows Dasein to explicitly orient itself upon a certain delimited whole of referential relations. When Dasein looks in the direction given by a pointer, not merely fixating on the arrow itself as a thing, it understands beings not as independent things, but as part of a whole of referential relations. The phenomenologist can start out from this implicit understanding to show how the sign explicitly enacts what is proper to innerworldly beings as such. In this way the sign constitutes an ontic affirmation of significance as ontological structure:

> Signs are not just at hand along with other utensils but rather through their handiness the surrounding world becomes explicitly

> accessible to circumspection. *A sign is something ontically at hand which, as this specific utensil, functions at the same time as something that indicates the ontological structure of handiness, referential whole (Verweisungsganzheit) and worldliness.* (82, tr. m.)

Heidegger's analysis of the sign thus searches for a being in which the ontological structure of innerworldly beings explicitly shows forth.[33] That is not the case with the objectively present thing, which draws all the attention to itself and thus causes the referring dynamic to cease. The sign also draws attention to itself—after all, it has to be noticed—but it only does this in order to immediately direct that attention to something else which does not show itself.

The utensil, the present thing, and the sign can now be recognized as the indifferent, inauthentic and authentic modes of the being of innerworldly beings. Clearly these modifications are respectively grounded in the way Present has not yet become, or has become, or is no longer predominant.[34] The formal structure that in these modes (1) not yet really appears, (2) does not appear, and (3) does explicitly appear, is significance as ontological structure of world. Thus, Heidegger seems to base his analysis of the being of innerwordly beings on the distinction between an indifferent, an inauthentic, and an authentic modification of a formal principle. This distinction he considers to be capable of letting this being appear as it is in itself—that is, of covering its different essential moments.

Something should be added here. There is a clear similarity between Heidegger's remarks on the present object and the sign in *Being and Time* and on objectifying and nonobjectifying concepts elsewhere. The formal indication is distinguished from usual concepts by its referring, nonobjectifying character. It is precisely for this reason that formal-indicative concepts, like signs, should be able to explicitly reveal the primordial dynamic of human life.[35] When Heidegger indicates how innerworldly beings can be thematized in either an inauthentic or an authentic way, his purpose is to discover what happens in the articulation of meaning as such. What is true of every articulation of meaning will also be true of the attempt to articulate the being of beings.

The analysis of utensils therefore cannot be taken in isolation. Ultimately, I think, this first analysis is already guided by the question concerning the possibility of a nonobjectifying ontology.[36] At the same time this analysis constitutes itself an example of such an ontology, insofar as it allows innerworldly beings to appear not only as perceivable and knowable objects. Heidegger's perspective allows this mode of appearing to be understood as an inauthentic modification of a formal structure that also underlies its indifferent and authentic modifications. This broader, nonpresentifying perspective thus permits the being of innerworldly beings to appear as itself. In that respect, the analysis of utensils is ontological. At the same time, however, it tries to answer the question concerning the possibility of ontology itself, which makes it a part of Heidegger's fundamental ontology. As I said earlier, the same applies for the entire analytic of Dasein. All aspects of this analytic constitute as it were a referential whole that ultimately refers to the question concerning being itself as the final "for the sake of which."

The distinction between a formal structure and its different modifications not only guides Heidegger's analysis of the being of Dasein and innerworldly beings, but grounds every thematization of phenomena. I will now show that Heidegger's interpretation of the concept of phenomenology in §7 of *Being and Time* is also guided by this methodical distinction. His concept of temporality will subsequently allow a better understanding of the little that he says here about his method.

4.4 Heidegger's Concept of Phenomenology in *Being and Time*

In §7 of the introduction of *Being and Time* Heidegger offers an initial and very provisional answer to the question concerning the meaning of his own method. We have seen how this question constituted a central preoccupation in the early courses. *Being and Time* now emphasizes that the concept of "phenomenology" relates exclusively to the method of philosophy, and does not determine its object at all (BT 27). With regard to the methodical principle of phenomenology, Heidegger refers to Husserl's maxim "to the things themselves," which entails that the analysis has to avoid all free-floating constructions, random findings, traditional concepts, and pseudo-questions (27–28).

He maintains, however, that the principle which underlies phenomenology is not in accordance with the way it actually occurs. Thus, in order to truly answer the question concerning phenomenology, it is not enough to look at the current phenomenology.

If he wishes to still view his own work as phenomenology, Heidegger will have to broaden or formalize the concept of phenomenology in such a way that its theme initially remains undecided. In this way the existing modes of phenomenology can be understood as inadequate modes of the formal principle of phenomenology. Heidegger's own phenomenology will then of course be able to appear as the mode that tries to retrieve phenomenology from its lapsing and bring it into its own.

The brief analysis of the concept "phenomenology" in *Being and Time* ensues directly from the deconstruction of Husserl's phenomenology that can be found in a number of Heidegger's courses from 1923 to 1925 and which, as noted earlier, does not appear in *Being and Time* itself.[37] Here I will sketch only the results of this deconstruction.

Heidegger's Deconstruction of Phenomenology

Much of the introductory part of the course *History of the Concept of Time: Prolegomena* is taken up by an analysis of the most important characteristics of Husserl's phenomenology. Heidegger here distinguishes three aspects: intentionality as the area of investigation; the a priori as that which is intended in this investigation; and finally, analytic description as methodical mode of access (GA 20:108). After this interpretation, he raises the question as to how far these aspects actually fulfill Husserl's own phenomenological maxim, and concludes that Husserl, despite making considerable progress compared with traditional philosophy, falls short on all points. Since Husserl's distinction between consciousness and reality rests in an uncritical adoption of the traditional concept of being (presence, as we know), it does not accord with the principle that things must be revealed as they are in themselves. While Husserl's phenomenological "seeing" thematizes the different modes of intentionality, the being of Dasein can only be revealed as itself on the basis of a modified perspective: the explicit articulation of what Dasein essentially is has to go along with the proper dynamic of what is being interpreted (189–90, cf. BT 37). The concept of the a priori that serves as the guideline in Husserl's intuition of essences will therefore also have to be modified:

> Heretofore, the a priori was determined as that which is always already there, that is, it was characterized on the basis of a particular concept of being, namely the specifically Greek concept of being. (GA 20:190, tr. m.)

Heidegger's attempt to modify Husserl's phenomenology is ultimately guided by the attempt to no longer understand being as constant presence. Philosophy, he argues, has to realize that it is always and ineluctably guided by a temporal horizon, even when it thinks it is only looking on.[38] When the being of Dasein is thematized, the preceding temporal perspective will have to be such that the being of Dasein can appear as existence—that is to say, not as a subject that persists amidst its successive experiences. The projective opening up of a temporal horizon dominated by Present may to a certain extent be adequate for thematizing the being of innerworldly beings, but is in all respects inadequate for revealing the proper character of Dasein. As long as philosophy fails to radically reflect on the character of its horizon, Heidegger contends, it will never lose its objectifying character.

One may now understand how Heidegger's answer to the question concerning the meaning of phenomenology is itself an example of his specific method. Starting from a certain concrete phenomenon (existing phenomenology), he attempts to go back to the principle that underlies this phenomenon (the temporal understanding of being), in order to subsequently indicate the possible authentic modification of that very principle. As I said, the criticism of Husserl sketched above does not appear in *Being and Time*, where Heidegger discusses only the meaning of phenomenology as such. He does this by analyzing the meaning of the words *phainomenon* and *logos* (cf. also GA 20:110–21).

The Meaning of Phainomenon

Heidegger begins his analysis by stating that the term "phenomenon" initially pertains to that which is immediately given in empirical perception. This characteristic allows him to formalize the everyday concept of phenomenon in such a way that it remains undetermined whether this concept pertains to beings or to modes of being. Heidegger then formally determines the meaning of the Greek *phainomenon* as that which shows itself as it is in itself, what is manifest (BT 28). This formulation indicates that what shows itself can be encountered in a direct way, without mediation of, for instance, opinions or arguments. This formal indication of the phenomenon "phenomenon" constitutes the first step:

> But if in the way we grasp the concept of phenomenon we leave undetermined which beings are to be addressed as phenomena,

> and if we leave altogether open whether that which shows itself is a particular being or a characteristic of the being of beings, then we have merely got hold of the *formal* concept of phenomenon. (31, tr. m.)

Both Husserl and Heidegger use the concept of "phenomenon" to indicate something other than what is given in sensory perception, namely, the fundamental structures of intentionality and the being of beings respectively. To further concretize this concept, Heidegger again starts out from what the *ontic* meaning of the term "phenomenon" entails.

The Greek *phainomenon*, he argues, pertains not only to that which shows itself as it is in itself, but also to that which appears as other than it is in itself. In the latter case, "phenomenon" has the meaning of "semblance" (*Schein*). He calls this semblance the privative modification of "phenomenon": in order to appear as other than itself, something must already be showing itself (31). More explicitly than Heidegger himself does, one could here distinguish between (1) the primordial self-showing that grounds the different modes of showing (2) the mode in which something does not show itself as itself (semblance) and (3) the mode in which something actually shows itself as itself.

After discussing the confusion that arises when the ways in which a phenomenon shows itself are understood as modes of appearing, Heidegger continues by elaborating the possible concretizations of the formal concept of phenomenon that he has gained so far. First, this concept can be deformalized to the "common" concept of phenomenon, from which the formal concept has just been "derived." The term "phenomenon" then relates to that which is given in empirical perception. Although this is an appropriate use of the formal concept, the *phenomenological* concept of phenomenon relates to something different. Heidegger therefore asks:

> Now with regard to what do we have to deformalize the formal concept of phenomenon to the phenomenological one, and how does this latter concept differ from the common one? . . . What is to be called "phenomenon" in a preeminent sense? (35, tr. m.)

The answer: "phenomenon" is preeminently that which *must* be explicitly thematized, because it initially and mostly does not appear of itself. What initially remains hidden is preeminently the being of beings:

> The phenomenological concept of phenomenon, that is, of that which shows itself, pertains to the being of beings, to its meaning, modifications and derivatives. (35, tr. m., cf. GA 24:466)

Since being—the being of Dasein, for example—is a phenomenon that initially and mostly does not show itself as it is in itself, it most of all demands a phenomenology that is capable of letting it come into its own.

By deformalizing the formal concept of phenomenon, Heidegger has now indicated what phenomenology proper should attempt to do. He has also implicitly established that the intentionality of consciousness is not a "phenomenon" in the most proper sense of the word. He then proceeds to suggest that either the being of beings has not been explicitly uncovered at all (this is the case in the natural attitude), or has become covered up (36) after being uncovered. This is the case—although Heidegger does not say so here—in traditional philosophy. What is called "semblance" with regard to ontic phenomena is called "concealment" (*Verdecktheit*) with regard to the being of beings. This concealment is the privative modification of the phenomenological concept of phenomenon. One might add that in traditional ontology the being of beings initially and mostly shows itself in the mode of concealment, that is to say, not as itself. However, insofar as even an essential structure that has become hidden still intimates something of itself, such a structure may be revealed as itself by a phenomenology that has retrieved itself from its presentifying tendency.[39]

Heidegger then goes on to distinguish between accidental and necessary ways of being covered up. The latter are said to be grounded in the constitution of what is uncovered itself, that is, not in an accidental mistake on our part (36). If that which is uncovered is the being of beings, is it then due to being itself that it does not show itself as itself? Are there only accidental mistakes or concealments when we are dealing with *beings*? If so, why is that? Again, §7 of *Being and Time* does not elaborate on these questions. In a course from 1923, however, Heidegger remarks:

> If it were to turn out that it belongs to the *ontological* character *of being* as it is thematized in philosophy *to be in* the way of *covering over itself* and veiling itself—and that not accidentally, but according to its ontological character—only then would the category "phenomenon" really be taken seriously. (GA 63:76)

Heidegger emphasizes in *Being and Time* that a phenomenological concept can also conceal a phenomenon. There is no guarantee whatsoever that a certain concept will be able to allow that to which it pertains to appear as itself. Constant self-criticism is therefore indispensable for phenomenological research (BT 36). Against the background of Heidegger's early courses, it may be added that concepts pertaining to the being of beings will in any case have to be formal-indicative. Only when a formal indication does nothing but delimit a realm of essential possibilities will it not necessarily infringe upon the proper character of that to which it pertains.

The Meaning of Logos

What Heidegger says about phenomena accords with his subsequent remarks on the meaning of *logos*. This is necessarily so: the science that pertains to the being of beings and the way in which that being appears are nothing but two sides of the same coin. In fact, in §7 he gives a very concise summary of his interpretation of Aristotle's concept of truth, which he elaborated in earlier courses such as *Logic. The Question Concerning Truth* (GA 21). Here I will only discuss how he interprets the term *logos* in such a way that it can be used for his concept of phenomenology.

Heidegger starts by pointing out the inadequacy of the usual translations of *logos*, such as statement or judgment. Since these translations pertain to the *logos* only insofar as it is spoken, he considers them to conceal the issue at stake (32). Heidegger himself, on the other hand, interprets *logos* in such a way that it first of all refers to the ontological structure of any discourse. He understands this primordial discourse (*Rede*) as a disclosing in which something can be explicitly brought to view. This disclosing has different modes, such as asking. However, Heidegger mainly concentrates on the apophantic *logos*, which is expressed in judgments. This specific mode of disclosing reveals something as true or false (32, cf. GA 21:133).

Subsequently, Heidegger—with Aristotle—distinguishes different modes of disclosing and truth. First, there is sensory perception, which precedes every mode of synthesis and therefore cannot be false (BT 33). This immediate mode of uncovering cannot yet be called apophantic.

Beings and being can only be explicitly disclosed and brought to light by means of the *logos*. With regard to beings, this occurs in statements which always pertain to something other than beings themselves—for example, "blackness" when the blackboard is disclosed "as" black (cf. GA 21:137). The apophantic *logos* underlying such synthetic judgments thus discloses beings with respect to a specific property; these judgments are not necessarily true or disclosing (like immediate perception), but can also be false. When a judgment reveals something *as* something, it is necessarily with respect to something other than the blackboard itself (cf. BT 34).

The third mode of disclosing that Heidegger distinguishes is *noein*, which he interprets as "a mere beholding apprehension of the simplest determinations of the being of beings as such" (33, tr. m.). Since this mode of disclosing, like sensory perception, does not rest on synthesis, it is equally impossible for it to be false—or at least so it seems. *Noein* thus unites the best of the other two modes of disclosing: the immediate character of empirical perception and the explicit, apophantic character of the mode of disclosing based on synthesis. Heidegger says in GA 21, still in line with Aristotle, that every knowing aims at this mode of seeing (GA 21:113).

Like the thematization of beings, the disclosing of the being of beings is grounded in the apophantic *logos*. However, in the latter case—I add—it seems that the *logos* does not necessarily have to be guided by something other than the thing itself. This mode of *logos* is naturally the *logos* that constitutes the second part of the concept "phenomenology." Thus, phenomenology now formally means nothing other than:

> To bring to view that which shows itself by starting out from it (*von ihm selbst her*), just as it shows itself of itself. (BT 34, tr. m.)

That is therefore precisely, and of course not accidentally, what is expressed by the maxim "to the things themselves." Heidegger's formalization and deformalization of the concepts *phainomenon* and *logos* thus allow "phenomenology" to be understood as disclosing the being of beings as it shows itself of itself—that is to say, not by means of categories that are foreign to it and thus conceal the being of, for example, Dasein. This is the principle of Heidegger's phenomenological ontology.

If we look carefully, which in this case can only be done by somewhat forcing the very concise text, we see that Heidegger is trying to interpret the *logos* so formally that the different modes of disclosing can be understood as modes of this *logos*. One might formally describe *logos* as the explicit disclosing or bringing to light of something as it shows itself of itself. Sensory perception discloses something, but not explicitly. Judgments that lie in synthesis do this, but because they are based on something other than the thing itself they must be regarded as inauthentic modifications of the *logos*. Ultimately, then, the disclosing of the *being* of beings is the only mode in which the formal concept of *logos* might enact itself in an authentic way. Heidegger does not bring out in the published part of *Being and Time*—and scarcely in GA 21—that he considers traditional metaphysics to be a mode of disclosing which, although it does pertain to the being of beings, is insufficiently capable of leaving behind the way of judging that allows innerwordly beings to be disclosed. Metaphysics thus remains tied to an inauthentic mode of apophantic discourse. I will return to this theme in 5.4.

In §7 of *Being and Time* Heidegger actually says very little about the specific character of his own method. On the basis of what has been said up to now about temporality, I will now attempt to elucidate how all Heidegger's analyses are guided by a mode of temporality in which Present does not gain dominance over the other temporal ecstases.

4.5 The Temporal Threefoldness of Heidegger's Method

I have indicated the proper character of Heidegger's method on the basis of various examples. The relation between the different moments of the being of Dasein and the formal concepts which bring that being to light must now be further specified.

In order to thematize the being of Dasein, formal indications are required. To this end, Heidegger takes a concept from everyday experience and deprives it of its ontic content in such a way that only a formal structure remains. This formal structure is then no longer only taken as the condition of possibility of the everyday phenomenon from which it was derived, but rather serves as the starting point for revealing the different possible modifications of that essential structure. After this step has been taken, the analysis relates exclusively to the being of beings.

The concepts are thus made suitable for ontological interpretation by a formalization of the ontic meaning and a deformalization of the obtained formal meaning at the ontological level. Within this deformalization Heidegger always (though not always explicitly) distinguishes an indifferent-inauthentic and an authentic modification, which indicate the essential possibilities of Dasein. A distinction must therefore be made between the ontic or "common" phenomenon from which the analysis starts out and the inauthentic modification of a formal structure that belongs to the *being* of Dasein. Thus, for example, there is a difference between the usual meaning of the concept "guilt" and the turning away from the always already being-guilty, which is an essential moment of the being of Dasein.[40]

Once a formal-indicative concept has been obtained, the being of beings can be further delimited. Such a concept refers to a primordial or formal structure in such a way that the inauthentic and the authentic modification of that structure can also be brought forth. The entire concept of a phenomenon thus comprises (1) the formal or primordial structure, (2) its indifferent-inauthentic modification (the "initially and mostly"), and (3) its authentic modification (the "possibly"). The being of beings, that is to say, the "essential," *is* nothing but the possible modifications in which that formal structure deformalizes itself. Although the order in which Heidegger thematizes the different moments can vary, this threefold structure gives the core of all his analyses.

We still have to answer the question as to how Heidegger understands the difference between this methodical threefoldness and the threefold that grounds the traditional concept of development. We have seen how Heidegger tries to understand the facticity of human life by means of a formal structure that grounds this facticity. Once this structure has been "seen," its most authentic modification can also be delimited. This is a possibility that belongs to facticity only *as* possibility, but as such nevertheless constitutes one of its essential directions. What essentially belongs to facticity is thus understood by conjoining it with a preceding condition of possibility and an authentic modification thereof.

Because Heidegger attempts to show how the indifferent-inauthentic modification of what Dasein essentially and possibly is always threatens to become the only tendency that determines facticity, both the formal structure and its authentic modification must lie *beyond* the realm of presence: what "precedes" is always already past and the "future" is only given as a *possibility* to come. The only, but decisive difference between Heidegger's methodical principle and, for example, that of Hegel, consists in the fact that Heidegger tries to reveal the formal structure and its authentic modification *as* that which retreats from the domain dominated by presence. From the metaphysical perspective, by contrast, the preceding origin (*archē*, ground, essence, idea) will always appear as that which is most present and real, and thus—sooner or later—also guarantees its own adequate actualization.

While the authentic mode of care pertains to the way in which factically existing Dasein bends itself back to the facticity of its own being, philosophy should bend itself back to the origin of everything that is or appears. If this preceding origin is understood as an origin which has never taken place and is always already past, then this is made possible by ecstatic Past. Heidegger tries to let his method be guided by Temporality in such a way that this Past delimits a realm within which being appears as an origin that itself does not belong to the realm of beings.[41] We could say that philosophy has always done this, but has never been sufficiently able to distinguish the proper character of the "preceding" from that which appears from within a horizon of Praesens. Past is then overshadowed by Present.

Just as Past opens up the preceding formal structure that constitutes one of the moments of being, ecstatic Future opens up the realm of the possible. The modification in which the preceding formal structure is possibly given its full due equally does not belong to the realm of presence.

Ecstatic Present appears to play a twofold role. As we know, it opens up the horizon of Praesens that allows beings to appear at all. Present sheds light on beings as they initially and mostly appear. The phenomenologist is able to understand this mode of appearance *as* the indifferent-inauthentic mode of a structure that itself does not appear from within Present alone. From Heidegger's perspective this temporal ecstasis remains embedded between the other two ecstases. Thus, Past and Future may delimit a horizon that allows being or the essential to appear as a presence that is radically pervaded by absence. Against this background the dynamic of human life may appear as itself.

It is difficult to give actual meaning to these abstract remarks. Temporality (*Temporalität*), as the purest mode of temporality itself, can hardly be thematized. This "time" may be said to primordially outstretch itself in a threefold way, such that the being of beings can be understood as (1) formal, preceding structure that (2) initially and mostly deformalizes itself by turning away from itself, but (3) has the possibility of coming into its own. It is important to emphasize, however, that this primordial threefold perspective has always already—that is to say, as soon as Dasein occurs—begun to confine itself. Hence, philosophy has never been able to do justice to the radical absence that constitutes the core of being itself.

The temporal horizon of the preontological understanding of being modifies itself in both everyday ontic involvement and metaphysics—that is, initially and mostly—into Praesens. Heidegger tries to resist this predominance of Present by going along with a primordial temporal projective preconception of being. This threefold projective preconception never actually occurred in history, and even for Heidegger himself it is a possibility that in a certain sense is impossible. Nonetheless, it is this possibility that guides his attempt to overcome the metaphysical projective preconception of being.

Everything that Heidegger tries to say about temporality, both concerning Dasein and concerning the deconstruction of metaphysics, in my view only gains full significance when it becomes clear how his own analyses are guided by a threefold Temporality. We know that this Temporality is a mode of the temporality that is revealed in *Being and Time* as the fundamental structure of the being of Dasein. In phenomenological ontology as a possible mode of existence, this temporality ultimately enacts itself as a projective, opening movement that allows the being of beings to occur in accordance with its essential threefoldness. Only from within such a temporal horizon might justice be done to the radical difference between beings and being.

The Meaning of the A Priori

Now that Heidegger's method has been interpreted against the background of his concept of temporality, his suggestion that the character of the a priori must be modified becomes more meaningful. Hints about the character of this modification are to be found, for instance, at the end of GA 24 and in GA 20. Here he remarks that the a priori has traditionally been understood as that which was always already there (GA 20:190). The concept refers to the "preceding," yet it has nothing to do with the time within which all events succeed one another. According to Heidegger, however, the fact that the a priori is not related to this time does not mean that it is above or beyond time. On the contrary; when the temporal meaning of the a priori is taken seriously, the concept pertains to what is "earlier" and thus makes beings possible with respect to their "what" and "how" (GA 24:461–62). Heidegger, then, takes the a priori to no longer pertain to essence, but rather to the whole of the formal structure and its different modifications. These constitute the being of, for instance, Dasein, and are "earlier" than the concrete individual.[42] Heidegger thus modifies the a priori in such a way that the "preceding" origin is no longer understood as that which was always already there and persists amidst all change, but rather as a condition of possibility, divided within and against itself, that withdraws from the reach of presence. Insofar as every essential structure can only be revealed from within Temporality, this primordial time must therefore itself precede even every a priori:

> Time is *earlier than any possible "earlier"* of whatever sort, because it is the basic precondition for an "earlier" as such. And because time as the source of all enablings (*Ermöglichungen*) is the earliest, all possibilities have, with regard to their enabling function, as such the character of the "earlier," that is to say, they are a priori. (GA 24:463, tr. m., cf. BT 419)

In 1925/26, Heidegger calls the mode of ontology that attempts to enact itself in accordance with this earliest Temporality "phenomenological chronology" (GA 21:199). Precisely because he traces back the apriorical structure of Dasein to temporality, his philosophy differs from what is usually understood by transcendental philosophy.

4.6 Deconstruction, Reduction, and Construction

What has been said up to now about the temporal character of Heidegger's method was, in my view, to have been elaborated in *Time and Being* and the third part of GA 24. In the introduction of GA 24 Heidegger gives a brief sketch of the themes of this part.

First, when the question concerning the possibility of ontology is at stake, it is necessary to thematize Dasein; this being constitutes the ontic (and not the only or final) condition of possibility of ontology.[43] The outcome of the analytic of Dasein would subsequently have constituted the starting point for Heidegger's reflection on the method of ontology. In the second chapter this would have taken shape as a "development of the methodical structures of ontological-transcendental differentiation."[44] Much of what I have said up to now about Heidegger's method would probably have been elaborated in this chapter. Third, the three basic aspects of the phenomenological method—reduction, construction, and deconstruction—would have been thematized (GA 24:28f). In the fourth chapter Heidegger would finally have been able to delimit more concretely the concept of philosophy. Here he would also have been able to come back to the confinement of the temporal perspective of metaphysics, with which the first part of GA 24 begins (cf. 32).

The meaning of deconstruction, reduction, and construction has as yet only been mentioned indirectly (cf. 3.3). Heidegger remarks in the introduction of GA 24 that these moments constitute a unity and must be grounded as a unity, but he does not indicate the character of that ground (31). On the basis of what has been said up to now, these three moments of the method can be understood as grounded in primordial Temporality. This places Heidegger's method in a rather broader perspective. From that perspective it will also be possible to summarize the aspects of Heidegger's method discussed hitherto.

In the introduction of GA 24 Heidegger characterizes philosophy as the mode of knowing that thematizes being (28, cf. 458). Since initially only beings appear, the investigation must start out from beings, in order to then change the perspective in such a way that the being of beings can be thematized. This "leading back of the investigative vision" from beings to their being Heidegger calls phenomenological reduction. Thus, he here explicitly adopts Husserl's terminology, while at the same time distancing himself from Husserl's conception of the meaning of that reduction (28–29). I would like to add here that the "reduction" of beings to their being is, like every mode of thematization, made possible by ecstatic Present.

According to Heidegger, the movement that leads thinking away from beings, which occurs in reduction, cannot be accomplished without a projective, opening movement that leads thinking to being in a positive way. Being must "each time be brought to view in a free, projective preconception." This is the phenomenological construction.[45] The phenomenologist can both explicitly assume and modify the temporal horizon that makes it possible to understand being. This projecting or constructing movement can be conceived as a mode of being-ahead-of-oneself. Thus, the phenomenological construction is itself grounded in ecstatic Future, although again Heidegger does not yet say that in the introduction of GA 24.

The projective preconception of being can only become a free projective preconception when thinking critically reflects on the metaphysical presuppositions that thwart the disclosure of the things themselves. Heidegger constantly traces these presuppositions back to an inadequate concept of being. This moment of the analysis is called deconstruction.[46] This dismantling entails a retrieval of the positive possibilities inhering in traditional philosophy. We recognize here the moment of retrieving repetition; being the authentic relation to Dasein's situated facticity, this moment is grounded in Past.

We can see how Heidegger as it were allows the thematization of being to arise out of a deconstruction of the traditional temporal horizon on the one hand and a constructing modification of this horizon on the other. This deconstructing-constructing dynamic ensures that the turn from beings to their being is enacted appropriately. In an authentic thematization of being, reduction will thus remain conjoined with the moments of deconstruction and construction, which are made possible by Past and Future. Heidegger clearly understands Husserl's phenomenology as a mode of philosophy in which the moment of reduction prevails to such an extent that the traditional understanding of being cannot be modified in an authentic way. In such a reduction Present has gained the upper hand. Heidegger argues that this has been the case throughout the entire history of philosophy.

If we now consider more closely the moment of reduction, we again encounter the temporal threefoldness within that reduction—namely, as the distinction between the formal structure of a phenomenon on the one hand and its different modifications on the other. I have shown how the threefold distinction between the formal structure, its indifferent-inauthentic mode and its authentic mode, is grounded in temporality as Temporality. If reduction enacts itself in an appropriate way, these moments of being will not appear as constantly present. In *Being and Time* and GA 24 Heidegger gives no direct indications about this. As far as I know, he only thematizes the temporal meaning of this methodical threefold in his interpretation of Hegel's *Phenomenology of Spirit*. This text will be interpreted in 10.3.

This is not yet the end of the story, however. The formal structure that shows forth in reduction as one of the moments of being, is itself structured in a threefold way, at least insofar as the being of Dasein is concerned. Care as formal structure has the moments ahead-of-itself, being-already-in, and being-with. These moments are distinguished with regard to the temporality (*Zeitlichkeit*) that constitutes the final a priori of human existence. This threefold temporal structure of care can modify itself in an inauthentic and an authentic way. A distinction therefore has to be made between the temporal threefoldness of care as such and the way in which this structure enacts or deformalizes itself. This deformalization pertains to the threefoldness which consists in (1) the formal structure itself, (2) its inauthentic modification, and (3) its authentic modification. This threefoldness constitutes the core of Heidegger's method and is grounded in time as Temporality.

I will try to summarize the above. As far as I can see, temporality plays a central part in Heidegger's analysis in three respects. First, with regard to the analytic of Dasein, this time constitutes the a priori of care as such. This structure modifies itself in human life in an inauthentic or an authentic way, depending on the extent to which Present has become predominant.

Second, the being of Dasein can be thematized in an inauthentic or an authentic way in *philosophy*, according to the modification of temporality that grounds philosophy itself. In a phronetic thinking this reduction will remain embedded within the deconstructive and the constructive movement.

Third, it is temporality as Temporality that allows being to be understood and thematized at all. An authentic modification of Temporality permits the formal structure of care and its different modifications to show forth respectively as (1) the preceding origin that recedes from the realm of presence, (2) the tendency that initially and mostly gains the upper hand, and (3) the tendency in which that preceding structure is possibly given its due.

It is quite understandable that these different modes of temporality are difficult to distinguish. After all, the Temporality that grounds every understanding of being is itself a specific modification of temporality. One could say that care as fundamental structure of Dasein modifies itself in authentic ontology in such a way that Past and Future are allowed to reach further into the absential than in all other modifications of temporality. Philosophy is itself a mode of life; it is the mode in which life explicitly comprehends itself. Thus, when Heidegger in turn tries to comprehend the character and the different possibilities of that self-conception, thinking takes on a vertiginous reflexivity. It does indeed seem hardly possible to explain these matters.

Yet the principle is simple. What Heidegger calls temporality is ultimately nothing more than a kind of construction that makes it possible to gain insight into the proper dynamic—divided in and against itself—of life, thinking, and the history of thinking. It is therefore meaningless to ask whether there is such a thing as primordial time. The character of the temporality that concerns Heidegger is in itself such that Present constantly threatens to break away from its juncture with the other temporal ecstases. This temporality is not brought about by human beings. It can, however, be modified in such a way that ecstatic Present no longer overshadows the other ecstases. It is not up to the thinker to let that happen. At most he can try not to thwart the primordial unfolding of threefold temporality. This compliance does, however, demand an active and constant resistance against Present, which inevitably prevails whenever anything is spoken or written.

The detours that Heidegger takes in order to reveal this dynamic can be understood as *indications* of something which is seldom if ever directly thematized. The detour in GA 24 is no more successful in reaching its aim than the analytic of Dasein in *Being and Time*. At the end of GA 24 it seems that Heidegger wishes to testify to this failure. He suggests here that his method has begun to thwart the course of his thinking:

> Precisely when a method is genuine and provides access to the matters at issue, the progress and the increasing originality of the disclosure which is due to this very method will themselves be the cause of its obsolescence. (GA 24:467, tr. m.)

This remark might relate to the phenomenological request that any interpretation should be in line with concrete experiences of Dasein. I have pointed out that this perspective almost inevitably takes the movement of life to be one of increasing actualization. Must Heidegger, in order to avoid that, also radicalize his own methodical principal? Can Dasein still be the starting point for a deconstruction of metaphysics? It may be that the whole idea of a method has to be relinquished, because the distinction between method and subject matter is based on the practice of the positive sciences. Heidegger will reflect on this for a couple of years. In the next chapter, still on the basis of GA 24, I will indicate how Heidegger uses his concept of temporality to try and understand not only the different possibilities of thinking, but also the different modifications of the "correlate" of philosophy: being itself. After all, the understanding of being and being as it is understood can never occur without one another. They even seem to be indistinguishable, as Heidegger suggests in 1930:

> Is, then, the relation between being and the understanding of being so elementary that what is true of being is true of the understanding of being as well, that being is identical with its disclosure? (GA 31:124)

5

The Turn toward Being Itself in *The Basic Problems of Phenomenology*

This chapter will concentrate mainly on part II of GA 24, that is to say, the part where Heidegger was to have thematized the meaning of being itself. Apart from the chapter on the ontological difference—the only one that is elaborated—the other three chapters of part II were to have thematized the following basic problems: the problem of the basic articulation of being, the problem of the possible modifications of being, and the truth-character of being.[1] The last of these themes appears to already constitute the transition to part III, where the relation between the understanding of being and time would have constituted the starting point for the question concerning the character of ontology itself. Having followed Heidegger from the being of Dasein to the ontology that thematizes being, we can now turn toward being itself as it is understood in ontology.

The principal way to gain access to the problems of the unwritten chapters of part II of GA 24 is the first part, which I have not as yet considered. Unlike *Being and Time*, GA 24 begins by deconstructing the history of the concept of being. Thus, Heidegger tries here, starting from a different angle, to reach the same point as in *Being and Time*. In this "historical" part he discusses four traditional theses concerning being. A critical, deconstructive interpretation of these theses was to clear the way for thematizing the ontological difference on the one hand, and the primordial articulation, the different modes, and the truth-character of being on the other. Since these four basic problems all ensue from the question concerning the meaning of being as such, this thematization would also have answered the question concerning being itself (GA 24:21).

In discussing the traditional theses, Heidegger is already working toward the issues that he would have dealt with in part II.

These hints, and passages in other texts that thematize the same problems, will serve as the starting point for my reconstructing interpretation. The emphasis in this interpretation will lie on Heidegger's *systematic* questions. Thus, I will try to thematize the four basic problems revealed by Heidegger's deconstruction of metaphysics, which he had wanted to elaborate in part II. This elaboration can be regarded as the counterpart of Hegel's *Science of Logic*. Heidegger, however, tries to break through to a level to which Hegel's perspective does not give access.

5.1 The Ontological Difference

Being can only be understood once the distinction between being and beings has been explicitly enacted. The first basic problem is therefore the problem of the ontological difference—that is, the access to being.[2] In order to thematize the ontological difference, Heidegger examines Kant's thesis that being is not a real predicate: whether something exists or not, does not say anything about its essence. Heidegger concurs with Kant insofar as the latter traces back "being," as positing, to the subject that posits the existence of something (103, 106).

However, since Kant (like Husserl) bases his understanding only on perception, Heidegger considers him to be incapable of questioning the character of the understanding of being that guides every intentional comportment to beings (106). The subsequent chapters also indicate that the traditional concept of being is determined either by beings that are perceived, or by an interpretation of beings as made or created. In other words, the horizon of Praesens within which beings can present themselves as present beings has always guided the thinking that has turned itself to the being of beings. From the outset, ontology enacts the ontological difference—that is, inquires into the being of beings or the essential—but is confined in its possible answers by its one-sided orientation upon Praesens. Since this theme has already been discussed in detail, I will not consider it further here.

5.2 The Basic Articulation of Being

In chapter 1 of part II, Heidegger concentrated mainly on "being" in the sense of existence, not yet broaching the traditional distinction between essence and existence. He now brings out this distinction as a distinction within being itself:

> Thus the difference between realitas (or essentia) and existentia does not coincide with the ontological difference. . . . [R]ather, it is precisely the two of them that make up the structure of being. The distinction between realitas and existentia *articulates* being more particularly in its essential constitution. (109, cf. 24)

Hence the ontological difference pertains to the distinction between "being" as primordial unity of "essence" and "way of being" on the one hand, and the whole of concrete beings on the other. The distinction between essence and existence shows that being is not an empty concept, but "reveals an ever richer structure within itself" (109). By speaking of a structure or articulation of being itself, Heidegger explicitly distances himself from the traditional conception that "being," as the most "empty" and general concept, cannot be further determined.[3] He considers that the indefinability of being in no way excludes that it is "determined" by something else:

> [T]he concept of being is in no way simple and just as little is it self-evident. The meaning of being is most intricate and the ground of being is obscure. (318; cf. BT 196)

In order to disentangle these "intricacies," thinking needs a guideline. Of this guideline—time—Heidegger says that it must be sought in Dasein's understanding of being (318). The perspective of metaphysics, by contrast, makes it impossible to inquire into the origin of the distinction between essence and existence.[4] Heidegger's thesis is now that this distinction intimates something of a "primordial articulation" of being (cf. GA 31:124). Traces of this primordial articulation remain in the traditional distinction between essence and existence, although there it does not show itself as itself. Initially and mostly—that is to say, up to now—this articulation of being could only appear as the distinction between a formal principle on the one hand and its actual realization on the other. After deconstructing this distinction, Heidegger would have been able to reveal in a positive way the primordial articulation of being in part II of GA 24.

We should keep in mind that Heidegger here is concerned with a manifold within being itself that is more primordial than the distinction between the different *regional* meanings of being. The different regions of beings, such as nature, number, humans, and life, each have their own whatness and mode of being, which constitute different modifications of the idea of being as such:

> Being means not only the multiplicity of regions and their respective *modi existendi* and *essendi*, but it means the idea of being insofar as it is essentially articulated into *existentia* and *essentia*. (GA 26:192–93, tr. m.)

In 1.6 I showed how Heidegger frees the concept *ousia* from inadequate translations such as essence and substance, understanding it as a primordial unity of "what" and "how." This meaning of *ousia* allows Heidegger to search for an articulation of being that is not twofold, but threefold. Since *ousia* has always been understood as that which is constantly present, this primordial threefoldness could never appear as itself.[5] When beings are approached with the question as to how their essence actually enacts itself, Heidegger will answer that a certain preceding structure enacts itself in either an inauthentic or an authentic way, and that the whole of those counter-striving possibilities is itself the "essential."

We know that Heidegger understands this threefoldness to be grounded in a threefold temporality which allows both the "preceding" and the "possible" to appear in their radical absence. Thus, the primordial threefold articulation of being itself modifies itself into the twofold distinction between essence and existence as soon as the horizon that guides the understanding of being is dominated by Praesens. Only a nonmetaphysical thinking will be able to let itself be guided by the primordial threefoldness of being.[6]

When the distinction between essence and existence is inappropriate to reveal the being of Dasein as it is in itself (GA 24:155–56), the traditional thesis that every being is determined by a "what" and a (possible) existence loses its universal reach:

> It is in no way proved and immediately evident that this thesis holds good of *every* being. . . . [I]f being does not coincide with existentia in the ancient sense of actuality, objective presence, then the thesis all the more requires an explicit foundation in its *restricted validity for those beings which are objectively present.* (157, tr. m.)

Because the concepts "essence" and "existence" are reserved for objectively present beings, space arises for introducing a different "articulation" of being with regard to the being of Dasein—namely, the distinction between the "who" and the way in which this "who" is enacted:

> It now appears that the ontological difference is becoming more intricate (*verwickelter*). . . . More intricate because under the

> heading *"being"* we now have *not only essentia* and *existentia*, but *also whoness* (*Werheit*) and *existence* (*Existenz*) in our sense. The articulation of being varies each time with the way of being of a being. (170, tr. m.)

The concept of being has now become so "developed" that two modes of "being" can be distinguished. The distinction between essence and existence pertains to the being of innerworldly beings insofar as that is understood as objective presence. Heidegger considers this meaning of being to be grounded in a "simplification" or leveling of the primordial threefold articulation of being. The distinction between who-ness and existence that characterizes the being of Dasein must, by contrast, be understood on the basis of the threefoldness of being that precedes every objectification. It is therefore inappropriate to comprehend the being of Dasein by means of concepts that are only able to thematize a specific moment of the being of innerworldly beings. While *Being and Time* merely suggests that the being of objectively present beings (as mere presence) and the being of Dasein are rooted in a common ground, this was only to have been elaborated in *Time and Being*. Thus, the introduction of *Being and Time* proposes that the relation between the "who" and the "what" be understood by starting out from the horizon that guides the question concerning being as such.[7]

The problem of the articulated structure of being yields of itself the third basic problem, namely, that of the different modes of being and the unity that grounds these modes. Hence, the distinction between who-ness and existence on the one hand and whatness and objective presence on the other does not have the final say in the matter:

> Interpreting existentiality as care and distinguishing it from reality . . . only brings forward more clearly the intertwinement of the problems concerning the question of being, its possible modes and the meaning of such modifications. (BT 212, tr. m., cf. GA 24:170–71)

5.3 The Modifications of Being

The third chapter of part II of GA 24 is entitled *The Problem of the Possible Modifications of Being and the Unity of its Manifoldness* (GA 24:33). This chapter concerns the regional distinction between the being of innerworldly beings and the being of Dasein. Unlike

Husserl, Heidegger does not take this distinction to be absolute, but tries to understand it from the perspective of being as such, which—in the history of ontology—modifies itself in different ways.[8]

In part I of GA 24, Heidegger seeks access to this problem by starting out from the traditional thesis that the being of nature on the one hand and the being of spirit on the other constitute the fundamental modes of being (172). His deconstruction of this thesis follows the familiar pattern: the distinction between object and subject points clearly to something essential, but at the same time conceals the matter itself—namely, insofar as this distinction is guided by an understanding of being as constant presence. Not only Descartes's idea of the *res cogitans*, but also Kant's concept of the moral person is ultimately considered inadequate to reveal the being of Dasein as itself (218). In determining the being of beings that we are ourselves, thinking has always been guided by an indifferent, leveled concept of being. This concept of being not only falls short in elucidating the being of Dasein, but also entails that innerworldly beings can only show forth as objects (233, cf. BT 201).

Having discussed the most important themes of the analytic of Dasein, Heidegger returns to the question concerning the unity that must underlie the different (regional) modes of being. The "encompassing concept of being" that guides metaphysics does not qualify; only when the radical distinction between the being of Dasein and the being of nature is taken seriously, can and must the question be asked concerning a "unifying concept of being" from which these modes of being originate:

> How can we conceive the unity of the concept of being in reference to a possible multiplicity of ways of being? How is the indifference of being, as it is unveiled in our everyday understanding of beings, related at the same time to the unity of an original concept of being? (250–51)

With regard to both the character of this primordial concept of being and its relation to the traditional indifferent concept of being, all Heidegger does in part I is ask this question.

Clearly, these questions indicate the same direction as the first two basic problems: the direction of the Temporality that grounds the threefold articulation of being. That idea gives rise to the following answer with regard to the question concerning the relation between the primordial and the indifferent concept of being. The increasing predominance of Present entails that the primordial threefold structure is increasingly overshadowed by the indifferent idea of being as objective presence. This occurs as soon as thinking begins. The indifferent mode of being has a certain right with respect to the thematization of objectively present beings, but it is used "improperly" as soon as it starts to function as the guiding principle in the inquiry into the being of Dasein.

I am not sure whether Heidegger himself would have used the terms *inauthentic* and *authentic* in connection with the different modifications of being as such. However, since he speaks of a primordial and an indifferent concept of being, and of different modes of the primordial concept of being, I think that the use of the terms inauthenticity and authenticity in this regard can be helpful. The inauthentic concept of being of traditional ontology then constitutes a *radicalization* of the indifferent concept of being that corresponds to the everyday understanding of being. On the other hand, the primordial structure of being appears most as itself—that is to say, modifies itself in an authentic way—when the being of Dasein is thematized as care. Being, that is to say, the essential, appears here as dynamic, threefold openness or transcendence.[9]

Besides care as the basic structure of the being of Dasein, Heidegger also searches for a mode of being that accords with the primordial structure of being at the level of innerworldly beings: the being of innerworldly beings cannot be adequately thematized on the basis of "being" in the sense of objective presence (249). We have seen how the beings with which we are involved every day become accessible through an awaiting and retaining way of making present. In this mode of temporality Present has not yet gained dominance over the other ecstases, although a horizon of Praesens has already been brought about. We can now conclude that Heidegger understands the being of beings at hand as a mode of being in which the "rich" temporal structure of being does indeed show forth, but yet is also already confined by Present.

Thus, the primordial threefoldness of being itself can be brought to reveal itself in an appropriate analysis of both the being of innerworldly beings and the being of Dasein. But if the temporality of care is also not yet the Temporality of being itself, then being itself will only be able to truly show forth as itself in an analysis that also takes its leave of the "region" of Dasein. That would therefore have been the task of part II of GA 24. I will now summarize the above by presenting a kind of "genealogy" of the different modes of being, as Heidegger (more or less clearly) must have intended in *Time and Being* and in GA 24; with regard to this, the introduction of *Being and Time* mentions "the ontological task of a genealogy—not a deductively constructing one—of the different possible ways of being" (BT 11, tr. m.).

The primordial, threefold concept of being that is pervaded by a radical absence grounds both the indifferent mode and the inauthentic and authentic modifications of being. In the preontological understanding of being which underlies every ontic involvement, being modifies itself in an indifferent way to presence. The self-increasing predominance of Present—that is to say, the dynamic in which the horizon of Praesens is brought about—has always already begun. This horizon constitutes the condition of possibility of the "natural attitude" or "world."

Ontology initially goes along with this primary direction of the understanding of being. When it explicitly thematizes the being of beings, Praesens becomes more predominant. Being thereby modifies itself in this ontology into constant presence. In that inauthentic modification the threefold structure of being recedes entirely from the way in which it appears. From within a horizon that only allows being as constant presence, metaphysical determinations of being such as substance, idea, essence, existence, subject, spirit, and will can then emerge.[10] One might add that the way in which Hegel in the *Science of Logic* unfolds the necessary relation of all pure concepts is also grounded in a conception of development as increasing self-presence. That conception too can only arise from within a horizon that is entirely dominated by Praesens.

Heidegger thus appears to understand the different "inauthentic" modes of being as resulting from the increasing predominance of Present. The light of Present allows beings to appear, yet also entails that being itself can only be understood as presence. This does not preclude, however, that thinking might be capable of resisting this predominant tendency. Thinking might try to twist free from the horizon that determines the natural attitude in a more radical way than metaphysics hitherto. The temporal horizon guiding this thinking would be such that the threefoldness of being can be given its due. That is also to some extent the case when in *Being and Time* the being of Dasein is thematized as care.

I would emphasize again here that Heidegger's question concerning the meaning of being pertains to the way in which being or the essential is *thought*. This only occurs explicitly in the history of ontology. The "meaning" of being which enacts itself in that history is not unifold, but encompasses the totality of (1) the primordial threefoldness of being, (2) its indifferent and inauthentic modification, and (3) the possible authentic modification of that threefoldness. The extent to which ecstatic Present conjoins with Future and Past constitutes the measure whereby these different modifications can be distinguished.

I would also like to point out that the distinction between a primordial structure and its different modifications is itself a distinction to which only an authentic thinking can truly do justice. This means that Heidegger understands the history of ontology as a movement in which beginning and end recede from that which has actually been and will be the case. From this perspective the end of fallenness will not appear as an attainable possibility.

Clearly the sketched "history" of being can hardly be distinguished from the history of ontology. This is a familiar issue in Heidegger's later thought. It seems, then, that this thought has already begun in *Being and Time* and has perhaps always already begun. As I hope has become clear, Heidegger already in GA 24 tries to accomplish the turning toward being itself that was also to have been accomplished in *Time and Being.* It is the turning to the possible temporal modifications of being that have determined "the questioning, findings and failures" of the history of thinking (BT 19).

5.4 The Truth-Character of Being

The last approach that Heidegger uses in part I of GA 24 to deconstruct the concept of being of metaphysics is the meaning of the copula. Here he first critically questions the traditional thesis that every being can be addressed by the "is" (GA 24:252). While traditional kinds of logic assume that judgments are the "place" where truth or untruth is brought about, Heidegger tries to understand truth as a phenomenon that grounds any truth or untruth proper to judgments. In one way or another the "is" will have to be related to the possibility of allowing something to appear *as* something.[11] In order to understand the copula on the basis of the understanding of being of Dasein, logic will thus in any case have to be taken back into ontology (254, cf. BT 213). The question is then whether the use of the "is" in a judgment necessarily entails the objectification of that to which the judgment pertains. While this question is thematized in the published part of *Being and Time* on the basis of the analytic of Dasein, part I of GA 24 starts out from a deconstruction of traditional logic. Here I will not thematize this deconstructive interpretation, but will try to sketch out the positive analysis that was to have followed in part II.[12]

Several passages in *Being and Time* explicitly refer to the third division with regard to the elaboration of the question concerning the meaning of the "is." Heidegger maintains, for instance, that the temporality of primordial discourse must be analyzed before the ontological meaning of the "is" and of the possibility of concepts can be elucidated.[13] I assume that Heidegger here particularly intended the possibility of ontological concepts, and that he had wanted to resume the analysis of primordial discourse in the first division of *Being and Time* from that perspective. The temporal condition of possibility that grounds every kind of significance would then have served as the starting point. Hence, the published part of *Being and Time* explicitly defers the question "whether every science and whether indeed philosophical knowledge aims at some sort of making present" (BT 363n, tr. m.).

We do, however, find an elaboration of this question in the course *Logic. The Question Concerning Truth* from 1925/26 (GA 21). The analysis of the phenomenon of truth recurs in a shorter version in §7 and §44 of *Being and Time*.[14] In order to elucidate what Heidegger had wanted to do in the last chapter of part II of GA 24 and in *Time and Being*, I will now thematize the analyses of the phenomena *logos*, language, and truth in GA 21. The course is somewhat misleading: Heidegger dwells at such length on the structure of ontic judgments, that he scarcely gets round to the question which was originally at stake. By drawing together what I have said on this theme in the foregoing chapters, my interpretation will try to make up for this.

Logos and Truth in GA 21

Sentences that pertain to the being of beings will have to do justice to the dynamic character of the essential structures and their different modifications. They usually do not; concepts tend to fixate what they bring to light. In order to reveal this "inauthentic" tendency, Heidegger in GA 21 begins by analyzing the disclosing that grounds any judgment. For this purpose he goes along with Aristotle's concept of truth.[15] Here he interprets the word *alētheia* as the unconcealment that precedes any (linguistic) determination of beings. Thus, unconcealment is the "correlate" of discourse or *logos*:

> The fundamental theme of the science of logos is truth in an entirely general sense. That is, one asks what truth as such is, further: how truth is structured and constituted, further: what possibilities and kinds of truth there are, and finally: what is the ground of that which we properly call "truth"? (GA 21:7)

This passage clearly shows Heidegger's methodical principle. In order to disclose the truth of the phenomenon of truth, it must be questioned with regard to its formal structure and the different modifications of that structure. The question concerning what grounds truth as unconcealment itself points in the direction of temporality.

The retrieving repetition of the analysis of truth with regard to temporality was to have been accomplished in the second and last part of GA 21.[16] The outline of the course indicates that Heidegger would here have thematized the foundations of truth as such (that is to say, temporality) and the different possible modes of truth, including the philosophical and the scientific truth (26). The first part, about Aristotle's concept of truth, should have prepared this theme. Much of the second part is, however, taken up with an analysis of Kant's concept of time. Only in the last section does Heidegger briefly return to his original question. Thus, as usual, he diverges from the plan sketched in the introduction and by this detour avoids his proper theme. I will try here to follow as far as possible the line of Heidegger's analysis as he sketches it in the introduction. In doing this I will discuss only those results—greatly simplified—of the first part of GA 21 that are important for the second part.

Aristotle argues that judgments are characterized by a bringing together (*sunthesis*) and by a distinguishing (*diairēsis*). According to Heidegger, this synthesis does not consist primarily in bringing together various words (141), but can be traced back to an "as"-structure. Judgments that bring beings to light always uncover something *as* something. Thus, in the judgment "the blackboard is black," the black blackboard is unfolded into "blackboard" and "blackness." This interpretation of the blackboard *as* black at the same time brings together the blackboard and the blackness (cf. 137, 145). Such a judgment explicitly reveals a being—namely, in relation to a certain property.

Heidegger understands the apophantic "as" of the judgment as a modification of the hermeneutic "as." Before I can reveal the blackboard as black or not black, I have already understood and interpreted it *as* blackboard. An assertion *about* the blackboard isolates this "as" from the whole of referential relations, such as a lecture hall; the "as" is thus "forced back to the uniform level of what is merely objectively present."[17]

In the apophantic judgment, moreover, the blackboard is brought together with something that does not essentially belong to the blackboard itself, namely, its blackness. The "as"-structure therefore always entails the possibility of mistake or untruth. This mode of untruth has ontic truth as its counterpart.

However, Heidegger continues, one can only be mistaken with respect to beings on the basis of a preceding familiarity with the environment within which something does or does not appear as itself. This "primordial disclosure of world" constitutes the condition of possibility not only of being mistaken but also of interpreting chalk as chalk and making judgments about a piece of chalk as white or about a circle as round.[18] In other words: every mode of ontic truth or untruth is made possible by a preceding unconcealment which itself could also be called "truth."[19] This unconcealment comes about in the preontological understanding of being, which is itself guided by the horizon of Praesens.

We know that Heidegger also regards the way in which philosophy thematizes being as an elucidation that makes explicit what has always already been understood. In Aristotle's view, this mode of thematization is not based on a synthesis:

> [T]he essence [is] something which is deprived of every "together" (*Beisammen*); thus, its being can basically not be understood in terms of a "together" and a unity of the "together."[20]

It therefore seems impossible to be mistaken when articulating the being of beings. The uncovering of being is an "uncovering for which there is no covering over" (182). Aristotle thus contrasts ontic and ontological judgments because the latter do not come about through a synthesis and hence cannot be false.

At the end of the first part of GA 21, however, Heidegger traces back the synthesis-structure of the judgment, via the "as"-structure of understanding, to a preontological making present that grounds every judgment.[21] The synthesis structure therefore no longer has to serve as the criterion in the distinction between ontic and ontological judgments. And that allows Heidegger to indicate the common ground of ontic judgments and the way in which traditional ontology thematizes the essential; from his perspective the ontological explication of the preontological making present constitutes precisely the highest mode of presentification:

> [T]he pure uncoveredness of beings (*reine Entdecktheit des Seienden*), such as conceived by Aristotle with regard to what is not complex (*das Einfache*), this pure uncoveredness means nothing but the pure, nonsuspended and nonsuspendable presence of present beings. . . . Thus, insofar as being is understood as presence (*Anwesenheit*) and uncoveredness as present (*Gegenwart*) . . . being as presence can be determined by truth as present. (193)

Like uncovering a piece of chalk *as* white or not white, or the bush *as* deer, the thematization of beings *as* beings thus occurs from within a horizon of Praesens. Ontic and ontological judgments are both grounded in the "as"-structure, which in the apophantic judgment expresses itself in the "is" of the copula.[22] Heidegger has previously shown that every "as" entails the possibility of covering over, so—in contrast to Aristotle's view—covering over must also be possible with regard to being itself. This must, however, be of a different character than the mistakes we can make with regard to beings: it is not accidental that "being" is initially and mostly understood as constant presence.

Thus, Heidegger's analysis has the same outcome as the second part of *Being and Time* and the end of GA 24. At the end of the first part of GA 21, Heidegger again concludes that "being"—although the Greek thinkers could have had no inkling of this "abysmal problem"—is understood against a temporal background (193–94). He proposes that the phenomena of judgment, truth, falsity, and synthesis should now be thematized with regard to their temporality (197–99). Since he has shown that these phenomena all originate in the as-structure, this retrieving repetition will have to concentrate on the temporality of the as-structure, of the leveling of the hermeneutic to the apophantic "as," and of thematization as such (207).

Heidegger sees his first step in this as to clarify what he understands by temporality. He does this by means of a short sketch of the analytic of Dasein and a long discussion of the history of the concept of time, focusing mainly on Kant's theory of schematism.[23] The conclusion he draws from his interpretation of Kant is also that time is the condition of possibility of being-in-the-world (406). After this long detour, Heidegger comes back at the end of GA 21 to the temporality proper to every judgment, and thus to the original theme of the second chapter. Only now does the fundamental-ontological character of his analysis show forth.

The "is" that characterizes every judgment does not so much serve to connect a subject with a predicate, but rather indicates that preontological making present is the basic function of the judgment, at least with regard to the uncovering of beings as objectively present (415). This mode of temporality is also expressed in the traditional determination of knowledge as intuitive beholding. Hence, in the judgment the "is" has the temporal meaning of presence, although this meaning could not be thematized by ontology itself.

Since being is always understood from within a temporal horizon, covering over can also occur in ontology. Being is then inappropriately understood as that which is constantly present and thus guarantees that reality can be known. Heidegger briefly indicates that "being" could also be interpreted in a different way, such that the interpretation goes along with the primordial temporality of Dasein:

> If the temporality of Dasein contained more radical temporal possibilities, then these would limit the domain of traditional logic and ontology. Whether philosophical research will gain enough intensity and strength to actually set this limit, is a matter of its destiny. (415)

These are the closing words of GA 21. The threefold temporal structure of care does not necessarily have to enact itself as mere presentification. Initially and mostly ontology adopts the act of making present that grounds every ontic involvement with beings. *All* ontological judgments must use the "is." But that "is" does not necessarily have to entail that something is made present:

> And when we use in our assertions (*Aussagen*) phrases like "time is this and that," "time is temporal," this "is" pertains to a specific phenomenological-categorial positing, which must have, insofar as it is spoken, the structure of a worldly assertion, yet does not primarily have the meaning of bringing to the fore something which is objectively present. . . . All assertions about the being of Dasein, all sentences on time, all sentences within the problem area of Temporality are spoken sentences which are to be characterized as indications: they merely indicate Dasein, while yet, as spoken sentences, primarily intending what is objectively present. (GA 21:410, cf. BT 39)

So we find ourselves back at Heidegger's first course from 1919, although much has also changed along the way. That to which ontological judgments refer cannot be grasped immediately, but only from a specific change of perspective. Heidegger maintains that this turning did not occur in Greek ontology and that the radical difference between categorial and empirical judgments therefore remained concealed (410n).

If, then, discourse or *logos* contains temporal possibilities more radical than making something present, the "is" in ontological judgments might have a meaning other than objective presence. Heidegger will try to write in such a way that the reader can follow the concepts to a different, broader meaning of being. In a certain sense, that goes against their proper character, and in any case is difficult to achieve. It is therefore understandable that Heidegger increasingly tries to replace the "is" with words that already have a dynamic character, such as *west*, *walten*, and *sich zeitigen*.

One may add to this that Heidegger's own use of the "as" will no longer result in a mere making present. In order to understand ontology *as* ontology, it will have to be thematized with respect to its essential structure and its different modifications. In order to understand being *as* being, it will have to be thematized as the movement in which it enacts itself as presence, constant presence, and possibly as a presence pervaded by absence. As long as ontology addresses beings as beings without accounting for the temporal horizon that guides every "seeing," it will reveal being as what it is not itself. From Heidegger's perspective this modification can be understood *as* the inauthentic mode that itself essentially belongs to the occurrence of the essential.

This may suffice with respect to the themes which Heidegger was to have elaborated in part II of GA 24. Starting out from the phenomenon "truth," he could have shown how any unconcealment is made possible by Temporality, while this analysis of Temporality is also already needed in order to understand how being itself modifies and could modify itself in the history of thinking. The four chapters are so closely related to each other and to the other parts that they hardly lend themselves to a linear development. In part III Heidegger could have thematized the problem of the method of phenomenology directly after the above analysis of the phenomena *logos* and truth. We will now leave behind the themes of GA 24 and *Time and Being*. We do, however, still have to consider why Heidegger did not get around to systematically elaborating these themes.

5.5 Why the Third Division Was Not Published

The question concerning Heidegger's reason for not publishing the third division of *Being and Time* is initially a rather external question, although it immediately leads to the problem of the turning. In this section I will first discuss the remarks that Heidegger made about the third division after the publication of *Being and Time*. This will allow a transition to be made to Heidegger's later work. I will try to show that the later texts are no less motivated than the earlier by the themes that *Time and Being* would have elaborated. *Time and Being* remains the—usually invisible—pivot of Heidegger's entire thinking: this is where it comes from and to where it seeks to return.

We cannot know how far Heidegger had elaborated the third division of *Being and Time* before he decided not to publish it. A note in *On the Way to Language* refers to *Time and Being* as follows:

> The failure to get through in 1923 to 1926 forced me to reflect on language and—to *not* publish the initially drafted parts. (US 161n)

So he mentions drafted *parts*. Since the first editions of *Being and Time* contain a reference to a chapter of the third division that is omitted from later editions, we may assume that while *Being and Time* was being printed Heidegger had at least decided which chapters this division was to contain.[24]

The course on Schelling from 1941 gives the most biographical information with regard to Heidegger's decision not to publish the partially elaborated text. This decision, he writes, was taken on the ground of the "lively and friendly discussions" with Karl Jaspers, whom he visited for a few days at the end of December 1926 to talk about the printer's proofs of *Being and Time*. During this visit, Heidegger realized that "the hitherto reached elaboration of this most important division (I,3) would remain incomprehensible" (GA 49:39–40). Presumably Jaspers could not follow Heidegger's effort to move away from the concrete existence of human beings. This must have been a serious blow to Heidegger, the more so because he had placed all his hope in Jaspers, as he wrote to him in June 1926.[25] Jaspers' lack of understanding will have considerably strengthened Heidegger's own doubts about the elaboration of *Time and Being*. However, this does not mean that he initially abandoned the project as such:

> At that time I took the view that in about a year's time, I would be able to say everything in a clearer way. That was a mistake. . . . It is essential however that the fragment itself gives enough hold to at least come upon the decisive *question*. And that in fact was all that mattered. (GA 49:40)

In a year's time: that is a reference to the course GA 24 from the summer of 1927. Here Heidegger does indeed start out with questions that no longer pertain to human beings, but he again fails to achieve his aim. In the summer of 1928 Heidegger has still not abandoned the idea of completing *Being and Time*. In his course from that year, he refers to the importance of the phenomenon "transcendence" in *Being and Time*, even though it is there not treated radically enough:

> But that it is possible to give an interpretation which is more radical than the ones I have given hitherto, will become apparent from the second part. (GA 26:215)

In September 1932, however, he writes to Elizabeth Blochmann:

> They have begun to think that I am now writing Being and Time II and they are talking about it. That is all right. But because Being and Time I was once a *way* for me which led me somewhere, and because this way is not taken anymore and is already beginning to become impassable, it has become impossible for me to write B.a.T. II. I am not writing a book at all.[26]

In various later publications Heidegger indicates that he considers *Being and Time* both to be a necessary way to the proper issue and to be inadequate to enact the turning from the human being to being itself. His best known remarks on this are found in the *Letter on Humanism* from 1946. Heidegger here indicates that the understanding of being is

> the ecstatic relation to the clearing of being (*die Lichtung des Seins*). The adequate execution and completion of this other thinking that abandons subjectivity is surely made more difficult by the fact that in the publication of *Being and Time* the third division of the first part, "Time and Being" was held back. . . . Here, everything is reversed. The section in question was held back because thinking failed in the adequate saying of this turning and did not get through to it by means of the language of metaphysics. . . . This turning is not a change of the view taken in *Being and Time*, but it is rather in this turning that the attempted thinking first reaches the location of the dimension out of which "Being and Time" is experienced.[27]

Heidegger here states clearly that the turning would have been enacted in the transition from *Being and Time* to *Time and Being*.

There the focus on Dasein would have been left behind, in favor of a thinking which starts out from the temporality of being itself.

This turning does not however refer only to a change in Heidegger's thinking. *In* that thinking the history of philosophy would for the first time no longer turn away from the temporal horizon which grounds everything that thinking brings about of itself. Facing this horizon is what Heidegger considers to be the proper possibility of this history, but also of being itself, which tries to make itself understandable in that history. In his letter to Richardson from 1962 Heidegger says:

> The thinking of the turning results from the fact that I stayed with "Being and Time" as that which was to be thought, that is to say that I inquired into the perspective which already in "Being and Time" (p. 39) was announced under the title "Time and Being." The turning is primarily not something which occurs in a questioning thinking; it belongs to the matter at issue (*Sachverhalt*) itself such as designated by the headings "Being and Time" and "Time and Being."

From *Being and Time* onwards,

> [T]hinking is called upon to accomplish a reversal that occurs in accordance with the turning itself. This, however, does not at all mean that the question of "Being and Time" is abandoned;

rather, it is

> brought to completion in a decisive way. . . . The "occurrence" of the turning . . . "is" Being (*Seyn*) itself. It only lets itself be thought from out of the turning (*aus der Kehre*).[28]

At the end Heidegger notes that the distinction between a Heidegger I and II made by Richardson is only justified if the early texts are understood as the initially indispensable way to gain access to the later work, in the sense that the early work itself is already a part of thinking the turning. I have shown how the analytic of Dasein itself already ensues from the question that arose around 1923 concerning the temporal meaning of being as such, and that this question itself could only be broached after the analytic of Dasein. Hence we might say that *Being and Time* would have come into its own, that is to say, to its most proper possibility, by turning itself into *Time and Being*.

In his letter Heidegger also argues against the conception that the turning was accomplished in the *Letter on Humanism.* Stating that his thinking has been motivated by the turning for about ten years, he implicitly refers to the *Contributions* from 1936 to 1938. Only in this work does he first attempt to actually make the leap that was merely prepared in both *Being and Time* and the texts between 1927 and 1936.[29]

In the *Contributions* itself we find one of the most important passages that Heidegger devoted to *Time and Being*. Briefly reflecting on *Being and Time*, Heidegger describes the question at issue in that work as apparently still bound to common representation: the question concerning the condition of possibility of the understanding of being still shares common ground with the metaphysical question concerning beings as beings. However, this is initially unavoidable:

> For a thinking which emerges out of the perspective of metaphysics, there is initially just no other possible way to explain the task of the question of being. This manoeuvre has the appearance of converting Being (*Seyn*) itself into an object (*Gegenstand*),

while in fact the opposite was intended. It is not enough

> to make clear that "time" is the reach of the projective movement which allows Being to appear (*der Entwurfsbereich für das Seyn*). . . . It thus became important . . . to overcome the crisis of the question of being as it initially had to be broached, and most of all to avoid an objectification of being (*eine Vergegenständlichung des Seyns*). That was to be done by holding back the "temporal" interpretation of Being and simultaneously making "visible" the truth of being without regard to that interpretation. . . . The crisis could not be defused by merely continuing to think along the lines of my questioning hitherto, but the manifold leap into the occurrence of Being itself (*in das Wesen des Seyns selbst*) had to be ventured. That also required a more primordial embedding in history (*eine ursprünglichere Einfügung in die Geschichte*). . . . Being itself announced its historical essence. (B 450–51)

This passage leaves no doubt as to why Heidegger considered *Time and Being* doomed to fail. Clearly, the transition from *Being and Time* to *Time and Being* only initially results in his focusing no longer on the structure and possible modes of being of Dasein, but on those of ontology. Although the deconstruction of that ontology constituted the starting point and goal of *Being and Time*, its inner movement seems to have prompted Heidegger to go even further than the issue of the history of metaphysics. The analysis of the different ways in which being is understood would have led him to the different ways in which being attempts to make *itself* understandable in the history of thinking. To a certain extent this is a reversal of the perspective with which *Being and Time* actually begins, and it does not necessarily ensue from the published part.[30]

The relation between being and temporality, as developed in *Being and Time*, appears not only to make possible the actual "leap," but also to increasingly thwart it. Enacting that turning was evidently not yet possible with the means at Heidegger's disposal. From his perspective, however, such an incapacity does not stem from thinking alone. Like the possibility of a turning to being itself, the lurking objectification of being is ultimately not grounded in thinking itself:

> Being (*Seyn*) is most threatened by a danger which time and again emerges from out of itself and belongs to it as its own time-space (*Zeit-Raum*); it is in danger of turning itself into something that "is" and of enduring the fixation which evolves from the beings. The history of metaphysics . . . attests to this danger and to the difficulty of coping with it. (B 476)

As far as I know, *Contributions* is the only text that explicitly refers to the need to hold back the thematization of temporality. Heidegger does indeed do this in the lectures after 1927—as we will see—but this does not mean that the problem of temporality is totally absent from those texts. Rather it shows itself as precisely that which is held back.

With regard to the failure of the transition to *Time and Being*, Heidegger repeatedly refers to the inadequacy of the language that at that time was available to him. In my view, however, that was not the only reason. *Being and Time* tries to leave behind the standpoint of modern subject-philosophy, but at the same time to radicalize the notion of finitude that he so esteemed in Kant's work. When the analysis of the temporal *understanding of being* leads to the question as to how being *itself* tries to make itself understandable in the history of thinking, Heidegger again crosses Hegel's path. Because how is one to understand this essential movement without taking up the "standpoint" of the absolute?[31] I take it that Heidegger deferred the explicit enacting of the "turning" in order to prevent "them" from unmasking him—unduly—as a second Hegel. It is therefore highly significant that in the penultimate section of *Being and Time* Heidegger distinguishes his own concept of time from that of Hegel.

The "battle of giants" concerning being (cf. BT 2) can be understood as the battle of Heidegger with Hegel and via Hegel with metaphysics from Plato and Aristotle onward. A thinking that wishes to confront Hegel at *his* level will first, with Hegel, have to twist free from a perspective oriented upon the subject. But at the same time it will have to develop a measure which makes it possible to also understand Hegel's philosophy as a philosophy that does not do justice to the proper character of being. Heidegger's concept of temporality allows him to understand the history of philosophy as a movement which does not consist in the increasing unfolding of a principle that from the outset inheres in history and guarantees its own actualization. In order to articulate the proper dynamic of this history, then, Heidegger will have to find a language that owes as little as possible to that of Hegel.

What Heidegger says on the last page of *Being and Time* about the strife with metaphysics can perhaps now be better understood:

> The *strife* concerning the interpretation of being cannot be settled *because it has not even begun to flare up*. And finally it cannot be "jumped into," while one first needs equipment to begin such a strife. The investigation presented here is solely *underway* to that. (BT 437, tr. m.)

Only in Heidegger's later work will this strife with metaphysics be able to really flare up, while temporality remains the "secret" weapon. Heidegger understands this strife between thinking and itself as ultimately a strife between the countering tendencies that being itself is. Being, that is to say, the essential, is in itself the tendency to become constant presence and the tendency to resist this presentification. This counterstriving needs Dasein in order to enact itself, although Dasein is unable to decide its outcome. Nothing is given except a free space, a battleground, a few essential possibilities.

In the texts after *Being and Time* Heidegger tries to take further his attempt to deprive Dasein of its central position and thus turn to the occurrence of being itself. These texts are more cautious than *Time and Being* would have been. Perhaps, Heidegger writes in *On the Way to Language*, he had ventured forth too far too early in *Being and Time*.[32] The later texts therefore observe a greater reticence. As though they are waiting until their time has ripened, yet knowing that such a time might always remain to come.

> In ripeness, the powerful capacity to become fruit and the greatness of its gift, lies at the same time the *most hidden* essence of the *not*, as not-yet and no-longer. (B 410)

II

Heidegger's Later Works

6

The Gigantic Strife of Being for Itself

The last chapter showed how Heidegger in GA 24 attempts to thematize the structure and the various modifications of being while no longer taking Dasein as his point of departure. This gives a broader scope to his early critique of the confined understanding of being that he considers to have dominated the entire history of metaphysics. He can now understand this history by starting out from the way in which being itself attempts to make itself understandable. This perspective permits a more radical interpretation of the relation between being itself insofar as it is understood and the time that opens up the realm for this understanding.

In this part I will reflect on what happens with temporality in Heidegger's later work. Although in his later texts Heidegger never discusses temporality in such detail as in GA 24, in my view this concept continues to ground the analyses that he actually does elaborate. Heidegger's understanding of the history of being is guided by the threefold distinction between a primordial possibility and the modifications in which this possibility enacts itself in an inauthentic way or an authentic way.

When it has been shown that the idea of temporality remains very important in Heidegger's later work, the continuity between the early and later work and the unity of that later work can be emphasized. I will thus try to show that the later texts all emerge from a common basic principle and that Heidegger, perhaps despite himself, remains an extremely systematic thinker. Only then will it also be possible to answer the question as to how Heidegger's concept of history differs from that of Hegel.

First, I will briefly indicate how Heidegger attempts to articulate the truth of being in the lectures after *Being and Time* without paying attention to the issue of time (6.1). On the other hand, he tries to no longer regard time and being as separate phenomena. The *Contributions* in particular concentrates on the question as to how being gives itself its own temporal horizon and thus attempts to make itself understandable. Being is now understood as an *occurring* of the essential (6.2), which takes place in and as the history of thinking (6.3). The different temporal modifications of being serve as Heidegger's guideline in his deconstruction of metaphysics, which takes shape especially in the courses from the 1930s and 1940s. Modes of thinking that precede metaphysics or try to break free from it are also thematized here (6.4 and 6.5). A thinking that is no longer guided by the confined metaphysical understanding of being might understand this history as itself—that is to say, no longer as a history in which a given principle increasingly actualizes itself.

However, Heidegger no longer thematizes the meaning of such an authentic mode of thinking by reflecting on his own method. The question concerning the proper possibility of thinking (6.6) entails the question concerning the essence of language: language is the "place" where the essential both discloses itself and withdraws from its disclosure (6.7). Finally, I will examine two texts that in my view most clearly show the relation between temporality and being: *The Anaximander Saying* from 1946 (6.8) and the lecture *Time and Being* from 1962 (6.9).

In order to structure the large quantity of material I will therefore—after a brief sketch of the transitional period between *Being and Time* and the *Contributions*—start out from the most formal mode of Heidegger's concept of being. The meaning of that concept will then be elucidated by means of his interpretation of the history of thinking. I will thus follow the structure chosen by Heidegger for the third division of the first part and the second part of *Being and Time*. This structure does not correspond to the order of his later texts; in these texts the systematic structure of Heidegger's thinking often remains in the background.

6.1 The Texts Published around 1930

In the lectures from the years after 1927 Heidegger tries in various ways to indicate a concept of being that differs from that of metaphysics. *What Is Metaphysics?* from 1929 suggests that any mode of presence is grounded in a certain primordial absence or nothingness. The nothingness that is at stake here is not the negation of that which is, but is an absence that belongs to the essence itself (WM 12 / PM 90). This "nothing" is to be understood as that which differs from beings—that is to say, being—and as such makes possible every encounter of beings. Heidegger here remarks that science wishes to know nothing of the nothing (4/84). Since metaphysics, like science, could only inquire into that which is, it could never do justice to the absence which primordially pervades being itself.[1]

On the Essence of Ground repeats that the difference between beings and being is grounded in the transcendence of Dasein. Dasein has always already transcended or surpassed beings and turned to their being. In line with *Being and Time*, Heidegger now defines this transcending movement as the projective preconception of world within which beings can appear as beings (35/109). This preconception he considers to be rooted in the ecstatic-horizonal structure of time (62/128). Heidegger again ventures this far—but then abruptly breaks off the line of thought.[2]

He repeats this movement starting from the question concerning truth in *On the Essence of Truth* from 1930. Truth as correctness (*Richtigkeit*) is grounded in a transcendence that allows beings to appear as beings. Heidegger now calls this primordial occurrence of truth "ek-sistence" (*Ek-sistenz*) (85/145). However, this essential occurrence of unconcealment necessarily entails that the nonessence of truth comes to power: the unconcealment of beings implies that being itself conceals itself (86/146). This concealment as primordial un-truth is not accidental, but belongs essentially to the unconcealment itself (89/148). The tendency of Dasein to take its standards from beings is called the insistence of ek-sistence (91/150). Heidegger considers this "persistence" to determine both Dasein's everyday existence and philosophy insofar as it is unable to face the primordial self-concealment of the essential (90/149). The turning away from primordial truth is now called "errancy." It is within the confinement of this errancy that every involvement with beings takes place.[3]

Heidegger's remarks on this issue remind us of the temporal ecstasis Present that, breaking away from its primordial threefold, has come to dominate the other ecstases and hence metes out the domain within which beings can show forth as present and being itself can solely be understood as presence. Only from within this errancy, however, does it become possible to no longer be led astray (93/151), that is to say, to no longer take one's standards from beings when the understanding of being itself is at stake. Heidegger here indicates very inconspicuously that metaphysics is grounded in and held by "something" that it cannot itself thematize (95/153). In order to understand what this means, he suggests that the question concerning the essence of truth be transformed into the question concerning the truth of essence—that is, the truth of the ways in which the essential mostly occurs and possibly might occur. This question is concerned with the truth of being itself. At this point Heidegger quite abruptly ends his essay.

In the aforementioned texts the idea of a primordial understanding of being that was lost in the ensuing history of thinking hardly comes to the fore. This is different in *Plato's Doctrine of Truth.* Heidegger here argues that with Plato truth in the sense of unconcealment began to leave the scene, to make way for truth in the sense of the correspondence between human vision and the ideas, which are conceived as always present and not susceptible of any change (136/176–77). The being of beings, that is, the "presencing of what is present," is no longer understood as the occurrence of unconcealment that allows beings to become present, but as that which offers thinking a firm hold—more than finite beings ever could (139–41/179–80). Here again, Heidegger refers to the tendency of metaphysics to cling to the confined domain of presence, precisely when thinking lets go of individual beings in favor of their *eidos*. As in the other texts from this period, Heidegger goes no further than indicating that this presentification of being is not grounded in human beings, but in the essence of unconcealment itself (143/182).

In the course *An Introduction to Metaphysics* from 1935, Heidegger ventures a little further into accomplishing the turning. He here attempts to thematize the different meanings—that is, ways of occurring—of being itself. The different meanings of being that determine the history of metaphysics are all said to be grounded in constant presence—which is but one specific meaning of being (EM 69, 154 / IM 92, 202). Whereas this meaning of being is itself grounded in a time that underlies any unconcealment of being, this temporality could never be brought to view from within metaphysics itself (157/205). According to Heidegger, this time must explicitly be taken as the starting point for the interpretation of being. He thus considers the title *Being and Time* to indicate a realm radically different from the realm that dominated the Western conception of being (156–57/205–6).

There is nothing very new in these texts compared with GA 24 and other courses around *Being and Time.* Heidegger is waiting, repeating, trying to elucidate what was at stake in *Being and Time*, and meanwhile preparing himself for the explicit accomplishment of the turning. This leads on the one hand to the *Contributions* and on the other to a number of courses on various episodes from the history of philosophy. These courses follow on from the deconstruction of metaphysics that was to have taken place in the second part of *Being and Time.* The themes that emerge in the texts from around 1930 continue to have an important place in many of Heidegger's later texts. The preparations for the "leap" must time and again be enacted—thinking is preparing. These repeating preparations do not, however, have any further vital function in Heidegger's thought.

6.2 Being Itself as the Occurrence of Being and Time

The threefold temporal structure that methodically guided the analyses of human life in *Being and Time* comes to serve in the later work as a guideline for interpreting the history of philosophy. It now allows Heidegger to distinguish between three modes of thinking, that is to say, between a thinking that is not yet, a thinking that is, and a thinking that is no longer metaphysical. He attempts in the *Contributions* to articulate the temporal threefoldness of being itself; here, the history of thinking is understood primarily as that which ensues from the occurrence of being itself (cf. B 176). This text, which is often highly impenetrable, may be regarded as the "source text" from which all the later texts originate. Since Heidegger here ventures further than in most other texts, it will play an important part in my reconstructive interpretation of his later work. I will not, however, attempt to give a comprehensive interpretation of this text. This would be quite impossible, in any case.

The *Contributions* consists of eight parts, in which thinking gradually breaks free from metaphysics and turns toward the history of being itself. Heidegger first indicates the attitude and attunement needed to accomplish this transition, and then shows how our time and the history of metaphysics deal with the question of being. An understanding of this history should prepare the "leap" into a thinking of the truth of being itself—that is, not merely the being of beings. The role of Dasein in this occurrence of truth can then also be indicated.

The question concerning the meaning of being recurs in the

Contributions as the projective preconception of "the occurrence of Being as *the occurrence of own-ing*."[4] This does not mean, however, that the ultimate answer to the question concerning the meaning of being can now be easily given. On the contrary. The work is made up of 281 short and sketchy fragments, often not clearly related to each other. There is no systematically elaborated line of thought—"The time of 'systems' has passed" (5). The structure of the book offers little help in understanding the separate fragments. They are dispersed on the pages like "blocks of a stone quarry" (421). It seems that Heidegger, probably inspired by the fragmented texts of both the late Nietzsche and Heraclitus, wishes to use this radical fragmentation to create a coherent whole that remains concealed *as* an unbroken unity.

I will try to show, however, that this fragmentation nevertheless springs from a rigorous, systematic line of thought, ensuing from what Heidegger had wanted to do in *Time and Being*. The time of systems does not pass quite as easily as Heidegger might have wished. I will concentrate on the fragments that may help to elucidate the systematic background of Heidegger's later work. As I said, this focus takes little account of the way Heidegger himself proceeds.

In a later marginal note to the introduction of *Being and Time*, Heidegger remarks that the concept of "horizon" was to have been overcome in the third division (BT 39). Initially, a retrieving thinking cannot avoid making use of such metaphysical concepts. As long as the analysis starts out from Dasein's understanding of being, being can come to the fore only as that which is understood, and time only as that which makes possible any understanding of being. Thus, the inner unity of both "moments" cannot become manifest:

> *Being and Time* does indeed intend to show that "time" is the realm within which Being (*Seyn*) can be projectively preconceived. Certainly, but if the analysis had not got beyond that stage, the question concerning being could never have been unfolded as a *question*, and could thus not have become a thinking of what is most questionable. (B 451)

The line of thought that was to have been elaborated in *Time and Being* now also turns out to be insufficiently radical. We know that Heidegger in GA 24 regards the problem of the ontological difference as the first of four basic problems. Only by starting out from the difference between the whole of beings and their being does it become possible to inquire how being itself has always been understood and might be understood. Only then does it also become possible to draw attention to the modifiable temporal horizon that guides every understanding of being. If, then, thinking increasingly succeeds in leaving behind a perspective that remains bound to the human understanding of being, it may conceive of time and being as two different moments of the one movement in which being itself makes *itself* understandable, that is, presents itself to human understanding. This is the step that is explicitly taken in the *Contributions*. Being itself, Heidegger now writes, brings about the temporal openness through which it can be understood as being:

> The projective preconception of Being can only be thrown by Being itself (*der Entwurf des Seyns kann nur vom Seyn selbst geworfen werden*). (B 447)

What is called Temporality in *Being and Time* and GA 24 recurs in the *Contributions* as "time-space" (*Zeit-Raum*). Unlike in the early works, this projective, temporal openness is now understood to be brought about by Being itself.[5] It is by virtue of its own projective movement that Being itself opens up the temporal horizon within which it can be understood as being and thus can enact the history of its different interpretations. That which opens up the temporal realm is now denoted by the word *Seyn*. Heidegger chooses this older spelling to indicate that which is even more primordial than the difference between being and time, because it is nothing but the occurring of this difference. What Heidegger now tentatively calls Being pertains to the differing movement in which Being divides off the temporal openness from itself and thereby opens up the space within which it can be understood as the being of beings and—possibly—as itself. This means that Being—due to its own temporal projection of openness—brings about the difference between itself and being insofar as it can be understood. Or, to put it another way, Being itself (*Seyn*) modifies itself into being (*Sein*) in order to become understandable, that is to say, to become the ultimate issue of ontology:

> Being (*Sein*) and Being (*Seyn*) are the same and yet they are fundamentally different. (B 171)

The difference between them is precisely the difference between ontology on the one hand and a thinking that attempts to think the truth of being itself on the other. This thinking

> enters into the beyond of the difference between beings and being, and therefore it writes being from now on as "Being."[6]

In the *Contributions* Heidegger repeatedly refers to the inadequacy of the concept "ontological difference." Because this concept presupposes that thinking has to start out from beings in order to gain insight into their being, the ontological difference can serve only as a transitional concept:

> The question concerning Being (*die Seynsfrage*)—the basic question—would have understood nothing of what is most questionable in this question, if it were not forthwith conducted back to the question concerning the *origin* of the "ontological difference." The difference between "being" *and* "beings" . . . can only . . . originate from the *essential occurrence* of Being (*die Wesung des Seyns*).
>
> The "ontological difference" is a passage (*Durchgang*) which becomes inevitable when—starting out from the guiding question (*Leitfrage*)—the necessity of posing the basic question (*Grundfrage*) is to be brought to view.[7]

The difference between the guiding question and the basic question also refers to the difference between traditional metaphysics and Heidegger's own thinking. As long as being is understood as the being of beings which can only be reached by starting out from concrete beings, being will appear from within a temporal openness that cannot do justice to the dynamic of Being itself, that is to say, to the occurrence of own-ing. Heidegger now attempts to think this occurrence itself and suggests that the difference between being and beings originates from a most abysmal cleaving (*Zerklüftung*) that from the outset divides Being against itself (244). The abyss to which Heidegger here refers is the time-space (*Zeit-Raum*) (379). Being (*Seyn*) must separate off temporality from itself in order to make itself understandable as "being." This differencing dynamic first enacts, as it were, the difference between beings and their being and thus grounds any mode of unconcealment or truth.[8] The ontological difference, then, is grounded in the originary movement in which Being distinguishes itself from itself and accomplishes itself as being. This most primordial difference has always already begun.

The temporal clearing (*Lichtung*) or truth that Being unfolds from out of itself does not guarantee that being can make itself understandable as *itself*. On the contrary; as soon as being is understood, the time-space modifies itself in such a way that being can only show itself as that which is preeminently present and constitutes the ground for everything that is. Metaphysics, turning itself to the being of beings, thus springs from the abyss of time and tries to establish a firm and stable ground for itself. The essential thinking, on the other hand, attempts to remain aware of the abyss by which it is borne (369).

What Heidegger calls *Seyn* is intended to elucidate that the way in which being mostly allows itself to be understood is an inauthentic modification of what it essentially is. This is the occurrence of dis-owning (*Enteignis*), which essentially belongs to the occurrence of own-ing itself; initially and mostly, Being can only occur as the movement in which it turns itself against its innermost possibilities. Since being—that is to say, the essential—has no power over the way in which it is understood in history, it can no longer be conceived as an ultimate ground which guarantees that reality can be known or that history will come to a good end. Heidegger's concept of temporality makes it possible to understand how every essential possibility from the outset thwarts its own fulfillment. The essential—always already divided in and against itself—can only occur as own-ing through a temporal openness within which being is initially and mostly understood as presence. The essential can therefore only come toward itself, or into its own, insofar as it constantly counters the tendency of presentification that it also is itself:

> Thus, while speaking of this matter becomes most difficult, the strife (*Streit*) is shifted to the ground of Being itself (*Seyn*). But this primordial enmity (*Feindseligkeit*) is the truest intimacy (*die wahrste Innigkeit*). (GA 39:273)

As being might not be able to resist its own persistence and presentification, its contention for its proper possibilities is dangerous and the outcome of this strife cannot be foreseen.

Being (*Seyn*) enacts itself as the distinction between time and being, which opens up the space within which thinking can understand, forget, or remember being. Being occurs as soon as meaning arises, as soon as there is world, or clearing. However, being can be determined further only when attention is focused on beings *as* beings: the history of being—that is to say, the history of thinking—only begins when the ontological difference is explicitly enacted. In this history, being is given the possibility of coming toward itself and resisting its prevailing presentification. In history, among human beings, a strife flares up between the counterstriving movements that being itself is: away from itself and toward itself. Being needs human beings to enact this strife, whereas human beings for their part come toward themselves by resisting the presentification that threatens time and again to determine all acting and thinking. However, the primordial self-differentiation of Being into being and time entails not only that being is understood, thematized, and misunderstood *as* the being of beings, but also that the time in which that misunderstanding is grounded itself disappears from view.

6.3 The History of Being as the History of Thinking

The history of philosophy is preeminently the "place" where being allows itself to be understood, yet gradually makes way for the constant presence that as nonessence belongs to being itself.[9] This modification entails that thinking initially turns away from its most proper possibility. Only by striving against its own nonessence might thinking liberate itself and turn to its authentic possibility.

The distinction between world history as the whole of successive events on the one hand and an essential occurring on the other is prepared in *Being and Time* with respect to the occurrence of Dasein, which mostly turns away from itself and possibly comes toward itself.[10] This "movement" is grounded in temporality and cannot be grasped in terms of linearity. In later texts the term history comes to relate explicitly to the history of thinking and thus to being itself that enacts itself in history.[11] I will now briefly indicate how Heidegger takes the temporal threefoldness of being as his guideline in interpreting the different phases of the history of thinking.

In the thought of Anaximander, Parmenides, and Heraclitus, beings are for the first time transcended in the direction of their being. One might say that being itself can now make itself understandable as that which essentially belongs to beings as such, and show forth as *phusis*, *logos*, or *alētheia*. In Heidegger's interpretation all these words pertain to the movement in which beings emerge from out of a preceding concealment into which they must always return. Because the horizon of Praesens from the outset grounds the understanding of being, we could say that in this first beginning of its history, being modifies itself in an indifferent way. The thinking that turns to being itself can initially not twist free from the horizon of Praesens intended or "destined" for the thematization of beings. According to Heidegger, this inauthentic tendency then leads to Plato's explicit fixation of the essential and, via Hegel and Nietzsche, culminates in a society that seeks to technologically control everything that is. On the other hand, being tries to modify itself in an authentic way in the poetry of particularly Hölderlin and in the thinking of Heidegger himself. Here the attempt is made to bring the essential to words *as* that which cannot serve as an ultimate and stable ground.

In this very brief summary of Heidegger's interpretation of the history of thinking, three essential moments can be distinguished—namely, (1) an originary temporal projective preconception of being, (2) the increasing predominance of presence within that projective preconception, and (3) the possibility of resisting that predominance of presence. Heidegger thus interprets the phenomenon "history of being" by means of the distinction between (1) a primordial structure, (2) its indifferent and inauthentic mode, and (3) its authentic mode. These three moments are called in the *Contributions* (1) *Wesung*, (2) *Anwesung* and *beständige Anwesenheit*, and (3) *Wesung* as *Ereignis*. These moments might be translated as (1) the (primordial) occurring of essence, (2) the occurring of essence as presencing and constant presence, (3) the occurring of essence as the occurrence of own-ing. They correspond to the distinction in *Being and Time* between (1) the primordial openness of Dasein, (2) everydayness and fallenness, and (3) resolute openness.

In an authentic modification of thinking, the proper dynamic of human existence and the history of being might show forth as itself. From Heidegger's temporal perspective, the primordial meaning of being has always already modified itself in an indifferent way, and the authentic modification of being is only preserved as a future possibility. But because every movement can only be understood by distinguishing between its beginning, middle, and end, Heidegger must nevertheless thematize origin and future of the movement as separate moments.

I will now first examine some fragments from the *Contributions* that relate to the different modifications of being itself. These may be regarded as examples; similar remarks often recur both in the *Contributions* and in the other texts.

> [T]he occurring of essence (*Wesung*) does not refer to something which would even lie *beyond* Being (*Seyn*), but brings to language what is innermost to Being, that is, the occurrence of own-ing (*Ereignis*). (B 286)

> The occurring of essence (*Wesung*) is the truth of Being itself and springs from it. Only when this occurring of essence can merely come to the fore as presencing, like it does in the first beginning, does *a separation* between beings and their "essence" ensue *forthwith.* (259)
>
> The first beginning thinks Being as presence (*Seyn als Anwesenheit)* against the background of presencing *(die Anwesung*), which is the first lightening of *one* of the ways in which Being occurs (*eine Wesung des Seyns*). (31)
>
> In the first beginning . . . only *presencing* (*die Anwesung*) could be grasped and retained as the measure for every interpretation of beings. (260–61)

When beings are transcended toward their being, Being can initially only show forth as presencing. The essential absence, or, one might say, the occurrence of absencing that belongs to the occurring of Being itself, is then not given its due: Being withdraws itself from the very outset.[12] This occurs with the first ancient thinkers. According to Heidegger, being is here experienced as occurrence of (un)concealment, but is scarcely thematized as such. The first thinking starts out from beings—that is to say, from Praesens—but in such a way that Present as yet remains more or less embedded within the threefold temporal horizon. Thus, presencing (*Anwesung*) may be understood as the indifferent mode of being, which corresponds at the level of the concrete existence of Dasein to the way in which innerworldly beings appear as at hand and, from a broader perspective, to everydayness. What Heidegger calls presencing pertains to the "not yet" of objectification. With respect to the articulation of being itself, this presencing tends to modify itself into constant presence. This presence is yielded by the primordial occurrence of being itself (478). This presentification is said to have occurred in the thinking of Plato and since then to have become ever more predominant:

> [T]he interpretation of being-ness as *idea* . . . projectively preconceives beings against the background of constant presence. . . . The occurring of essence as presence and permanence (*die Wesung als Anwesenheit und Beständigkeit*) does not leave room for the un-satisfactory (*Un-genügen*) . . . ; it confirms itself. (220)

Heidegger appears to understand presencing and constant presence as the two moments of being that set the standards for the history of philosophy hitherto. They are combined in the term "presence" (*Anwesenheit*).[13] *Being and Time* also understands the indifferent and the inauthentic mode as two phases of the same temporal dynamic. In both meanings of being, Present overshadows the other ecstases, albeit to a different extent:

> Presence (*Anwesenheit*) turns out to be *one* specific appropriation of the truth of Being, in which Presentness (*Gegenwärtigkeit*) has been specifically favored above Past (*Gewesenheit*) and Futurity (*Künftigkeit*). (B 297)

According to Heidegger, this predominance of Present should be resisted. Being itself might then for the first time occur as an occurring of essence in which absence is no longer excluded—that is, as the finite occurrence of own-ing:

> [B]ecause the occurrence of Being (*das Wesen des Seyns*) from now on refers not only to presence, but to the full occurring of the temporal-spatial abyss and thus of truth. (32)

> The beginning reverberation of Being (*der Anklang des Seyns*) wants to retrieve Being in *its full essencing occurrence*, that is, as the occurrence of own-ing . . . (*will das Seyn in seiner vollen Wesung als Ereignis . . . zurückholen*). (116)

> Remembrance and preparedness (*Erinnerung und Bereitung*) open the free time-space of Being (*den Zeit-spiel-raum des Seyns*); "Presentness" (*Gegenwärtigkeit*), the primary and only determination which this space received hitherto, is a determination that thinking must renounce. (257, cf. 390)

> In the ripeness, the powerful capacity to become fruit and the greatness of its gift, lies at the same time the *most hidden* essence of the *not*, as not-yet and no-longer. Starting out from here, one might surmise how intimately that which has the character of the "not" occurs within Being. (410)

> Thus, one should attempt to projectively preconceive being itself and the way in which it is essentially pervaded by the shadows of nothingness. (GA 49:58)

This cannot be done by following on from the first thinkers, where the withdrawal of being itself in favor of presencing has already begun. While this first beginning determines the entire actual history of philosophy, Heidegger attempts to enact an other beginning.[14] The "first" of the first beginning must be understood as that which initially takes place, and not as the most primordial, which as possibility preceded every actual occurrence. Heidegger always considers that which initially shows itself to be the indifferent modification of a primordial structure that has never occurred as itself. A thinking that turns back to the origin of the history which has actually taken place can try to take over the temporal projective preconception that grounds that history in such a way that Present does not get the chance to become predominant.[15] This has never yet occurred in history, and can at most be prepared; the origin toward which thinking reaches withdraws itself from what can be reached.

The series of "meanings" of Being that may be distilled from the *Contributions* already show a remarkable coherence at the level of the words chosen by Heidegger. The term *Wesung* refers to *Wesen* in the sense of essence, although it now denotes the occurring or enactment of the "what," that is to say, the primordial unity of the essential and its possible modifications.[16] The word *Anwesung*—presencing—still intimates the dynamic character of the *Wesung,* but at the same time already refers to the meaning of being as presence. *Anwesung* is a modification of being, which occurs as soon as thinking transcends (present) beings toward their being, but this mode is such that the concealment which grounds every unconcealment of beings is still more or less given its due. Presencing, however, yields of itself the tendency to modify itself into constant presence (*beständige Anwesenheit*), so that the essential can henceforth merely appear as *ousia* and idea. The meaning of being as *Wesung* has then entirely disappeared into the background. The word *Anwesenheit* finally expresses the common ground of *Anwesung* and constant presence.[17] As far as I can see, Heidegger is reasonably consistent in his use of the words that indicate the different moments of Being. That is also the case when he equates "being" with presence; then "being" is understood as the being of beings—that is to say, as Being *insofar* as it—initially and mostly—makes itself understandable as presence.

Although the first thinkers' understanding of being as presencing (*Anwesung*) did more justice than the ensuing metaphysics to the preceding and future absence within being itself, this was less than Heidegger considered necessary. In their understanding of being, being thus seems to modify itself in an indifferent way: the presentification of being has not yet become predominant, but is indeed already inherent in it as an inevitable tendency.

In order to prepare an other, more appropriate beginning of thinking, however, Heidegger regards a return to the thinking that precedes metaphysics as a necessary step. The texts of the first thinkers are a *better starting point* for understanding being itself as the movement in which it comes toward itself—the occurrence of own-ing—but they are no more than that. Heidegger writes of the relation between the first and the other beginning that they are "totally separated according to the character of their origin."[18] This means that Heidegger's interpretations of the first Greek thinkers must be read as preparatory detours just as much as, for instance, the analytic of Dasein. In my view, the miraculous unconcealment of beings is therefore not the main focus of Heidegger's thinking, although it may appear so in some texts. The interpretation of the first beginning can at most serve as an intimation of his own thinking, while conversely this interpretation itself is only possible on the ground of his own projective preconception.[19] However, it is often difficult to distinguish where Heidegger is only interpreting and where he is trying to draw attention to his specific perspective—temporality—itself.

In his reflection on the history of thinking, Heidegger tries to explicitly distinguish himself from Hegel's and Nietzsche's philosophy of history. He considers that they indeed try, however differently, to restore the broken relation with the Greeks, but:

> neither of these two attempts . . . is original enough, because they are not motivated or supported by *the* question, the one through which beginning Greek thinking must surpass itself toward an other beginning.[20]

Heidegger regards Hegel and Nietzsche themselves as representatives of the metaphysics that should be left behind in favor of a different possibility of thinking. With regard to Hegel, Heidegger does not want to regard the first thinkers as the "germ" of what originated from them, nor Hegel's philosophy itself as the ultimate completion of what they first articulated (cf. GA 55:78–79). The history of metaphysics should be regarded as more an impoverishment of this first beginning than an enrichment. This means that Heidegger's view of history is guided by a different—although not entirely different—law than Hegel's dialectic. The "law" that Heidegger finds in concrete history could not be revealed by that history itself:

> [T]he rich, innermost change of the essence of metaphysics [follows from] a law, still hidden from us, of a hidden history. (GA 53:28)

This law entails that the history of thinking is neither a history of increasing development nor one of increasing decline. According to Heidegger, history is precisely characterized by the tragic and insurmountable strife between the two tendencies, which can only be understood as a unity on the basis of the idea of a primordial time-space in which Present respectively is somewhat, is and is no longer predominant. On the basis of the primordial free space that it is given, then, the history of thinking is on the one hand the attempt to come to its most proper possibility (*Ereignis*) and on the other the repeated failure of this attempt (*Ent-eignis*), since all progress confirms rather than overcomes the predominance of Present.

The more metaphysics develops, the more it *seems* to definitively overcome itself. And the more difficult, but also the more necessary, it becomes to expose how, for instance, even Hegel and Nietzsche still cling to an inadequate preconception of being. The completion of metaphysics means that thinking has exhausted all the essential possibilities of its basic projective preconception. Heidegger does not take this to mean that thinking after Hegel and Nietzsche has twisted free or can twist free from that frame. The metaphysical projective preconception becomes ever more predominant, both in philosophy and in the relation of human beings to the whole of beings:

> The end never sees itself, but takes itself to be the completion, and thus will be the least prepared and ready to expect or experience the *last* (*das Letzte*).[21]
>
> The end of the first beginning will for a long time infringe on the transition period (*Übergang*), and even on the other beginning. (B 227)
>
> The fact that the history of metaphysics has come to an end (with Nietzsche) implies not at all that metaphysical . . . thinking has henceforth been extinguished, on the contrary: this thinking shifts its unfaltering habits to the realms of worldviews and of the increasing scientification of everyday's hustle. . . . The history of metaphysics does not end, because it is now converted to the non-historical, which it indeed first opens. (431)

Heidegger regards the ontological-temporal horizon within which everything on earth is conceived as technically controllable as the perishing (*Verendung*) of metaphysics, which can hardly be resisted, if at all. Yet thinking must unremittingly attempt to bring metaphysics to an end in such a way that another beginning of thinking, of history, and of being itself becomes possible:

> History as it has been hitherto [should] not perish (*Verenden*), but must be brought to its end (*zu ihrem Ende*). (411)

Heidegger maintains that a temporal projective preconception that allows being itself to occur as a presence thoroughly pervaded by absence will be able to let the being of Dasein and of history appear in an appropriate way. The interpretation of concrete texts that is based on that preceding projective preconception should then be able to reveal the essential of these texts. Thus, Heidegger's interpretation of, for example, Heraclitus and Parmenides attempts to retrieve their thought from inadequate metaphysical interpretations, including that of Hegel (cf. GA 55:30–31). I will now focus on Heidegger's interpretation of the first beginning of the history of thinking, and the place of Nietzsche and Hölderlin in that history. This interpretation is particularly elaborated in the courses from the 1920s and 1930s. Heidegger's confrontation with Hegel will be deferred until part III.

6.4 Heidegger's Interpretation of the First Thinkers

Unlike the deconstruction of philosophy that Heidegger was to elaborate in the second part of *Being and Time*, his later work mainly draws attention to the "not yet" and the "no longer" of metaphysics. Precisely by embedding the actual history of metaphysics between a primordial possibility of thinking on the one hand, and its possible future on the other, Heidegger attempts to understand what metaphysics itself is. He basically interprets the first beginning of Western thinking in two ways. On the one hand he dwells on central words and fragments of the first thinkers, but on the other, starting out from this interpretation, he tries to indicate that which is essential for the first beginning as such. These analyses are often highly contrived. The very fact that the first thinkers did not understand the character of their own "situation" he takes to be an important difference between the first beginning of thinking and his own radicalizing retrieval of what could only be intimated in this first beginning. Heidegger elaborates his conception of the first beginning in, for instance, an interpretation of the words *phusis* and *logos* in the courses on Heraclitus from 1943 and 1944 (GA 55). In *Parmenides* (GA 54) he mainly focuses on the meaning of *alētheia*. I will now briefly describe the principal themes of these courses.[22]

From the early 1920s onward, Heidegger regards the basic

word *alētheia* as highly significant, because it indicates that truth as unconcealment is grounded in a primordial concealment (cf. GA 54:38). The word thus refers to the primordial openness or clearing (*Lichtung*) that allows beings to show forth (214). According to Heidegger, however, the essential conflict between concealment and unconcealment as it is expressed in the one word *alētheia*, could not be explicitly experienced by the Greeks themselves.[23] Although the essence of truth primordially occurs as *alētheia*, it does so "in such a way as to conceal itself forthwith." This concealment is considered to determine the course of Western history (218).

This change in the essence of truth entails that concealment increasingly makes way for mere unconcealment and presence. Because the counter-striving essence of *alētheia* showed itself only to withdraw forthwith, the *concept* of truth could modify itself on the basis of this withdrawal into, for example, the correspondence between seeing and that which is seen. Untruth can then only show forth as lack of correspondence (95). This transition is said to take place with Plato; his thought allows the first beginning to appear for the last time while it also enacts the forgetting of this beginning.[24] According to Heidegger, Plato's concept of truth does not *bring about* a modification of the occurrence of truth, but rather *responds* to it. He sees this modification as determining the whole history of metaphysics.

In a possible other beginning, thinking—in contrast to what happens in the first beginning—will illuminate itself and its essential domain—that is to say, the essence of *alētheia* (202). This can only mean that thinking will then explicitly understand itself and its history by letting itself be guided by the temporality that grounds every unconcealment. Heidegger begins his course on Parmenides by describing the transition from the beginning of thinking to metaphysics as an increasing alienation from that beginning (2). This does not mean, however, that the first thinking gained something that it subsequently lost. At most, the originary has become less lost at the beginning of the history of thinking. In the *Contributions* Heidegger notes concerning the collapse (*Einsturz*) of *alētheia* that occurs in the Greek questioning of being:

> What collapses is not something that had already been established, let alone something that had been founded. Neither the one nor the other was achieved in primordial Greek thinking. (B 360)

In the first course on Heraclitus this collapse—which has always already begun—is called the primordial out-of-joint (*Unfug*) that belongs to *phusis* as such.[25] Heidegger interprets *phusis* not as "nature" or "essence," but as the clearing (*Lichtung*) that allows beings to appear at all (GA 55:163). The word *phusis* is said to refer to *alētheia* (157, 175) and hence to being itself as the occurrence of unconcealment. From this perspective, beings can be experienced as emerging from out of a preceding concealment to which they will have to return. In the Greek meaning of *phusis*, however, the unconcealment that grounds the appearing of beings is said to already prevail above concealment.[26] Heidegger himself tries to understand *phusis*—starting out from Heraclitus, but for the first time explicitly—as the harmonious unity of unconcealment and concealment. He suggests that these two moments (primordially) grant each other the space to accomplish themselves, as it were in friendship. Presence then accords with concealment and does not yet prevail at the expense of the proper character of concealment, as—which Heidegger does not say explicitly—will increasingly be the case in metaphysics.[27]

Starting out from the word *phusis*, Heidegger thus tries to sketch out the beginning of Western thinking as a situation in which presence has to some extent already begun to become predominant, although he still takes the word to also express the "friendly" conjuncture of unconcealment and concealment.[28] Since unconcealment threatens from the outset to come out of joint, this conjuncture must also be understood as a strife (cf. 133). In GA 55 and elsewhere Heidegger calls this essential strife that which is counter-turning (*das Gegenwendige*).[29] The counterstriving movement in which being as presence turns against the absence that it essentially also is, cannot be reconciled in a higher unity.

According to Heidegger, the words *alētheia*, *phusis*, and *logos* all refer to being itself as the counterstriving unity of concealment and unconcealment (371). Hence, the second course on Heraclitus, which has the *logos* as its central theme, follows largely the same scheme as the texts on *alētheia* and *phusis*. Insofar as the first thinkers understood *logos* as language, Heidegger maintains that they did not understand the essence of the *logos* (238–40). The *logos* must therefore be thought more primordially than it was by Heraclitus (344). In line with *Being and Time* Heidegger now translates *logos* as "gathering" (*Versammlung*) (280), that is to say, as the event that gives rise to the primordial coherent whole that allows beings to appear as beings (322, 376). This event is, of course, being itself (278) and it therefore pertains not only to discourse (*Rede*) as human capacity of articulation.

The word *logos*, more than the other basic words, allows Heidegger to reveal the relation between human speaking and being itself. Every human *logos* as mode of gathering is guided by the primordial *logos* as unconcealment (309, 317), and this—he suggests—in an inauthentic or an authentic way. That speaking usually fails to rightly pertain to the *logos* seems to be grounded in the essence of this *logos* itself:

> [H]ow can this same *logos* entail that human beings do not reach their proper essence (*sein eigentliches Wesen*) and do not even come close to its limits? (317)

Heidegger identifies this *logos* with the "Present" in which all beings are gathered (338, 371), but gives no further indication of how the different modes of this temporal open space determine the inauthentic and authentic possibilities of human speaking.

In his interpretation of the first thinkers, Heidegger goes along with their own words to indicate what has always already been enacted behind their backs. In the same way, the explication in *Being and Time* goes along with the way in which Dasein understands being, although without knowing it. I will now turn to Heidegger's interpretation of Nietzsche and Hölderlin. He takes them to respectively mark the final episode of metaphysics and the first attempt at an other beginning, although without knowing it.

6.5 Nietzsche and Hölderlin

Nietzsche

Between 1935 and 1955 Heidegger devoted many texts to Nietzsche. Although they differ in some respects, their tenor is in general that Nietzsche realizes the most extreme possibility of metaphysical thinking.[30] Heidegger considers the way in which Nietzsche distances himself from metaphysics not to result in the defeat of metaphysics, but rather in the confirmation of its most fundamental principle (HW 200 / QT 61). This means that the tendency toward increasing control that Heidegger sees in Nietzsche's thinking culminates in a thoroughly technological approach to reality (N II, 20–21 / N 3, 175). Heidegger's attempt to situate Nietzsche's thinking within metaphysics is often somewhat forced and does not do justice to the ambiguity of his texts. I will here indicate only briefly the projective preconception that leads Heidegger to regard Nietzsche's thinking as merely the culmination of the metaphysical tradition.

Heidegger must have agreed with much of Nietzsche's critique of the history of metaphysics. The proclamation that God is dead means that it is no longer possible to posit an ultimate being which orders reality and maintains this order.[31] Nietzsche's "deconstruction" of metaphysics as Platonism is based on the idea that every determination of values and truths is directed toward self-preservation. Philosophy maintains itself by determining ultimate, unchangeable values or ideas, but in doing so inevitably turns itself against its own vitality. Maintaining the distinction between a sensible and an ideal reality leads to a rigidity which negates life as will to power; the increase of power that constitutes the dynamic of life can only take place if the necessarily established values are also left behind.

The will to power can only fully accomplish itself if life no longer clings to a world beyond this world where there is no suffering. The insight that there is not a better world waiting for us may on the one hand lead us to an experience of things having no sense. Nietzsche claims that all Western philosophy is grounded in this nihilism, but is unable to recognize this. On the other hand, we may also try to expressly affirm reality as it actually is. When one acknowledges that suffering cannot be overcome and will always recur, one can accept that life consists in the movement in which it engenders and tries to maintain values, but is then forced to leave them behind or destroy them.[32] In so doing, life affirms the self-transcending dynamic of the will to power. The doctrine of eternal recurrence of the same therefore does not lead to a powerless nihilism, but confirms the human possibility of creatively transcending oneself.

Heidegger tries to understand the will to power and the doctrine of eternal recurrence as two moments of the same fundamental thought, which as a countermove ultimately remains tied to the confined horizon of metaphysics.[33] He considers Nietzsche's basic doctrine to be the idea that the will to power enacts itself as a process of constant becoming. Since Nietzsche regards the traditional distinction between being and becoming as subordinate to life as constant becoming, in Heidegger's view he does not do justice to the radically finite dynamic of human life and of being as such.[34] Insofar as Nietzsche still suggests that the way in which the will to power tries to increasingly affirm itself is a process of increasing self-actualization, his concept of the will to power is considered to remain indebted to the Aristotelian concepts *dunamis*, *energeia*, and *entelecheia* (N I, 76–77 / N 1, 65).

Nietzsche's conception of life as constant increase of power implies that the authentic possibility of life—the *Übermensch*—is understood as the ultimate concentration of power. Even when this does not pertain to any mode of political or economic power, human beings are still the central focus of this perspective. The place that has been vacated by God's death is taken by the human being, which autonomously brings about values and truths. Heidegger regards this conception as the ultimate expression of subject-thinking and hence as the complement of Hegel's absolute consciousness.[35] As long as the human being takes itself as a standard, the essence of the human being withdraws itself—in the same way as being itself.[36] According to Heidegger, Nietzsche's conception of the will to power as the essential dynamic underlying everything that is, is ultimately grounded in an understanding of being as constant presence and even constitutes the culmination of the forgetting of being.[37] He suggests that the eternal recurrence of the same should be understood against the background of "primordial 'time,'" which could not be done by Nietzsche himself.[38] Thus, Nietzsche could not turn back to the primordial beginning of thinking and went along with "the beginning which has already come to a halt" of metaphysics (N I, 469 / N 2, 205, tr. m.).

One might add to this that Heidegger, from within a modified temporal horizon, does not regard the self-affirmation of the will to power as the most proper possibility of life, but rather as the affirmation of one's own finitude—that is to say, of the incapacity to actually accomplish what one is aiming at. Nietzsche's supposed lack of this temporal perspective leads Heidegger, despite perceiving a certain kinship, to mainly emphasize the difference between his own thinking and that of Nietzsche. A note in the *Contributions* clearly expresses this ambiguity:

> [T]o venture the confrontation with Nietzsche as the one who is nearest, and yet acknowledge that he is the furthest removed from the question concerning being.[39]

This nearness means that Nietzsche also prepares the transition to something other than metaphysics. In this respect he seems to be closer to Hölderlin than Heidegger usually acknowledges.

Hölderlin

It is well known that from the mid 1930s Hölderlin's work had a great influence on Heidegger. He regards Hölderlin as the first and—besides himself—the only one who truly attempts to modify the perspective that determined the entire metaphysical tradition. Through Heidegger's interpretations, the poet of the great hymns emerges as the poet par excellence and ever more as his only kindred spirit. It is of utmost importance for Heidegger to extricate Hölderlin from German Idealism. In Heidegger's view, Hölderlin's work attests a temporal perspective that does justice to the past and future absence that grounds the occurrence of the essential.

Whereas Nietzsche is regarded as mainly thwarting an authentic turning away from metaphysics, in Heidegger's interpretations Hölderlin shows forth as the first to be truly able to free himself from Hegel's grasp and thus to resist the presentification of being.[40] It seems that Heidegger via Hölderlin's works—which he apparently considers a kind of proper modification of German Idealism—wants to affirm his own closeness to Hegel's philosophy, without however giving up the fundamental difference between his own thinking and metaphysics. As Heidegger tries to win Hölderlin for his own side, his interpretations perhaps say more about Heidegger's relation to Hegel than about Hölderlin himself.

Heidegger regards Hölderlin as a poet who gives rise to being itself in a new way and thus enacts a new history.[41] Being a poet, however, Hölderlin could not explicitly understand the turn that he brings about; that is, according to Heidegger, the exclusive task of the thinker.[42] The latter must try to retrieve what is brought to words for the first time in the poems. In this respect, Hölderlin is no different from Heraclitus and Parmenides.

Heidegger's interpretation of Hölderlin is again not solely concerned with a historically accurate representation (GA 52:4). His attempt to draw Hölderlin from the shadow of Hegel and to draw him closer to his own thinking may be less forced than his interpretation of Nietzsche, but it is certainly not without problems with regard to the textual analysis. Here too, however, I will only try to sketch out the fundamental truth that Heidegger thinks is to be found in Hölderlin. This truth takes various shapes in the poems. The three central motifs in Heidegger's interpretations are (1) the holy and the gods, (2) source and river, (3) being not at home and going homeward. These motifs are often intertwined within the texts and take turns to appear in the foreground.[43] Here I will separate them as much as possible and discuss them in a highly simplified way.

1. The Holy and the Gods

There is no doubt that Hölderlin's poems allowed Heidegger to retrieve Christian belief to such an extent that the fragility and absence of the holy could be given its due. This retrieval leaves behind metaphysical theology—insofar as it still regards God as creator, first ground, or ultimate being—but does not, on the other hand, entail a merely antithetical attitude toward the holy. Heidegger is not interested in the theological question concerning the existence or nonexistence of God, but in the question as to how that which is called God presents itself and withdraws from the way it presents itself.[44]

Just as Heidegger goes along with Aristotle or Kant to reveal in their work what could not be thought by those thinkers themselves, from the mid 1930s he uses words like "the holy" and "the gods" to bring something to light that has very little to do with belief in God. These words allow him to elucidate that human beings are part of a history of which they are neither the center nor the cause.[45] However, God may not be conceived as the origin or ground of reality either. To show that the appearance of God also rests on an understanding of the essential as such, Heidegger interprets the "holy" that appears in Hölderlin's work as the unconcealment or openness that grounds every occurrence of being. This temporal unconcealment is brought about by Being itself and makes it possible for innerworldly beings, humans, or gods to be encountered. Heidegger calls the holy "the pure lightening," which as the oldest time first makes it possible for the gods to appear.[46] This holy is misunderstood by humans (GA 4:63), which means that the gods—which remind humans of their essential finitude—withdraw and abandon humans to themselves.

The time in which the old gods have fled and the coming God has not yet arrived is the time in which Hölderlin finds himself. He intimates the "falling apart of the holy" in his poems by keeping silent about it (66). Thus the poet stands his ground in the midst of a double absence: that of a no-longer and a not-yet (44).

If the holy refers to the temporal unconcealment of being, the flight of the gods and the possible arrival of a last God must respectively be grounded in an inauthentic and an authentic modification of the holy. The authentic modification of the holy would mean that heaven, earth, humans and gods are held together by a center that Heidegger sometimes calls "fourfold" (*Geviert*). This authentic modification of unconcealment, in which neither humans nor the gods are at the center, is as it were constantly thwarted by the hardly resistible power of the fixating, objectifying perspective that Heidegger calls "frame" (*Gestell*).[47] What Heidegger, with Hölderlin, describes as the flight of the gods refers to this forgetting of being:

> How far has the God moved away from us, the God which has assigned us as founders and creators because he needs these for his occurring (*weil sein Wesen diese braucht*)? He is so far away that we are unable to decide whether he is moving toward us or away from us. (B 23)

Hölderlin's language thus lends itself to expressing the issue that most concerns Heidegger: being itself as the history in which it enacts itself and withdraws itself from the way in which it appears. Only in the work of Hölderlin can the flight of the gods be experienced as flight. Hence, the mood that underlies his poems is that of mourning.[48] Precisely this taking leave or letting go allows one to be open to a future arrival of the divine (GA 39:95), although in such a way that one, in awaiting that possibility, endures the deferral of this arrival.[49] According to Heidegger, this "most proper dynamic" is grounded in the primordial time through which "our existence exceeds itself into Future and Past."[50] This is one of the few passages in the courses on Hölderlin that explicitly refers to temporality.

2. Source and River

Hölderlin's river poems are pivotal in Heidegger's interpretations. What is said about the Rhine and the Danube is taken—rightly, I think—to pertain not only or primarily to the actual rivers, but to the dynamic of being itself, which may be recognized in the character and flow of the rivers. Hence, the river as it appears in the poems is for Heidegger not a metaphor in the sense that an empirical meaning is raised to a more abstract level.[51] There is rather a primordial dynamic that grounds not only the being of the actual river, but also the movement of history, human life, and poethood.

Heidegger identifies this—initially concealed—essential dynamic with "Being as a whole" (238). This means that in these poems, being or the essential is understood not only as preceding origin, but as the *whole* of the origin and that which springs from it. The stream is the whole of the source and the river that springs from that source.[52] Just as the source that itself remains concealed enacts itself as stream, being itself is also the way in which it enacts itself—that is to say, comes toward itself and turns away from itself.

As may be expected, Heidegger also recognizes this counter-striving dynamic of being in Hölderlin's description of the river's flow. The spring and the stream "come into conflict with one another" because the stream leaves or changes its original direction.[53] The will to take a different direction than originally intended Heidegger calls "the breaking through of a will that counters the original will of the river." The origin can only find a course for itself—against the flow—and come toward itself by resisting this essential countercurrent:

> Only through this counter-will does the origin become endangered and thereby come to itself. . . . Only if the origin which has sprung forth meets resistance and has to force its way through, does the being of the river become a destiny (*Schicksal*). (234–35)

If the countercurrent takes its own course, and continues to do so, this does not mean that the origin loses itself in it: being the beginning, it leaps over the stream that has sprung, to be preserved as the authentic *end* of the river (241, 247). The enmity between the original direction of the river and its countercurrent constitutes the unity of being (241, 249), that is to say, its intimacy (*Innigkeit*). Heidegger sees this intimacy as fundamentally different from Hegel's concept of the absolute.[54] From Plato onward, the counter-striving dynamic of being itself is considered to have stabilized itself to such an extent that being could only show forth as idea or essence, that is to say, not as itself (cf. GA 53:95). Hölderlin, like Heraclitus, is said to have succeeded in doing justice to the essential counterstriving dynamic that being itself is.

By enacting itself counterstrivingly, being opens up world, unfolds the whole of relations between beings and thus enables human beings to dwell in the world (GA 39:264). On this basis, Heidegger can also understand the being of the actual river as that which makes human dwelling possible and gives it meaning.[55] Both the stream and the poet bring about relations between beings and hence belong to the essence of being itself: being enacts itself both in the being of the river and in the work of the poet.

Heidegger's interpretation appears to be aimed at finding something in Hölderlin's poems about the Rhine and the Danube which—as origin—initially does not show forth and threatens to get lost in the flow of words. Clearly, he regards moving away from the text as the only way to come closer to the essence of the poems, or to let the poems turn themselves homeward, to bring them home. Against the current of traditional interpretations.

3. Being not at Home and Going Homeward

In GA 53 in particular the structure sketched above returns as the movement in which the poet, the human being as such, the stream, history, and being itself attempt to go homeward. Hölderlin's work is said to express for the first time the law of being-not-at-home and going homeward.[56] The turning toward one's own can only take place from out of a being-not-at-home: the "home" is not behind us, but arises only from within homelessness as a future possibility. This is the hidden law that Heidegger tries to find in the works of Hölderlin:

> The historicity of history is essentially the return to what is one's own, whereas this return can only take place by departing for what is foreign. (GA 4:90)
>
> In that case, however, to dwell in what is one's own comes last, rarely succeeds and always remains most difficult. (GA 53:24, tr. m.; cf. 179)
>
> Being-not-at-home (*das Unheimische*) . . . is the fundamental trait of the human dwelling among beings. (113, tr. m.)

Only from within a history in which being has withdrawn itself might being be experienced as an occurring of presence that is pervaded to its core by absence. It is important that Heidegger distinguishes between two modes of being-not-at-home. First, there is the forgetting of being in which one clings to beings and does not know what is being forgotten; second, there is the possibility of responding to being's refusal to present itself.[57] This authentic mode turns itself against the forgetting of being, yet not against the insurmountable homelessness. In the going homeward that concerns Heidegger, all that takes place is the affirmation of the impossibility of actually being at home. To turn homeward is nothing but to dwell in the journeying itself.[58] Thus, Heidegger seems to reject the traditional scheme of "at home—on the way—at home." There is only the movement which of necessity turns away from its origin or source and risks not being able to return to it. While on the way, however, the origin can be kept in view as a future possibility. Like the gods, being itself is nearest when kept at a distance (cf. GA 4:23). Yet this mode of nearness will always be threatened by the predominance of Present:

> Whatever human beings undertake, turns . . . counter to what they are fundamentally seeking from it, namely, finding themselves at home (*das Heimischwerden*) in the midst of beings. (GA 53:104, tr. m.)

Sometimes the essential can be said quite simply. The tragic character of human life is grounded in the counterstriving dynamic proper to the occurrence of being itself.

Hölderlin's poems try to articulate something essential. They allow being to return homeward, that is to say, to come nearer without presentifying itself. They therefore respond to the "stream" of the essential that enacts itself in language and thus attempts to come into its own. In this way the poet also turns himself to that which is most proper to him. If Hölderlin is only concerned with this movement (GA 53:60), then this concern of itself entails the care for poethood:

> One is tempted to say: his writing is solely concerned with poetry and the poet. Hölderlin is the *poet of poets*, just as the thinker who is most akin to the poet in his highest creating wishes to think and know, indeed *must* wish to know, what thinking is and who the thinker is. (GA 39:30)

In this passage we recognize the movement of *Being and Time* that was to have resulted in the question concerning the character and the possibility of thinking itself. The question concerning the proper character of poetry and thinking seems hardly distinguishable from the question concerning the occurring of being itself. The relation between thinking, being, and language will be thematized in the next two sections. We thus turn ourselves from that which is thought to the way in which that thinking occurs.

6.6 Being and Thinking

Heidegger's later work no longer explicitly deals with the issue of his philosophical method. Since the occurrence of being preeminently enacts itself in thinking, it is scarcely possible to distinguish between method and theme.[59] Nevertheless, Heidegger does not give up the principle of phenomenology as he understands it in *Being and Time*. He wishes no less to let things appear as themselves. The early Heidegger takes the phenomenological attitude to consist primarily in holding back interpretations that are foreign to the things themselves. The following passage from *Heraclitus* is highly reminiscent of the definition of phenomenon in *Being and Time*:

> Is it not finally time to recognize that that which reveals itself in the *logos* . . . gives us the proper intimation of how to grasp the essence of the *logos*, *purely according to what the logos itself lets us perceive of it and about it*? (GA 55:256–66, italics mine)

Metaphysical interpretations must be pushed aside "to let being occur from out of its own truth (*aus seiner eigenen Wahrheit*)" (279). In relation to Hölderlin, Heidegger calls the approach which lets that which it approaches appear as itself a beckoning or greeting:

> Greeting is a letting be of things and human beings . . . a reaching out to what is greeted, a touching . . . which however disturbs nothing; a grasping which does not need to "grab" because it is at the same time a letting go. (GA 52:50)

This description of the possibility of touching something without disturbing it differs in tone, but not in meaning, from the way Heidegger from the earliest courses onward understands the proper possibility of thinking.

In Heidegger's later work, being itself as it enacts itself in the history of thinking becomes the preeminent phenomenon. This means that the appearance of being as constant presence is revealed as inauthentic mode of an origin that has never taken place as itself and always already differs from what springs forth from it. The different essential moments in the history of thinking are revealed by means of a temporal projective preconception in which Present holds back itself in favor of Past and Future. Heidegger cannot, however, merely "project" this projective preconception onto history, but must show *from within history itself* what is essential in that history. His interpretation must therefore go along with what presents itself in the history of thinking, but does not initially come to the fore. This often creates problems with respect to actual, “correct” interpretations of texts.

Letting being appear as itself means opening oneself to what being itself, occurring as the history of being, has to say. In various texts Heidegger regards listening to this address (*Zusage*) as the authentic attitude of thinking: every question is grounded in a preceding susceptibility to what lets itself be thought. The questions that appear to the thinker are announced by the history of being itself and do not spring from the accidental thoughts of an accidental thinker (GA 55:187). This move from asking to listening may be considered a critical retrieval of the beginning of *Being and Time*, but it does not conflict with the principle of reticence, which is already important in *Being and Time*. In this connection, we may recall what Heidegger says in *Being and Time* about the proper mode of social concern: Dasein does not impose itself, but allows the other to come to its proper possibilities.

In the *Contributions* and in many other later texts Heidegger indicates that being cannot come toward itself without human beings. Only human beings bear the responsibility of letting being occur. On the other hand, human beings can only come to their most proper possibilities by letting the essential occur in an authentic way.[60] Human beings have been given the task of responding in an authentic way to what being itself is: that which withdraws itself, and initially and mostly does not give itself as itself.[61] Thus, being occurs hesitantly, wavering, as it were, between promising and refusing itself. Only insofar as being draws itself back does a time-space open up within which being might possibly begin to occur as itself:

> However, that which both promises and refuses to give itself (*das Sichversagende*) does so hesitantly, it thus grants us the possibility of the gift (*Schenkung*) and of coming into our own (*Ereignung*).[62]

Being withdraws itself, yet does so hesitantly. Its refusal, its “no,” first opens up the possibility of a “yes” and always continues to hold open this possibility as a promise; the ambiguous *versagen* means both refusal and promise. It is to this hesitating, suspending reticence of being that thinking must be able to respond. Not to bring about a decision, but to affirm the hesitation as proper to the way in which being enacts itself. This reticence of thinking must leave being the space to enact itself as occurrence of own-ing:

> In reticence (*Verhaltenheit*) reigns . . . the turning toward Being's occurrence (*die Wesung des Seyns*) as hesitant promise and refusal of itself (*zum zögernden Sichversagen*). Reticence stands *midway* between . . . anxiety (*Erschrecken*) and diffidence (*Scheu*). From them, and especially from diffidence, springs the necessity to keep silent, and this keeping silent is that which . . . allows Being to occur as occurrence of own-ing (*Ereignis*). (B 15–16)

An authentic thinking will respond as far as possible to the occurrence of own-ing itself, and will not resist it. It will try to articulate the essential movement itself in such a way that beginning and end of this movement show themselves as withdrawing from the realm of Present. Only then can the essential and insurmountable counterstriving of being itself show forth. This approach runs entirely counter to the prevailing tendency of language and can never entirely succeed. And yet there is no other way.

6.7 The Language of Being

In the *Contributions* Heidegger scarcely touches on the meaning of language. Only at the end of this work does he suggest that the essence of language should be understood by starting out not from beings, but rather from Being itself (B 497–99). In *On the Way to Language*, the interpretations of Hölderlin and other courses, Heidegger tries to understand language as that in which and through which being is preeminently given the opportunity to come to light, but at the same time is in the greatest danger of not being able to appear as itself.

This danger also threatens the articulation of what language itself essentially is. In the everyday and theoretical modes of language, language refuses as it were to bring itself to language; it holds itself back and "sends" itself only as what it is not itself—for example, as a means of communication.[63] Heidegger resists this tendency and tries to bring to language that which language essentially is. If he is to succeed at all, language itself will have to reach the appropriate words:

> But when is language itself put into words as language? . . . But when one attempts to let something come to language which has never yet been spoken, then everything depends on whether language gives or withholds the appropriate word. (US 161–62 / OWL 59, tr. m.)

The question as to how being occurs and might occur in language reminds us of the question concerning a mode of speaking that would prevent being from becoming objectified; this is the question that motivated Heidegger from the earliest courses and prompted him to take all kinds of detours.[64] The impasse that occurred at the end of *Being and Time* impelled him to develop a language better able to respond to being itself. An authentic mode of speaking should be able to go along with the way in which the essential lodges itself in language, but is always on the point of withdrawing itself from it. I will now elaborate in more detail what that means for Heidegger.

In *Being and Time* Heidegger proposes that not concrete beings, but only their *being* is dependent on the human understanding of being.[65] This simply means that concrete things also exist if they are not spoken about. Heidegger is not concerned with the existence or nonexistence of things, but solely with the question as to how they appear to us—that is to say, become meaningful.[66] Beings are dependent on the understanding of being only insofar as their meaning is concerned; the openness that Dasein itself is allows them to appear as belonging to a coherent whole. Even the appearance of something *as* existing is only possible on the basis of a preceding unconcealment of beings as such.

The gathering of beings—the *logos*—is enacted as soon as beings become meaningful, appear as something, are articulated. *Being and Time* shows that this occurring of unconcealment or world already takes place before anything is actually spoken; the involvement with tools is already grounded in a familiarity with the coherent whole from which all beings derive their meaning. Heidegger's later works focus no less on a showing forth of meaning that precedes all actual speaking. In various texts he calls this event *logos* or primordial poetry.[67] He now emphasizes more, however, that the gathering which allows beings to appear as meaningful preeminently takes place in language, that is to say, as soon as human beings have begun to articulate what and how beings are.

The primordial articulation of meaning that opens up world thereby also brings about the distinction between world on the one hand and the beings that owe their meaning to this openness on the other.[68] Then it also becomes possible to bring to words not only beings, but also the being of beings. The essential begins to indwell language as soon as human beings begin to speak, but initially remains itself concealed in favor of the unconcealment of concrete beings. Only through the language of poets and thinkers—who each in their own way are concerned with the being of beings itself—is being allowed to come into its own, that is to say, to go "homeward."[69] At the same time, however, the homecoming of the essential is made increasingly impossible by this very language: the concepts that are developed in philosophy—and could not have been developed in any other way—are only appropriate for comprehending beings.

In the lecture *Hölderlin and the Essence of Poetry* Heidegger indicates that the showing forth of beings which occurs in language is grounded in temporality. Words grant a certain permanence or identity to beings. This identifying capacity of language is said to be grounded in the self-differencing dynamic of the three temporal ecstases that give rise to presence in the first place:

> But the one and the same can only be manifest (*offenbar*) in the light of that which is perpetually and permanently there. However, permanence (*Beständigkeit*) and perpetuity (*Bleiben*) only appear when persisting (*Beharren*) and presence (*Gegenwart*) come to light. But that occurs when time opens itself up by stretching itself out into its ecstases (*in ihren Erstreckungen sich öffnet*). . . . Only since the "tearing time" has torn itself open into Present, Past and Future has it become possible to agree on that which remains. (GA 4:37)

Only when presence has been brought about can language create unity and thus let beings appear as a coherent whole. This possibility entails a danger, however. Referring to Hölderlin, Heidegger even maintains that language is the preeminent danger because it clears a way for being to be threatened by beings (34). Being or the essential threatens to get lost through the presentifying tendency of language. The word "house," for example, allows all houses to appear explicitly as house. But in thus enacting the difference between the essence of the house and all concrete houses, the word that makes a house a house threatens to become an empty, general concept that does not do justice to the proper structure of the being of beings. With such concepts and their corresponding grammar, language enacts itself in a way that does not accord with its most proper possibility:

> Thus, language must always bring itself within a semblance which it has brought about itself, and thereby endanger what is most proper to it: genuine speech. (35)

> The holy grants the word and comes into the word itself. The word is the own-ing occurrence (*Ereignis*) of the holy. (74)
>
> When the holy becomes word, its innermost essence comes to waver (*kommt ins Wanken*). (70)
>
> This remaining of the holy however is threatened by the mediation—which stems from itself— . . . of the word of the song. (71)

The most proper possibility that is meant here is the articulation of being itself. But as soon as that happens, the temporal openness that grounds every speaking turns itself against this possibility. Language thus comes to have two essentially counterstriving sides. On the one hand, it preeminently allows the human being to come to its most proper possibilities; on the other, it opens up the bottomless realm of fallenness and idle talk that threatens to make this future impossible. As nonessence of language, this latter side belongs essentially to language itself and cannot be overcome.[70] The poet and the thinker may, however, try to accord with the wavering proper to language as such.

We can see that Heidegger links the enactment of language with the unconcealing and concealing of being as that occurs in the history of thinking. It is in language that being itself—as occurrence of own-ing—comes or does not come to itself:

> The saying (*Sage*) which is grounded in the occurrence of own-ing (*Ereignis*) has an indicating character and is as such the most proper mode of this own-ing occurrence (*die eigenste Weise des Ereignens*). . . . The saying is the way in which the occurrence of own-ing speaks. (US 266 / OWL 135, tr. m.)
>
> Being comes, while lightening itself, to language. It is perpetually underway to language.[71]

The essential that attempts to lodge itself in language can hardly come home in it. We may recognize here the dynamic of a given possibility that thwarts its own actualization and tends to make it impossible. The strife between presentification and the effort to resist this prevailing tendency unfolds as soon as one tries to articulate something essential.[72] The concepts brought about by philosophy give no shelter to the essential; it does not feel at home in them. Being withdraws from the realm of Present, waiting until language is able to do justice to its radical difference from beings. Heidegger considers this withdrawing movement of being itself—that is to say, the not arriving of the essential in language—to be the "first" movement that really takes place; no real arrival has preceded it. At most, being has briefly, and barely, intimated itself in words like *phusis* and *alētheia*—although thinking could not truly receive their meaning as a gift. Even the first beckonings of being were already beckoning in farewell:

> For only the de-tour leads to the need of refusal (*die Not der Verweigerung*) and to the necessity of bringing to a decision what in the first beginning was only the hint of a gift (*phusis, alētheia*), and which then could not be grasped or preserved. (B 434)

The hints or intimations of language itself are to be taken over and passed on by the poet and the thinker.[73] A speaking that wants to let being arrive as itself will as far as possible have to leave behind words that presentify the essential and force it to become identical to itself. It will have to direct itself no longer toward beings but toward what language itself has to say:

> Man only speaks when he responds to language by listening to its appeal (*Zuspruch*). . . . Language beckons us, at first and then again at the end, toward the essence of a matter. . . . But the responding in which man authentically listens to the appeal of language is the saying which speaks in the element of poetry.[74]

This does not mean, however, that human speech is merely dependent on the appeal that takes place in language. After all, the essential can only occur in language insofar as human beings actually speak.[75] When Heidegger indicates that thinking shares its element with poetry (US 188–89 / OWL 83), he means that in both modes of speaking essential structures—which language itself as primordial poetry offers—can be brought to light. While the poet is said to "found" being and thus to first enact the strife between concealment and unconcealment, philosophy will intensify this strife and in so doing run the greatest risk of seeing this strife decided in favor of metaphysics (cf. GA 39:257). To resist that lurking possibility, thinking will have to take over and take further the primordially given possibilities of language in its own way. Heidegger's own work is naturally the clearest and most extreme example. Words like *alētheia*, *Ereignis*, and *Es gibt* become in his interpretation highly significant. Even though this may sometimes lead to contrived etymological escapades, I think that his attempt to evade the power of metaphysical concepts should be taken seriously.

The thinker who believes he is called upon to bring being to language will not only have to attune himself to the way in which being announces itself in language, but will also have to do as much justice as possible to the radical absence with which being is pervaded. In order to give room to this absence, thinking will have to adopt the restraint proper to being itself. Only a mode of speaking that is able to beckon the essential by keeping silent about it might allow the essential to appear as itself. This silence within speaking increasingly takes over the role of a methodical principle in Heidegger's work.[76] I will now briefly thematize the different modes of keeping silent that can be found in that work.

Heidegger's own texts are often structured in such a way that a possibility or question given at the outset postpones its own actualization or answer as much as it keeps it open. The text is thus not only what it actually is, but is also its most proper possibility. The reader should therefore be aware that the actual text is always on the way to this possibility, trying to come into its own, to come home. Authentic reading means keeping open this authentic possibility and not fixating oneself on what is said. In *Being and Time* the question concerning the meaning of being functions as such a postponed possibility.

The later courses and lectures are also written in such a way that the reader should be able to take Heidegger's thinking further than what is explicitly stated. His preliminary analyses should lead the way and allow the reader to pursue the indicated direction him- or herself. Heidegger, then, often indicates in his courses that he holds back or keeps silent about what is at stake, or that he can only give a few intimations:

> What finally matters in a really philosophical lecture, for instance, is not what is immediately said, but what in this saying is kept silent (*erschwiegen wird*). (GA 39:41)

> Keeping silent means here: to say everything that is to be said (*alles Zu-sagende*) in such a way that one can become aware of it as that which is kept silent. (GA 52:136)

Keeping silent (*Erschweigen*) is a mode of speaking in which the secret (*Geheimnis*) is intimated as that which withdraws itself.[77] *Being and Time* also refers to keeping silent as such an authentic mode of speaking; here too this mode pertains more to allowing the unsaid to resonate than to simply being silent.[78] The unsaid cannot occur without language, though any mode of speaking entails the danger of completely drowning out the silence which sought to make itself audible.

Clearly, the attempt to indicate what is at stake by keeping silent about it is not an accidental idiosyncrasy of Heidegger's style. To respond appropriately to being itself, the essential must be held back, but in such a way that what is said can lead the attention to what remains absent. This means that language must become a *sign*. Words then no longer draw attention to themselves, but rather refer to what remains unsaid:

> To give a sign means: to reveal something (*etwas entbergen*) which, while it appears, points to something which is concealed. . . . The essence of the sign is the revealing concealment (*die entbergende Verbergung*).[79]

We can see how the analysis of the sign from *Being and Time* recurs here within a different context. In *Being and Time* the sign functions as the authentic mode of innerworldly beings. The sign can be thematized without becoming an object—that is to say, without Present prevailing over the other temporal ecstases—and hence can refer to what recedes from view. In later texts the mode of the sign comes to pertain to the hints of language itself which the poet and the thinker each in their own way receive and pass on (GA 39:32). Heidegger thus retrieves the motif of the formal indication from the early courses. In such a referring mode of speaking, the absence that grounds and pervades any presence can come into its own. This demands of the reader the capacity to read in such a way that what is explicitly said is left behind in favor of the unsaid from which the said ensues and to which it refers back. The reading of the text as a "sign" is also only possible on the basis of a projective preconception in which Present restrains itself in favor of the other temporal ecstases. This modification cannot be easily brought about and risks failure time and again.

Heidegger's unceasing attempt to shelter being in language inevitably tends to make the texts inaccessible to the reader, who after all starts out from the perspective of metaphysics and can only attempt to depart from it out of this factic situation. Heidegger's interpretation of the history of philosophy is intended, I think, to help the reader take that step. The actual interpretations should be understood as detours that prepare the articulation of being itself as the occurrence of own-ing.

The way in which Heidegger holds back what is finally at

stake becomes over the years increasingly integrated in the actual texts. *Being and Time* just breaks off, in the hope that the fragments will give the intelligent reader sufficient ground to understand where the text is going. This also applies to GA 24 and the lectures around 1930. The later courses allow that which is kept silent to show through from within that which is actually said. They bear their lack more as a core within themselves and try to preserve it as a lack. In the *Contributions*, finally, Heidegger has twisted free from metaphysics to such an extent that this work scarcely risks being interpreted in a fixating way. This text therefore runs the greatest risk of not being interpreted at all. But perhaps it was not so much meant to be interpreted, but rather to serve as a source for all the texts that spring from it.

In the last two sections of this part I will interpret two texts that in my view summarize the entire thinking of Heidegger's later work. These are *The Anaximander Saying* from 1946 and the lecture *Time and Being* from 1962. In both texts temporality is pivotal.

6.8 *The Anaximander Saying*

Heidegger's text on the Anaximander fragment—published in *Holzwege*—was not written as a course or lecture, and is therefore one of the most difficult, but also most important texts of his oeuvre. As is often the case with Heidegger, the text opens with a deconstructive move: the common, philological interpretations of the fragment are said to be based on metaphysical presuppositions that block the possibility, as it were, of letting the meaning of the fragment appear as itself.[80] Heidegger considers his own approach to be guided by a different, nonmetaphysical horizon, which casts a different light on texts such as the Anaximander fragment. It should be stressed, however, that Heidegger's reading of Anaximander is not an interpretation in the traditional sense.

Starting out from the fragment handed down to us, Heidegger attempts to say something about the beginning and the ensuing development of the history of being as such. He takes Anaximander's fragment to retain more traces of this beginning than later texts.[81] Hence, comparing Heidegger's texts on Anaximander with the fragment of Anaximander itself can only result in disappointment. Because the fragment is questioned solely in order to turn our attention toward the concern of thinking as such, I will disregard the text itself as much as possible and focus on what Heidegger tries to do with it. In my opinion, Heidegger's "interpretation" has to be understood against the background of what has been said about time in the foregoing analyses.

Heidegger divides the saying of Anaximander into three parts, and "translates" its key words in such a way that they come to pertain to the occurring of the being of beings as such. An English translation of Heidegger's preliminary, literal translation of Anaximander's fragment runs as follows (I add the most important Greek terms):

> (1) But that from which things arise (*genesis*) also gives rise to their passing away (*phtora*), (2) according to what is necessary (*kata to chreōn*); (3) for things render justice (*dikē*) and pay penalty to one another (*tisis*) for their injustice (*adikia*), (4) according to the ordinance of time. (HW 303 / EGW 20)

I will now follow Heidegger's interpretation in broad outlines and consider in turn parts 1, 3, and 2 of the fragment.

The Transitional Character of Beings

Although it is uncertain whether the formulation of the first section of the fragment is genuine, Heidegger assumes that Anaximander must have said something about the genesis and decline of beings in general. Since it is not specified which beings are at stake, he infers—rightly, I think—that the fragment is concerned with an essential feature of beings as such. Heidegger takes any statement about beings as beings to be based on an answer to the implicit question concerning the meaning of being as such. This guiding answer must itself be brought to the fore. In order to understand Anaximander's saying as an articulation of the meaning of being, Heidegger forces the various key words to refer to that which makes possible the appearance of beings as such, that is to say, to the (temporal) structure in which every openness is grounded. His reading is based on the assumption that the specific meaning of being which underlies Anaximander's saying differs from the understanding of being which characterizes the ensuing metaphysical tradition. Philosophy from Plato to Nietzsche is considered to be guided by a specific understanding of being (307/23). Heidegger regards Anaximander as one of the thinkers who is not yet under the spell of metaphysics; in early Greek thinking, the improper presentification of being has already begun to take place, but has not yet got the upper hand. Thus, Heidegger will try to show that the fragment still speaks of a meaning of being that was lost in the ensuing history of metaphysics; he suggests that this first meaning of being determines the meaning of all basic Greek concepts, without ever having been elucidated itself (308/23–24). However, even the first attempts to express the being of beings already failed to bring being itself to the fore as itself. Being itself conceals itself as soon as beings are revealed as beings; this epoch opens up the realm within which beings can receive meaning and thereby enacts the—erring—history of being (311/26).

As I mentioned above, Heidegger presumes that the first section of the fragment deals, one way or another, with the genesis and decline of beings (315/30). He understands this process as the one movement in which beings arrive in unconcealment, linger awhile, and return to the concealment from which they originated (322/37). What is said in the fragment about genesis and decline is thus to be understood not so much as an expression of the perishability of all things (316/31), but rather as an indication of their transitional character: what becomes present arises out of and returns to an absence or concealment that underlies and pervades every lingering in presence:

> What is presently present always lingers awhile (*Das gegenwärtig Anwesende weilt jeweils*). It lingers while it comes to the fore and withdraws. Lingering (*das Weilen*) is the transition from coming to going (*der Übergang aus Kunft zu Gang*). What is present is what always lingers awhile (*das Je-weilige*). Lingering in a transitional way, it still lingers in where it comes from (*Herkunft*) and already in where it goes to (*Hingang*). The present beings which linger awhile, those which are present, occur from out of absence (*Das jeweilig Anwesende, das gegenwärtige, west aus dem Abwesen*). (323/37, tr. m.)

Beings are experienced as lingering between their coming and going. Thus, the presence of these lingering beings is embedded between the absence out of which it arises and the absence to which it returns. Heidegger suggests that this experience of the lingering of beings is based on a certain understanding of the meaning of being itself: only when being itself is understood as a presence which is, as it were, thoroughly pervaded by absence, can the way in which beings occur be understood as a lingering.[82] This Greek experience he considers to be also expressed by Homer when, in the Iliad, he characterizes the seer Kalchias. Kalchias surveys what has been, what is, and what will be, and thus gathers in his seeing both what is actually present and what is absent:

> All that is present and absent is gathered and preserved in *one* presencing for the seer. (321/36, tr. m.)

Every experience of beings as emerging from concealment and returning to it is guided by an understanding of being itself as presencing. It is essential for this presencing to be embedded in a twofold absence:

> The while [Heidegger uses the word *Weile* to indicate the openness which makes possible the lingering—*das Weilen*—of beings] occurs between coming to the fore and withdrawal. Between this twofold absence the presencing of all that lingers occurs. . . . In both directions, presencing is conjoined with absencing (*Anwesen ist nach beiden Richtungen in das Abwesen verfugt*). Presencing occurs in such a juncture (*Anwesen west in solcher Fuge*). (327/41, tr. m.)

Being itself is understood as a presencing that reaches into a twofold absence. Heidegger suggests that this "broad" meaning of being as such underlies Anaximander's understanding of the transitional lingering of beings. He clearly attempts to understand the Greek experience of the transitional character of beings as grounded in a modification of primordial time in which Present is still conjoined with Past and Future. Just as the appearance of beings at hand is made possible by a temporal horizon whose three temporal ecstases are still more or less conjoined, the first Greek thinkers are understood to have experienced beings from within a horizon that is not yet exclusively overshadowed by Present. But because their understanding of being itself could only start out from present beings, being itself could only enact itself, take place, or occur as presencing. Heidegger would say that as soon as being is understood as presencing, it is not allowed to occur in such a way that its innermost absence can come to the fore as itself.

Joint and Out-of-Joint

The words *dikē* and *adikia* in the third part of the fragment allow Heidegger to further articulate the way in which both beings and being itself are conjoined and disjointed. He renders *dikē* as "joint" or "juncture" (*Fug* or *Fuge*) and not, as is usual, as "justice."[83] To express the contrary of this conjoinedness, Heidegger chooses the word *Un-Fug*, which normally means something like impropriety or unruliness. Thus, the meanings of *Fug* and *Un-Fug* are formalized in such a way that they can pertain to an essential structure that underlies every kind of justice and injustice. Evidently, Heidegger attempts to develop a concept of *dikē* that as yet has no ethical or juridical connotations (305/21). The question concerning the ethical relation between human beings is postponed in favor of the question concerning that which—as juncture and out-of-joint—underlies all human actions. This is, in fact, very similar to what Heidegger in *Being and Time* tries to say about ecstatic Present, which time and again threatens to disjoint itself from its juncture with the other ecstases, and thus underlies any kind of inauthenticity or impropriety. In his interpretation of Anaximander, Heidegger again tries to make clear that threefold temporality—which is always already out of joint—grounds every inauthenticity and every effort to extricate oneself from it.[84]

What, then, does Heidegger say about the juncture and the out-of-joint in the Anaximander fragment? He suggests that Anaximander seems to conceive of *adikia* as the basic structure of beings and subsequently argues that beings can only become disjointed if a certain conjoinedness belongs to being itself:

> Present beings (*das Anwesende*) as such, being what they are, are out of joint. Both juncture and the possibility of being out of joint must belong to presencing as such (*Anwesen*).[85]

Heidegger, implicitly shifting the perspective from beings as beings to being itself, thus tries to indicate a conjoinedness and disjointedness within being itself that is not mentioned in any way in the fragment. But this most fundamental structure can be clarified only, if at all, by first considering the disjointedness that characterizes all beings.

Heidegger starts out from what he considers to be the Greek experience of the transitional character of beings to give his own account of the out-of-jointness of beings. Beings not only linger in unconcealment insofar as they emerge from and return to concealment, but it belongs essentially to their being to resist this primordial transitivity. Beings that have arrived in unconcealment tend to establish themselves as present things, to insist on their presence and thus to refuse to acknowledge both their origin and their future return to concealment:

> Beings which linger awhile (*das Je-Weilige*) occur as lingering within the juncture (*Fuge*) through which presencing (*Anwesen*) is conjoined between a twofold absencing (*zwiefaches Abwesen*). However, precisely the beings which linger and thus become pre-

> sent—and only they—can at the same time abide in their while. What has arrived may even insist on its while, solely to remain more present, that is, to persist. That which lingers perseveres in its presencing. In this way it withdraws itself from its transitory while. . . . It stubbornly sticks to . . . the constant continuation of its presence. (327–28/42, tr. m.)

Lingering beings tend to remain in the unconcealment meted out to them and to resist their transitivity. This resistance is not, however, grounded in beings, but in the out-of-joint of being itself:

> The out-of-joint consists in the fact that whatever lingers awhile seeks to stubbornly stick to . . . what is merely permanent (*das nur Beständige*). . . . *In presencing itself (im Anwesen selbst), which always lets present beings linger in the realm of unconcealment, arises the insistence on presence (steht die Beständigung auf). Through* this revolt of the while (*das Aufständische der Weile*) the lingering beings insist upon sheer permanence. (328, 43, italics mine, tr. m.)

Heidegger understands this persistence in presence as the disjointedness of beings. It is important to stress that the possibility of the revolt of beings against their own lingering is opened up by the lingering itself; it is grounded in the movement of presencing that has always already begun to take place. This movement of presencing, as a way in which being itself occurs, underlies every resistance or disjointedness that may take place on the level of beings. Giving rise to the horizon that allows beings to linger in unconcealment, Present must from the outset have begun to disjoint itself from the other ecstases and tends to only intensify this disjointedness. Being as presencing thus modifies itself into constant presence and expels from itself the absence by which it is pervaded.

The difficulty of the text is partly due to the fact that Heidegger seeks to articulate something about beings as such, without differentiating between, for instance, human and nonhuman beings. In *Being and Time*, Heidegger works with this distinction in order to focus the analysis on the being of human beings. Like *The Anaximander Fragment*, however, the analytic of Dasein is ultimately motivated by the attempt to show that the being of *all* beings is grounded in one fundamental temporal structure. The tendency of beings to persist in presence is at work in both innerworldly beings and in Dasein. Innerwordly beings tend to lose their original practical meaning and to lend themselves to objectification. Dasein on the other hand tends to flee its own original past and future, and thereby detaches itself from the threefold temporality that constitutes its being.

The same is the case with philosophy itself as a specific mode of human life: its articulation of the essential tends to modify that which it articulates into some sort of permanent and stable presence. This tendency to presentify being and to expel its absence means that metaphysics refuses to acknowledge the finite temporal threefoldness that underlies all understanding of being.

Heidegger tries to understand the tendency toward pure presence that can be said to determine the being of innerworldly beings, of human life, and of the history of thinking as due to a disjointedness in being itself that is—in a way—always already at work and can hardly be resisted. In his view, however, there is no disjuncture without the possibility of overcoming it (329/43); note that the term *Verwindung* that is used here most often indicates the possibility of thinking to twist free from metaphysics. According to Anaximander, all beings are essentially marked by *adikia*. But these beings also have the possibility of no longer insisting on their permanence and thus of bringing about something like *dikē* or juncture. How, then, can such a modification take place? How is it that beings can overcome their improper tendency and turn themselves toward their own and proper possibilities? Or, as Heidegger puts it:

> How should lingering beings, when they abide in disjuncture, be able to bring about or give juncture (*Fuge geben*)? Can they give what they do not have? (329/43, tr. m.)

Heidegger notes that the fragment does not answer these questions. He then turns to the word *tisis* to elucidate what it means for beings to do justice to one another, that is, to give each other their due. *Tisis* is usually translated as penalty. Heidegger, in contrast to other interpretations, chooses to relate *allēlois* (one another) only to *tisis* and not to *dikē* (330/45). This enables him to subsequently distinguish between a bringing about of juncture that is not yet to be determined on the one hand, and a mutual giving due that may occur between beings on the other. He first considers the latter.

The tendency of beings to persist in presence, Heidegger now adds, implies that they no longer care for the being of the other beings.[86] The structure that grants every being its proper place and takes into account the being of the beings to which it relates, falls apart. To understand this, one might again recall the analysis of utensils in *Being and Time*. The carpenter may or may not be able to let his tools function as tools, that is, let them appear as themselves. Dasein's objectifying gaze is shown to pull the beings out of their original joint or context, so that their practical meaning can no longer come to the fore. In a certain sense, this possibility might be understood to pertain to the relation between innerworldly beings as well. The hammer, for instance, could be said to enable the nails to function as nails and thereby let them appear as themselves. On the other hand, a resistance of the hammer to comply with its surrounding context breaks down this context as such and thus makes it impossible for the beings involved to function in accordance with their being.

It should be noted that in both *Being and Time* and *The Anaximander Fragment* it is neither the carpenter nor one of the tools that finally brings about meaningfulness. Only in and through the movement of presencing can Dasein encounter innerwordly beings, other human beings, and itself. Whereas in *Being and Time* the word *Rücksichtslosigkeit* indicates only the improper mode of consideration for other human beings (BT 123), in the text on Anaximander *all* beings are said to have the possibility of doing justice to other beings. This is what Heidegger reads in the word *tisis*. In order to free *tisis* from its juridical meaning, he finally translates it not as care, but as *Ruch* (332/46). This word, which in common German is only used in the negative form *Ruchlos*—reckless—is thus molded to indicate all possibilities of beings—whatever they may be—to reck other beings, to care for them and give them their due. The recking "turns itself to something so that it may remain in its essence (*in seinem Wesen*)" (332/46, tr. m.). The introduction of the word *Ruch* is important not only because it refers to a possibility of both human and nonhuman beings to show consideration for the being of other beings. It also enables Heidegger to distinguish more clearly between the level of beings and the level of being itself. He claims that the meaning of justice or order cannot be fully understood if only the relationship between beings is taken into account. Every ontic injustice or disorder that is to be overcome rests on a disjuncture that occurs, and necessarily occurs, within being itself. This does not mean, however, that beings can only follow the improper movement of being, that is, insist on presence. On the contrary: juncture or *Fug* within being itself can only take place insofar as beings give one another their due:

> The overcoming of the out-of-joint properly occurs through the assignment of recking. (333/47, tr. m.)

The relation between *Fug* and *Ruch* or *dikē* and *tisis* is to be understood in such a way that the possibility of *Fug* within being itself depends on the capacity of beings to care for the being of other beings, whereas this possibility of beings to give one another their due is both given and threatened by the occurrence of presencing itself. Thus, beings have to assume all possible responsibility to let a certain kind of justice occur that cannot, on the other hand, be reduced to something purely ontic. Bringing about juncture means trying to surmount the ontological out-of-joint that has always already begun to take place and can never be fully overcome.

What is possible though, in Heidegger's view, is a certain resistance on the part of beings that prevents the improper tendency within being itself from definitively getting the upper hand. It may be clear that it is most of all the task of human beings to give other beings their due, and thus to resist the tendency toward constant presence of being itself. In his interpretation of Anaximander from 1941, Heidegger makes the following remarks concerning the possibility of a proper modification:

> However, insofar as lingering beings accord with the essential occurrence of presencing, they do not insist on and stubbornly stick to persisting in constant presence. . . . They comply with the juncture. . . . When beings themselves thus give being its juncture, they are such . . . that they by themselves also allow every single being to be what it is. (GA 51:119)

> To bring about juncture and acknowledge one another—that is in itself the overcoming of the out-of-joint (*die Verwindung des Unfugs*). Constant presence is not overcome in the sense that its essential possibility is . . . sublated (*Aufhebung*). On the contrary. (119)

The out-of-joint of being itself has always already begun to take place and will never end. However, being itself is in itself also the movement in which it tries to resist this disjointedness (122). A thinking that attempts to give being itself the space to do this will have to accord with the transitional character of being itself and be attentive to the absencing within every occurring presence. In this, traditional philosophy has always failed:

> What is present . . . comes to presence out of absence. This must be said precisely of whatever is truly present, although our usual way of representing things would like to exclude all absence from it. (HW 323 / EGT 37, tr. m.)

Heidegger here implicitly refers to the mode of philosophy that understands being itself as *eidos* or *ousia*, and thus cannot do justice to its transitional character.

To Chreōn. *Handing Over*

Clearly, in Heidegger's view the question of how juncture can be established cannot be adequately answered if one only takes account of the relation between beings. It was precisely the difference between beings and being or *Anwesendes* and *Anwesen* that could not be acknowledged as such in the history of metaphysics (336/50). Heidegger therefore turns his attention not only to this ontological difference, but also, yet more radically, to its origin. The primordial openness within which beings can be encountered as meaningful occurs only insofar as their being or "essence" is understood—that is, insofar as being itself is implicitly distinguished from concrete beings. He conceives of this differentiating movement as made possible by a certain kind of original "giving" that hands over being to beings. It is in and through such an original giving that the ontological difference occurs—yet mostly fails to occur properly.

Heidegger has to make some complicated interpretive turns to understand Anaximander's word *to chreōn*, normally rendered as "necessity," as this original giving gesture. Whereas Anaximander seems to tell us that the genesis and decline of beings happens according to a certain necessity, Heidegger maintains that *to chreōn* refers to the handing over of being to beings, which allows them to appear as beings, to be disclosed by language, and so come to their truth.[87]

Only if being is given to beings can they possibly give each other their due, that is, allow one another to come into their own. Insofar as this most difficult giving succeeds, being itself will not insist on pure presence, but will comply with the jointed threefoldness of Temporality. It is only through the primordial disclosing gesture that being can accomplish itself as presencing or as constant presence. It is the same gesture that gives being its original transitional character and sets free its tendency to persist as constant presence: the giving gesture necessarily hinders and even tends to make impossible the promised gift, that is, the coming into its own of being itself. Heidegger chooses to translate *to chreōn* with *Brauch* to indicate this double gesture:

> While it gives juncture (*Fug*) and reck (*Ruch*), *Brauch* sets free the whiling and leaves the beings each time to their lingering. This entails that beings are constantly in danger of petrifying this lingering into mere persistence. Thus, *Brauch* remains in itself as much the handing over of presencing in the out-of-joint (*die Aushändigung des Anwesens in die Un-Fug*).[88]

A satisfying translation of *Brauch* does not seem possible; the German word is incomprehensible enough in this context. It is clear, though, that Heidegger uses it to indicate something—which is nothing—like an original giving gesture, which gives something it does not have beforehand, while withdrawing itself in the movement of giving. In the lecture *Time and Being* from 1962, among others, this same disappearing hand appears in the expression *Es gibt* (cf. 6.9). Being is given the possibility of occurring in accordance with its own absence and so of granting beings their transitional character. On the other hand, this very same giving delivers being to the danger of persistence. Juncture can only be brought about insofar as beings are capable of preventing constant presence from definitively getting the upper hand.

It is, Heidegger would say, especially the task of thinking to turn itself against the disjuncture of being that has occurred throughout the history of metaphysics and thus to do justice to the absence that pervades any presencing. Being occurs only insofar as human beings try to articulate the essential. It *needs* human beings for its accomplishment, as Heidegger suggests in many other texts as well.[89] Yet it is absolutely uncertain whether that which is needed will actually be given: the detours that have to be taken—language, for instance—may very well irrevocably thwart the course of being toward itself that Heidegger calls the history of thinking.

How, then, are we to understand the relation of human beings to being itself? The ontological difference only occurs when human beings think and speak. It is only through language that being can arrive and give beings their meaning; this language allows the essential to occur as itself yet at the same time always threatens this occurrence. In the end, being itself cannot but divide itself against itself, and in so doing must radically threaten its own possibility of coming toward itself. When human beings nevertheless attempt to allow being to accomplish this innermost movement, they also come toward their innermost human possibilities.

Although Heidegger in *The Anaximander Fragment* scarcely mentions the difference between Dasein and innerworldly beings, we may infer from *Being and Time* that Dasein is capable of facing a past and future nothingness (its being-thrown and imminent death respectively) in a far more radical way than the innerwordly beings that do not resist their past and future concealment. Innerwordly beings, insofar as they appear, are always determined by presence and therefore by common chronology. Human beings are as much determined by this common time as all beings, but are, as Dasein, further constituted by the threefold ecstatic temporality that makes possible any encounter of beings. Radical nothingness, one might say, can only take place insofar as being is understood, that is, insofar as Dasein exists.

The Anaximander Fragment mentions two different kinds of human beings: first, the seer Kalchias, who gathers absence and presence in their juncture; and second, at the end of the text, the man who rises against his finitude and tries to master the world and its historical course (343, 57). Kalchias and this rebellious man represent two possibilities of human existence, in which we may recognize the proper and the improper mode of existence as analyzed in *Being and Time*. These contrary possibilities delimit the battleground in which the struggle that constitutes human life and human history takes place.

As I noted above, it is especially in philosophy that the essential absence that pervades all presence might be acknowledged. Yet this very philosophy threatens the absential with exclusion from being in the most radical way. Insofar as Anaximander is considered to already understand being as presencing, this expulsion of the absential from being occurs as soon as thinking begins. Heidegger attempts not only to let his own ontological questioning be guided by a different, nonmetaphysical modification of being, but also—ultimately—to no longer understand being from the perspective of beings at all. Only when this ontological perspective has been surmounted can both presencing and constant presence be understood as two privative modifications of being that do not cover all its essential possibilities. A modification of being in which the absential is fully acknowledged for the first time would be a modification which, for Heidegger, is still to come and belongs to a future that can never become present.

Heidegger does not mention in *The Anaximander Fragment* that the realm within which presencing can occur is itself opened up by a primordial time that belongs to being itself. He might have used the word *chronos*, which is mentioned in the last part of the fragment, for this purpose, but he chooses not to. The hidden temporal character of being is mentioned only once (311). In GA 51, *chronos* is interpreted as the incalculable time meted out to all beings (GA 51:121). There is more to be said about time than this, however: Anaximander does not say that time itself is that through which being, as presencing, can occur (121). *The Anaximander Fragment* does not elaborate on the relation between the *Brauch* that hands over being to beings, presencing, and time. The lecture *Time and Being* from 1962 is much clearer in this respect. There is no doubt, however, that Heidegger's interpretation of the Anaximander fragment is also guided by the idea of a primordial threefold temporality in which Present again and again tends to reduce this threefoldness to a unifold horizon. Insofar as Heidegger succeeds in thematizing the three different modes or moments of being—that is, its primordial possibility that never took place, its improper tendency, and the possibility of countering that tendency—his text allows being to occur or take place as itself. This means nothing more than that Heidegger attempts to bring that which is essential to language—for better or for worse.

6.9 *Time and Being* from 1962

The lecture *Time and Being* may be regarded as supplementing *The Anaximander Fragment*. In comparison with this text, *Time and Being* at first sight has a very clear and simple structure. Heidegger here no longer takes the detour of interpreting a philosophical text or poem, but directly broaches the question concerning the relation between being and time. He thus not only returns to the issue of the third division of *Being and Time*, but also goes along more directly with the *Contributions*. Articulating the relation between being and time means that being as it is understood by metaphysics, which gains access to being through beings, cannot be the last word or answer: being as presencing is something that has been "given" and is therefore not the primordial "giving" that makes possible every mode of unconcealment.[90]

To indicate the distinction between giving and that which is given, Heidegger now uses the expression "it gives" or "it is given" (*Es gibt*). This expression, which has the idiomatic meaning "there is," is already used in the earliest courses with respect to that which appears or is given in one way or another, without existing in the same way as beings. In *Being and Time* Heidegger says repeatedly that being, in contrast to beings, "is" not, but is given insofar as it is understood.[91]

While Heidegger initially used the expression "it gives" merely to avoid the "is," in *Time and Being* it takes on a more emphatic meaning. The "it" that is nothing but the gesture of giving pertains to that which is described in many later texts as the movement in which presence or presencing is both handed over and handed out to beings. The "it" gives being and time, while it withdraws itself from what it gives. This giving—which has to be taken over by human beings—gives beings the possibility of appearing as beings. Like the words *Seyn* and *Brauch*, *Es gibt* thus refers to that which precedes the distinction between being and time.

In *Being and Time* temporality was considered to be the condition of possibility of the understanding of being. While confirming this relation between being and time, *Time and Being* also tries to no longer let time be the last word. On the basis of the *Contributions*, Heidegger now indicates that time as clearing or lightening belongs to the occurrence of being itself. He emphasizes that the only purpose of *Time and Being* is to bring being to the fore as the occurrence of own-ing (SD 22 / TB 21). I take that to mean that Being can only occur as the movement in which the essential as such attempts to come into its own when Temporality delimits the realm within which being can be understood as being. In that respect, temporality is more primordial than being. But it is not more primordial than the *Seyn* or the *Es* which lets itself be understood as being and to this end distinguishes itself from temporality. In that respect, time just as much as being is something that is given.[92] In order to emphasize the difference between the gift of being and the gift of time, *Time and Being* uses the word *reichen*—to reach or to hand—to indicate the gesture by which time is given; the word *schicken*—to destine or send—is reserved for the gift of being:

> A giving which only gives its gift, but in this giving withholds and withdraws itself, is a giving that we call destining (*das Schicken*). According to this meaning of giving, being that is given (*das es gibt*), is that which is destined to us (*das Geschickte*). (8/8, tr. m.)

> We call the giving which gives authentic time (*die eigentliche Zeit*) the lightening-concealing reaching (*das lichtend-verbergende Reichen*). (16/16, tr. m.)

Being is destined to us by the giving gesture that differentiates itself in a *schicken* and *reichen*; this gesture opens up the temporal realm or reach (*Bereich*) that makes possible the unconcealment of beings and thus the history of being. Precisely because time is *reached* to us as Present (*Gegenwart*) and being is *destined* to occur as presencing (*Anwesen*), the "it" that gives both time and being withdraws itself from what it gives. Human beings receive this gift of being and time, but are initially and mostly unable to do this in an appropriate way; it is, so to speak, taken for granted and grasped in such a way that the gesture behind it remains hidden.

All that is indicated by words such as *Geschick* and *Schickung* is the tendency of metaphysics to comprehend that to which it pertains, the essential, as that which is preeminently present. This tendency may be understood as the incapacity to leave behind the horizon of Praesens. Although all metaphysics is determined by this *Geschick*, thinking should not merely resign itself to a kind of fatal destiny.[93] On the contrary: only if inadequate concepts are as emphatically as possible left out might a different kind of *Schickung* of being begin to occur. In *Time and Being* Heidegger concentrates so much on the "it" which releases being and time that he gives little attention to the different possible modifications of the temporal realm and of being as it appears within that realm. He does, however, note that presencing has come to have a very large reach:

> The vast reach of presencing (*das Anwesen*) shows itself most oppressively when we consider that absencing (*das Abwesen*) too, and more than anything else, remains determined by a presencing which at times prevails in such a way that it is unsettling.[94]

Heidegger here suggests that the occurrence of absence also always concerns us in one way or other. If something shows forth as belonging to the past or future, then this showing must be grounded in a handing over of presencing that is not confined to mere presence (13–14/13). The primordial interplay of Present, Past, and Future makes it possible for presencing to be given to us in a threefold manner—that is, in such a way that the absence of what is no more and not yet can play its part. By starting out from the ontic level of past and future events, Heidegger in *Time and Being* indicates a mode of presencing within which the occurrence of absence is allowed to take place. Tacitly and inconspicuously, he subsequently transfers this broader meaning of presencing to a level that no longer pertains to events that occur, but to the reach of unconcealment itself. The three temporal ecstases thus together open up a time-space within which being can be understood as presencing:

> How are we to determine the reaching of presencing which occurs in Present, Past and Future? . . . What do they reach one another? Nothing other than themselves—which means: the presencing which in them is reached to us (*das in ihnen gereichte An-wesen*). What we call time-space (*Zeit-Raum*) brings itself to light (*lichtet sich*) in this reaching. (14/13–14, tr. m.)

In this primordial interplay of the temporal ecstases, their "dimensions" are both held together and held apart, and they thus give rise to a presencing that does not yet have the character of constant presence. The ecstases are near one another, which implies that they are essentially different. Their interplay is not yet disturbed by the dynamic in which Present overshadows the other ecstases such that the primordial threefoldness is reduced to mere presence. The temporal ecstases can be held apart insofar as presence is denied to Past and Future.[95] This allows the essential to appear as a possibility that is always already behind us and, while it enacts itself, remains preserved as a future possibility. This means, in the words of *The Anaximander Fragment*, that presencing is conjoined with a twofold absence. As we saw, Heidegger hardly touches on the possible modifications of this initial reach. He focuses instead on the "it" that allows being and time—that is, unconcealment—to occur at all.

When being and time are assigned to human beings, being itself is given the possibility of occurring as presencing and—possibly—of coming into its own. Likewise, the given time can occur as the whole of the interplaying ecstases and thus turn itself to its innermost possibility. This enactment or occurring of presencing and clearing is what I understand Heidegger to mean by *Ereignis*:

> The movement in which being is destined to us and in which time is reached to us, reveals an own-ing (*ein Zueignen*), a handing over (*ein Übereignen*): being is handed over as presence (*Anwesenheit*) and time as the realm of openness; thus they are handed over into what is their own (*ihr Eigenes*). What determines both, time and being, in their own, that is, in their belonging together, we shall call: *the occurrence of own-ing* (*das Ereignis*).
>
> Accordingly, the "it" that gives . . . reveals itself as the occurrence of own-ing. (20/19, tr. m.)

The "it" that gives time and being refers just as much to the occurrence of unconcealment as the word *Ereignis*. This last term, however, indicates more clearly that it pertains to a dynamic which encompasses more than merely the initial moment of the gift. The giving of being and time means—in formal terms—that the possibility is given of coming into one's own.[96] This means that unconcealment can accomplish itself, that beings can appear as beings, that the essential can occur as itself and that human beings, history as such and the history of thinking can come toward their most proper possibilities.[97] Thus, the word *Ereignis* pertains no longer to a (special) event that may or may not take place (21/20), but—although Heidegger does not say this explicitly—to the radically finite occurring of the essential as such that grounds every mode of coming toward oneself.

In allowing temporal unconcealment to occur, that in which that occurring is grounded withdraws itself from the unconcealment that it makes possible (23/22). Owing to this withdrawal, time accomplishes itself as Present and being as presence or presencing. The occurring of absence then withdraws in order to give free play to presence; this is the condition of every impossibility of coming to oneself, of every alienation or inauthenticity. The time that lets being occur also entails that being itself is "forgotten" *as* divided in and against itself and thus as radically finite. The time that gives Dasein the possibility of thinking being and thus of turning toward itself, thwarts this very movement as well. Hence, to the occurrence of own-ing that grants being, history, and human beings the possibility of coming into their own, essentially belongs the occurrence of dis-owning—*Enteignis*—which counters that movement (23/23). Thus, the essential itself is nothing but the one counterturning movement in which it turns against and toward itself. Being has to divide itself against itself in order to possibly come toward itself. It thus enacts the history of being, that is, the history of philosophy in which being is understood and, initially and mostly, misunderstood.

Heidegger does not specify what he means by this occurrence of dis-owning. But he does end the lecture with the remark that a thinking which no longer wishes to approach being by starting out from beings has many obstacles to overcome. One of these is language, whose grammatical structures can only be used to make statements about beings (25/24). He does not, however, relate the obstacles that thinking encounters to the remark in the beginning, that the occurring of absence is largely determined by presencing.

The lecture *Time and Being* is followed by a summary of a seminar that was held on this text in 1962. Here we also find passages in which Heidegger defends himself against a superficial comparison with Hegel's philosophy. Although Heidegger's own share in the discussion is difficult to infer from the report, it is not without significance that the only philosopher explicitly considered is Hegel. Little more is said, however, than that presence is also prevalent in Hegel's dialectic (36/34). Moreover—at least according to the participant Jean Beaufret—in Hegel's philosophy the finitude of the human being, insofar as the absolute can come to itself in and through it, has been sublated (53/49). Heidegger's project may be understood as an attempt to reveal and overcome the concealed confinement of Hegel's philosophy, and hence Western metaphysics as such. In the next part I will thematize the constant challenge that Hegel constituted for Heidegger. Heidegger's thinking as it has been presented up to now will therefore be "repeated" with respect to his relation to Hegel.

III

Heidegger and Hegel

Introduction

When Heidegger in 1915 is completing his habilitation, he seems to know precisely what philosophy has to accomplish. It has to engage in the strife against Hegel.[1] The fact that the entire nineteenth century has been dominated by attempts to recapture the finite, historical, singular, and groundless from Hegel does not mean for Heidegger that those attempts have been successful. From his perspective—as revealed at least by a later text—these countermovements remain bound to what they contest.[2] Heidegger will therefore have to find a different way to overcome Hegel, that is to say, a more radical one.

Nevertheless, Hegel is not only Heidegger's great opponent, but also someone with whom he has a deep kinship. What is at stake in his strife with Hegel is the projective preconception guiding Hegel's philosophy. Heidegger tries to modify this preconception in such a way that being, or the essential, can accomplish itself without losing its proper dynamic. Since Hegel also conceives the essential as movement—that is to say, as concept—it is extremely important for Heidegger to reveal the confinement of Hegel's system.

In order to understand Hegel's thinking as the culmination of the metaphysical tradition, Heidegger will have to radically criticize the *character* of the movement that constitutes Hegel's point of departure. He will have to show that the "total absence of presuppositions" which Hegel considers the precondition for truly scientific philosophy (Enc. I, §78 rem.) is itself based on a "presupposition" that drives Hegel's thinking, yet cannot be thematized by it. Hegel may say that the dignity of thinking consists in "throwing off all our individual opinions and prejudices, and submitting to the sway of the matter itself" (Enc. I, §23 rem., tr. m.). Heidegger for his part will have to show that Hegel's system no less forces the matters at stake to hold back what is most proper to them.

In the following chapters I will start out from Heidegger's texts on Hegel in order to understand how Heidegger tries to twist free from the metaphysical tendency of Occidental philosophy. Heidegger's texts on Hegel will not, however, have the final say; at least as important is what Heidegger does *not* say about Hegel. In many texts he tries to secure his distance from Hegel, and not to emphasize that Hegel is also a dangerous competitor. Hegel is not only the philosopher who completes metaphysics, but also the one who comprehends the history of philosophy as a whole and, in his own way, achieves its deconstruction. Exactly the same motivation inspires both Hegel's and Heidegger's critique of a discursive metaphysics that obstinately holds on to oppositions such as that between subject and object, or seeks an ultimate foundation in the transcendental subject. But even when Heidegger explicitly confirms his kinship with Hegel, he does this in order to separate from him:

> The problem will make no further progress . . . as long as Hegel . . . is not comprehended. And this means always that Hegel must be both overcome and appropriated by radicalizing the way in which the problem is put. This overcoming of Hegel is the intrinsically necessary step in the development of Western philosophy that must be made for it to remain at all alive. (GA 24:254, tr. m.)

Heidegger's use of such terms as "overcoming" and "appropriation" brings him dangerously close to Hegel's sublation, and he also seems to enter Hegel's territory with regard to the "necessity" of a subsequent phase in the history of philosophy; this indicates the complexity of Heidegger's critical confrontation with Hegel. In later texts the need for such a confrontation continues to be an important theme. Thus, Heidegger in 1942 writes about a thinking

> that finds itself being driven into . . . the confrontation (*Auseinandersetzung*) with absolute metaphysics and thus becomes prepared for the pain of the separation from it (*der Schmerz der Entzweiung*). (GA 68:136)

This slightly pathetic passage clearly shows Heidegger's awareness that his philosophy is part of a necessary movement. This is, however, a movement in which the separation no longer serves the purpose of an ultimate reconciliation.

In my view, it is precisely Heidegger's interpretation of Hegel that confirms the relation between Heidegger's concept of time and his method. I will try to show that his interpretation of Hegel is always based—even though this is often far from explicit—on the idea of a temporality which sheds the light that allows the being of beings to appear as itself or not as itself. In fact, in none of Heidegger's hitherto published texts on Hegel does he really elaborate how Hegel's philosophy is methodically dominated by temporality, and how his own method is a modification of this. We will have to infer it from the usual sparing hints, which will be followed in the direction indicated by what has previously been elaborated.

The texts that Heidegger published during his life give the impression that he thought he could deconstruct Hegel on the basis of his concept of time; §82 of *Being and Time* was for a long time the only early text to explicitly thematize Hegel. Heidegger's earliest Freiburg courses, however, evidence his primary interest in the function of negativity in Hegel's dialectic. Most of the remarks on Hegel in the early work therefore relate to the *Science of Logic*. Heidegger appears to understand that a deconstruction of Hegel's philosophy would have to focus on this text. This is also why passages about Hegel in *Being and Time* very often refer to the *Logic*.[3]

In the introductory section about the deconstruction of the history of philosophy, Heidegger maintains that Greek ontology "still determines the foundations and goals of Hegel's Logic" (BT 22). When during the course of history the subject comes to acquire a central position, Heidegger considers that either the traditional ontological categories are applied to this being or "dialectic is called upon to help with an ontological interpretation of the substantiality of the subject" (22). If this is intended as a characterization of Hegel, it naturally offers much scope for argument. Here and elsewhere, however, Heidegger seems mainly to direct his attack toward neo-Hegelians who force the dialectical "mediation-machine" to run.[4]

As I take the view that Heidegger's discussion with Hegel mainly pertains to the meaning of dialectic, negativity, and movement, the *Logic* will play an important part in my interpretation of that discussion. I consider this text pivotal for understanding the overall structure of Hegel's thinking. I therefore intend to let the strife between Heidegger and Hegel be fought at the level of the *Logic*. Since Heidegger never elaborated a deconstructive interpretation of the *Logic*, and since the quotations that he gives are mostly drawn from the prefaces, the introduction, and the first part, one may doubt whether he intensively studied the entire work. It could be that his turn away from the dialectical machinery prevented him from taking the *Logic* really seriously.[5] I think, however, that what I suggested in part I concerning Heidegger's method offers a good starting point to show that Heidegger's strife with Hegel does indeed pertain to the "logical." I will focus my interpretation on the difference between Hegel's and Heidegger's methodical threefoldness—which Heidegger tries to understand by means of his concept of temporality—in order to thematize something that extends much further than merely a methodical issue. After all, for Heidegger no less than for Hegel, method is not an external instrument; both thinkers would agree that the way in which things are brought to light cannot be reduced to an activity of the subject.

In my presentation of Heidegger's discussion with Hegel, I will not only examine Heidegger's texts. However, neither do I intend to compare Heidegger and Hegel in an external manner; they themselves consider the comparison to be an inferior mode of comprehension.[6] I will rather use Heidegger's interpretation of Hegel to show how Heidegger's thinking springs from metaphysics and turns itself against this origin, without turning back to it, yet equally without standing entirely outside it. The history of Heidegger's discussion with Hegel, insofar as we can speak of this, will be ordered by reading Heidegger's *actual* interpretations of Hegel in the light of what I consider to be the *principle* underlying those interpretations. As I said, Heidegger takes this principle to be the temporality that grounds every understanding of being, without metaphysics being aware of this fundamental background or being capable of modifying it. This principle is not, according to Heidegger, external to Hegel's philosophy. On the other hand, I will try to present Hegel as a very strong opponent.[7] Thus I hope to be able to elucidate the different aspects of Heidegger's relation to Hegel, without the chronological order of Heidegger's texts having to play a decisive part.

This final part will repeat the most important themes of the preceding parts and relate them to Heidegger's attempted deconstruction of Hegel. To introduce the context of Heidegger's critique, I will start out from his thesis that time is more powerful than the concept. The issue will then be further introduced via a brief discussion of the meaning of negativity in Aristotle's concept of movement and of Heidegger's and Hegel's interpretations of Kant (chapter 7). Chapter 8 will thematize Hegel's *Science of Logic*. This leads us to Hegel's concept of time, which Heidegger contests in *Being and Time* (chapter 9). I wish to show that this discussion is of subordinate importance, and that the strife between Heidegger and Hegel ultimately concerns the problem of method. Chapter 10 is devoted to this issue, and will mainly draw on passages from the courses *Basic Problems of Phenomenology* from 1919/20 and *Hegel's Phenomenology of Spirit* from 1930/31. In the last chapter I will consider Heidegger's later texts on Hegel. This chapter will focus on Heidegger's conception of history, which he develops by means of a modification of the temporality that underlies Hegel's logical principle.

With two actors now on the stage, the role of the interpreter becomes rather more complicated. It is not my intention to take sides, but rather to intervene as a kind of director in such a way that the drama of Heidegger's break with Hegel can unfold more neatly than in fact was the case. Such a staging will have succeeded if it suggests that what is enacted could not have happened in any other way, and if we seem to be merely its spectators.

7

The Power of Time

7.1 Time and Concept

Being and Time attempts to show that the temporal horizon of metaphysics, however "absolute" it pretends to be, is brought about by the movement in which ecstatic Present becomes increasingly predominant. An authentic thinking tries to resist this predominance. In the only course devoted entirely to Hegel, *Hegel's Phenomenology of Spirit* from 1930/31, Heidegger concisely expresses his "program" with respect to his deconstruction of Hegel's philosophy:

> It is important to show—formulating it with Hegel—that it is not the concept which is "the power of time," but that it is time which is the power of the concept. (We should however note that by "time" Hegel understands something different from what we do). (GA 32:144, tr. m.)

This is a response to a thesis from Hegel's philosophy of nature in the *Encyclopaedia*. Whereas all finite beings are transient and governed by the power of negativity, Hegel considers the concept not to be subjected to this time or negativity:

> The concept however, in its freely existing identity with itself . . . is in and for itself absolute negativity and freedom, and is consequently not only free from the power of time, but is neither within time, nor something temporal. It is rather the *concept* which constitutes the power of time. . . . [T]he true . . . the idea, spirit, is eternal.[1]

These two passages concisely summarize the strife between Heidegger and Hegel. It will be important, then, to understand what distinguishes Heidegger's concept of time from the time that can be overcome by the concept—that is to say, from the time that can be incorporated in the movement of the concept. Also when Heidegger writes that his dialogue with Hegel is located at "the crossroads of finitude and infinity," he is concerned with a finitude that is radically different from the finitude that is overcome in absolute knowing.[2]

We know that Heidegger especially develops his concept of time in *Being and Time* and GA 24. In the latter course he maintains that Hegel has seen everything that is possible, but that by moving within the circle of philosophical problems, he could not see the *center* of this circle.[3] In order to reveal this center, Heidegger himself tries "to get beyond being to the light from which and in which it itself comes into the brightness of an understanding" (GA 24:400). This metaphor of light recurs in several of Heidegger's texts on Hegel, one of which is a text from 1969:

> Speculative dialectic is a mode in which the matter of philosophy of itself comes to appear (*zum Scheinen kommt*) for itself, and thus becomes present. Such appearance necessarily occurs in a certain clarity (*Helle*).[4]

Heidegger maintains here and elsewhere that metaphysics has no understanding of the clearing which makes it possible for something to be brought to light. In GA 24 he indicates that *time* is the center of the circle of philosophical problems, in other words, the light that makes it possible for being to be understood (GA 24:406, cf. 402). Heidegger will have to show that even Hegel's philosophy, despite the semblance of the opposite, is based on an understanding of being as constant presence, and hence confirms the starting point of the entire tradition, instead of overcoming it.[5] In 1930 Heidegger describes Hegel's concept of subjectivity as the "sheer self-comprehension of the whole of beings" (GA 31:110). He then quotes the passage from the *Encyclopaedia* in which Hegel characterizes spirit as the eternal, and the eternal as "absolute presence."[6] This evidently suits Heidegger very well:

> This Present . . . , which stands with itself and of itself, [is] in itself reflected duration; a presence which is most constant and which can only be given by egoity (*Ichheit*), the being-with-itself. (110)

We will see that Heidegger in various texts tries to retrace Hegel to the tradition of Descartes, and thus fails to do justice to Hegel's speculative overcoming of traditional philosophy. Nothing is said here about Hegel's view that what is real only brings about its "duration" in a continuous movement, which certainly cannot be reduced to an ego that is present at itself. If Heidegger is to truly free himself from Hegel, he will have to show that Hegel understands the highest mode of movement as the *energeia* which has overcome all restlessness and uses it for its own purposes. Such a concept of movement in fact confirms the meaning of being as constant presence. Hegel conceives this highest mode of movement as the structure of the concept as such; to understand what this means, we will have to turn to the *Logic*.

In GA 31 Heidegger maintains that Hegel consciously holds fast to the intrinsic relation between his thinking and antique metaphysics (111). He considers Aristotle—not unduly—to be the "father" of Hegel's *Logic*. Heidegger for his part tries not to further sustain this genealogy, but to prepare another, new lineage.[7] Before considering Hegel's *Logic*, I will prepare the ground by showing that Heidegger's critique of Aristotle is also aimed at Hegel. Since I believe that the same holds for Heidegger's interpretation of Kant from 1929, I will dwell on *Kant and the Problem of Metaphysics* by way of a further preparatory detour. Aristotle and Kant are pivotal both for Hegel and for (the early) Heidegger. Heidegger's interpretation of these thinkers may clarify how he time and again seeks to turn against Hegel. A short sketch of Hegel's early interpretation of Kant will then serve to introduce the chapter on the *Logic*.

7.2 Aristotle's Interpretation of Negativity and Movement

Chapter 1 sketched out how Heidegger already around 1922 tries to deconstruct Aristotle's concept of movement. In 1931 he gives a course that follows on from this early interpretation (GA 33). In this course, in which the distinction between *dunamis* and *energeia* plays an important part, Heidegger usually stays close to Aristotle's text, and only occasionally suggests where he actually intends to go. In *On the Essence and Concept of Phusis*, a text from 1939 included in *Pathmarks*, he circles around the same theme, but in certain respects is more explicit. I will therefore let the two texts elucidate each other. Heidegger's early preoccupation with the problem of negativity is very evident in the following passage from *Being and Time*:

> It is true that ontology and logic have expected much of the not, and thus at times made its possibilities visible without revealing it itself ontologically. Ontology found the not and used it. But is it then so self-evident that every not means a *negativum* in the sense of a lack? Does its positivity get exhausted by its constituting the "transition"? Why does every dialectic take refuge in negation, without grounding it *itself* dialectically, without even being able to locate it *as a problem*? Has anyone ever made the ontological origin of notness (*Nichtheit*) a problem at all? (BT 285–86, tr. m.)

One can only deal with this problem, Heidegger continues, within the context of an explicit elucidation of the meaning of being as such. This means that the questions raised here will for the time being have to be deferred. GA 33 tries to find a way of approaching this problem by analyzing Aristotle's concept of movement.

Heidegger's interpretation of the concepts *dunamis* and *energeia* in GA 33 tries to show that Aristotle's analysis does indeed *start out* from the movement of beings (*kinēsis*) but always *intends* movement as essential structure.[8] He maintains that Aristotle was the first to understand "being-moved" as a fundamental mode of being (WM 314 / PM 187)—that is to say, as a mode of presencing (*Anwesen*) (331/200). Aristotle understands the movement of things that are produced both by man and by nature on the basis of the difference between *dunamis* and *energeia*. Wood has in itself the capacity to become a table, and that which is "proper" to this wood—Heidegger speaks of *Eignung*—actualizes itself while the table is being produced (cf. 355/217–18). This also applies, at least to a certain extent, for the *eidos* of the table, which actualizes itself in the concretely existing table.[9] Since such a table is susceptible of decay, it will always require an *energeia* in order to continue being a table. On this level, no movement can entirely achieve its aim and hence come to rest.

This rest, as the ultimate mode of *energeia*, only occurs in "seeing" the unchangeable *eidos* of the table *in* the concrete table; this *eidos* itself does not change. Only in that pure beholding does the movement have "itself in its end," as Heidegger translates *entelecheia*.[10] The *ousia* then appears as "constant presencing" (337/204, tr. m.) to a beholding that thus also reaches its own accomplishment. The "not yet" proper to every finite movement has here been overcome (357/219). Aristotle thus understands essential movement as the increasing development of a *dunamis* that is there from the outset. The "not" that is proper to the *dunamis* and animates the movement is increasingly overcome during that movement. With regard to the movement of concrete beings themselves, this can only succeed to a certain degree. Their movement demands as it were to be completed by thinking.

Since Aristotle, in contrast to his predecessors and contemporaries, moves beyond the opposition between that which is and that which is not, he is able to conceive the essence of movement.[11] He understands movement not only as *kinēsis* but also, and primarily, as development—that is, as the process in which something that was always already present increasingly unfolds and actualizes itself. Heidegger takes this to mean that Aristotle must also regard the mere *having* of a certain capacity as a mode of reality or objective presence—namely as the first phase in a process of self-accomplishment (cf. GA 33:177/152). *Dunamis* and *energeia* thus constitute two "modes" of reality or presence: "Enactment is practicing, thus presence . . . of something which is already present" (185/158). Aristotle must interpret the "not yet" of the *dunamis* as a mode of presence in order to "save" the phenomenon of movement. Heidegger suggests, however, that in this interpretation something is also lost.[12] Because Aristotle's predecessors only regard that which has realized itself as present, they *in principle* leave open the possibility of understanding that which is not, which is merely *dunamis*, as the *absent* with respect to every presence: "The possible, however, is the not-yet-objectively-present." (170). Heidegger considers that this does more justice to the *character of possibility* of the *dunamis* than Aristotle's perspective. Hence, precisely when the phenomenon of movement is first thematized and understood, the understanding of being which guides that interpretation undergoes a confinement. When the absent or the "not yet" is brought within the domain of presence, being presentifies itself. From within a horizon dominated by Present, movement can only show forth as a process of actualization in which the "not" from which the movement started out is increasingly left behind.

This is exactly what Heidegger criticizes. Turning against Aristotle, he tries to understand movement as an event in which the "not" that inheres in the *dunamis* does not disappear, but is, by contrast, allowed in and preserved. In everything that enacts itself, the possibility is then preserved as that which is not objectively present and does not actualize itself.[13] This is mainly important with respect to the "movement" that is enacted *meta logou*, that is to say, in human acting and knowing.

In GA 33 Heidegger, following Aristotle, thematizes at length the difference between physical movements and the movements that are enacted by human beings. Aristotle himself sees that precisely in acting there always exists the possibility of failure of an action, so that skill and knowledge are required in order to bring the action to a good end.[14] Heidegger makes use of the concept *sterēsis* to radicalize the meaning that Aristotle gives to negativity. Aristotle uses the term *sterēsis* to refer to the lacking of something (cf. 108/92). Now Heidegger suggests that it is especially the *dunamis* which is characterized by this lack.[15] He later indicates that the *dunamis meta logou* is always already divided within itself (157/134): the *logos* that makes it possible for an *eidos* to constitute the "motivation" of the acting brings about a "realm" within which a possibility can develop either in accordance with that *eidos* or not in accordance with it. From Heidegger's perspective, however, the "not" that is given by this *logos* is not accidental, but essentially pervades any human action:

> Every production of something, in general every *dunamis meta logou*, prepares for itself, and this necessarily, through its proper way of proceeding, the continually concomitant opportunity for mistaking, neglecting, overlooking, and failing; thus every force carries *in itself* and *for itself* the possibility of sinking into *un-force*. This negativum does not simply stand beside the positive of force as its opposite but haunts this force in the force itself (*lauert dieser in ihr selbst auf*), and this because every force of this type according to its essence . . . is invested with a "not." (154/131, cf. 163/140)

The "not" that lurks within the *dunamis* itself gets the opportunity to "strike" precisely when that capacity begins to enact itself. This clearly pertains to something other than *sterēsis* in the Aristotelian sense. Heidegger seems to suggest that when the "lack" of human acting is understood as an accidental and surmountable moment, the dynamic of human life is unduly understood in terms of increasing self-presence. He considers that this perspective does not do justice to the radical counterstriving of human life: as soon as the *logos* comes into play, the movement that tries to attain its *telos* is always and fundamentally thwarted by a negativity *which cannot serve as a surmountable moment in a process of self-actualization*. As soon as something begins to enact itself, the "not" that from the outset inheres in the *dunamis* gets the opportunity to develop. This means that the acting itself reveals a "not yet" and a "no longer" that cannot be brought within the realm of presence. This "not" is that which withdraws itself from the process of self-actualization—that is to say, it is an absencing that occurs within presencing:

> *Steresis* as absencing (*Abwesung*) is not simply absence (*Abwesenheit*); rather, it is a *presencing* . . . in which precisely the *absencing*—and not absent beings—occurs (*anwest*). (WM 366–67 / PM 227, tr. m.)

Heidegger has here taken the step from the lack of *something* to an essential absence; in so doing he raises Aristotle's analysis to the level of being as such, convinced that this is in line with Aristotle's own intentions. He justifies his ontological interpretation by drawing attention to the fact that Aristotle, much more concretely, considers the *sterēsis* to be a kind of *eidos*: in producing or acting we are not only concerned with a certain *eidos* as *telos* (such as health), but also relate to its opposite—the lack of health—as a kind of *eidos*.[16] Hence, the "lacking" is an essential part of the realm of the essential—that is to say, of the *ousia* of the being of beings. This is the point that Heidegger wanted to reach. We could say—though Heidegger does not say this here in so many words—that human acting mostly aims at letting the "not" that inheres in the *dunamis* merge as much as possible in the fullness of the *energeia*. The *sterēsis* is then understood as a surmountable lack.[17] When this pertains to the work of the doctor or the carpenter, one can clearly not object. However, when it pertains to the way in which human beings are concerned with their own *being*, they should attempt, according to Heidegger, to do justice to the "not" that, while it withdraws itself, constitutes the core of any presencing. This would not change our actual doings, but would certainly shed a different light on them. At this level, the *sterēsis* is usually no less taken as that which constitutes the *dunamis* but is increasingly lost in the actualization.

Heidegger translates *sterēsis* as withdrawal (*Entzug*) (GA 33:108/92). He evidently understands the realm of possibilities opened up by the *logos* as the realm within which being is understood, but usually cannot show forth as itself. Due to the predominance of Present, the "not" only comes into play as that which is to be overcome and actually can be overcome. As necessary as that may be for the doctor who wishes to do his work well, it is "fatal" for philosophy, which has to take care of being—that is to say, of the absence that is harbored by any presence and that tries to unfold itself. The movement in which Present breaks free from the other temporal ecstases may be conceived as a "negativity" which casts its spell precisely on a thinking or acting that thinks it has mastered all negativity. For Heidegger, authentic life and authentic thinking consist in an appropriate relation to a "not" that cannot be overcome. With respect to human acting, then, he is concerned with a mode of existing that does justice to the radical finitude of that acting:

> And because, then, the force which is directed by discourse is in an original sense nihilating (*nichtig*), that is, pervaded by this not and no, the how is . . . always decisive for this force. (157/134, tr. m., italics mine)

Since the *energeia* of human acting is essentially pervaded by the "not," it is precisely here that the difference between an inauthentic and an authentic mode of acting—the "how"—comes to be very important. This is much less the case for the way in which, for example, a plant develops. What Heidegger says here is directly related to the following passage on care in *Being and Time*:

> *Care itself is in its essence thoroughly permeated by nothingness* (*Nichtigkeit*). . . . Existential nothingness by no means has the character of a privation, of a lack as compared with an ideal which is set up but is not attained in Dasein. . . . Still, the *ontological meaning of the notness* of this existential nothingness remains obscure. But that is true also of the *ontological essence of the not as such.*[18]

We see here how Heidegger relates the "not" of human existence to the "not" within being itself, and thus also to the philosophy that tries to bring being to words. In his text from 1922 on Aristotle, Heidegger briefly remarks that Hegel's dialectic has its roots in the concept *sterēsis*, insofar as the object "is posited in a specific kind of movement" with regard to the "not yet" and the "already" (something is already there, but has not yet actualized itself) (A 259, tr. m.). Here again Heidegger relates the *sterēsis* to the difference between *dunamis* and *energeia*, and hence to *an entirely determined kind of movement.* Hegel himself also understands the basic movement of his thinking on the basis of these concepts, and would probably therefore not disagree with Heidegger on this point.[19] When Heidegger attempts to critically question the Aristotelian concepts *sterēsis* and movement, he is also intending Hegel, who indeed allowed negativity as the source of every movement, yet only to deprive it of its power.

The question concerning the essence of movement led us to the relation between temporality, negativity, and thinking. I will come back to this in the following chapters. First, however, I will try to clarify how Heidegger in his interpretation of Kant starts out from the problem of subjectivity to broach the same issue.

7.3 A Tug-of-War for Kant

The text *Kant and the Problem of Metaphysics* from 1929 is devoted to Kant's *Critique of Pure Reason*. In this book, Heidegger attempts to show that the subjectivity of the subject which according to Kant founds every experience of beings is not an ultimate ground, but is itself grounded in primordial time. Heidegger, aware of the contrived character of this interpretation, admits in a later preface that he unduly sought an advocate in Kant.[20] Like Kant, he realizes that the inquiry into the possibility of knowledge in general and metaphysical knowledge especially should start out from the finitude of human beings. But since Heidegger tries to radicalize Kant's understanding of this finitude, he not only follows Kant, but simultaneously undermines his subject-philosophy. Thus contesting human subjectivity its central position, Heidegger must have been conscious of the similarity between his critical approach to Kant and that of Hegel. Heidegger emphasizes, however, that the *aim* of his own interpretation runs counter to Hegel's intentions; precisely by no longer starting out from the human subject, it should become possible to "found" the radical finitude of human understanding as such and of philosophy itself.[21] Heidegger thus seeks to overcome Kant's philosophy of the subject without adopting the position of Hegel. Hence Heidegger's interpretation of Kant ultimately testifies, I think, to his strife against Hegel. Just as Hölderlin in his later interpretations, Kant is considered an ally against Hegel's renunciation of finitude.

Heidegger's Interpretation of Kant

In *Kant and the Problem of Metaphysics* Heidegger emphasizes that the *Critique of Pure Reason* should be understood as an inquiry into the possibility of ontology, that is to say, as an attempt to found metaphysics (KM 17). Even when the inquiry is actually concerned with the possibility of empirical, ontic knowledge, it ultimately intends the "faculty" that brings about the free space within which beings can be encountered as standing over against the human being (77, cf. 198). The categories can only bring about unity in the multiplicity given by the senses insofar as they are reliant on this "horizon of what can be thematized" (84, tr. m.). The preceding orientation upon this horizon is an *ontological* orientation; in order to understand its character, it is inadequate to conceive sensibility and understanding as two separate faculties. Time as universal pure intuition (which makes it possible for beings to be experienced as occurring in time) and the categories (which bring about unity in the experiences of beings) must have a common ground (22, 58). This ground, a third "faculty," makes it possible for sensible perception to relate to things in an immediate way, and for understanding to relate to things through the mediation of the senses (23). This preceding capacity brings about a pure, ontological synthesis, from which all the other syntheses originate (38–39, 63).

Kant himself has doubts concerning the possible common root of understanding and sensibility (37). Because he indicates transcendental imagination as the capacity to bring about synthesis at all (63), however, Heidegger interprets this imagination as the capacity of "pure synthesis" (65), which is the "unifying middle" and source of pure sensible intuition and pure thinking (64, 78). Pure, transcendental imagination enacts the primordial synthesis that brings about the horizon within which beings can appear as beings (90). This free, open space first makes it possible for both sensible intuition and understanding to relate to beings in their own way and thus to produce knowledge. The horizon itself is not a being; transcendental and empirical imagination have in common that they give rise to something that does not exist and is "nothing" in itself. While empirical imagination produces images or representations, pure imagination brings about the horizon which makes it possible to imagine, apprehend, or represent something at all; this horizon is itself "nothing" compared with the totality of beings:

> This holding oneself into (*Sichhineinhalten*) the nothing is . . . an event which underlies all instances of finding oneself in the midst of beings which already are. (238, tr. m., cf. 143–44)

This is the first step. Heidegger then tries to show that this projective preconception of imagination is not self-dependent, but is a root that is itself rooted in time (196, cf. 202). He does this by means of an interpretation of Kant's doctrine of schematism.

Every empirical concept, such as "dog," has a schema, which gives the rule that allows us to classify all kinds of concrete dogs under the concept "dog." It is through the schema that we are able to imagine the content of the concept, which itself is not given by empirical intuition. The schema concretely indicates, as it were, in what the "essence" of something consists (cf. 98–101). Now, Kant states that the categories as *pure* concepts also need such a schema in order to actually pertain to sensible intuitions. Or, as Heidegger puts it, categories also need their discernability (102). This sensibilization or schematization of the categories is brought about, in Kant's view, by relating them to time. Thus, the schema of the category "substance" can be described as that which persists in time amidst all changes (106).

Though Kant intends time as a sequence of now-moments, Heidegger sees something more fundamental happening here: the schema of substance refers to constant presence, and it is only within "the horizon of such constant presence that this or any 'present presence of an object' as such can show itself" (131–32). Heidegger may now conclude that time makes it possible to gain access to the objectivity by virtue of which beings can appear as beings.[22] This primordial transcendental schematization originates from transcendental imagination, which differentiates itself into pure intuition (142–43) on the one hand and into the schemata of the categories on the other:

> [T]he apparent achievement of pure understanding *(des reinen Verstandes)* in thinking unities is a pure basic act of transcendental imagination. (151, tr. m.)

Hence Heidegger considers pure understanding and pure intuition to be two modes of a "representing preforming of the unifying horizon" (150, cf. 143).

Like pure imagination itself, these modes must be grounded in primordial time. Thus, the pure time that gives rise to the sequence of now-moments is itself grounded in the time that as ecstatic Present opens up a horizon (180). Heidegger also considers that the constitution of unity, which Kant believes to be founded in the "I think," is made possible by the temporal horizon within which something can be held before us at all (186). Heidegger's attempt to "grasp the selfhood of the self as inherently temporal" (187) thus annuls the opposition between understanding and sensibility: both faculties have their ground in primordial time, which as it were through these faculties makes possible every "letting-stand-against-of . . ." (190). This means that "all representing including thought is . . . subject to time" (183). This time is called a "transcendental primal structure" (242).

Heidegger notes how in the second edition of the *Critique of Pure Reason* Kant's hesitation about the status of the imagination has led him to yield to the tradition, fixated as it is on the *logos*, and to reduce imagination to a function of thinking (160f, 167). This function of the imagination is then even more strongly emphasized in German Idealism (197). According to Heidegger, the first version still allows the function of time to be interpreted in such a way that it shakes the predominance of reason to its very foundations, while, partly because of the second edition, this possibility is later entirely annulled by Hegel (243–44). Hegel's metaphysics can thus more radically than ever before become a *logic*, that is to say, confirm the power of reason (244). Before turning to Hegel, we should follow one more step in Heidegger's interpretation.

If primordial time, by means of transcendental imagination, opens up the realm within which beings can present themselves as present beings, then this very time must also constitute the condition of possibility of ontology:

> [T]ranscendental imagination, on the ground of its indissoluble, original structure, opens up the possibility of the laying of a ground for ontological knowledge, and thereby for metaphysics. (197, cf. 202–3)

Being a possibility of a *finite* thinking, ontology depends as much as empirical knowledge on this pregiven horizon, and should be able to face the finitude that such a horizon entails (124). By means of a retrieving repetition, Kant's attempt to found metaphysics must now be brought toward its innermost possibility; this means that the possibility of understanding being as such has to be elucidated (203, 226). Thus, Heidegger has again come back to the fundamental ontology of *Being and Time*. In the everyday and Greek understanding of being, being is always understood as presence (239–40), that is to say—I add—from within a horizon that is only appropriate to bring about ontic knowledge.

Heidegger does not thematize Kant's transcendental dialectic, in which Kant himself also shows that metaphysical knowledge fails when it makes use of the means that are intended to bring about empirical knowledge. If that—to use Heidegger's terms—means that ontology requires a different temporal horizon than empirical knowledge, the question arises whether the transcendental imagination is capable in itself of bringing about such a different horizon. Kant, for his part, maintains that reason is capable of relating to ideas that are not given in experience, yet necessarily orient empirical knowledge. These ideas should not be brought within the realm of presence, or at least not in the same way as beings are.[23]

For Kant it is pivotal that this other involvement should not be called knowledge; for Hegel, on the other hand, true knowledge only begins once the domain of empirical knowledge has been left behind. Heidegger would say that ontology does indeed consist in transcending the perspective that guides the empirical experience of beings. He emphasizes, however, that Hegel unknowingly takes over and confirms this perspective *in* his turn to the "essential," rather than leaving it behind. Since Kant still preserves a kind of difference between understanding and reason, Heidegger considers him to do justice to the finitude of a thinking that cannot bring the two areas into unity without becoming entangled in contradictions.

Hegel's Interpretation of Kant

Just as for Heidegger, but for a different reason, Kant's interpretation of sensibility and understanding as two separate basic faculties is also a stumbling block for Hegel.[24] He maintains that Kant's doctrine of schematism merely relates understanding and sensible intuition in an external way, and does not penetrate to the true unity of these faculties—namely, an intuitive understanding.[25] In *Faith and Knowledge* he expresses his approval of Kant's idea of transcendental imagination. He considers that Kant here has seen "the idea of true a priority," yet only to subsequently annul it (FK 316/79, tr. m.). In this early text, then, Hegel like Heidegger—who was probably inspired by Hegel—takes transcendental imagination to be the origin from which spring both the subject and the objective world (insofar as it is brought about by the syntheses of intuition and understanding) (308/73). Sensible intuition and thinking are thus not isolated faculties standing over against each other, but have the same primordial synthetic unity as their principle (305/70). The difference between these faculties consists in the fact that intuition relates to this unity as still fully immersed in the manifoldness, whereas discursive understanding actually brings about this unity *as* unity. While the understanding can merely do this in a relative way (305/70), only reason as pure, intellectual intuition is able to grasp the total identity of unity and difference. Reason thus explicitly brings about the primordial synthesis of the imagination.

Now Hegel comprehends this imagination as reason *itself* (308/73). Thus, he no longer understands reason as one of the synthetic faculties, but as the one principle of identity that unfolds itself in different ways to actually accomplish this primordial identity. From this perspective there is no "manifold of faculties and capacities of spirit" (308/73), but only the one and only movement of imagination—that is, of reason—which enacts itself as understanding and sensible intuition, posits these faculties over against itself as separate faculties, yet ultimately comprehends its own absoluteness and gains insight into the true unity of intuition and thinking.[26]

Hegel agrees with Kant insofar as he understands empirical knowledge as bringing about a unity, albeit relative, of concept and being. This unity is made possible by the pure synthetic judgments. Because these judgments—the categories—create unity without having to rely on the senses, they must contain the difference without which no true identity can be brought about within themselves. Hegel argues that the plurality of categories should be traced back to a primordial, pure synthesis that also comes about by dividing itself within itself. This synthesis cannot be regarded as identical to Kant's "I think," since this expresses an *abstract* or *formal* identity that remains posited over against any kind of manifold.[27] Thus, Hegel assigns to transcendental imagination as primordial synthetic faculty the place that Kant gives to reason. He considers Kant himself to stubbornly hold fast to the empty identity of reason which, contrary to understanding, is unable to produce valid knowledge (318/81).

The way in which Kant clings to fixed oppositions is seen by Hegel as a symptom of the power of understanding *within philosophy itself*, that is to say, within the domain proper to reason. He calls Kant's philosophy a triumph of an understanding and a finitude that declare themselves absolute with "loud jubilation" (321/85, tr. m.). It is hard to "see the highest idea corrupted with full consciousness, while reflection and finite cognition are exalted above it."[28] On the other hand, the development of subject-philosophy, characterized by "establishing the different dimensions of the totality as absolute," also first makes it possible for true philosophy to annul this positing and thus manifest itself as the perfected appearance of philosophy (431/198). Here again fixed oppositions must be brought about: true identity can only come about in the annulment of those oppositions.[29] Philosophical reason thus needs the understanding, and must let the understanding, which is one of its own moments, become independent and go its own way:

> In the struggle between understanding and reason, understanding is only entitled to strength to the degree that reason forsakes itself; the success of the struggle thus depends on reason itself.[30]

Hence reason evidently always has the capacity to annul the increasing absoluteness of the understanding (D 23/92). Or more precisely: it is reason itself that "tempts" the understanding to venture onto foreign ground—the limitless, the totality—where it cannot maintain itself, so that it entangles itself and gets stuck (cf. 26/95). Apparently, reason only has to wait and watch the obstinate understanding gradually becoming capable of enduring the sublation of all this confusion and finally giving up its independence (35/102).

This very brief and perhaps rather free account of Hegel's interpretation of Kant shows that Hegel also relates the problem of the relation between discursive understanding and reason to the possibility and actual incapacity of philosophy itself. According to Hegel, Kant did indeed found the relative identity of being and thinking that is brought about by experience. But since he remained bound to the perspective of ordinary, discursive understanding, he was unable to also found the *absolute* unity of being and thinking. When reason brings about this absolute unity, it also overcomes its own position as subjective faculty.[31] Reason then understands itself as a manifestation of the absolute synthesis which unfolds itself *as* human reason or imagination, and subsequently *as* the different faculties, although it cannot be reduced to them. This primordial, absolute synthesis has no opposite over against it—this only seems to be the case from the standpoint of reflection (59/125)—but bears the absolute difference within itself. This synthesis is to be understood, I add, as the pulsating dynamic of the pure concept which, dividing itself within and against itself, brings about the absolute identity of that which divides and that which is divided.

Hegel takes this pure movement as the starting point of his system. To a certain extent, this principle springs from his interpretation of Kant, namely, insofar as it ties in with the primordial synthesis that he considers to inhere in transcendental imagination. Hegel identifies this "root" with reason and leaves time as pure intuition in the place that Kant assigned to this form. This intuition is understood as a necessary, but subordinate, moment in the unifying movement of reason itself. Heidegger may indeed say that Hegel's concept of time leaves everything as it was (GA 21:203–5).

There is more to be said, however. Both Hegel and Heidegger regard imagination as the most fundamental human "faculty." Hegel, conceiving this imagination as the primordial synthetic faculty, identifies it with reason. In order to enact itself, this intuitive thinking has to divide itself within itself and become sensible intuition and understanding. This means that the concept—that is, the universal—cannot be conceived immediately, but only by starting out from beings as they initially appear to us. To put it differently: the *nous* needs the *logos* in order to occur as human knowledge. Heidegger, for his part, considers transcendental imagination itself to originate in temporality and hence takes a further step back. What is ultimately at stake, then, is the difference between the dynamic structure of Hegel's absolute concept and this primordial time. That difference will have to be elucidated on the basis of the *Science of Logic*.

Heidegger would say that the possibility of both ontic and ontological knowledge is grounded in the increasing predominance of Present, which brings about a horizon of Praesens. This occurs by means of what Kant calls transcendental imagination. According to Heidegger, authentic ontology consists in the possibility of undoing this predominance of presence. This runs counter to the usual direction of the imagination, which tries to bring everything it produces within reach and lacks the force to endure the "not" of that to which it pertains. The movement that counters this tendency seems very similar to Hegel's negation of the negation, but is, as will be seen, not to be identified with it. Concerning this, Heidegger repeatedly maintains that speculative reason may well negate the apparent self-dependency of all finite moments, yet cannot annul the predominance of Present in which this self-negating negation is itself grounded. However much reason distinguishes itself from the understanding by subjecting it to its power, the domain of Present is and remains their common ground. In GA 21 Heidegger quotes and agrees with Kant, who says that philosophy thematizes the "secret judgments of common reason." A little further on, he proceeds:

> And perhaps it will become clear that our philosophy hitherto has as yet only to a small degree become philosophical reason, and only in very few domains. Rather, it is to a large extent still thoroughly dominated by common reason; and only insofar as common reason is driven out by philosophical reason can the latter claim to be science and the fundamental science. (GA 21:198–99)

Although no names are mentioned, Heidegger here undoubtedly also includes Kant and Hegel in the "philosophy hitherto." I take him to mean that Hegel rightly conceives the faculties which Kant distinguishes as different modifications of one principle—that is, rightly sets everything in motion—yet is unable to understand the ultimate condition of possibility of this dynamic. Hegel, then, could not understand this dynamic as grounded in the horizon of Praesens which entails that transcendental imagination usually, though not necessarily, enacts itself as a making present. It is striking, however, that Heidegger in his critique of philosophy *including* Hegel again comes very close to his opponent. In a later text Heidegger asserts that not understanding, but "reason, glorified for centuries, is the most obstinate adversary of thought."[32] According to his course on Heraclitus, the relation between ordinary and essential thinking is such

> that essential thinking everywhere and necessarily is time and again enlightened by the peculiar light that ordinary thinking incessantly spreads around itself. (GA 55:120)

In the same text Heidegger remarks that the obstinacy of ordinary understanding—and reason seems to be included here—must be brought to a standstill in order for essential thinking to occur. When he adds that one should nevertheless not conceive this movement as dialectical (116–17), he seems to suggest that the horizon which determines the metaphysical tradition will not necessarily of itself be able to annul the predominance of Present.

8

Hegel's *Logic* as a Deconstruction of Metaphysics

Everything that is owes its meaning to the movement in which it takes shape. This movement first makes it possible for a content to distinguish itself from its form and to actually become content. Now Hegel conceives the pure concept as the principle that grounds meaning as such.[1] The *Science of Logic* manifests how the movement in which the pure concept increasingly determines itself and overcomes its one-sidedness grounds the appearance of everything that is. This self-unfolding of the concept reaches its ultimate mode when thinking no longer has to pertain to that which it is not itself and becomes entirely transparent for itself. The *Logic* thus results in the comprehension of the necessity of its own method.[2] As I will try to understand Heidegger's relation to Hegel by focusing on the problem of method, this chapter will mainly be devoted to the way in which the *Logic* provides the foundation of its own method. However, since Hegel establishes that the opposition between form and content cannot be maintained, it will be necessary to consider the basic structure of the whole work. This can only be done by maintaining a certain distance to the very complex text and not entering into its details.

8.1 Passing through Contrariety

Hegel starts out from the idea that the movement in which meaning comes about also brings about its own petrification. When essential distinctions are made, the difference between the one and the other will be fixed in such a way that the unity of that which is distinguished vanishes from sight. When concepts in this way come to stand over against one another as independent units, they must lose their lives. Thus, whenever thinking takes place, death also comes onto the scene.

Hegel finds himself in a history of philosophy that has always brought about a difference between the one and the many, the essential and the accidental, spirit and nature, that which remains identical to itself and that which cannot maintain itself in the process of change. This same philosophy has also always asked the question concerning the relation between the two domains, without having being able, in Hegel's view, to answer that question in a satisfactory way. What is distinguished always threatens to posit itself as something independent and to free itself from the living, dynamic totality in which it was included (cf. D 20–22/89–91).

For Hegel, however, this phase is a necessary condition of the real and first coming to life of this preceding unity. Whenever duality and contrariety occur, philosophy has the task of turning this phase of decline to advantage. The absoluteness of fixed oppositions can be negated by revealing this duality as a moment of the movement in which something that was always already there increasingly actualizes itself. The duality that tends to posit itself as absolute must be made transparent in such a way that the unity—which constitutes the "past" and "future" of the duality—can manifest itself through that duality. These three moments characterize the circular movement in which something comes back to itself by dividing itself within and against itself, and increasingly appropriating that which then appears as the other of itself. Only in this way is self-actualization possible. Since this movement sublates all otherness, and ultimately no longer relates to anything that it is not, only the movement itself, in its purest form, may be considered absolute.

Hegel also understands the philosophy of his own time as a thinking in which the dichotomy has come to be independent and cannot appear as a subordinate phase in a movement. The philosophy that since Descartes has centered on the question concerning the relation between subject and object, turns out to be incapable of truly comprehending the unity of the one who experiences and that which is experienced. Hegel regards Kant's transcendental turn as a great step forward, insofar as he shows how the conditions of possibility of the experience also constitute the conditions of possibility of that which is experienced. Thus, objectivity comes about in and from out of subjectivity: the experience of something and that which appears in the experience constitute two sides of the same coin. If the subject is to recognize itself, its own share, in that which it knows, then that which it experiences should initially appear as that which is foreign and other. Unity, here between subject and object, can only come about on the basis of an established difference between the understanding and that to which it pertains.

According to Kant, however, the unity between subject and object which comes about in empirical knowledge can only be a relative one, subordinate to an insurmountable opposition between transcendental apperception, as subjective principle of unity, and a thing-in-itself that constitutes the beyond of the plurality given within time and space.[3] Although knowledge brings about unity according to objectively valid principles, this unity—that is, objectivity—does not coincide with reality as it is in itself. Kant recognizes that thinking is dominated by a persisting urge to transcend the domain within which this relative objectivity is brought about. But he shows how the understanding, when it exceeds the limits of its proper realm, cannot hold fast as truth that which it held to be true, entangles itself in contrarieties, and must collapse: when understanding takes possession of the realm of reason, death enters the scene of thought.

This will be confirmed by Hegel. Contrary to Kant, however, he regards this "death" as a necessary *passage*. He proposes that precisely when the fixating, discursive understanding gets stuck, space opens up for speculative reason to understand the concepts that were fixated by the understanding as independent entities, as subordinate moments of a single movement.[4] Kant's own philosophy, insofar as it holds on to an insurmountable difference between what is and what can be known (and subsequently also to the independence of the different subjective faculties), is thus considered by Hegel to be still too dominated by ordinary understanding to bring about true unity (L I, 38/45). Hence, he considers it necessary to radicalize Kant's philosophy in such a way that every duality, and not least that between thinking and that to which it pertains, can be understood as a necessary, yet subordinate moment. Hegel does this, as I said, by always understanding duality in the light of a movement in which unity can only truly come about by dividing itself within itself, positing the other of itself over against itself, comprehending that opposition as semblance, and finally sublating it.

In concrete terms, this means that Hegel has to show how nature and spirit, substance and subject, being and concept, are not only opposed but constitute a continuity within which that opposition is subordinate. This program is outlined in the early text *The Difference between Fichte's and Schelling's Systems of Philosophy*.[5] Kant himself already prepares the idea of that continuity by recognizing that nature cannot be understood from the discursive perspective of mechanical and chemical causality alone. To understand nature, thinking must orient upon something like a principle of self-organization that animates nature and brings about the multiplicity of organic forms. Thinking itself might then be considered the highest and purest expression of this forming principle, and hence the ultimate *telos* of nature.[6] But Kant, as always, emphasizes that we have no means to determine nature as it is in itself: the necessary orientation of thinking upon such an organizing principle—which cannot be discursively fixated—may not lead us to conceive nature itself as teleological. He thus preserves the opposition between a free subject and a nature that can only be known insofar as it is determined by causality.

Hegel's *Logic* might be understood as a work in which the continuity between nature and spirit is founded in a purely conceptual way. If this project is to succeed, Hegel has to proceed beyond a thinking subject that somehow has disposal of the pure judgments that bring about knowledge of nature. The pure concepts from which Kant starts out, the categories, are merely ordered on the basis of the different forms of judgment that are actually *encountered* in thinking. Hegel, on the other hand, considers true knowledge to be able to reveal the pure, nonempirical origin of what is initially merely encountered (L I, 30/39). It goes without saying that all conceptual distinctions are actually brought about by thinking. Insofar as those concepts have a nonempirical origin, however, Hegel maintains that it must be possible to trace them back to a pure, logical principle that precedes any kind of human subjectivity. *All* conceptual distinctions that have arisen during the course of history must be brought to light as moments of the movement in which that pure principle—the concept—seeks to determine itself.[7] That principle itself may for now be described as the movement in which it divides itself within and against itself in order to bring about unity.

Since empirical knowledge always remains dependent on that which is *given* by the senses, at this level there necessarily remains a difference between a thinking that orders what is given to it and that which is ordered. This difference does not, however, occur at the level of the pure concepts, which pertain to the essential or the universal. Now Hegel conceives as "real" precisely what is not transient and only occurs insofar as it is thought. In founding the true, absolute unity between thinking and the reality that it brings about, that unity will therefore have to be sought in the concepts which do not have an empirical origin.

Looking at science and philosophy hitherto, however, Hegel finds many nonempirical concepts that at first sight are not coherently related. These concepts always appear as fixed oppositions and are not embedded as moments within a totality. The metaphysical concepts are thus the only ones to have the possibility of bringing about true unity, but in fact they always get stuck halfway into their movement: although pertaining to the essential, the universal, and the identical, they simultaneously bring about a separation between the universal and the individual, between what persists and what is transient, between the infinite and the finite. Understanding the universal only as the abstract in relation to the concretely given manifold brings about a divide which, according to Hegel, cannot be undone as long as discursive understanding holds sway over philosophy.

Hegel's *Logic* primarily aims at understanding and sublating the inadequacy of discursive metaphysics. All essential distinctions brought about by thinking in order to understand reality are incorporated in such a way that they lose their independence and become part of a living whole—that is to say, of the movement in which the concept increasingly determines itself. Thus, metaphysics itself is reduced to a phase within a development in which the opposition between the universal and the individual—which was brought about in that metaphysics—can be truly sublated. However, the *Logic* is not a history of philosophy in the usual sense of the word; the rise and fall of discursive metaphysics are thematized only *insofar* as the determinations brought about by that thinking can be understood on the basis of their pure origin. Hegel as it were rewrites that history without accounting for all the accidental entanglements that characterize the actual history. In his lectures on the history of philosophy he thus maintains

> that the historical sequence in the systems of philosophy is similar to the sequence in the logical deduction of the conceptual determinations of the idea. I maintain that if the fundamental conceptions of the systems appearing in the history of philosophy be entirely divested of what regards their outward shape . . . the various stages in the determination of the idea itself are found in their logical concept.[8]

When the actual history is kept at a distance in this way, the question arises as to how the many concepts that came about in this history may be systematically ordered. After all, chronology cannot serve as the ordering principle. If the discursive tendency in philosophy is to be truly overcome, *all* existing conceptual distinctions should no longer be taken as absolute. This can only succeed if the existing concepts are incorporated in a movement that of itself brings about the totality. This movement is actually sustained by a constant strife between the understanding that brings about oppositions and the reason that tries to save the unity of that which is distinguished. Hegel proposes that this movement is a necessary development that accomplishes itself independently of subjective interventions. The movement of the *Logic* thus accomplishes itself because Hegel, like a theater director, lets thinking time and again strive against its own objectifying tendency, without that movement being reduced to a confrontation between subjective faculties.

Since Hegel concentrates on the way in which the concepts develop out of *one another*, this strife is mostly not explicit in the *Logic* itself.[9] It is Hegel who ensures that the self-developing movement of the concept proceeds as it logically should. While in the actual history that "logical" course can only be recognized to a certain extent, the *Logic* excludes this externality from its realm and thus allows the movement that is at stake to enact itself in its purest form. The concepts brought about in that actual history are only given a place in that movement if and insofar as this is logically necessary.[10]

Hence, the *Logic* is the place where the pure concepts can first manifest their lively, organic totality (cf. L I, 49/54). Here is opened up the space within which the development of the one concept out of the other can take place. If this movement is to reach its end, it is clearly of utmost importance to let it start from the right point. Hegel's choice of starting point is based on the following idea. Everything that is marked by a lack will in one way or another seek to overcome this shortcoming. Every kind of becoming, life, or development, consists in this attempt to annul the "not" that something has within itself. This applies for the germ that cannot bear to remain only a germ, for a living being that, for example, satisfies its hunger, and for human beings who strive to overcome that which they have actually become.[11] Everything that is confined or finite acquires independence and reality—that is, being-for-itself—by appropriating the possibilities that it has in itself.

Now Hegel lets this principle of self-actualization also apply for concepts, which thus equally acquire a certain kind of life. As long as a concept is merely formal, it will try to overcome its lack of being-for-itself. It does this by determining itself. In this way it gains content, though initially only by losing its universality. The concept divides itself into an abstract universality on the one hand and a concrete content on the other, and, in doing so, will attempt to regain its universality. The universality that is brought about *in* that movement will no longer be formal, but will have incorporated the determinateness within itself. This means that the concept has enriched itself: it has become the totality of itself and that which was opposed to it. This entails, however, that it has become a different concept. As long as a concept is finite, it will time and again posit itself over against a "not" that it has within itself and try to sublate this opposition. According to Hegel, this movement is guaranteed to go toward its own completion. It comes to an end only when the concept has incorporated every otherness within itself. Discursive understanding always brings the concepts to make themselves independent and thus to thwart their own movement; Hegel, on the other hand, reveals this opposition as a necessary, but surmountable moment within the movement in which the formal concept actualizes itself.

The movement of the *Logic* is divided according to the basic concepts "being," "essence," and "concept." The three parts of the *Logic* show the proper development and self-determination of these concepts. This development culminates when thinking understands itself *as* the manifestation—and indeed the purest manifestation—of the concept itself. I will now try to sketch out this movement; in doing this I will discuss the "content" of the *Logic* only insofar as it is relevant for the comprehension of Hegel's method.

8.2 The Rise and Fall of Discursive Metaphysics

Being, Nothing, and Becoming

The movement of the concept that enacts itself in the *Logic* begins with the emptiest and most undetermined concept: being. More than any other concept, "being" will attempt to undo its lack of determination. "Being" is the category that is the condition of possibility underlying every involvement with beings. Our involvement with beings is from the outset determined by many different viewpoints or categories. These allow us to bring about coherence and unity in the manifold of phenomena. Whenever something is determined as, for example, a thing that is large, black, or a table, these acts are already preceded by the basic determination that it "is." This "being"—which Heidegger would call "objective presence"—is a category that in itself means nothing at all. The concept "being" is entirely indifferent to the objects of which it is predicated. It is the most universal of what can be said about something, and precisely for this reason it says nothing about the matter itself.[12] Since the concept "being" is more than all other concepts characterized by a lack of determinateness, nothing more can be said about it from the perspective of discursive understanding. Hegel, however, makes it possible for the concept "being" to further determine itself, that is, to accomplish the movement which is proper to every concept, but to which the understanding is blind.

Whenever we say of something that it *is* something, this statement already implies that it is *not* something else. When I say of a being that it is white, then I have also expressed that it is none of the other colors. Everything that is, is in one way or another characterized by a "not." *Preceding* every specific ontic predication there is thus not only an orientation upon "being" as such, but implicitly also already upon the "not" as such. Nothing can actually be said about these emptiest concepts. Nevertheless, Hegel maintains that they must be regarded as the concepts that underlie all the distinctions that allow us to actually encounter beings. In order to thematize the *determined* relations between "being" and "not," Hegel begins the *Logic* with the concepts "being" and "nothing" insofar as they do not yet relate to one another. That is a logical, but difficult beginning. To make it rather less difficult, we could say that the assertion that something does or does not exist, or has one property and not another, is in Hegel's view made possible by the purely logical categories "being" and "nothing." These most universal, empty concepts do not in themselves say anything—and therefore also cannot be distinguished from one another—but rather constitute the precondition of everything that can be said about beings and hence of all determined concepts.[13] Thus, concepts such as "existence," "something," and "substance" are further determinations of the concept "being." A concept such as "being-other" can only arise from out of a preceding orientation upon an undetermined "nothing" as such.[14]

After beings have been understood as determined by a "being" and a "not," this determination demands to be further qualified.

When the understanding enters the domain of philosophy, it will insist on the opposition "being" and "nothing" (cf. L I, 95/92). Hegel permits that opposition to occur, but only for a short time. Close observation shows that beings are always engaged in sublating a "not" or lack. The least complex form of this movement is "becoming." This pure "becoming," as the transition from a "not" to a "being," always guides our experience of beings, for instance when we concretely determine that something is white. Close observation shows that "being white" in fact means: "having *become* white." And that implies: being able to become *other*. If we take a closer look, this just means that everything which *is* can be understood as that which has *become*. Beings try to annul their lack, and as long as they do not entirely succeed in this, they will remain in a process of becoming. Only the pure concept "becoming" makes it possible for "being" and "nothing" to be distinguished as different moments (83, 95/82–83, 91–92).

"Becoming" is the first category that has an otherness within itself; only because it is thus distinguished within itself does it have a certain determinateness. This concept, which may then be further determined as "coming-to-be" and "ceasing-to-be" (112/105), constitutes the basic category of *The Doctrine of Being*. Insofar as beings are approached from an ontic perspective—that is to say, by means of the senses—they appear as susceptible of many different qualitative and quantitative changes, all based on the fact that these beings are in the process of becoming. From this perspective beings remain transient, however much they may try to sublate their lack and gain self-dependence; according to Hegel, true self-dependence or being-for-itself is not granted to them.

It is here neither possible nor useful to consider in detail the way in which Hegel lets the concepts develop in *The Doctrine of Being*. Basically, this part systematically introduces all pure concepts that give access to nature as it appears through sensible intuition. Starting from the difference between qualitative and quantitative determinations, Hegel covers the entire realm of immediate involvement with beings—that is to say, the realm of the natural orientation of consciousness and, following on from this, of the positive sciences and mathematics.[15] Since the *Logic* is only concerned with the "logical" aspects of this natural involvement, time and space are excluded from the analysis (L II, 257/586). These only come back into play in the philosophy of nature.

The pure concepts that are developed in *The Doctrine of Being* constitute the conditions of possibility both for the sciences of nature and for the (immediate) appearing of nature itself. These conditions of possibility are rarely if ever explicitly thematized in the sciences themselves, but only in philosophy (cf. L I, 235/205). Hegel is therefore also always concerned with traditional, discursive philosophy, which could not do justice to the logical interrelatedness of the pure concepts. These two levels—the science whose possibility must be understood and the philosophy that has done this in an inadequate way—are not always easy to separate.

In *The Doctrine of Being* the concepts that make possible every ontic experience are not only ordered, but develop out of one another in such a way that they take on a necessary character. Yet Hegel, in thus providing the foundation of the sciences, at the same time also reveals the confinement of this ontic orientation. The positive sciences try to discursively create unity and coherence in that which is given by the senses. However, they can only do this to a certain extent. The constantly returning dissatisfaction with what it has achieved leads knowing, when it has entirely exhausted the basic possibilities of its perspective, to exceed its own domain and engage in a new movement to become philosophy. *The Doctrine of Being* must therefore primarily be read as an analysis of the perspective that *precedes* philosophy proper.[16] When thinking begins to inquire into the essence of what is, it emerges from the natural, discursive understanding of nature and has this understanding as its "past." *The Doctrine of Essence* then thematizes the understanding that extends its power and enters the domain of philosophy. Philosophy, as external reflection, lets its questioning be unduly (but unavoidably) controlled by the understanding and therefore cannot see through the semblance of the oppositions that it brings about. Finally, *The Doctrine of the Concept* proceeds toward a mode of philosophy that is able to do precisely this and thus assigns to the understanding its rightful, subordinate place. The *Logic* itself then turns out to be the preeminent example of this philosophy. Hence, Hegel's own thinking proves to be the science that constitutes the true "future" of philosophy. These three moments constitute the phases of the pure history which is accomplished in the *Logic*.

At first sight, however, it is not self-evident that the *Logic* describes the provenance and future of philosophy. Hegel thematizes this movement primarily by starting out from the movement in which the concept determines itself. The pure concepts do indeed come about in thinking, yet ultimately do not ground in finite subjectivity. The illusion that this movement might depend on subjective interventions is thus avoided as far as possible. I believe, however, that it may be clarifying to also take this "subjective" side of the *Logic* into account. The "life" of the concepts and the movement of thinking that gives rise to these concepts can hardly be separated, as Hegel indicates at the beginning of *The Doctrine of Essence*:

> When this movement is pictured as the path of knowing, then this beginning with being, and the development that sublates it, reaching essence as a mediated result, appears as an activity of knowing. . . . But this path is the movement of being itself. (L II, 13/389)

The Doctrine of Essence can thus be read as an analysis of both the possibilities and the incapacity of a thinking that turns its gaze to the essential. The path of the concept "essence" is also the path of metaphysics seeking to reach its innermost possibilities.

Essence

When a sheet of paper and a swan are said to be white things, this is an inadequate way to bring about unity in the manifold of given impressions. The things themselves are indifferent to such predications. As thinking strives for unity, it finds no satisfaction as long as it confines itself, guided by pure concepts, to that which appears through sensible intuition.[17]

The mode of thinking that raises itself above this domain and becomes philosophy thus allows a new basic category to come into play: "essence." This category opens up a realm within which an identity or universality can come about that is not foreign to the concrete beings; these beings can now be conceived as manifesting their identity as their essence. Since the essence of something remains identical to itself *in* all its appearances, it has acquired greater independence than concrete beings (cf. L I, 451/379). From this new perspective, beings, for their part, lose their relative independence and become determined as semblance, or as that in which essence appears. This swan is then no longer a thing that is white, but is that in which the essential of the swan can appear.

The essence of something cannot be revealed in an immediate way, but is brought about in and through the movement of bending back to itself which Hegel calls "reflection." It is important to stress that Hegel conceives this reflecting movement as issuing from the movement of the pure concept itself; the concept "being," overcoming its one-sidedness, negates itself of itself and thus yields the concept "essence" (L II, 13/390). Thus, reflection does not originate in the human subject, but in the dynamic of essence itself. Essence needs beings in order to confirm itself *as* the essential. It distinguishes semblance or appearance from itself, posits these moments over against itself as that which is other than itself, and is able to recognize itself in its own otherness as in a mirror. Thus, essence may be understood as the reflecting, self-returning movement in which it brings itself to itself.[18] Hegel lets essence divide itself initially into essence and semblance; when essence subsequently distinguishes itself from itself as appearance, it grants a greater independence to the other of itself, while essence and appearance nevertheless remain dependent on one another.[19] Using a simple example, we may perhaps conceive the relation between essence and appearance as follows.

The concept "bird" may be regarded as a concept that is brought about in a process of abstraction and pertains to that which all birds have in common. That is the common, discursive perspective. One may also, as Hegel does, begin from the other side. The concept "bird," taken in its abstraction, then appears as characterized by a lack of determinateness that it tries to overcome. It only acquires meaning and can only come into its own when the "bird" is seen *in* all concrete swans and thrushes. These beings then reflect their bird-character in such a way that the essence of all birds can mirror itself in those concrete birds and can thus confirm its own identity or universality. The essential bird-character sets itself in motion, divides itself within itself and specifies itself as swan, thrush, and all other kinds of birds, which are then concrete enough to "animate" the actually existing birds.

"Essence" thus becomes the principle that grants these beings their form. This means with respect to beings that they each in their own way, as thrush, sparrow, or swan, embody what belongs to birds as such and derive their identity precisely from that embodiment. Beings therefore also need their opposite, essence, to confirm themselves in what they are: they thus "reflect" themselves as much in essence as essence reflects itself in its appearances. From Hegel's perspective the individual can only show forth *as* the individual against the background of something universal; the universal, for its part, can only show forth *as* the universal when it has specified itself and has become the animating, organizing principle of individual beings.

In the reflection of the bird as such *in* concrete birds, the concept "bird" gains its being-for-itself and self-dependence. It can acquire a universality that is not abstract, but has its determinateness within itself. The extent to which essence is able to reflect and recognize itself in concrete beings depends on the way in which human beings actually think. Thinking must grant things the capacity to appear in such a way that they are neither entirely transparent nor entirely opaque.

Now the negation of the immediacy that is accomplished in reflection *entails of itself* that essence and that in which it appears are not only distinguished, but come to be posited over against one another as two separate domains. Hegel reserves the basic category "essence" for the movement that brings about a difference between the universal and the concrete, *without* allowing the true unity of the two movements to be fully restored (cf. L II, 125/480). The character of reflection entails that there must remain a difference between that which reflects itself and that *in* which it reflects itself. Since essence always tends to posit itself over against the things in which it appears, the movement in which essence tries to reflect itself in beings gets, as it were, stuck halfway. Reflection, then, is nothing other than the movement in which the essence attempts to return to itself and in that movement brings about immediacy, as semblance or appearance. That semblance will, however, pretend to be the first, as that from which reflection *starts out.* In this way the circular movement of essence vanishes from sight, and the reflecting movement of essence becomes a merely *external* reflection.[20]

If this same movement is viewed from the perspective of the philosophy in which all this takes place, it is the understanding—the faculty of this external reflection—that clings to the opposition between essence and appearance. The understanding is not aware of the unity that precedes this opposition and thwarts the movement in which true unity could possibly come about.

On the other hand, philosophy will always try to overcome the discursive perspective and bridge the gap between essence and that in which it appears. It does this by freeing the concept "essence" of its abstract character. This further determination, however, only entails that the opposition between essence and semblance modifies itself into the opposition between identity and difference, ground and that which is grounded, form and matter, cause and effect, an independently existing world and an appearing world, inside and outside. All these oppositions arise from within the perspective that is opened up by the basic category "essence."[21] The essential unity and universality which by means of this category can be brought about *among beings*, thus leads to a divide between the immediate and the reflected that cannot be truly sublated from this perspective. As long as external reflection holds sway, the fixated difference between essence and that which appears will yield ever new oppositions. Until that process has come to an end, the thinking that seeks true unity will be unable to find rest and satisfaction. If essence does, however, succeed in entirely recognizing itself in its appearances, it is no longer "essence," but has become "concept."[22] The specular reflexivity of the concept thus opens up a perspective that sublates the one-sidedness of the categories "being" and "essence."[23]

8.3 The Concept

If philosophy is guided by the concept "essence" in everything it approaches, it will necessarily bring about its own downfall. Hegel conceives essence as a failed concept, that is to say, as the "not yet" of the concept (L II 182/526). The lack that inheres in the concept "essence"—and that is also the lack of a metaphysics which remains dominated by external reflection—demands to be annulled itself. The sublation of this lack has to consist in a true accomplishment of the reflecting, self-returning movement in which essence gets stuck halfway. That it is actually possible to find such a way through and that this is not only something which *ought* to take place, is shown in the *Logic* itself, three-quarters of which we have now covered. Hence, Hegel's own perspective is not guided by the basic category "essence," but by the basic category "concept." From the perspective that is opened up by this category, he maintains, the issues that concern philosophy should at last be able to appear in their true dynamic and truth. The universal is now no longer posited over against determinateness, but is itself the movement in which it brings about determinateness and becomes true, nonabstract universality. In the self-determining movement of the concept, the usually despised individuality becomes "the profundity in which the concept seizes itself" (297/619). The concept as such consists precisely in the movement in which the universal understands and recognizes itself in the individual. This principle structures all Hegel's work and constitutes the heart of the speculative method.

Before I further thematize the concept as methodical principle, the way in which the concepts "essence" and "concept" are developed may serve as an example of Hegels' method. When Hegel asks what the concept "essence" is, he is not satisfied with an answer that defines the "what" of the essence in an abstract way. His analysis of the concept "essence" distinguishes three moments. First, essence is the universal and identical in relation to the manifold that appears. But in order to confirm itself *as* the universal, essence must actually bring about what it always already is. It does that by, second, dividing itself into essence and appearance, in such a way that this appearance appears as the other of itself. This leads to essence and appearance becoming independent of one another. The third moment then consists in essence fully recognizing itself in that otherness, thus retrieving appearance as a moment within its own movement of self-actualization. We have seen that when that has been accomplished, essence has become concept.

The concept "essence" owes its finitude precisely to the fact that it cannot come to itself without becoming a different concept. In any case: only when essence is understood in these three moments—that is to say, *as* the movement in which it tries to sublate its own lack—is it truly understood. Furthermore, this perspective makes it possible to understand the concept "essence" as being itself a moment within an encompassing movement, that is, to understand it with regard to its "origin" (being) and its "future" (the concept). Looking back over the course of the *Logic*, one sees that the difference between being and essence is a difference that was brought about by the concept itself. In this most primordial difference, the concept determines itself in such a way that it becomes itself a moment within its own movement: as essence (universality) it comes to stand over against being (determinateness). The concept lets these two domains become independent of one another and, when their one-sidedness forces them to give up this independence, retrieves the two moments into itself.[24]

In *The Doctrine of the Concept* Hegel founds the possibility of truly scientific philosophy by showing how the movement of the essence sublates of itself its own lack and thus becomes the concept. But that is only the beginning. He still has a long way to go before he can thematize the concept as the absolute principle that also structures his own thinking: there is still a considerable difference between what is usually understood by "concept" and what Hegel understands by it (cf. 252/582). In the last part of the *Logic*, Hegel elaborates the different concrete manifestations in which the absolute structure of the concept appears in such a way that the concept itself can increasingly manifest its own purity by means of those manifestations. Up to now, Hegel has followed thinking in the way it involved itself with reality by means of the various pure concepts. In *The Doctrine of the Concept* Hegel lets thinking turn to itself. This will at last allow the opposition between subjectivity and objectivity to be sublated. He initially focuses on the way in which thinking itself has traditionally understood its own part in the coming about of truth. This brings us to the traditional logic.

Hegel tries to breathe new life into these "dead bones of logic" (L I, 48/53). This means that the different forms of thinking (concept, judgment, syllogism) which traditional logic considers to be separate are thematized in such a way that they emerge out of one another to constitute an organic totality (41/48). This order is guided by the idea that these subjective modes of the concept in one way or another try to express the true unity of the universal and the individual. This is already the case when I call this thrush a "bird" (cf. L II, 277/603–4). But in order to really bring about this unity, the difference between the universal and the individual must actually be expressed. This occurs when a subject and predicate (for example, "this bird" and "whiteness") are distinguished and related in a judgment. The various judgments try to bring about unity, each in its own way, but this entails that the universal and the individual are always distributed between the two moments of the judgment in such a way that their unity cannot really show forth.[25] The judgment is thus the preeminent instrument of discursive understanding (cf. 304/625).

Hegel considers this lack of the judgment to be sublated in the syllogism (351/664). Hence the syllogism is the highest manifestation of the concept that can occur within the limits of traditional logic. That is to say, the syllogism expresses the movement in which the universal determines itself to become the particular and returns to itself in the individual. Thus, the universal here determines itself by dividing itself within itself *without* in that movement losing its universality. The circular movement of the syllogism thus manifests the pure structure of the concept as such. Yet, no matter how much the syllogism twists free from accidentally given contents (393/697), all its manifestations remain merely subjective forms of thinking.

Hegel therefore subsequently turns to the way in which the concept expresses itself in thinking about nature. When we let thinking turn itself to nature, we see that the pure concept here attempts to acquire objectivity as the end of natural processes (*Zweck*). The teleological structure of nature indicates a universal principle which *from within* animates and gives shape to nature in all its forms. Hegel calls the concept that has acquired an *adequate* reality "idea."[26] This idea first takes shape as "life" (468/760). The principle of self-organization or self-determination that manifests itself in everything that is alive, expresses the movement of the concept as such. A clear manifestation of the concept as idea may be found in the structure of human knowing itself: the concept here not only *is* in accord with its reality, but also *comprehends* that unity. In this self-comprehension the idea becomes truly for-itself (486–87/774) and thus acquires true independence. Knowing is no longer understood as subjective faculty of judging, but in its own reality: as form of life, as living self-relation. The subject now appears as the movement in which it divides itself into consciousness and self-consciousness, but does not lose itself in its many different experiences. The way in which the subject distinguishes itself from itself does not lead to an alienation that must then be sublated, but is precisely the way in which it comes to itself. Self-consciousness

> is just the *existent* pure concept, and therefore *empirically perceptible*, the absolute relation to itself that, as a separating judgment, makes itself its own object and is solely this process whereby it makes itself a circle. (490/777–78)

The subject that is able to become an object for itself accomplishes the identity of itself and its object and affirms itself as this identity. Nevertheless, it is not able to understand *all* otherness to which it relates as that which it has itself brought about (497/782). This knowledge remains dependent on what is *given* through the senses. Thus, a difference still remains between concept and being, or between subjectivity and objectivity.

For Hegel the ultimate mode of knowing—and hence of "life"—consists finally in a knowing that can fully recognize the reality to which it relates as that which it has itself brought about. This absolute unity of subjectivity and objectivity is called the "absolute idea."[27] This idea does *not* pertain to the empirically given reality: what remains of this after we disregard the way in which this reality is brought about by the subject is nonessential matter that does not deserve the name "reality" (cf. 258/587). Everything that has some meaning owes that meaning to pure, transcendental imagination: by means of the pure concepts, this imagination opens up the realm within which something can first show forth. The reality that thinking brings about entirely of itself is the totality of pure concepts which constitute moments of the self-actualization of the concept as such. Thus, the object is what it is through

> the determinations of thought and of the concept. . . . Therefore these determinations are in fact the sole thing that matters; they are the true subject matter and content of reason, and anything else that one understands by subject matter and content in distinction from them has value only through them and in them. (L II, 560/833, tr. m.)

Precisely because these concepts are understood with regard to their pure, nonsubjective origin, a knowing that understands this cannot cling to itself as finite subject (548/823). Absolute knowing, capable of leaving behind all subjective one-sidedness, understands itself as *that* manifestation of the idea in which the concept has fully comprehended itself and its own history. When the absolute concept accomplishes itself as the method of true philosophy, then that method is not external to a given content; it is the concept itself which, as pure form, determines itself and turns itself into its own content.[28] Hence it is in the *Logic* that the concept finally understands itself as the one, pure principle of self-becoming and self-organisation which animates nature and truly actualizes itself in the human spirit. The concept, then, is nothing other than the movement in which the universal brings itself about by distinguishing itself within itself, *while remaining indifferent to that difference.* Since it is itself also the modes in which that has not yet been achieved (being and essence), the concept as such is the most encompassing and most primordial category.

Since Hegel regards the "concept" as the movement in which the one-sidedness of "being" and "essence" is sublated, this means in concrete terms that true philosophy can only come about when the perspective that makes it possible to relate to concrete beings and the perspective that raises itself above this have exhausted their limited possibilities to bring about unity and have given up their independence. Absolute knowing is thus capable of really bringing the movement of reflection—in which the concept returns to itself in such a way that it becomes entirely transparent for itself—to a good end.[29] When the moment in which that which reflects itself distinguishes itself from its mirror is understood as a necessary, but subordinate moment within that movement, thinking has become speculative philosophy. This philosophy allows the distinguishing power of the understanding in everything that it understands, insofar as this is necessary, and brings about true unity by annulling the independence of what is distinguished.

This "work" of philosophy means nothing other than that it lets the absolute concept's own dialectical movement take its course. This entails that every apparent independence ultimately annuls itself. The shortsighted understanding cannot grasp the movement in which the essential determines itself and in that self-determination confirms its own universality. Since everything that is essential is constantly in motion, the understanding which determines something as true and clings to this truth will see this truth of itself turn into untruth, and hence its own capacity into incapacity.

The dialectical principle which entails that the understanding gets stuck insofar as it obstinately clings to oppositions does not, however, have the last word in speculative philosophy. Breaking the power of the understanding, this dialectic solely results in a skepticism that no longer has anything to cling to. This side of the dialectic in itself constitutes only the negative, deconstructive moment of the speculative method and must be accompanied by a positive involvement with the unity in all oppositions.[30]

I will now briefly analyze how Hegel at the end of the *Logic* understands his own method as absolute method. This self-comprehension starts out from the thesis that everything which is finite strives to sublate its lack. It tries to become the totality of what it already is and what it not yet is, but indeed *could* be. It wishes to actually become what it has within itself as its *dunamis.* In every finite concept, just as in finite beings, there "lives" a contradiction between what it is in itself and what it could become. Thus, it has within itself a "not" that is just as determined as the concept itself. From this negativity originates all internal restlessness and self-movement, which makes it possible for unity to restore itself.[31]

In the *Logic* Hegel lets the proper movement of the concept occur by confronting it with its specific lack. To this end, he presents the concept firstly as that which is universal in itself (566/837). The specific lack of this concept then proves to consist in a lack of determinateness or being-for-itself. When a concept sets itself in motion in order to incorporate its otherness—that is, to determine itself—this initially leads it to annull its own universality. Hence, it turns into the opposite of what it was (561/834). However, since that negation is a *determined* negation, the first universality of the concept is preserved as a moment.

Both sides will then in their one-sidedness become independent of one another; this is the work of the understanding that time and again threatens to thwart the immanent dynamic of the concept.[32] The power of the dialectic, however, entails that the universal and the determined cannot sustain their independence and must again become part of the movement of the concept. This deserves a closer look.

According to Hegel, the negation of the first universality has its otherness within itself. This brings the moment of determinateness into conflict with itself, and it enacts the movement in which it sublates this contradiction (562/835). In other words, this moment—again driven along by absolute negativity—negates itself as determinateness. Thus, universality is once again brought about; however, it has now incorporated within itself the moments of formal universality and determinateness.[33] Hence the concept is no longer merely formal, but comprehends the totality of the moments that it distinguished in its own movement, and comprehends itself as this totality (566/837–38). The "other" can now no longer appear as opposite. The concept has thus become richer and more concrete. But in that self-determination it has also acquired a different "not" over against itself, to which it must once again relate. This process continues until the concept has incorporated all otherness within itself and has truly become the absolute concept.[34] In this way all concepts can become part of the encompassing movement of the concept itself.

This movement begins with a still entirely undetermined "being"; this is the concept in which the difference or the contradiction has not yet in any way unfolded itself. During this movement, the concept determines itself in such a way that while it does indeed surpass itself in the concepts that it yields, it does not lose itself: *in* and *through* these externalizations the concept gathers itself and returns into its "simplest depth" (570/841). This takes place explicitly at the end of the *Logic*. The concept then understands—as Hegel puts it—its own simplicity or unifoldness as the most primordial principle that grounds both the absolute method and the totality of pure concepts which have unfolded in the history of thinking and constitute the content of the *Logic*. Hence, the concept also underlies everything that, through those pure concepts, appears as meaningful. This concept Hegel considers to be

> the absolutely true being and the eternal . . . just because it is . . . the unity *of itself and its other*; it cannot therefore pass into that

> other as though it altered itself in it, for the very reason that it is itself the *other*, that is, determinateness, so that in this transition it only comes to itself. (492/779, tr. m.)

The universality that is not opposed to its determinateness and hence is capable of persisting amidst all changes, has gained true self-dependence and reality. While essence remains dependent on the beings in which it appears, the concept—that is, the movement of inner self-determination—is no longer posited over against something other than itself, but is itself the source of all otherness.[35] The way in which a concept yields its own concrete determinations can only be grasped from a perspective that is oriented upon the nonempirical origin of concepts—otherwise a difference will always remain between what is given by the senses on the one hand and what is thought on the other. When the absolute concept enacts itself in and as human reason, it thereby enacts the history in which it conceives the totality of pure concepts and, so to speak, *gives them to itself.* Insofar as this true being-in-and-for-itself of the concept is actually brought about by philosophy, philosophy here also reaches its ultimate self-actualization. Reason now accomplishes itself as intellectual intuition and actually grasps the pure concepts that always already underlie any mode of knowledge. In so doing, the difference between what is given and what is brought about or between what is presupposed and what is posited entirely disappears. The *Logic* thus completes the movement in which both the concept and thinking gain their truth and become completely transparent for themselves.[36]

8.4 The Eternal Movement of the Concept

Having sketched out the course of the *Logic* in a very provisional and simplified way, I will now thematize again from an even greater distance the relation between the basic concepts "being," "essence," and "concept." Hegel comprehends the intrinsic relation between these concepts by considering them to be different modes of movement. In general, movement for Hegel means that something tries to preserve itself by appropriating that which it is not. From this perspective, the highest form of movement consists in the movement which constantly remains identical to itself *in* that process of appropriation.

That is not in any case granted to transient beings. They

encounter the other over against themselves and try to confirm their identity by annulling this otherness. The way in which they do this, however, does not lead to true self-subsistence. The germ cannot cling to itself as germ, and has to give up itself for the sake of the plant that it in itself already is and wishes to become. Living beings can ultimately only preserve themselves by reproducing their kind; for the sake of that universality, however, the individual itself must perish. Thus, everything that is finite will be unable to cling on to what it is and will become different from itself while attempting to come to itself.

From Hegel's perspective this also applies for the "life" of finite concepts. We have seen how Hegel also regards the concept as a self-relation in which the concept tries to actualize its in-itself. The extent to which this succeeds or fails constitutes the difference between the basic categories being, essence, and concept. The movement of the concept "being" is still entirely abstract and the most difficult to perceive. Being does not really distinguish itself from itself, but keeps the determinateness of beings as the other over against itself, opposes itself to them. The empty "being" is absolutely indifferent to determinations such as white, big, or bird. Opposing the other is a very poor way to affirm one's own identity. Hence, "being" is characterized by an abstract self-relation (L II, 553–54/828), which is not capable of including the other within itself and thus acquiring content: it is "nothing." While being itself has no movement whatsoever, the beings that appear on the basis of the category "being" are for their part still entirely at the mercy of "becoming."

Contrary to "being," "essence" is characterized by a real relation to itself. That is to say, it itself brings about the difference between essence and appearance, so that it can confirm itself *as* essence by way of the otherness that it brings about itself. Since the reflecting movement enacted by essence must, however, cling on to the otherness of appearance, it gets stuck in the dichotomy between itself and the other of itself. The concepts "being" and "essence" bring about objectivity. Insofar as essence is a reflecting movement, it already has the structure of subjectivity, although this structure only comes into its own in the movement of the concept. Thus, *The Doctrine of Essence* constitutes the transition to *The Doctrine of the Concept*, which Hegel calls subjective *Logic*.

The concept is distinguished from essence because it no longer has to posit the other of itself over against itself. It can therefore continually remain itself in the movement in which it determines itself. Unlike being, it does not do this in an abstract way, but always recognizes itself in that which it distinguishes from itself. It is thus always present at itself in the other of itself. That is freedom. The concept yields its own content and in doing so does not posit itself as the universal over against determinateness. This means for the speculative method as the purest manifestation of the concept that in *all* the different analyses the dynamic structure of the pure concept remains visible—transparent for itself. In the *Encyclopaedia* Hegel summarizes the three modes of "advancing" as follows:

> The abstract form of the advance (*Fortgang*) is, in being . . . *transition* into an other; in essence *showing* in the opposite; in the concept, the distinction of *individual* from *universality*, which *continues* itself as such into, and is as an *identity* with, what is distinguished from it.[37]

I take this passage to concern the modes of movement proper to immediately given beings, essence, and the concept respectively. The three modes of movement to which the concepts "being," "essence," and "concept" give access are distinguished with regard to the extent to which they are able to truly appropriate what is other than themselves; this measure assigns the concepts their place in the all-encompassing movement of the concept. In "being"—which opens up the perspective of immediacy—this appropriating movement has not yet really been enacted. "Being" remains itself and leaves beings to their fate, that is to say, to their becoming and perishing. "Essence," the domain of reflection, actually relates to the other of itself, but does not succeed in bending itself back to its own beginning, because it holds fast to the opposition between being and essence. Only when the concept annuls and sublates this opposition and thus opens up the perspective of speculative philosophy has the movement of self-appropriation truly accomplished itself. This perspective is no longer bound to the mediating function of discursive understanding, but gives rise to the immediacy of intellectual intuition.[38]

Summarizing, the three modes of movement proper to the three basic concepts can be characterized as not yet relating to itself at all, bending back to itself in a finite way and truly returning into itself. The "logical" continuity between these movements allows Hegel to comprehend the actual continuity between nature and spirit.

We may also conceive this continuous movement as the movement which opens up the three horizons or ontological perspectives that constitute the conditions of possibility of all knowledge. The perspective of being first opens up the domain proper to discursive understanding. Transgressing its limits, this understanding then enters the domain of essence—that is, of philosophy—and thus comes to dominate the actual history of philosophy. Finally, the perspective of the concept succeeds in assigning the understanding its rightful, subordinate position. Viewed from Heidegger's perspective this would mean that the horizon of Praesens, while necessary for the appearing of beings, wrongfully remains dominant when thinking raises itself to become philosophy.

Hegel's conquest of the confined horizon of discursive metaphysics means for Heidegger, by contrast, that thinking more than every falls prey to the power of Present. He regards the threefold movement of the concept as equally developing from out of the self-increasing predominance of Present. Hence, for him the total "recollection" of the absolute concept itself rests on a forgetting of the temporal horizon, which grants every concept a limited reach. This is what the concept itself, however transparent it may be for itself, cannot comprehend. In order to annul this one-sided presentification, it is not enough to deprive the objectifying understanding of its independence. According to Heidegger, the "complete transformation" (L I, 13/25) that Hegel claims to accomplish in relation to metaphysics hitherto precisely confirms that metaphysics. Thinking therefore needs to accomplish an even more radical turning.

Hegel considers the sublation of otherness and negativity to be the basic principle of every movement; this sublation attains its ultimate possibility in the philosophy that is able to fully recognize reality—insofar as it is essential—as its own product. This idea seems to be mainly based on the relation between a knowing subject and a known objectivity. When Hegel tries to sublate every opposition between subject and object, he does this by starting out from the idea that the "other" or the "not" which the subject encounters can be fully appropriated and overcome, at least when knowing itself raises itself to the standpoint of true science. Heidegger for his part tries to do justice to a "not" that precisely demands to be *admitted*. What is other than presence needs human thinking in order to occur as that which recedes from its reach. Here a different "givenness" also comes into play than the empirical givenness that is assigned a subordinate position in Hegel's philosophy. The "it" that first grants thinking its thoughts and demands to be thought itself is not a result of the concept and therefore cannot be internalized by it. One might say that Levinas and Derrida, each in his own way, also start out from this issue.

9

Concept, Time, and History

We have seen that Hegel in the *Logic* defers the analysis of time and space, so that the part played by subjectivity in bringing about objectivity can be understood purely by means of the self-determining movement of the pure concept. The result is that the concept fully sublates the opposition between subjectivity and objectivity, and understands itself as the absolute unity of that difference, that is to say, as absolute idea. However, it still remains unclear how the absolute concept that gives access to reality is related to *time*. We know that Heidegger attempts to deconstruct Hegel's conception of the relation between concept and time. In this chapter I will therefore first thematize how Hegel understands that relation, and then consider Heidegger's remarks on Hegel at the end of *Being and Time*. Heidegger here suggests that Hegel's concept of time most radically manifests the "vulgar" understanding of time (BT 428). In the last section I will discuss the relation between what Heidegger understands by "temporality" and the "vulgar" concept of time. But I will begin by following further the course of the *Logic*. Having brought itself to its end, the *Logic* becomes aware of its confinement, exceeds its bounds, and unfolds itself into an all-encompassing system. It does this by bringing space and time back into play.

9.1 Concept and Time in Hegel's System

Absolute knowing is the manifestation of the concept in which the concept has fully determined itself. It has recognized the essential aspects of reality as being brought about by itself. It knows that it beholds itself in everything that it beholds. This logical movement can be understood in its purity—which happens in the *Logic*—but only really takes place in history. The *Logic* has every essential determination within itself, and yet turns out not to be self-sufficient. The concept that has been able to fully unfold itself and no longer has any essential otherness external to it, still finds itself over against reality insofar as it is given through time and space. This reality appears initially as the nonlogical, nonessential, and nontransparent manifoldness where accident and changeability have free play.[1]

The concept does not tolerate that opposition between its own purity and this impure reality, and must attempt to also sublate this most encompassing opposition. It will have to be able to find or recognize itself in reality as this is actually given. This means that thinking will now have to repeat and understand reality as it took place in time and space from the perspective of the concept. The *Logic* thus surpasses itself to become philosophy of nature and spirit.[2] While the different moments of the concept are only considered in the *Logic* with respect to their pure, nonempirical origin, these sciences try to find the pure concept *in* the spatiotemporal givenness.

In Hegel's system, the absolute idea that was the result of the *Logic* is given the opportunity to "repeat" its history. This means first that the idea divides itself from itself in such a way that it appears as completely other than the concept—as nature. The development of the idea then consists in the increasing sublation of this otherness; in this return of the idea to itself the idea accomplishes itself as spirit.[3] When spirit at the end of the history of its essential determinations has reached its highest possibility and has become absolute knowing, the idea has understood its own absoluteness not only with respect to the necessary, pure movement of the concept, but also with respect to the way in which that concept has actually accomplished itself in time and space. The concept that freely leaves its own domain and releases itself in reality, only does this in order to ultimately confirm itself all the more as the principle that animates every single aspect of reality (cf. L II, 573/843–44).

This absolute self-confirmation is only possible when the idea does not posit time and space over against itself, but succeeds in recognizing them as moments of its own development. Hegel now calls the externality of space and time the *form* of the determinateness of the idea.[4] When the absolute idea determines itself as nature and spirit, it becomes accessible (for us) through space and time. Thus, the absolute idea does not externalize itself into space and time, but rather into nature as *determined* by space and time. Hegel suggests that time and space are forms of intuition, that is to say, give access to reality as nature:

> Time, like space, is a *pure form* of *sensibility* (*Sinnlichkeit*) or *intuition*, it is the unsensible of the sensible (*das unsinnliche Sinnliche*). Like space however, time is indifferent to the difference between objectivity and a distinct subjective consciousness. (Enc. §258 rem., tr. m.)

Hegel here clearly draws on Kant's analysis of time and space. However, since he no longer considers these forms to be subjective principles, the question concerning their relation to the pure concept that unfolds itself in the *Logic* becomes highly relevant. Although the texts of Hegel that I have studied do not give a conclusive answer to this question, and therefore do not explicitly support my interpretation, I will here try to provide a possible answer. For this, I turn once more to the pure concept.

We have seen how the pure concept develops in the *Logic* from the still abstract "being" that gives access to nature into the pure concept that fully comprehends itself and the reality that it has brought about. In speculative philosophy this concept has acquired its highest form of reality: this is the absolute idea. Life and (finite) knowing are also manifestations in which the concept has acquired objectivity, that is to say, has become idea. In the *Logic* these manifestations are only thematized with respect to their logical development, although these manifestations of the idea actually always appear on the basis of the pure intuitions space and time.

Now, since these forms may not be foreign to the concept that unfolds itself in the *Logic*, the pure concept must have distinguished itself from the outset into the emptiest category "being" on the one hand (which then unfolds itself into essence and concept) and the pure intuitions space and time on the other.[5] Hegel thus seems to let the Kantian opposition between pure concept and pure intuition be preceded by a concept that of itself enacts this difference. Space and time, then, constitute the moment of the concept that makes possible every externality. Time is thus, as it were, the "capacity" of the absolute concept to bring about external distinctions. Hegel therefore seems to assign to time the same function that he assigns to discursive understanding. Just as reason distinguishes itself from itself as subjective principle in order to let the understanding go its own way, the pure concept distinguishes itself from itself as time. Understanding and time are both characterized by the abstract and external character of their movement. They are needed, but insofar as they resist their subordinated position they also constitute the most intimate "enemies" of reason and concept.

When the pure concept distinguishes itself into "being" on the one hand and space and time on the other, it opens up the realm within which plurality and contingency can take place. The concept gives itself the external forms of space and time; taking shape in this way, it brings itself to life and becomes the idea which can now manifest itself—with regard to its content—as nature. Hence time and space are moments of the movement of the concept itself; Hegel therefore also calls time the merely *intuited* concept.[6] Since space and time constitute the greatest externalizations of the concept, it is not evident at first sight that the pure concept already manifests itself here. One needs a speculative gaze to see this. I will now indicate how this external side of the concept, which could not be thematized in the *Logic*, is itself also characterized by a certain development.

Nature manifests itself as the totality of the beings that occupy space and are in motion. Extensiveness and movement can only be perceived by means of the pure, abstract-sensible intuitions space and time. In the philosophy of nature that constitutes the second part of the *Encyclopaedia*, Hegel does not leave these two forms unrelated to one another. He describes space as the intuition that gives access to an as yet entirely indifferent and static self-externality (*Außersichsein*) (Enc. §254). The difference that can appear *within* this extensiveness is that of the point; this point negates the pure indifference proper to space and thus brings about the difference between point, line, and plane (§256). From the perspective of the concept, which sees everything in the light of increasing self-determination, "space" can be understood as a form that tries to sublate its own lack of determinateness. This occurs when we not only let the point develop *within* the domain of space into line and plane, but let it acquire an independence or determinateness such that the point negates space *as such* and posits itself over against it. The point that in this way acquires a certain being-for-itself (§257) brings about a difference which has become less indifferent than that of the spatial point: this is where the point becomes the "now."

The "now," however, is completely unable to retain its for-itself. It yields of itself the difference between a "before" and an "after" and cannot maintain itself at all in that difference. Precisely because the "now" constantly differs from itself, it constitutes the uninterrupted continuity of time, which allows beings to appear as becoming—that is to say, against the background of the transition from "being" to "nothing" and vice versa (§259). Hegel remarks that time itself is the "becoming," or "the Cronos which engenders all and destroys that to which it gives birth" (§258 rem.). Time is the "total negativity" that entails that all finite, limited beings, which have the other of themselves outside themselves, are constantly driven by the restlessness to sublate this difference, but do not succeed:

> That which is real . . . is limited, and the other involved in this negation is *outside* it. . . . That which is finite is transient and *temporal* because, unlike the concept, it is not in itself total negativity, but . . . it relates to negativity as to its *power*. The concept however, in its freely existing identity with itself . . . is in and for itself absolute negativity and freedom, and is consequently not only free from the power of time, but is neither within time, nor something temporal. It is rather the *concept* which constitutes the power of time, whereas time is this negativity merely as externality. (§258 rem., tr. m.)

Time is negativity *as* externality—that is to say, it is the movement which brings about difference insofar as this movement can be *intuited.* Time brings about a difference between a "before" and an "after" which makes it possible to experience movement. Finite beings are *subjected* to this dynamic, they are forced to go along with a flow that they have not themselves brought about and that compels them to become other. The concept, by contrast, is *itself* this movement of distinguishing itself from itself. It brings about its own manifoldness and unity and thus determines *itself*, rather than being determined by the external negativity of time:

> [I]nternal self-movement proper . . . is nothing else but the fact that something is, in one and the same respect, self-contained and deficient, the negative of itself. . . . Something is therefore alive only insofar as it contains contradiction within it, and moreover is this power to hold and endure the contradiction within it. . . . Speculative thinking consists solely in the fact that thought holds fast contradiction, and, in it, its own self, but does not allow itself to be dominated by it as in ordinary thinking. (L II, 76/440–41)

Negativity is that which entails that everything that is differs from itself and attempts to overcome this difference. This differencing movement can be intuited in an immediate way as time:

something that is in motion both is and is not at a certain point (L II, 75–76/440). Now the concept is the mode of negativity which has *its source of movement in itself.* Differencing itself within itself without thereby becoming different from itself, it can, unlike the "now," truly resist the power of the all-devouring Cronos. Hegel therefore asserts that the true, the idea and the spirit are not subjected to time, but are *infinite.*[7] This leads us to the question as to how *finite* spirit, as it accomplishes itself as history, is determined by time. The movement of finite spirit is on the one hand no longer characterized by the "becoming" that perpetually accomplishes itself in nature, but on the other hand is still subjected to time. Referring to a possible "metaphysics of time," Hegel remarks:

> [Spirit] constitutes its existence and posits itself as external to itself. . . . One of the modes (*Weise*) of externality is time however, and this mode requires to be further examined both in the philosophy of nature and in the philosophy of finite spirit.[8]

Since the *Encyclopaedia* thematizes time and space *only* insofar as these forms give access to nature, this text does not make clear that time itself undergoes a certain development. I will now try to sketch out this proper movement of time.

The time that gives access to the totality of beings insofar as they change, are in motion, arise, and perish, is the time that Hegel terms "intuited becoming" (Enc. §258). This form is a manifestation of the concept in which the proper movement of the concept has not yet come into its own. In the *Logic* "becoming" is understood as a movement that does not allow any essential progress. It is only a transition from the one to the other, in such a way that the moving object cannot hold fast its own identity. In the concept of time that grounds this form of movement we thus find a repetition of what in *The Doctrine of Being* was only brought about by means of the movement of the pure concept.

The movements that take place in nature are entirely dominated by the externality of time. The return from nature of the idea—as spirit—entails on the one hand that being unfolds itself into concept, and on the other that the externality of space and time is increasingly sublated. The history of spirit evidences a time in which movement can indeed accomplish itself as self-actualization. Since the manifestations in which spirit externalizes itself are not lost, but are incorporated in the next manifestation, history is characterized by progress.

The development of history is such, however, that the dividedness is not yet entirely sublated; every result will again come into conflict with itself, and again have to set itself in motion to overcome that conflict. Here one may recognize the character of the movement which in *The Doctrine of Essence* is attributed to reflection: something is on the way to itself by recognizing itself in the other of itself, but does not reach its aim, and must therefore time and again become different from what it was. Thus, although the movement here already displays the structure of the pure concept, the power of time has not yet been sublated. This means that the movement is indeed already "reflexive," but is not yet able to return to its starting point.

The movement of pure self-externalization which is called time entails that what sets itself in motion can never return to the point where it began.[9] As long as the beginning and end remain different from one another, the result of a certain development must again find an otherness outside itself and must again engage in a new appropriating movement. The externalization that is intended to gain itself for itself is here still accompanied by a self-loss that cannot be entirely annulled. We thus see how finite spirit on the one hand is able to accomplish the self-determining movement of the concept, but on the other is still subjected to the power of time. This time entails that the difference between the in-itself and that which actually exists will recur time and again.

According to Hegel, all the external distinctions that come about in that movement can be sublated by spirit. From his perspective the history of finite spirit appears as the movement in which the externality of space and time is increasingly sublated, so that the movement of the concept can accomplish itself with ever-increasing purity. History is thus understood as the movement in which spirit becomes increasingly conscious of its freedom and actually brings this about.[10] History as it were arises from out of the situation in which time still completely dominates nature, and moves toward a situation in which the differencing time has had to completely renounce its power. The movement of finite spirit occurs in this way within the tension between the linear movement of time on the one hand and the circular movement of the pure concept on the other.

The development of the idea as spirit culminates in the moment in which thinking is able to *freely* break the power of time. Spirit is then able, *from within* its temporal factic situation, to truly sublate the difference between the in-itself and the for-itself. In the *Logic* itself the pure and infinite circular movement of the concept can manifest itself *as itself*; this movement does not occur in time, but constitutes the infinite, animating principle which gives shape from within to both reality and the thinking that pertains to this reality.[11] The concept thus manages of itself to fully withdraw from transience:

> Time is *the concept* itself that *is there* and which presents itself to consciousness as empty intuition; for this reason, spirit necessarily appears in time, and it appears in time just so long as it has not grasped its pure concept, that is, has not annulled (*tilgt*) time. Time is . . . the merely intuited concept, when this latter grasps itself it sublates its time-form, comprehends this intuiting and is a comprehended and comprehending intuiting. Time, therefore, appears as the destiny and necessity of spirit that is not yet complete within itself.[12]

Time is the intuited negativity through which all beings become different from themselves and can never fully overcome this difference. Finite beings are unable to maintain themselves in the movement in which they try to sublate their lack, and will perish. As intuited "becoming," time is not yet able to truly accomplish the movement of the concept. It is able to do this to a certain extent in the movement that grounds history, but only in absolute knowing does time achieve its highest aim—that is, its own perishing. Here the power of time is broken; spirit comprehends that time is not so much a subjective intuition, but constitutes a moment of the pure concept itself. In the movement that is enacted by absolute knowing, the negativity which enacts that movement leads only to the self-actualization of the concept: during this movement nothing more has to be relinquished.

From the perspective of speculative philosophy, time can be understood as the externalization of the concept which constitutes a necessary, but subordinate moment of the movement in which the absolute idea confirms its purity. The movement of the concept itself turns out not to depend on time, but to have posited time as the other of itself over against itself in order to truly occur and to ultimately sublate the externality given with time.

Philosophy can therefore also understand its own history as a moment of the movement in which the idea moves toward the sublation of its own externality. Spirit itself is thus ultimately able to fully comprehend what is "logical" in natural and historical reality.[13] It may then be seen how the idea manifests itself in nature as its forming, animating principle, but in such a way that this principle initially remains fully immersed in the rampant manifoldness of nature. The return from this manifoldness, as it is enacted by the idea as spirit, also means that nature can now be understood with respect to its principle, and can manifest itself—for spirit—*as* nature.[14] This will initially entail that thinking posits itself as understanding over against nature and is not able to understand itself and nature as two moments of the movement of the idea. When it is able to do this, thinking—having become a true science—is also able to incorporate time within the encompassing movement in which the absolute concept confirms its absoluteness. Thus, the circle of circles closes itself (L II, 571/842).

We, for our part, will have to go further. Satisfaction again turns into dissatisfaction and gives rise to a new history. It is this absolute movement of the concept that we have so resisted since Hölderlin, Schelling, and Kierkegaard. Hegel's very powerful system, however, appears to pursue its own way unaffected, indifferent to most of our objections. Can the omniscient storyteller be reduced to a character in a story that is still to be told? Or the director to one of the leading actors in a drama of which neither the beginning nor the end can be seen, and which is not at all certain to have a happy ending?

To let Hegel's system give up its own absoluteness, it may itself have to be revealed as a relative moment within a movement—a different kind of movement than that of the concept. But how much imagination does that require? And who would be able to comprehend that "semblance" without falling prey to the absolute?

> With regard to the essential grounding of the truth of Being, "logic" itself is a semblance, but the most necessary semblance that the history of being has known hitherto. The essence of "logic" itself, which has reached its highest shape in Hegel's metaphysics, can only be understood from out of (*aus*) the other beginning of the *thinking* of Being. (B 461)

Someone who says that he no longer makes claim to absoluteness (439), yet still *thinks* in terms of "most necessary semblance," will have to be very cautious. Heidegger's confrontation with Hegel can begin.

9.2 Heidegger's Interpretation of Hegel in *Being and Time*

After Heidegger in *Being and Time* has shown how temporality grounds the being of Dasein, he tries in the last two chapters to understand both history and the usual representation of time by starting out from this primordial time. Within this framework, he thematizes in §82 Hegel's concept of time, which he considers to be the most radical elaboration of the usual, vulgar understanding of time (BT 428). He maintains that on the basis of this concept of time, Hegel could not understand primordially enough the way in which spirit enacts itself as history in time (435). Heidegger acknowledges a certain kinship between his thinking and that of Hegel, insofar as the latter also thematizes the relation between spirit and time. But precisely for this reason it is important for Heidegger to show that his own interpretation of that relation moves in a direction that is opposite to Hegel (405). What Heidegger says about Hegel is thus exclusively intended to contrast his own perspective with that of Hegel, and hence to elucidate it in an indirect way (406, 408). However, it can hardly be inferred from this text that Heidegger tries to no longer understand the movement which is proper to history in terms of increasing self-actualization.[15]

Heidegger starts out from a passage in which Hegel asserts that it is in accordance with the concept of spirit "that the development of history takes place in time (*in die Zeit fällt*)."[16] If this development takes place in time, then spirit itself must be related to time (428). Hegel would certainly agree with Heidegger on this. Heidegger then suggests that Hegel can only understand this relation in a formal way, namely, by conceiving the structure of both time and spirit as the negation of a negation:

> The most appropriate expression for Hegel's interpretation of time thus lies in the determination of time as the *negation of negation*. . . . It is only in terms of this formal and dialectical concept of time that Hegel can produce a connection between time and spirit. (BT 432, cf. 435)

Heidegger's question is, then, whether that basic structure of time and spirit does not itself spring from primordial time. If that were the case, the formal structure of the concept indicated by Hegel could not be the final answer to the question concerning the relation between time and spirit (435). That Hegel, from his perspective, could not be aware of this time is elaborated by Heidegger in §82 of *Being and Time* only with respect to Hegel's concept of time in the *Encyclopaedia*.

Heidegger considers it symptomatic that Hegel only thematizes time within the framework of his philosophy of nature

(428–29). He maintains that Hegel's concept of time, following on from Aristotle, is exclusively directed to the everyday understanding of time (421, 428). From that leveling perspective, time can only be understood as a continuous succession of now-moments; in contrast to the time that we experience in everyday life, this time is stripped of all meaning.[17]

While Hegel understands time by means of the point, which becomes a now-moment by negating spatiality as such, Heidegger proposes that this point—posited as independent—constitutes itself a negation of a negation; that is to say, the point itself is already a negation of space (430, 432). He does not, however, mention the difference between the way in which Hegel lets the concept "time" dialectically develop from out of the concept "space" on the one hand, and the structure of time itself on the other. Yet with regard to time itself, what matters is not so much that it negates the indifferent externality of space, but that the "now," considered independently, brings about a difference between a "before" and an "after" that it immediately annuls. The difference that time constantly brings about and sublates makes it actually possible to perceive movement and becoming. Heidegger in fact quotes the passage where Hegel calls time intuited becoming, but sees it only as a confirmation of his thesis that Hegel understands time with respect to the "now" (BT 430–31, cf. 434–35).

As negation of a negation, time refers to the structure of the concept as such. However, in *Being and Time* Heidegger understands this structure primarily with respect to the structure of self-consciousness: since thinking has the form of comprehending *itself* in the other of itself, the essence of spirit, the concept, can also be conceived as self-negating negation.[18] Heidegger objects not only to this formalization of the structure of spirit, but also to Hegel's attempt to consider the movement of time as already a form of subjectivity—that is to say, of the concept. Whereas Hegel would say that time remains identical to itself while constantly distinguishing itself from itself, and thus shows in a still abstract way the structure of the subjectivity of the concept, Heidegger maintains in GA 21 that time is *not* related to subjectivity.[19]

Heidegger merely notes that Hegel characterizes both time and spirit as negation of a negation, and considers this formal similarity to ground Hegel's concept of history. Heidegger's further remarks on this are very concise and difficult to interpret. He quotes some passages in which Hegel maintains that the "progress" of spirit consists in the strife with and overcoming of itself.[20] The freedom of spirit comes about in the movement in which spirit determines itself by dividing itself within itself and then sublates that difference, but only to once more divide itself within itself. Since, according to Heidegger, this movement consists in the negation of a negation, it is in accordance with the concept of spirit to take place in time (BT 434).

One may add to this the following remarks. Because the spirit that accomplishes itself as history incorporates what it has actually become in a subsequent manifestation, progress in history is possible; the various manifestations do not succeed one another in a random way. However, this development of spirit is only possible if the manifestations are *also distinguished* from one another. This after-one-another is precisely the external difference brought about by time; the concept as such is not able to do this. Hegel says on this:

> It is in accordance with the concept of spirit that the development of history takes place in time. Time is determined by negativity. We relate to something, an event, in a positive way; but the fact that its opposite can also be the case, this relation to nonbeing (*Nichtsein*) is time.
>
> In the sphere of spirit . . . it becomes apparent that higher forms are produced through the transformation of earlier and less advanced ones. . . . [A]nd the fact that each new form is the transfiguration (*Verklärung*) of its predecessor explains why the appearing forms of spirit take place in time.[21]

This is how Hegel answers the question as to why history has to occur in time. Whereas the different *natural* species appear as unrelated to one another, the manifestations of spirit are *both* distinguished from one another (by time) *and* constitute part of a movement in which that difference is sublated. The development of finite spirit—I add—would then only be possible in the interplay of time (which distinguishes the moments of spirit, that is to say, lets them appear as following one another) and the concept, which constantly incorporates those moments in a higher unity. But that is expressed too mildly: the "play" is the infinite strife between time and concept in which freedom is ultimately at stake. What I add here does not necessarily contradict Heidegger's remarks; in fact, he says too little for this to be the case. He does, however, try to establish a relation between history, in which every "not" is overcome, and time:

> The "progression" of spirit . . . contains a "principle of exclusion." However, this exclusion does not lead to the detachment of what is excluded; this is *surmounted.*
>
> The "excluding" that belongs to the movement of development contains a relation to nonbeing. That is time, understood in terms of the self-inflating now (*das sich aufspreizende Jetzt*). (BT 434, tr. m.)

The principle of exclusion to which Heidegger here refers means for Hegel that spirit does not merely surpass itself, but increasingly realizes its own freedom. Hence a choice must continually be made between what does and what does not contribute to this self-actualization. Only spirit is capable of making this choice.[22] The "not" as that which makes no (further) contribution to the actualization of freedom is not, according to Hegel, excluded from history—that occurs only with nonessential, accidental facts—but is sublated and overcome.

Heidegger recognizes in this relation to the "not" the structure of the self-negating negation. He is not interested in how Hegel understands the difference between time and history, but sees in both movements the *same* relation to the "not": it is only admitted in order to be overcome. This specific "relation to nonbeing" entails that every "not" is increasingly annulled, so that history *in* all its detours can head directly for its goal. If the history of spirit is to occur in time in order to overcome time, it will have to "comply" with the structure of time as negation of a negation.

Heidegger in *Being and Time* further indicates only that the self-negating negation which constitutes the essential structure of spirit is itself grounded in primordial time (435). One may add that, according to Heidegger, Hegel's interpretation of history as a movement in which the "not" is only admitted in order to be sublated is grounded in the mode of primordial time in which Present has become predominant at the expense of the other temporal ecstases. An authentic modification of this same primordial time would make it possible to understand the proper movement of spirit, if we may still speak of spirit, as a movement in which the "not" is neither excluded nor sublated, but is actually admitted. The movement of history can then no longer be understood as a process of self-actualization. When thinking starts out from the temporality that makes possible every understanding of being, it is no longer appropriate to speak of a time in which spirit takes place, or, as Heidegger puts it, into which spirit "falls":

> "Spirit" does not fall *into* time, but factic existence "falls," as fallen, *out of* primordial, authentic temporality. This "falling," however, has its existential possibility in a mode of accomplishment that belongs to temporality.[23]

Although Heidegger does not say so in this passage, we know that this mode of temporality consists in the increasing predominance of Present.[24] This predominance first makes it possible for time to accomplish itself as now-time and as the time in which history occurs (436). Heidegger's analysis of temporality aims at understanding the relation between the dynamic of temporality and the different modes of "movement" which are grounded in this. However, if one wishes to read this in Heidegger's summary remarks in §82, one will have to look very carefully; he does not actually say this. Not yet. It is still there only as a germ, but a germ that hesitates to really manifest itself. That is something of which the germ that Hegel so often takes as an example is never capable—it can only move forward.

The way in which Heidegger in his first confrontation with Hegel seeks a concept of movement and history that cannot be thought from within the Hegelian perspective, I consider to be useful and important. The extremely sketchy text itself, however, evidently gives rise to questions. From a rather more critical point of view, I will now show that Heidegger and Hegel are closer than Heidegger suggests.

Being and Time and GA 21 do not permit us to infer whether Heidegger is aware of the difference between the pure structure of the concept as such and the way in which this structure concretizes itself in time and spirit. In his interpretation of Hegel's concept of time, Heidegger on one occasion calls time the objectively present concept:

> Time is . . . the differentiated self-differentiation that can be immediately found, the concept that "is there," that is, objectively present (*vorhanden*)." (434–35, tr. m.)

He also quotes the passage where Hegel characterizes the "ego" as the concept that really exists, but does not thematize the way in which Hegel understands the *difference* between the structure of time and that of spirit. As I said, Heidegger seems to regard the concept as identical to the structure of self-consciousness, and not to understand the latter as one of the manifestations of the concept as such.

Neither does he thematize the relation of Hegel's philosophy of nature to the *Logic*. His thesis that Hegel is not able to clarify the origin of now-time (435) is shortsighted. Hegel's concept of time is not independent, but is grounded in the structure of the concept as that is unfolded in the *Logic*.[25] Insofar as both Hegel's "concept" and Heidegger's "time" constitute a source or origin of vulgar time that cannot be reduced to a human capacity, there is a greater kinship between Hegel and Heidegger than the latter acknowledges—both basic concepts constitute fundamental conditions of possibility of the appearance of reality as such.[26]

Heidegger thus seems not to see—or not to want to say—that time and spirit as they are understood by Hegel *both* spring from the concept as such. It is not enough to understand their relation by means of the formal principle of the self-negating negation. Spirit can only accomplish itself as history because the pure concept has always already distinguished itself into concept on the one hand (being, essence, and concept) and time and space on the other. The concept *as* time brings about the externality that makes possible, but also constantly thwarts, the development of the idea (as spirit). Spirit develops from out of nature by increasingly overcoming the power of time and *can* only accomplish itself in its strife against externality. Time tears finite beings away from what they have become. Spirit, by contrast, is able to always remain identical to itself *in* the movement in which it divides itself within itself, and thus to resist the power of time. The history of finite spirit is in my view determined by the countering forces of the concept as such and the time that the concept has distinguished from itself in order to actualize itself as idea.[27] If that is the case, then Heidegger in *Being and Time* is wrong to suggest that Hegel understands the movement of the history of spirit by means of natural time (cf. GA 32:208). However, since Hegel himself primarily thematizes time in his philosophy of nature, he does pave the way to this misunderstanding.

The way in which Hegel understands the movement of spirit by means of a fundamental interplay of forces, then, is not entirely foreign to the way in which Heidegger understands the tendency of temporality to let its ecstases be overshadowed by Present. Heidegger's concept of time, however, allows him to thematize a movement which has neither the structure of becoming (nature) nor that of increasing self-unfolding (spirit). Later texts will confirm that Heidegger understands the movement of the pure concept as a movement in which a "not" that cannot be incorporated is excluded from the outset. From Heidegger's temporal perspective it becomes possible to understand history as an event in which a primordial possibility always—or increasingly—threatens to be lost in favor of that which actually unfolds itself. If the "past" and "future" of a historical movement really resist the realm of Present, the beginning of the movement can in no way guarantee its good end. This makes it in principle impossible for the strife between the force and its counterforce, however one wishes to further concretize this, to be decided. This is what grants the history where this strife takes place its radically finite character. Since Present, which constitutes the time-space of this history, always threatens to bring origin and future within its realm, Heidegger considers that philosophy has done little if any justice to the finitude that also characterizes its own history.

9.3 From Now-Time to Temporality

Within the limits of *Being and Time* Heidegger cannot avoid that one reads his interpretation of time independently of its context; what is really new in his conception of time, temporality as the horizon for the understanding of being, was after all only to have been thematized in the third division. In the course *The Metaphysical Foundations of Logic* from 1928, Heidegger explicitly distances his own thinking from the "usual isolated philosophical speculation about time."[28] He asserts here that his analysis of temporality is not independent, but is guided by the insight that the understanding of being is somehow related to time (GA 26:178). The analytic of Dasein itself is one of the possible ways to gain access to the problem of temporality.

When Heidegger has seen this way reaching a dead end, he chooses soon after, in the second part of GA 24, a different starting point: the concept of time as first articulated by Aristotle. In this course Heidegger traces back, more clearly than in *Being and Time*, "vulgar" time to temporality. He tries to show how the different manifestations of time—which are partly also thematized in traditional philosophy—originate in a "time" that itself hardly deserves the name time. Since he again fails to really achieve his aim, the different phases in the analysis threaten to focus attention on themselves, and thus thwart the movement of thought.

I will sketch out this movement here only in order to show that the issue of vulgar time did not deserve all the attention it has received. The aspects of Heidegger's concept of time which I thematized in part I will therefore now be repeated briefly, starting out from a different point. In this I follow the structure of part II of GA 24; this will make it easier to clarify the systematic place of the different aspects of the analysis of time in *Being and Time*.

Heidegger considers Aristotle's conception of time to exemplify the philosophical interpretation of the everyday concept of time (BT 421; GA 24:324f). He conceives this time as a series of now-moments, which constitute the constantly shifting border between past and future. In everyday life, we always calculate with time, namely, by comparing the events that occur with the continuous, even movement of the sundial or the hands of the clock. But the counting of time is not the only way to experience time, and for Heidegger certainly not the most primordial. In everyday life we also always already take account of time, without having to look at the clock. The time that shows forth in this practical involvement Heidegger calls world-time (BT 414; GA 24:370). This time, unlike objective time, is meaningful: a certain point in time is not identical to another, but is suitable or not suitable for doing or not doing something. In everyday life we experience a time that has a certain "span," can last for a short or a long time, and is datable (GA 24:381). This meaningful time cannot, according to Heidegger, be thematized from the perspective of the tradition (BT 422).

The first phase of Heidegger's analysis of time thus consists in a kind of phenomenological description of how we experience time in our everyday life, which precedes the objectifying measuring or counting. Here one can recognize the difference between handiness and objective presence. Heidegger then tries to trace back these modes of *experiencing* time to a dynamic temporal structure that is the condition of possibility of all our acting and knowing. He thus turns to the being of Dasein. Every involvement with beings, according to Heidegger, is made possible by an anticipatory understanding of possibilities and a familiarity with an already existing interrelatedness. As we know, he calls this structure the making-present that awaits and retains. In one single movement, Dasein outstretches itself in these three directions.[29] This specific dynamic of anticipating and retaining gets stuck at the moment when beings are objectified. This makes the structure of world vanish into the background and allows beings to appear as objects to a knowing subject (BT 360f). It is also only this change of perspective that allows time itself to appear as now-time (GA 24:383f).

Heidegger then traces back the temporal structure of the involvement of Dasein with innerworldly beings to the temporality that grounds the being of Dasein as such. In order to expect, hope, or fear something, Dasein must always already be open for the possible as such. Because Dasein is always already ahead of itself, it is able to go toward its most proper possibilities. This is always accompanied by an equally primordial involvement with its own factic situation, which makes possible every actual remembering or forgetting.[30] The dynamic that allows Dasein to outstretch itself toward that which it always already has been and that which yet remains to come is grounded in the interplay of the temporal ecstases Future, Past, and Present. In this primordial temporal dynamic, Present always threatens to overshadow the proper character of the other ecstases; that is the temporal condition of possibility of fallenness.

This mode of temporality does not, however, have the last word. The concrete involvement with things, with fellow human beings and with itself, is only possible if Dasein from the outset is familiar with the being of beings. The temporality that grounds this understanding of being as such, and constitutes its purest or most primordial manifestation, Heidegger calls, as we know, Temporality (BT 19, 23; GA 24:429). The three dimensions or ecstases of Temporality delimit the realm within which something like "being" can first appear.

With this turning, which is only prepared in *Being and Time* and briefly indicated in GA 24, Heidegger again leaves behind the domain of the being of Dasein. This domain as it were opens up the hardly accessible terrain of the temporality that grounds the different modifications of ontology. The dynamic that occurs on the level of Temporality also consists in the increasing "narrowing" into Present of the realm within which being can be understood. A thinking that could succeed in resisting this dominant tendency would be able to do justice to the fundamental absence that permeates the essential as such.[31]

Thus, by starting out from the vulgar concept of time we have again reached the question concerning the temporality of thinking itself. There is hence an intrinsic relation between what Heidegger understands by temporality and the problem of method as the way in which something, whatever it is, is given the opportunity to manifest itself as itself. He regards *Hegel's* method as a mode of thinking which hinders the primordial "not" from appearing as itself—that is to say, as that which resists the power of the concept:

> But . . . why nihilation (*das Nichten*) comes to the fore through this dialectic but at the same time is veiled in its essence, cannot be discussed here.[32]

When Heidegger uses this standard expression, one has to listen carefully to what is kept silent. In his course on Hegel, Heidegger calls *Being and Time* the preparation that is needed to venture "a confrontation with real philosophy in its core" (GA 32:212). Hegel is then named. Because Heidegger, if he wished to elucidate the difference between his own philosophy and that of Hegel, would also have to admit his kinship with Hegel, this is a dangerous enterprise.[33] In *Being and Time* the confrontation has indeed hardly begun.

10

The Threefold of Thinking: Heidegger's and Hegel's Conception of Method

In chapter 4 I showed how Heidegger's methodical difference between a primordial structure and its inauthentic and authentic modification is grounded in threefold temporality. In this chapter I will again thematize the temporal ground of philosophical method and will now base my interpretation of Heidegger's relation to Hegel on this.

Heidegger's course on the *Phenomenology of Spirit* from 1930/31 (GA 32) is the only course entirely devoted to Hegel. Since it is the only text in which Heidegger indicates that Hegel's method is also grounded in temporality, it will be the main focus of this chapter. The question concerning the relation between the phenomenological method and dialectic already arises in Heidegger's earliest courses, especially in *Basic Problems of Phenomenology* from 1919/20 (GA 58). This course will be thematized in the first section.

GA 32 indicates a possible answer to the question concerning philosophy's own method; this is the answer to which Heidegger was on the way in *Being and Time*. During the following years, Heidegger must have realized the one-sidedness of the *question* concerning the method—this leads him to the insight that the projective preconception of being that guides thinking ultimately does not originate in thinking, but in being itself insofar as it tries to make itself understandable.

This turning may be observed more clearly than in GA 32 in two later texts on the *Phenomenology of Spirit*. In *Hegel's Concept of Experience* and part II of *Hegel* (GA 68)—both from the early 1940s—Heidegger presents an interpretation of the introduction of the *Phenomenology of Spirit*. These texts are very closely related to each other and to GA 32, and they will be discussed separately only insofar as they differ from this course. In this way the transition from the early to the later work can once again be briefly indicated; GA 58 and Heidegger's interpretation of the introduction of the *Phenomenology of Spirit* from 1942/43 constitute as it were the origin and future of Heidegger's course on Hegel from 1930/31. With regard to Heidegger's interpretation of the *Phenomenology of Spirit*, I will concentrate mainly on the passages that reveal the deconstructive aspect of Heidegger's interpretation.

10.1 Traces of the Dialectic in Heidegger's Early Work

Thinking means distinguishing. What something truly is, is only adequately expressed by the movement in which it divides itself within itself, brings about an opposition between itself and the other of itself, and then sublates this opposition. Only if the form of thinking is threefold can the difference between the one and the other be incorporated in a higher unity in such a way that it is preserved as relative difference. This principle can, however, deteriorate into an external schema:

> Formalism has, it is true, also taken possession of triplicity and adhered to its empty *schema*; the shallow ineptitude and barrenness of modern philosophical *construction* so-called, that consists in nothing but fastening this schema on to everything without concept . . . and employing it for an external arrangement, has made the said form tedious and given it a bad name. Yet the triteness of this use cannot detract from its inner worth. (L II, 565/837)

This is Hegel, who seems to anticipate the words of Heidegger. In his early courses, Heidegger also distinguishes between a dialectic that is able to express the "not" in a primordial way and the dialectical machinery that, without considering its origin, blindly goes its own way. Heidegger emphasizes, however, that a danger lurks within *any* dialectic. With respect to the formal meaning of the "not,"

> the dangerousness of any dialectic reveals itself, regardless of whether it has gained a critical awareness of the significance and the origin of its interpretation (which in fact runs counter to its own meaning) or (which is therefore most often the case) of whether it proceeds like a machine, and is inclined to be blind to itself . . . and to ward off discussion. (GA 61:146)

Whereas Hegel does not consider the formalistic *application* of the dialectic to threaten the inner worth of this method, Heidegger criticizes the way in which the dialectic as such relates to the "not." He admits, however, that even phenomenology cannot entirely proceed without the dialectic; the phenomenological "seeing" alone does not suffice to articulate the dynamic of factic life.

In his course from 1921/22 Heidegger characterizes factic life as fall (*Sturz*) (GA 61:144). Life is such that it initially throws itself into the world and is not aware of itself (148). This mode of existing constitutes the "not" with respect to the primordial possibilities of life, but as such essentially belongs to life itself: life has in itself the character of a detour (88, 145). In order to do justice to the "not" of factic existence, philosophy will have to thematize first the primordial possibilities of this life, second the way in which this initially and mostly does not realize itself (*Ruinanz*), and third the possibility of resisting this tendency (*Gegenruinanz*).

We could say that in the inauthentic modification of existence a contradiction has arisen between the formal structure of existence and the way in which this actually accomplishes itself. In an authentic modification of existence, on the other hand, this formal structure comes into its own. Heidegger realizes that this tripartite structure is not entirely foreign to the *dialectical* threefoldness. In GA 58 he suggests that phenomenology has to face the lack of that which actually appears:

> Factic life manifests itself in a specific *deformation*. This taking shape of life in objectifications must be undone. That is why one constantly says "no" in phenomenological descriptions.—This is the basic meaning of Hegel's dialectical method (thesis, antithesis, synthesis).—In this method the negation gains a creating force, which is the driving force of the *concepts of expression*. (GA 58:240, cf. 148)

Heidegger here comes into close proximity with Hegel. Only when that which initially appears is understood as deformation of a primordial, preceding structure that might also modify itself in an authentic way, can a phenomenon like human life show forth as itself. What initially appears is then no longer independent, but is understood as part of the movement in which it comes about and has to give up its self-sufficiency. It takes more than an immediate intuition to make the "not" of human existence "transparent" in such a way that the origin and future of this inauthentic modification can manifest themselves.[1]

According to Heidegger, however, the dialectic may not pretend to bring about meaning of itself. But because that which is seen must also be *determined*, the dialectic *is* suitable "as the form . . . in which pure intuition is expressed" (184). Heidegger calls it a characteristic of "absolute seeing" that the intuited phenomena "can only be fully expressed phenomenologically by a counter-seeing" (110). What can be seen only manifests itself by going back and forth between what a matter is in itself and what belongs essentially as "not" to the matter itself.

When the dialectic is assigned its proper place, says Heidegger at the end of his course, it becomes "dia-hermeneutics" (263). This method regards the phenomena that it encounters as determined by a "not" in relation to primordial life. This primordial realm, which is the authentic theme of philosophy, may not as the general be separated from what is actually encountered. Phenomenology as it existed hitherto—and we know who is intended by this—does indeed yield essential, that is to say, eidetic knowledge, but unduly conceives of "essence" as genus (*Gattung*). Heidegger will thus have to seek a *different concept* of essence, which not only pertains to the general, but encompasses the different moments of factic life.[2] Thus Heidegger, turning away from Husserl, comes face to face with Hegel, who like no other succeeded in thematizing concrete and historical life in a philosophical way:

> If one chases the problems of history from the perspective of phenomenology, one does not view life in its liveliness. That is the significance of Hegel's philosophy for phenomenology. This philosophy should not, however, be comprehended in a shallow way. . . . One rather must seek to fathom Hegel's ultimate motives. (238, cf. 246)

The dialectic is able to bring forth the dynamic of human life; life that actually accomplishes itself is here regarded in the light of its origin and future. With respect to this meaning of the dialectical method, Heidegger acknowledges his kinship to Hegel. In order to understand the *difference* between dia-hermeneutics and the speculative dialectic, Heidegger will have to investigate wherein Hegel's dialectic is grounded. We have seen that Heidegger repeats this question at the end of *Being and Time*. Two years after GA 58 Heidegger asserts that Hegel's method does not consider its own provenance and, fleeing from it, establishes itself as autonomous (GA 61:150). Evidently, Heidegger here attributes characteristics of fallenness to Hegel's philosophy. He maintains that authentic philosophy, by contrast, is always prepared to engage in the strife with its own factic ruinance (153). Even though Heidegger does not take account of the fact that Hegel does indeed understand his methodical principle as based on the structure of the concept as such, it is perhaps right to assert that Hegel's philosophy does not bend back far enough toward its own origin.

It is 1922. Heidegger is wrestling with the question as to how he can develop a concept of essence that on the one hand does not pertain only to the general, but on the other hand is also not identical to Hegel's modification of the traditional concept of essence. The way in which the dialectic brings the "not" into play makes it possible for Hegel to understand life and history as movement, yet only as a very specific kind of movement.[3] Heidegger will only be able to distinguish his own methodical principle from Hegel's by means of the concept of temporality that he develops around 1923. The question concerning the difference between Hegel's dialectic and dia-hermeneutics is for the time being deferred. Only Heidegger's course on the *Phenomenology of Spirit* from 1930/31 offers suggestions which allow the relation between Hegel's and Heidegger's method to be understood on the basis of Heidegger's concept of temporality.

10.2 Absolvent Knowing

Whenever Heidegger discusses the *Phenomenology of Spirit* he assigns this work a central position. He repeatedly refers to the fact that Hegel published the *Phenomenology of Spirit* in 1807 as the first part of his scientific system. The second part was to have covered the logic and the philosophy of nature and spirit.[4] But when the first part of the *Science of Logic* is published in 1812, it is no longer presented as the second part of a system: in the meantime the *Phenomenology of Spirit* has been excluded from the system, which now begins with the *Logic* and later takes shape in the *Encyclopaedia*. As we know, within that new system the *Phenomenology of Spirit* is assigned a subordinate position in the philosophy of spirit (GA 68:70).

Heidegger considers this change to be a "decisive swerving back into the basic constitution of metaphysics hitherto" (71). He maintains that the *Phenomenology of Spirit* played an "all-determining part" (96) in the system proposed by Hegel in 1807, and thus fails to appreciate that Hegel from the very beginning regarded this introductory part of his scientific system as a necessary preparation. Heidegger clearly tries to rescue the *Phenomenology of Spirit* from the later system, dominated as it is by the *Logic*. This allows him to affirm his kinship with the "unique" *Phenomenology of Spirit* and to seriously engage with Hegel.[5] He now protects Hegel's work from the formal dialectic of "Hegelianism, which was dead from the beginning" (GA 32:129, cf. 162). This does not mean, however, that Heidegger is not intending a deconstruction of the *Phenomenology of Spirit*. He takes Hegel to understand the being of beings by starting out from the *logos* or the concept (17–18, 92). In order to radically criticize this starting point, Heidegger tries in GA 32 initially to indicate what his thinking has in common with that of Hegel. As one might expect, this text does not enter into a real confrontation with Hegel either.[6]

Heidegger indicates how the mode of consciousness that constitutes the starting point of the *Phenomenology of Spirit* step by step and of its own accord manages to retrieve itself from its confinement. Thus a knowing turns out to be possible that frees itself from that in which it was initially lost:

> For knowledge to be qualitatively other than relative knowledge . . . it must not remain bound but must liberate and ab-solve itself (*sich losmacht, sich ablöst*) from what it knows and yet as so ab-solved, as absolute, still be a knowing. (21, tr. m.)

Spirit's "absolvence from the relative" culminates, as Heidegger remarks, in absolute, infinite knowing.[7] By using the word absolvence—which for good reason pertains to the movement rather than the result—Heidegger brings out the kinship between his own thinking and that of Hegel. Heidegger also tries to free his thinking from the confined perspective of traditional philosophy. He can therefore regard absolvence as the point where his path crosses Hegel's, albeit only in order to then take an entirely different direction (cf. 92). While Hegel, according to Heidegger, unduly conceals the *finite* character of absolvent, self-freeing knowing (92, cf. 195), Heidegger seeks a thinking which rather accomplishes the absolvent movement in such a way that it faces its insurmountable finitude. Heidegger calls the finitude of the discursive knowledge that is overcome in Hegel's absolute knowing a nonprimordial mode of finitude (55). It is not *this* mode of finitude that he wants to defend (56).

Heidegger seems to conceive absolute knowing and his own thinking as the inauthentic and authentic modification respectively of a radically finite absolvence. If every mode of inauthenticity is grounded in the predominance of the temporal ecstasis Present, then Hegel's philosophy must also remain dependent on the horizon that determines the mode of consciousness which is related to things. That this is the case is mentioned, but not really elaborated, in the texts on the *Phenomenology of Spirit*.

GA 32 does not thematize the *Logic*, which according to the 1807 plan was to follow the *Phenomenology of Spirit* and thus constitute the second part of the system. Here absolute knowing, having come into its own element in the first part, was to have truly unfolded itself.[8] Heidegger remarks, however, that his interpretation of the *Phenomenology* already contains indications concerning the meaning of the *Logic* (25). We could even say that Heidegger's interpretation of the *Phenomenology* concentrates mainly on the "logical" side of Hegel's philosophy. Thus, Heidegger says that he wishes to focus attention on "the *inner law* of the work" (63). This law, he notes a little further on, consists in the infinite affirmation that accomplishes itself as the negation of a negation (66). He asserts that this law grounds both "the kind of dynamic which inheres in the occurring of the history of spirit" (63, tr. m.) and absolute knowing itself (cf. 66). Since every method is guided by a preceding projective preconception, the difference between method and content is as relative for Heidegger as it is for Hegel. Heidegger is mainly interested in the character of that preceding projective preconception itself. His remarks on Hegel's method in GA 32 may elucidate how he tries to deconstruct the perspective that guides Hegel's method.

10.3 The Problem of Method in *Hegel's Phenomenology of Spirit*

Most of GA 32 is taken up by a sympathetic interpretation of the first part of the *Phenomenology of Spirit*, in which consciousness develops from sense certainty into understanding and self-consciousness. Although Heidegger sees that consciousness only becomes truly free in reason, he holds that the character of this liberating movement can also be shown with respect to the transition from consciousness to self-consciousness.[9] His interpretation, which I here briefly summarize, initially follows Hegel quite closely.

The *Phenomenology of Spirit* systematically unfolds the different possible modes of knowing. The "history" of these modes begins with the most one-sided and empty mode of knowledge—namely, a consciousness that merely relates to a "this-here"—and ultimately results in absolute knowing. Heidegger rightly asserts that the poorest mode of knowledge never occurs as such, but that the analysis must initially disregard the other elements of actual knowledge (80, 102). Once this poorest knowledge has been taken as the starting point, Hegel no longer has to intervene, but can just look on how knowledge increasingly frees itself from its one-sidedness. Since even the simplest sense certainty is already a mode of absolute knowing (47), but has not yet actualized itself as such, this mode of knowing is dominated by the longing to annul the contradiction between what it actually is and what it essentially is (cf. 127). Hence the movement of the *Phenomenology* consists in the increasing sublation of the difference between consciousness and absolute knowing (38). This means that consciousness increasingly withdraws from the world, turns toward itself, and ultimately entirely annuls the difference between itself and that to which it relates. The difference between the spectator of the development of consciousness and the consciousness that goes through that—painful—development is then also sublated (cf. 188).

Heidegger repeatedly asserts that Hegel lets consciousness develop in the light of an absolvent projective preconception that precedes the actual analysis (129, 163). The way in which Hegel systematically orders the different modes of consciousness is based on the principle whereby everything that is tries to sublate the difference between what it is in itself and what it has actually become. If this dialectical movement is conceived as infinite return to itself (111, 113), the different manifestations of consciousness may be systematically ordered.

The "movement" in which consciousness comes toward itself as self-consciousness, but has not yet reached that manifestation, may then appear as the movement in which the simplest and most immediate relation to things turns into perception and understanding. Perception and understanding are thus no longer conceived as independent, but as moments of a movement in which consciousness is forced to leave behind its most elementary certainties. This movement of consciousness may be taken as an example to elucidate Hegel's methodical principle. This is what Heidegger in fact does.

From the perspective of absolvent knowing a phenomenon is always divided into three different moments—namely, the moment in which no difference has yet been enacted, the moment in which a difference has been enacted, and the moment in which that difference has been sublated. Heidegger remarks that this movement can also be expressed by means of the distinction between the immediate, the "middle," and the immediate that is the result of the mediation by that middle:

> Hence, absolvent cognition proceeds in a threefold (*in einem Dreischritt*).[10]

This methodical threefold allows the different aspects of consciousness to be unfolded. Perception then appears as the transitional middle which on the one hand refers back to its origin in sense certainty and on the other refers forward to understanding (115–16). On this Heidegger says:

> Perception knows no rest. . . . It *is* only *what* it is in its *Past and its Future*. If we here deliberately point to the *temporal* moments in the "being" of what is to be known in an absolvent manner, we do so knowing full well that we are going beyond Hegel . . . in a direction which, if actually taken, would turn against him. But this would only happen if the fundamental problematic, that is to say, the problematic of time, is unfolded *from out of the problem of being itself*. (116, tr. m.)

This is a rare and crucial passage, where Heidegger at the decisive moment again does *not* take the indicated direction. Again there is no space for unfolding the problem of temporality. It therefore remains unclear how Heidegger, having acknowledged his kinship with Hegel, thinks he can overcome the confinement of his perspective. He does, however, say that Hegel's methodical threefold ensues from the structure of the judgment, in which different aspects of something are distinguished in order to bring about the unity of that which is distinguished. He maintains that this structure fully manifests itself in the "ego."[11] Whereas Hegel thus understands "being" by starting out from the *logos* or the concept, Heidegger himself claims to understand being by starting out from time (143). According to the above passage, however, the "articulation of the dynamic of the dialectical movement" (173, tr. m.) is no less grounded in the temporality that Heidegger does not want to elaborate than the threefold articulation of his own thinking.

Heidegger evidently understands the three moments that ground the movement of the concept—and hence also Hegel's method—as *temporal* moments. When Hegel asserts that absolute knowing has overcome time and enacts itself as pure circular movement, Heidegger would not disagree.[12] But he maintains that this circular movement is itself grounded in a modification of temporality which has very little to do with the time that is overcome by the concept.

I showed in part I how the temporal ecstases Past, Present, and Future delimit the space within which being or the essential is understood. This background allows philosophy to thematize, for instance, the essential moments of consciousness and history. I am convinced that Heidegger wanted to show how Hegel's methodical principle is grounded in a temporal projective preconception in which Present overshadows the proper character of the other ecstases. The primordial threefoldness that is brought about by Temporality somehow shines through in the dialectical threefold: in it, the primordial threefoldness has modified itself in an inauthentic way. If the origin and future of a movement only show forth in the light of Present, this movement will be conceived as a movement that initially alienates itself from its origin, but ultimately is able to turn back to its own starting point.

The beginning that already has everything within itself will then certainly be able to accomplish itself. However much the necessary detour also constitutes a "not" in relation to that which is left behind, and however much this path is characterized by pain and contrariety, it is a path that ultimately will succeed in overcoming every resistance. In the light of the increasing predominance of Present, the most essential movement can thus merely appear as the increasing actualization of what was always already there. Only then can the transition from the one manifestation to the next appear as necessary advance:

> It should be noted that we understand the transition from perception to understanding only if we register in advance that . . . perception is already placed in the perspective of absolute knowledge; only then is further advance a necessity. (138–39)

If the most essential movement is advance as return, then the obstacles that spirit encounters along its way will always appear as surmountable.[13] Even if, as Heidegger remarks, Hegel considers that it essentially belongs to consciousness to "stick to its own place" (161), the absolvent movement will from Hegel's perspective always find a way through. Heidegger regards the principle of the self-negating negation—although he does not explicitly say this in

GA 32—as a principle that does not do justice to the proper, radically finite movement of the being of Dasein, of history, and of being as such. He will therefore have to intervene in a different manner than Hegel in order to let this movement accomplish itself of itself.

10.4 Heidegger's Modification of Hegel's Methodical Principle

We have seen that Heidegger in §82 of *Being and Time* doubts whether Hegel's philosophy is indeed grounded in a primordial ontological basis (BT 435). It is now possible to elucidate why he takes this not to be the case. Hegel interprets everything that he sees by means of the structure of the concept as negation of a negation, but is not able to see how the movement of the concept itself is made possible by the inauthentic modification of Temporality that dominates the entire history of metaphysics. This is the time which, according to Heidegger, has more power than the concept (GA 32:144). The way in which Hegel looks on now turns out to be less neutral than it appears:

> Indeed, we read again and again in Hegel that . . . we only "look on" (*zusehen*). . . . This is indeed the way it is. But the question is: What is this "looking on"? . . . This looking on is a looking with the eyes of absolute knowledge. (75, tr. m., cf. 119)

In GA 32 and in the later texts on the introduction, Heidegger quite extensively thematizes the question as to how far every philosophical looking on contributes something to what it sees. In doing this, he draws on passages in the *Phenomenology of Spirit* where Hegel asserts that thinking does not have to contribute its own criteria to the testing of the development of consciousness: consciousness compares itself with its own concept and continually tries to sublate the difference between what it essentially is and what it has actually become.[14] This movement unfolds itself for the eye of absolute knowing—but not as easily as it seems. For when consciousness experiences the untruth of that to which it relates, it cannot merely turn to something else, but has to thematize this insufficient knowledge itself. Only then, according to Hegel, does the new object necessarily ensue from the previous one. In this way,

> the new object shows itself to have come about through a *reversal of consciousness itself*. This way of looking at the matter is some-

> thing contributed by us (*ist unsere Zutat*), by means of which the succession of experiences through which consciousness passes is raised into a scientific progression—but it is not known to the consciousness that we are observing.[15]

The necessary sequence of the manifestations of consciousness thus accomplishes itself behind the back of consciousness itself. Only absolute knowing sees how consciousness is compelled to abandon the truth it had attained and to comply with the dialectical movement of the absolute concept. Just as transient beings are compelled to let themselves be dragged along by time, consciousness that is brought forth cannot resist the power of the pure concept. In GA 68 Heidegger emphasizes that the concept does not intervene in consciousness in an external manner:

> If, however, the overturning is our "addition" (*Zutat*) to the "looking at" (*Zusehen*), then this "addition" "adds" nothing foreign to consciousness. The addition merely drives the looking-at to the enactment of its innermost essence. The addition is the first and highest act of the looking-at, which thus watches in advance, that is to say, takes care that . . . the absolute is being respected and that only the absolute and nothing else comes to appearance.[16]

Every seeing, however much it has freed itself from the one-sidedness of natural consciousness, enacts itself, according to Heidegger, within a given horizon. Something like "pure immediate description" is impossible in philosophy (GA 32:74). Heidegger thus knows just as well as Hegel that the seeing of the things themselves always requires a contribution from thinking. This contributed construction may not be arbitrary (71), but must accord with the movement of the essential as such. Also in this, the two thinkers are still in agreement.

This means for Hegel that philosophy may not cling to the opposition between essence and that in which it appears, but must accord with the dialectical movement in which the essential determines itself. We know that Hegel chooses the term "concept" to designate this movement. *As* concept, the essential itself brings about the otherness in which it appears and through which it returns to itself.

Like Hegel, Heidegger criticizes the static opposition between essence and existence.[17] Heidegger, however, also considers Hegel's sublation of essence into the concept to still be an inauthentic modification of what he himself understands by the essential. Heidegger also understands the essential as movement, but not as a movement in which every "not" that appears is subsequently sublated. For the essential that comes toward itself without ultimately becoming identical to itself, Heidegger chooses the word "being." Thus, whereas the Hegelian concept replaces what is usually understood by "essence," Heidegger's dissatisfaction with the traditional concept of essence leads him to return to what he calls "being." This means that Hegel's "concept" and Heidegger's "being" both pertain to the movement in which the essential accomplishes itself. What Heidegger understands by "being" thus encompasses more than Hegel's concept of being. According to Heidegger, Hegel conceives "being" as "objective presence," that is to say, as a *specific mode* of what he himself understands by "being" (59). Heidegger concludes:

> Thus, from first to last being means something radically different for Hegel than it does for us. But this is not the difference between two points of view that are side by side but indifferent. . . . Rather, it is difference *itself*, which is possible only . . . through commitment to what is simple, unique, one, and essential. (60)

The "one" refers to being as such, which from Hegel's metaphysical perspective can only manifest itself as presence. Heidegger does not, however, mention here that "being" for Hegel constitutes only one mode of the absolute concept. It is highly important therefore to investigate the relation between what Heidegger understands by "being" and what Hegel understands by "concept." Only once does Heidegger say anything about this relation:

> The named infinity is the *absolute concept*; it is . . . the universal which is in itself the differentiated in its difference and is therefore simultaneously unity. Hegel says of the absolute concept that it is "the simple essence of life, the soul of the world," but *we* can say that it is *the essence of being*. (180, tr. m.)

Heidegger here seems to mean that the absolute concept is a way in which being enacts itself, but only *insofar as* being is understood as presence. "Being" and "concept" in Hegel's sense, then, constitute for Heidegger merely two sides of the same coin; both the presence of something and the self-presence proper to the concept are only possible if the essential as such is already understood as presence.[18] While even absolute knowing is not able to turn itself to the predominance of Present that takes place behind its back, it is precisely this turning that Heidegger tries to accomplish.

By means of a modification of Hegel's dialectical threefold, Heidegger tries to let himself be guided by Temporality in such a way that it casts a different light on the way in which the essential accomplishes itself. When thinking accords with the primordial threefoldness of time, being will not appear as constant presence and its movement will not appear as the increasing coming toward itself of what was always already there. Origin and future of the movement then withdraw from the realm of Present, and pervade this realm only as the radically absent in relation to every presence. When Present restrains itself in favor of Past and Future, the essential can appear as a primordial possibility, which in no way guarantees its own actualization and constantly threatens to be lost in the movement in which it tries to come toward itself. The counterstriving character of the way in which the essential accomplishes itself then no longer appears as a subordinate moment in the movement in which a primordial unity actualizes itself, but as an event that has always already begun and cannot be sublated.

Against *this* background Heidegger tries to thematize the radical finitude of the movement in which Dasein turns away from itself and comes toward itself. Just as in the *Phenomenology of Spirit* Hegel's looking on ensures that the absolute, and not something else, comes to appear, so Heidegger's contribution should ensure that being itself and the being of Dasein appear as characterized by a counterstriving that does not serve the purpose of an imminent reconciliation. In Heidegger's eyes—and these eyes are *different* from those of absolute knowing—authenticity means nothing other than the attempt to admit and endure the radical "not" that is proper to factic existence, that is to say, to affirm the insurmountable finitude of human existence.

In order to bring to light the being of Dasein as radically finite dynamic, Heidegger as much as Hegel has to distinguish between a beginning, a middle, and an end. Only when the factic turning away from itself appears against the background of Dasein's proper possibilities on the one hand, and a possible appropriation of those possibilities on the other, can this turning away be revealed as the predominant tendency. Heidegger will have to be continually on guard to ensure that from the perspective of his own threefold the preceding and future moments will not be understood as modes of presence.

I pointed out earlier that the difference between a primordial structure and its inauthentic and authentic modification cannot entirely prevent Heidegger in *Being and Time* from presenting the movement of Dasein as a kind of development (cf. HW 132 / HCE 53). This perhaps shows that it is almost impossible to distinguish the beginning, middle, and end of a movement in such a way that the beginning appears as a possibility which is always already past, the "middle" as the mode in which that possibility realizes itself in an inauthentic way, and the end as a possibility which does not increasingly actualize itself, but in that movement is preserved *as* possibility.

10.5 *Being and Time* and the *Phenomenology of Spirit*

In GA 32 Heidegger calls the *Phenomenology of Spirit* "the fundamental ontology of absolute ontology," and indeed the last possible foundation of ontology (204). He thus acknowledges the kinship between the *Phenomenology of Spirit* and *Being and Time*. Whereas Hegel founds the possibility of an absolute ontology, Heidegger in *Being and Time* seeks a fundamental structure that not only makes possible an authentic mode of life and thinking, but also constantly threatens it. This means that his own fundamental ontology tries at once to reveal the radical finitude of every ontology and to understand why philosophy is usually not able to face this finitude.

When Heidegger rightly defends himself against the critique that the problematic of *Being and Time* already exists in the work of Hegel (GA 32:208–9), it does not follow from this that his own fundamental ontology is entirely foreign to that of Hegel. In the retrieving repetition of the metaphysical tradition that occurs in *Being and Time*, Heidegger tries to do justice to the primordial possibilities which in this tradition could only appear in a concealed way.[19] Thus, Heidegger largely adopts the structure of the *Phenomenology of Spirit* in *Being and Time*, albeit *for the purpose of* deconstructing the projective preconception on which that structure is based.

Since the *Phenomenology of Spirit* is based on a movement that already indwells consciousness itself, it can reveal human spirit without external intervention. That is, of course, also the ideal of Heidegger's phenomenology. Just as Hegel lets consciousness, which itself is already a manifestation of absolute knowing, develop step by step into absolute knowing, so Heidegger lets Dasein, starting from its everyday involvement with innerworldly beings, gradually gain insight into its own being and the meaning of being as such.[20] I have shown how also in *Being and Time* this was to have led to a concept of philosophy itself as a specific possibility of human existence. The third division of *Being and Time* occupies the same place as the *Logic* in the system of which the *Phenomenology* was to have been the first part. In fact—as I mentioned earlier—Heidegger in 1928 suggests that fundamental ontology should turn back to the totality of beings that *also* constitutes the theme of the positive sciences. He notes that a metaphysics of human existence might also fit in here.[21] Thus, Heidegger explicitly goes along with the difference between a *metaphysica generalis* and a *metaphysica specialis* that Hegel had already adopted as the difference between logic on the one hand and philosophy of nature and spirit on the other.

However, Heidegger's retrieving repetition also entails a critical renewal. He tries to free Dasein from its world in such a way that it is finally no longer involved with its proper being or with being as such, but with the temporality that grounds every understanding of being. From a perspective guided by Temporality, fallenness can no longer be regarded as a surmountable moment in the self-actualization of spirit. While Hegel lets knowing become increasingly conscious of its own infinity, Heidegger by contrast brings Dasein to understand that every movement which is enacted *meta logou* is radically finite.

Hegel is no less aware of the essential obstinacy of consciousness, but his projective preconception does not allow that resistance to appear other than as a subordinate moment in the absolving movement of absolute knowledge. For only when the mediation lets the unity that precedes every opposition come toward itself, can the achieved result serve as the starting point for a subsequent movement and is it guaranteed that the whole of possibilities will develop in a systematic way. Heidegger considers this *logical* movement—which according to Hegel must necessarily accomplish itself in history—to be incapable of thematizing the proper character of those movements that are animated by the *logos*.

A deconstruction of Hegel's logical principle should, in my view, start out from the *Science of Logic*. In one form or another, the *Logic* also already grounds the *Phenomenology of Spirit*. As I said, Heidegger in fact restricts himself to interpreting the *Phenomenology of Spirit*, although he ultimately intends the most fundamental, "logical" aspects of Hegel's philosophy. This means that Heidegger does not sufficiently distinguish the way in which consciousness develops into absolute knowing from the movement of the concept as such, which only accomplishes itself *in* absolute knowing.[22] Even though Hegel designates the movement of the absolute as absolute subjectivity, he has already left behind what is usually understood by subject-philosophy. This is less evident from the *Phenomenology* than from the *Logic*.[23] Heidegger's interpretation of the introduction of the *Phenomenology of Spirit* from the early 1940s is in this respect less one-sided. This interpretation also makes clear how much Heidegger was aware of the analogies between the *Phenomenology of Spirit* and the analytic of Dasein.

10.6 The Obstinacy of Absolute Knowing

In *Hegel's Concept of Experience* Heidegger seems to closely follow the introduction of the *Phenomenology of Spirit*, just as sympathetically as in GA 32.[24] The result of his interpretation is that the consciousness at issue in Hegel's work sometimes becomes remarkably similar to Dasein. It is precisely this appropriation, however, that allows Heidegger to give a twist to the introduction that turns him against Hegel.

Hegel shows how the consciousness that has abandoned itself to what it is not contradicts its own concept. This self-contradiction is what compels consciousness to set itself in motion. Heidegger emphasizes that natural consciousness is not the same as the sensible consciousness from which the *Phenomenology* starts out, but manifests itself on all levels (HW 137 / HCE 62). This consciousness "presents, regardless of whether what is present is perceived by the senses, or is a nonsensible thought" (133/56, tr. m.). Later on, Heidegger interprets natural consciousness—as he says, cautiously and with some reservation—as ontic consciousness (161/105). Even when this consciousness directs itself toward its own knowing, he considers it to do this in an ontic way. In his view, this natural, representing consciousness can only fall prey to beings if from the outset it understands the being of beings: it is both ontic and preontological, but does not yet explicitly comprehend the being of beings.[25] The difference between Dasein's preontological understanding of being and its ontic involvement entails that natural consciousness tries to sublate that difference, that is to say: to become ontological. As preontological consciousness,

> it has already been brought on the way to its truth. But on the way, it is already constantly turning back, and remains "for it." . . . It opposes the looking on (*das Zusehen*). (163–64/109, tr. m.)

Afraid of the absolute that manifests itself in this absolving movement, representational consciousness opposes the movement that compels it to abandon its certainties (149/82). Heidegger remarks that this opposition is also often a proper characteristic of philosophy, which then clings to ordinary opinion (164/110). Insofar as consciousness steadfastly resists the movement that belongs to its own nature (146/78), philosophy must as it were let the absolvent movement occur behind the back of consciousness (174/127). The intervention of absolute knowing—enacted in the *Phenomenology*—compels consciousness to no longer oppose the experience that raises it above itself and leads it to the ontological perspective. Thus occurs the will of the absolute, which actualizes itself *in* the course of appearing knowing and needs this course to come into its own (151/85). Absolute knowing accords as it were with the will of the absolute and thus breaks the resistance of consciousness to its own self-sublation.

Heidegger refers repeatedly to the passage where Hegel remarks that the absolute is already with us and wants to be with us.[26] It comes to us, insofar as appearing knowing comes to its truth (GA 68:100). This self-revelation or *parousia* belongs essentially to the absolute. The idea that the absolute *wants* to appear and offers no resistance to knowing, constitutes for Heidegger the presupposition that underlies the entire *Phenomenology of Spirit*.[27] Only in this way can the greatest self-alienation of absolute knowing open up the realm within which consciousness goes through its experiences and returns to the absolute knowing that it has always already been. Thus,

> this turning away [is] *merely* a turning *round* (*Umwendung*), in which absolute consciousness does not give itself up and does not abandon itself. Only this turning round to externalization discloses to consciousness the outstretching (*Erstreckung*) of a distance from itself. . . . And only when this passage (*Durchgang*) opens itself does absolute consciousness have the possibility of returning to itself. . . . The turn to externalization is necessary for the sake of the absolute. (GA 68:122, cf. HW 176 / HCE 131)

> The turning round (*die Umkehrung*) first brings about the essential free space for the dialectic of the movement; experience, the being of consciousness, accomplishes itself as such a dialectical movement. (HW 177 / HCE 132, tr. m.)

The consciousness that in the experiences that it goes through sublates the difference between its concept and its existence, establishes itself as present at itself (cf. 170/120). From this one may infer that absolute knowing—that is, the mode of consciousness that has become ontological—is oriented upon presence as much as the consciousness that it has left behind: the absolute reveals itself as absolute self-presence for and in absolute knowing. Natural consciousness, *as* preontological consciousness, understands the being of beings from the outset as presence. The turning that takes place in the *Phenomenology of Spirit* is not so radical as to let consciousness overcome this preontological understanding of being. On the contrary:

> Natural knowledge is alive in all manifestations (*Gestalten*) of spirit, lives all of them in its own way—including especially the manifestation of absolute knowledge, which occurs as absolute metaphysics, although that is visible only occasionally to a few thinkers. (137/62, tr. m.)

Only those who look very carefully can see that speculative philosophy is dominated by the very understanding of being that guides representational thinking. Since Heidegger regards this temporal understanding of being as the condition of possibility that grounds representing consciousness, the way in which absolute knowing overcomes this consciousness appears from his perspective as a very relative overcoming—regardless of what absolute knowing leaves behind, it is neither able nor willing to relinquish its attachment to presence:

> Praesens (*Präsenz*) however . . . is a mode of presence (*Anwesenheit*) which . . . occurs (*west*) from out of a yet unthought occurring of a hidden time (*aus einem noch ungedachten Wesen einer verborgener Zeit*). (142/69, tr. m.) [28]

Yet being, he continues, does not necessarily have to only appear as the presence of the present. Perhaps it does not *want* to be understood as such at all:

> It is, to be sure, an altogether different question whether and in what way subjectness is an essential destiny proper to being, in which the unconcealedness of being . . . *withdraws* itself, thus determining an epoch of its own. (176/132, tr. m.)

Being *can* initially only manifest itself from within a horizon of Praesens. Every form of absolvence necessarily accomplishes itself by starting out from a thinking that has initially abandoned itself to the world. From Heidegger's perspective, the liberating movement of the *Phenomenology of Spirit*, despite the semblance of the contrary, also remains bound to the temporal horizon of Praesens. Thus, it seems that even behind the back of absolute knowing an essential movement still tries to occur, which that absolute knowing strenuously resists.[29] Granting passage to *this* movement calls for a different reversal, a different contribution, and a different light.

We see that Heidegger takes over Hegel's idea of a liberating movement, but radicalizes that from which thinking has to liberate itself in such a way that Hegel's philosophy itself comes to belong to the phase that must be left behind. He takes absolvence proper to then consist in a thinking that directs itself toward the temporality which constitutes its most radical condition of possibility. This time grounds every projective preconception of being, but also constitutes the insurmountable situatedness of thinking. For Heidegger, a thinking that is able to occur in accordance with the primordial temporal threefoldness can distinguish the beginning and end of the movement to which it pertains in such a way that they recede from the realm of Present. Since this temporal ecstasis has always already broken away from its juncture and draws all power toward itself, this can hardly be realized; to think is to do something extremely precarious.

Precisely because Heidegger intends to radicalize the movement of the *Phenomenology*, he can sympathetically follow this movement and express his admiration of Hegel.[30] Or so it seems. In the next chapter I will show that Heidegger also in his other later texts on Hegel intends a repetition that in the end radically turns against Hegel's project.

11

Bound by the *Logos*: Heidegger's Later Texts on Hegel

In his texts on the *Phenomenology of Spirit* Heidegger mainly brings out his kinship with Hegel, but in other texts he often emphasizes the difference between Hegel's metaphysics and his own thinking. While chapter 10 focused mainly on the issue of consciousness, in this chapter I will especially thematize Heidegger's deconstructive interpretation of Hegel's concept of history. The concept of negativity will play an important part here. Although some texts on the *Phenomenology of Spirit* are from the 1940s and the *Contributions* from 1936/38 already contains important passages on Hegel's concept of negativity, this order largely follows Heidegger's turn from Dasein to the history of being.

Since Hegel understands the most essential movement as absolute self-actualization, Heidegger considers Hegel's philosophy to be the culmination of a history that has increasingly turned away from what it could possibly be. His own understanding of this history is not, however, entirely foreign to that of Hegel, but rather constitutes a modification thereof. Heidegger can understand Hegel's philosophy as an inauthentic modification by means of the "construction" of a primordial possibility to which, in his view, only his own thinking attempts to do justice. Since their different interpretations of history each ensues from a different logical principle, it will be necessary to thematize Heidegger's modification of Hegel's logical principle. In GA 55 Heidegger calls what is usually termed logic "a task which as yet has never been assumed in a primordial way."[1]

I will show that Heidegger tries to take over the "logical" in an authentic way by tracing it back to the threefold temporality that grounds every conceptuality. The "logical" will thus have an important role in this chapter as well, albeit no longer with respect to the method. Heidegger's modification of Hegel's logical principle constitutes the basis of his temporal-ontological perspective. Since Heidegger in his later work increasingly refuses to unfold his thought in a systematic manner, it is often difficult to see that his thinking starts out from Hegel in order to turn against him. I would here like to show how Heidegger enacts this movement in his later work.

Although I am aware that something is lost by not following closely the various texts on Hegel, I will only use these texts to sketch out the line of thought that in my view constantly guides Heidegger's interpretation of Hegel. This line of thought can be broadly traced back to Heidegger's critique of metaphysics from the 1920s. My interpretation will start out from the passages in the *Contributions* which relate to Hegel.

This work already contains in a way the whole of Heidegger's later thought. The first part of GA 68, *Negativity. A Confrontation with Hegel Starting out from Negativity*, was written during the same period as the *Contributions* (1938/39) and was equally not intended for immediate publication. Published in 1993, this text is very similar in style to the *Contributions* and in some parts just as inaccessible. Since Heidegger also goes further in GA 68 than in the texts that were intended for publication, I will give quite a lot of attention to this text. Better known texts on Hegel, such as *The Onto-Theo-Logical Constitution of Metaphysics* in *Identity and Difference* and *Hegel and the Greeks* in *Pathmarks*, will play a less prominent role in my interpretation.

11.1 The Sembling Self-Dependence of Thinking

Heidegger remarks in the *Contributions* that German Idealism "seeks once more to permanently secure itself against any insecurity," without knowing that in doing so it flees from the truth of being (B 203). Before turning to Heidegger's often difficult and abstract texts, I will briefly reflect on this passage.

According to Heidegger, the principle that constitutes the secure basis of philosophy ensues from a more primordial principle that it excludes from itself. He calls this principle—although often not by name—temporality. This "time" constitutes the source of every understanding of being, but equally of every misunderstanding. By means of this temporal basic structure, Heidegger can show that a possible mode of understanding of being could not be given its due in the history of philosophy. If it is true that absolute knowing has been unable to incorporate this possibility in its own movement, but "owes its life" to excluding this possibility, this knowing can no longer be considered as the highest possibility of spirit. Looking back on its own history, spirit sees how every "not" necessarily annulled itself. It sees itself everywhere, yet does not see that this infinite "self" can only be identical to itself insofar as it does not admit a different, more primordial principle into itself.

This primordial principle exists only insofar as it is thought, and it is only thought because it might shed a different light on the dynamic of history and human life as such. In this different light, history will no longer appear as a development in which a principle given at the outset actualizes itself by externalizing itself only to increasingly annul this externality. Heidegger's perspective allows us to see how that which tries to actualize itself in history will come into conflict with the other of itself in such a way that this otherness constantly threatens to get the upper hand. This is, in his words, being as constant presence. It is from this unquestioned presence that he considers philosophy to derive its sembling self-sufficiency.

When Heidegger takes his "step back" toward that which makes this very presence possible, his intention is to destabilize philosophy and make it less confident of itself. Thinking should be able to face the insurmountable contrariety between what is intended and what actualizes itself. Whereas metaphysics always seems to decide the strife between being itself and that which it distinguishes from itself in order to accomplish itself—that is, presence—in favor of this presence, Heidegger tries as it were to give the strife of being with the other of itself the chance to unfold itself.

This is the background against which I should like to approach Heidegger's later texts on Hegel. It perhaps seems rather strange to interpret Heidegger in terms drawn from Hegel, when Heidegger himself chooses his own, most proper words so carefully. I take the view, however, that precisely when these words are translated in such a way that Heidegger can meet Hegel on his most speculative level, it may also become clear what is at stake in Heidegger's own thinking. To ensure that the dialogue in which Heidegger says he wishes to engage Hegel does not entirely end up in mutual misunderstandings or a long silence, I will try to let them speak in a more or less common language. But before this final act really begins, I will briefly turn to Heidegger again:

> Therefore, when we attempt a thinking conversation with Hegel, we must speak with him not just about the same matter, but about the same matter in the same way. But the same is not the merely identical. In the merely identical, the difference disappears. In the same the difference appears. . . . Thinking can stay with its matter only . . . if for it the strife concerning this same matter becomes ever more undecided. (ID 35/45–46, tr. m.)

If this "matter" is being, then Heidegger's dialogue with Hegel should allow the strife of being against its unavoidable presentification to come to the fore as it is in itself.

11.2 A Different Philosophical History of Philosophy

In the *Contributions* Heidegger calls Hegel the first to have achieved a truly philosophical comprehension of the history of philosophy. For Hegel's perspective allows the different historical manifestations of philosophy to be understood as phases of a necessary development.[2] Since Heidegger regards this approach as the first adequate interpretation of the history of thinking, but at the same time as the last possible of its kind (B 214), the question arises as to what a different history of philosophy—just as philosophical as Hegel's—might be like (221). Everything that has been tried in this respect since Hegel is described by Heidegger as a learned, yet helpless stammering (214).

Heidegger's philosophical approach to the history of philosophy is similar to Hegel's in that it starts out from a certain unity of the different phases of that history and a certain necessary sequence of those phases. This can only be done by approaching that history by means of an encompassing projective preconception. In order to distance himself from his great predecessor, Heidegger characterizes the realm within which the history of metaphysics unfolds itself as a realm within which being only makes itself understandable as presence.[3] This realm is the place where thinking comes into its own and feels at home, yet is further from home than it will ever be able to admit.

In *The Onto-Theo-Logical Constitution of Metaphysics* from 1957, Heidegger calls the realm within which Hegel's thinking moves the realm of the "completely developed certainty of the knowing that knows itself" (ID 39/49, tr. m.). Hegel's conception of being as the emptiest and most general concept that in a dialectical way attains its completion as absolute knowing (cf. 43/53) is based, according to Heidegger, on a specific "light":

> But here, too, being gives itself only in the light that lightened itself for Hegel's thinking. (59/67, tr. m.)

The way in which being gives itself always depends on the light that is cast on being; this "epochal molding" (59/67, tr. m.) can only be revealed when thinking turns itself toward the source of that light. It should attempt to withdraw from metaphysics and focus attention on a realm which until now has been skipped over by metaphysics (39/49). Heidegger considers that the step back into this primordial realm will make it possible to survey the entire history of thinking, and to do so with regard to the source of that thinking:

> Thinking recedes before its matter, being, and thus brings what is thought into an over-against-itself, in which we behold the whole of this history, and do so with respect to what constitutes the source of this whole thinking in that it first establishes for this thinking the realm of its abode.[4]

The idea that the whole of history can be understood in a philosophical way once again brings Heidegger close to Hegel. He emphasizes however the difference between his stepping back and Hegel's sublation by saying that only the first makes it possible to understand that whole from out of its source—that is, its light source—which first grants metaphysics its realm. Only this perspective might be able to reveal the primordial origin and possible future of metaphysics.

A thinking that turns away from its true origin will increasingly come to regard *itself* as the ultimate ground. In the *Contributions* Heidegger says that thinking not only brings about the unity of beings, but in modern philosophy becomes the preeminent identity, namely, the identity that understands itself as identity (B 198). This means that knowing itself is determined as that which has achieved the highest possible mode of being and as such constitutes the ground of the being of beings. When Hegel regards absolute knowing as absolute reality, he expresses the idea that thinking has become the unconditional guideline for determining the being of beings. But this event might be considered the result of something else:

> When, however, the *pure relation* of the *I-think-unity* . . . thus becomes unconditional, then this means that *self-present present* (*die sich selbst gegenwärtige Gegenwart*) is the measure (*Maßstab*)

> of all beingness. . . . [T]he more thinking becomes the unconditional guideline, the more decisive *presentness* (*Gegenwärtigkeit*) as such, that is, "time," gives, entirely concealed and unbidden, beingness its truth in a primordial sense. . . . The guiding line . . . which, as such, conceals itself, grounds and gives rise to the horizon for the interpretation of beingness.[5]

Thinking can only become the guideline by virtue of the openness brought about by primordial time. Heidegger suggests that a thinking which understands itself as that which grounds the being of beings as it were takes the place of time, whereas this "replacing" is itself made possible by a temporal realm that is increasingly dominated by Present. It is only within this realm that thinking can separate off itself from its origin and regard itself as the unconditional (201) which is capable of grounding itself. In the last part of the *Contributions* Heidegger repeats that the idealistic determination of being as presentness is guided by the idea that the subject is the being that itself decides about the way in which the being of beings can appear:

> Thus, absolute idealism manifests that beings are given here even more priority over beingness . . . insofar as Being here determines itself on the basis of the subject, that is to say, simultaneously on the basis of the object. With regard to the history of being, this determination is only a *modification* (*Abwandlung*) *of constant presence* into the being-posited-for-itself of the subject. Absolute idealism therefore completely . . . deprives being of its power in favor of the uncontested and boundless predominance (*Vormacht*) of beings.[6]
>
> [O]bjectivity as such is already with respect to its essence—*to say nothing of the way it originates in the history of being*—. . . determined . . . as a specific interpretation of beings *on the basis of* the object. (B 427, first italics mine)

From these passages we may infer that Heidegger's critique of Hegel takes two lines. Heidegger usually concentrates on showing that all metaphysics—as onto-theology—has the tendency to base its comprehension of the being of beings on a specific being (the subject or God). He maintains that the errancy of German Idealism consists in the attempt, based on Descartes and Kant on the one hand, and Christian dogma on the other, to understand the *ego cogito* in an absolute manner (202–3). Heidegger here often keeps more or less silent that the attempt of philosophy to take subjectivity as the ultimate ground is itself grounded in the increasing predominance of Present. We know that Heidegger considers a certain predominance of Present to constitute the condition of possibility of any encounter of beings; this predominance tends to intensify itself as soon as philosophy, *starting out from* beings, turns to the being of beings. Being itself *must* distinguish itself from itself in order to make itself understandable as presence and to enact the history of thinking. This history, then, concerns itself less and less with being insofar as it *differs* from the way in which it appears.

Heidegger must have had his reasons to be reticent about the temporal source of the history of being. It is indeed perhaps easier to explain that metaphysics unduly conceives the ground of beings as an ultimate being, than to show how this conception rests on a destining that precedes every human action. It could be that Heidegger was afraid that this latter approach might bring him too far in Hegel's direction. But what he thinks he *can* say about Hegel is not always very convincing. In various texts Heidegger seems to get stuck at the point where he regards thinking or subjectivity as the basic principle of Hegel's philosophy. He then tries to situate Hegel within the tradition of Descartes, and seems not to see that the movement of the pure concept even precedes every form of (relative and absolute) knowing, and only *manifests* itself in, for example, the structure of the finite subject. If that is the case, Hegel's philosophy cannot be simply reduced to a thinking that considers thinking itself the ultimate ground.[7]

I believe that Heidegger's critique of Hegel would have been more convincing if he had systematically shown that the realm within which Hegel's thinking accomplishes itself is delimited by the temporal ecstasis Present. I will try to bring out this underlying line of thought more than Heidegger himself often does—the conception of temporality on which this approach is based seems to be one of the best weapons in the lasting strife with Hegel.

When Heidegger formulates his critique of metaphysics *from* the perspective of that metaphysics itself, his conception of the history of being stays more or less in the background. This conception distinguishes itself as it were from itself, so as to initially show only its external side. Heidegger does, however, sometimes indicate that this side constitutes only one side of the story that should be told. I will now first turn to *The Onto-Theo-Logical Constitution of Metaphysics.* Then, focusing on the *Contributions* and GA 68, I will sketch out the line of thought that I consider to underlie Heidegger's interpretation of the history of being.

11.3 The Origin of Onto-Theology

The Onto-Theo-Logical Constitution of Metaphysics from 1957 starts out from the ontological difference in order to thematize the confinement of traditional metaphysics. Heidegger remarks that the difference between being and beings delimits the realm of metaphysics, while metaphysics itself was unable to inquire into the origin of that difference (ID 41/51). The way in which this difference occurs is now called the carrying-out (*Austrag*) of this difference (60/68, tr. m.). Only when being carries out itself as presence can beings on the basis of that presence arrive as present beings; the ontological difference then enacts itself as the difference between the being of beings on the one hand and the whole of beings on the other. This carrying-out of the ontological difference entails that being reveals itself to metaphysics as the ground or *logos* of all beings (48/57). It is scarcely possible to infer from this text that this carrying-out is itself grounded in a difference which occurs within being itself.[8] At the beginning of the text Heidegger does mention, however, that the "matter" of thinking—that is, being itself—is itself that which is at strife:[9] being's strife within and against itself needs the encounter between thinkers to actually occur, that is to say—though Heidegger does not say this here—to make itself understandable as presencing, constant presence or otherwise.

Heidegger remarks that the carrying-out of the ontological difference that delimits the realm of metaphysics "pervades the destining of being from its beginning to its completion" (60/67, tr. m.). He adds, however, that this continuous pervading (*Durchgängigkeit*) is not to be understood as a kind of dialectical law. Evidently, Heidegger again tries to distinguish his thinking from Hegel's concept of history. He seems to do this by granting the word *Durchgängigkeit* an unusual ambivalence: on the one hand the term pertains to that which always continues to take place and hence resembles a universal principle. On the other hand, however, the term also suggests that what is taking place has the character of a passage (*Durchgang*). According to this double meaning, one could understand the actual history of metaphysics not only as always continuing, but also as a history that might grant passage to another mode of thinking. In that case, presence would no longer impose itself as the one and only meaning of being.

One might say, perhaps, that presence constitutes the inevitable "passage" for being insofar as it occurs in the history of philosophy, but that this passage tends to "forget" itself as a passage and to let itself continue endlessly. This persistence of presence threatens to thwart the movement in which being, *through* its modification into presence, attempts to come into its own. Although being needs its course through metaphysics as a necessary "means," this means has the tendency to rise against that for which it was intended and to no longer serve the original purpose. From Heidegger's perspective it is no longer possible, then, to decide whether being, in its history, will be able to find a passage through presence and turn toward itself. Being, having divided off presence from itself in order to occur in the history of thinking, must continuously strive against this prevailing mode of being to maintain itself as pervaded by absence, and it will always threaten to lose this strife.

In *The Onto-Theo-Logical Constitution of Metaphysics* Heidegger does not mention that the way in which being is destined to metaphysics—and on the basis of which being can present itself in the history of thinking as, for instance, *phusis*, *logos*, idea, objectivity, subjectivity, or will to power (cf. 58/66)—is grounded in the predominance of Present. Owing to this predominance, the realm of metaphysics has always had a confined reach. Heidegger emphasizes that the various ways in which being is molded cannot be taken together in a general concept, but he does not say that being itself is from the outset given as the presencing that of itself tends to modify itself into constant presence.[10] This means nothing other than that philosophy each time in a different way, but always on the basis of the same principle, attempts to order the totality of phenomena in such a way that this order ensures certainty, truth, and stability.

Let me turn to Heidegger's remarks on Hegel in this text. At the beginning of the lecture, he distinguishes his own thinking from that of Hegel with respect to the latter's conception of the history of philosophy. Without mentioning possible similarities, he immediately states that Hegel's thinking is part of a certain epoch of that history.[11] He indicates that the realm within which being gradually unfolds itself and determines itself as the mode of knowing which is absolutely sure of itself and of its matter is grounded in the carrying-out of the ontological difference; this carrying-out first makes it possible for being to take shape as the ultimate ground on which the totality of beings rests:

> Insofar as being occurs as the being of beings, as the difference, as the carrying-out, grounding and founding keep moving away from and toward one another, being grounds beings and the being that

> most of all "is" becomes the ground of being as such. . . . Speaking from the perspective of the difference, this means: the carrying-out is a circling, the circling of being and beings around each other. (61–62/69, tr. m.)

The carrying-out entails that the difference between the being of beings and beings as such—that is, between the essential and the beings in which it appears—is enacted as the difference between a ground and that which rests on that ground. Heidegger takes this founding relation to also underlie Hegel's conception of the relation between being and thinking; Hegel's perspective reveals being as the ground that is able to actually comprehend itself as ground by developing itself as thought. Thus, by means of the thought that is engendered by being itself, being is able to affirm itself as the ground of all beings (48/57). Metaphysics up to Hegel has always conceived this self-founding being as ultimate ground or *causa sui*, that is, as God (51, 64/60, 71). Insofar as this ground is considered to be that which is most real, being itself can only be represented as the highest being. Heidegger remarks that Hegel's *Logic* therefore also begins with God.[12]

He does not mention, however, that Hegel in the *Logic* radically criticizes the metaphysical conception of the relation between the ground and that which rests on that ground. In his own way, Hegel overcomes the perspective of traditional metaphysics by subordinating the fixed opposition between the ground and what is grounded to the circular movement in which the ground—the absolute concept, that is—affirms itself as the true ground (cf. L I, 70–71/71). Heidegger seems to consider this modification to be precisely the ultimate affirmation of the metaphysical molding of being. However, it is difficult to see how, according to the passage quoted above, he can interpret the self-founding movement of the absolute as a movement in which beings and being circle around one another. When Hegel explains how the absolute externalizes itself to become being and to return to itself as absolute knowing, he leaves behind the traditional representation of God as highest being: the absolute is nothing but the movement in which it engenders the totality of finite conceptual determinations and through them accomplishes itself. Hegel does maintain, however, that the absolute is the movement in which every lack can be sublated, and in which the absolute can be entirely present at itself. The instances in which Heidegger indicates that being can only take the shape of an ultimate ground if it has made itself understandable as presence show much more convincingly that absolute knowing owes its absolute self-dependence to an "occurring" which refuses to be absorbed by the circular movement of the absolute concept.

Although, to my knowledge, the term *onto-theology* does not occur until Heidegger's course on the *Phenomenology of Spirit*, one can trace back this determination of metaphysics to the second half of the 1920s.[13] According to Heidegger, metaphysics has always answered the question concerning the being of beings in terms of a principle capable of accounting for the unity and coherence of all beings. This principle could only be understood as that which *is* in the most preeminent sense of the word—that is to say, as something that is not, like all finite beings, marked by a lacking.

Thus, the carrying-out that delimits the realm of metaphysics gives rise to a difference between an infinite being which is not affected by the "not" and the totality of beings, which is. Hegel succeeds in sublating this opposition by admitting negativity within the core of the absolute itself. Yet, by conceiving the ground of everything that is as the self-grounding movement of the absolute concept, Hegel more than ever affirms the infinite power of this ultimate principle. Heidegger does not really make clear that his lecture precisely intends to criticize the idea of such an absolutely powerful principle. Other texts will have to show that being itself, insofar as it *differs* from the way in which it is understood from out of beings, is itself radically finite; thoroughly pervaded by an insurmountable "not," it is unable to become the bearing ground of the whole of beings.[14]

Heidegger remarks toward the end of *The Onto-Theo-Logical Constitution of Metaphysics* that the carrying-out may come to refer to a realm within which the difference between being and beings, or between the ground and that which rests on it, no longer suffices. Such words merely pertain to "what is different in the difference" (63–64/71–72, tr. m.), that is, to being insofar as it is represented as the highest and most universal principle. Especially in the *Contributions* and in GA 68, Heidegger attempts to show that being in this sense has already become different from what it essentially is.

11.4 Heidegger's Radicalization of Hegel's Concept of Negativity

The first part of GA 68 explicitly thematizes the meaning of Hegel's concept "negativity." We have seen that the question concerning the "not" is also discussed in *Being and Time*.[15] As early as in his outline for the book on Aristotle from 1922, Heidegger suggests that life can only gain access to itself by means of a deconstruction. In the movement that counters the tendency of life to lapse, a "negation" is enacted that gives life access to its (usually ignored) proper possibilities (A 14). This second negation should not lead to a determination of the content of what the human being essentially is, but should rather bring out the fundamentally questionable character of human life. Life can then no longer be accommodated in some kind of reassuring world. This negation of a negation thus does not culminate in an unconditional "yes," but on the contrary confirms an insurmountable lacking of life with respect to what it essentially is. This is what Heidegger takes to constitute the difference between his own conception of negativity and that of Hegel. In the *Contributions* and GA 68 Heidegger tries to comprehend Hegel's interpretation of negativity as an inauthentic modification of an insurmountable "not" that essentially belongs to being itself.

In GA 68 Heidegger remarks that thinking can only develop into absolute knowing because it turns away from "the most secret condition, of which it is not able to free itself."[16] This renouncing must itself be deconstructed (GA 68:14). It is clear that Heidegger conceives his own deconstruction, here called *Abbau*, as a negation of what is negated in the metaphysical tradition from Plato to Hegel. For Heidegger, this negation is to lead philosophy back to the temporality in which the ontological difference is grounded, so that philosophy might assume its hitherto neglected possibilities. He considers that his "second negation" thus does not conclude the history of thinking, but prepares a possible overturning thereof.[17]

According to Heidegger, Hegel's philosophy accomplishes a "complete *dissolving* of negativity into the positivity of the absolute" (14). If negativity functions as the "'energy" of unconditional thinking" that enacts thinking, keeps it going and brings it to itself, then the nothingness (*das Nichthafte*) has from the outset already been abandoned and expelled. The negativity that is understood as negation of a negation is founded, Heidegger asserts, in a "yes" with regard to a self-consciousness that founds itself (14) and is thus rendered harmless:

> *Hegel's negativity* is no negativity, because it never takes seriously the not and nihilation (*das Nicht und Nichten*),—it has already sublated the not into the "yes."[18]

Heidegger, by contrast, tries to understand the "not" as the abyss which denies us the possibility of turning to beings for firm ground and security.[19] When this ground fails and the primordial abyss is allowed to open up itself, it also becomes possible for the seemingly decided strife between the countering modes of being—being as constant presence and being as pervaded by the "not"—to flare up. The "not" that belongs to being itself may then be rather affirmed:

> Da-sein as the "yes" to the truth of Being (not approval and acceptance of beings), the yes to nihilation (*Nichtung*) and to the necessity of the "no." . . . The yes to nihilation as the yes to the abyss (*Ab-grund*) is the questioning of what most deserves to be questioned. (47–48)

When Heidegger conceives the "not" as that which entails that Dasein can no longer cling to beings, this is—in contrast to what he suggests—still completely in line with Hegel. However, Hegel lets the turn to being or the essential culminate in the absolute self-satisfaction of thinking, which thus finds an ultimate firm ground in itself. According to Heidegger, even this ground must be left behind.

To this end, Heidegger repeatedly asks about the origin that gave rise to Hegel's idea of absolute negativity.[20] It seems obvious to turn for an answer to the beginning of the *Logic*, where, according to Heidegger, nothingness as it were appears in person (17–18). But the "nothing" that Hegel introduces here pertains, like "being," only to the being of beings insofar as that is understood as undetermined immediacy. This immediacy can only appear from a perspective that takes its standards from mediation.[21] Since this dialectical mediation is proper to absolute knowing, Heidegger considers Hegel's concept of being to come about from within the "perspective of that which is thought" (30). Hegel thus understands being—in Heidegger's encompassing sense—from the outset as "pure presence" (31). The absolute idea constitutes the highest form of being and is therefore to the greatest extent determined by this presupposition:

> What holds for Hegel's nonconcept of being however, holds in a more essential way . . . for being in a broader sense, for the absolute idea—that is, for the sightedness (*Gesichtetheit*) that sees and mirrors *itself*, that is to say, for self-present presence. (31)

When the *Logic* begins with "being" as the empty and undetermined pure concept that grounds all our relations to beings, being has thus already acquired a meaning which Hegel cannot as such comprehend (cf. BT 2–3). The nothingness that concerns Heidegger has then already vanished from sight:

> Hegel's "negativity" precisely *not* to be understood by starting out from "nothing" (*das Nichts*) and its identity with "being"; for here no "difference" (*Unterschied*). . . . Being and nothing no difference—and yet: being something that is *"distinguished"* (*ein "Unterschiedenes")*, the "negative" of *proper negations*. Of which? (GA 68:19)

This question is not answered. From this vague and difficult passage one may in any case infer that Heidegger thinks that the origin of Hegel's concept of "negativity" must be sought elsewhere than in the *Logic*. When Hegel identifies the empty "being" with the "nothing," then being which—as presence—makes itself understandable *has itself already been distinguished* from something that withdraws from the realm of absolute knowing. This is being itself insofar as it is thoroughly pervaded by an insurmountable "not." There is thus a difference between being which is pervaded by the "not" and being which has expelled the "not" from itself. Because of this negation of what it essentially is, being can present itself in metaphysics as that which guarantees not only the presence of beings, but ultimately also the total presence of thinking at itself. The primordial "not" that in fact fundamentally threatens this possibility can within the realm of metaphysics only return as a negativity through which everything becomes divided within and against itself, yet is ultimately also reconciled with itself. For Heidegger, this negativity constitutes an improper modification of what he himself understands by nothingness.

The *Contributions* thematizes this in more detail. Heidegger here asks:

> The intimacy of the not (*die Innigkeit des Nicht*) and that which is at strife within being itself (*das Strittige im Sein*), isn't that Hegel's negativity? It is not, although he has . . . experienced something essential, yet sublated it into absolute knowing; negativity, only to disappear and sustain the movement of sublation. Precisely not the occurring of essence (*Wesung*). Why not? Because Being as beingness (reality) on the basis of thinking (absolute knowing). (B 264)

Thinking should be able "to experience nihilation . . . within being itself."[22] This "not" must be distinguished from the negativity that is rendered harmless by reducing it to the force which drives the absolute toward its own completion. We may now infer that the "strife within being itself" pertains to the strife between a mode of being that is pervaded by the "not" and a mode of being that expels this "not" from itself to become constant presence, and thus to prevail in the history of philosophy. There is no doubt that Heidegger considers his own thinking to reveal this strife within being itself as it is in itself, while the perspective of metaphysics could not but conceal its radical character. The passage cited above is preceded by the following note:

> [T]he origin of the strife in the intimacy of the not within Being! Occurrence of own-ing. (264)

Such an exclamation point is rare. When Heidegger notes that the strife within being itself originates in a "not" which essentially belongs to being itself, he seems to suggest that this "not" or "lack"—remember the *dunamis*—is that which first enacts the movement of being. Being always already shelters an otherness that it has not created and that it cannot overcome. But it is due to this lack, so it seems, that it cannot withstand the prevailing presence that it also is itself. Precisely because the "not" of itself withdraws from presence, it allows being to confine itself and become constant presence.

To put it differently: insofar as Being distinguishes itself into being and time, being can make itself understandable, albeit initially and mostly merely as presence. Being can only occur in history if it distinguishes itself from itself and allows the other of itself to go its own way. This movement initially nihilates the primordial "not" proper to being. One could say that being thus negates what it essentially is. This negation itself then demands to be negated itself; by means of this second negation, the "not" that originally pervades being might possibly be given its due in the history of thinking.

Since Present always threatens to break away from its primordial juncture, there is no guarantee whatsoever that the second negation, which being needs in order to occur in accordance with its primordial possibility, will actually take place. According to Heidegger, it is entirely uncertain whether the most essential movement, grounded in an insurmountable difference, will be capable of maintaining this difference throughout its actual history. The strife between the mode of being which, as constant presence, dominates the domain of metaphysics and the mode of being which does not expel the "not" by which it is pervaded, has not yet been decided.

Such a thought is unthinkable from Hegel's perspective. His concept of negativity and movement is such that every contrariety between what actually is and what should be appears as a subordinate moment of the movement in which a preceding, albeit formal identity increasingly actualizes itself. I think that Heidegger, on the contrary, would maintain that all the concepts developed in the *Logic* rest on an expulsion or suppression of a "not" that resists its sublation into the movement of the concept. Hegel will always consider the moment in which a concept divides itself against itself to be an essential, yet subordinate moment in the self-actualizing movement of the concept.

From Hegel's perspective, the self-externalization that the concept needs in order to occur and return into itself is a loss that will ultimately be reversed in its complete self-possession.[23] This self-actualization he considers to be the highest possible mode of movement. By distinguishing between being, essence, and concept, Hegel in his own way throws light on the origin and future of metaphysics. But when the absolute concept succeeds in sublating the metaphysical "lack" of true reflection, it becomes less possible than ever to keep open the difference between being itself and the way in which the *logos* allows it to appear.

Heidegger repeatedly indicates that the Hegelian system only lets the primordial "not" appear as a negativity which is and remains subservient to the life of spirit. This negativity yields every mode of self-alienation, but in one and the same movement brings about spirit's return to itself. Concerning a passage from the *Phenomenology of Spirit*, Heidegger remarks:

> Negativity as being torn apart and as separation is "death"—*the absolute Lord*, and "life of absolute spirit" means nothing but enduring and *accomplishing* (*austragen*) death. (But this "death" is not taken seriously, no *catastrophe* possible; neither hurling down nor overturning (*Sturz und Umsturz*) possible; everything intercepted and smoothed out (*alles aufgefangen und ausgeglichen*). Everything is *already unconditionally* secured and given its place.) [24]
>
> Philosophy as *ab*-solute, as *un*-conditional, has *to include negativity* in a specific way, and that means that it ultimately cannot take it seriously. Unwinding as retaining (*Los-lösung als Behalten*), everything completely smoothed out. (GA 68:24)

Heidegger's projective preconception of being as such differs from Hegel's in that it allows being to be pervaded by a "not" that cannot be sublated. This difference between Heidegger and Hegel entails that they also understand the way in which human beings relate to their death in a different way. I will not dwell on this. Heidegger indicates in these passages that Hegel's philosophy does acknowledge negativity, but only to incorporate it in such a way that the "not" cannot announce itself as that which recedes from the movement of the concept and radically undermines its stability.

The system that is able to internalize negativity as its driving force cannot account for the possibility that this force forever turns itself against the movement of spirit's self-accomplishment. The words *Sturz* and *Umsturz* that Heidegger uses here recall the "ruining" and "counter-ruining" movements in his early Freiburg courses; being part of one counterturning dynamic, they never take place without one another. If Heidegger here mentions the possibility of a catastrophe, this should not be understood as fatalism. Even if one faces the possibility of this ruining tendency to become increasingly predominant, it can never be excluded that this tendency may somehow be resisted.

Although absolute knowing incorporates negativity in such a way that it forces discursive understanding to increasingly abandon everything from which it had stubbornly sought security, Heidegger suggests in the passage cited above that this tearing loose is grounded in a stubbornness of absolute knowing that it cannot acknowledge itself. This knowing no less clings to the temporal realm within which being as presence seems to guarantee an ultimate stability (cf. GA 68:14). Metaphysics continues to hold fast to presence. This is what Heidegger considers the one and only "catastrophe" of the history of philosophy. His thinking consists solely in the effort to resist this threat, which indwells the *logos* as such. Heidegger's projective preconception permits him to understand how the "not" which as primordial lacking enacts the occurring of the essential threatens to be nihilated in and by the course of that very movement. Not every given possibility engenders its self-actualization—what lies in the seed will not necessarily unfold itself so as to bear fruit. One has to accept, then, that death, suffering, and dividedness can no longer be conceived as granting life the passage to its truth. Only when one is able to face this will it be possible to do justice to the withdrawing movement of what is always already behind us and remains to come.

In deconstructing Hegel's concept of negativity, Heidegger

attempts to no longer conceive increasing self-actualization as the highest kind of movement. When from this perspective he brings to light the radically finite movement of history, he must of course again cross the path of Hegel.

11.5 The Hidden Movement of History

Although Heidegger tends to conceive Hegel's thinking as the culmination of subject-philosophy, it is clear that neither of them still regards the subject as the ultimate ground. Only when the subject is no longer central does it become possible to understand history in a truly philosophical manner. The dynamic of the pure concept enables Hegel to understand not only how the reality experienced by the subject is brought about, but also how the different historical manifestations of this reality necessarily ensue from one another and constitute a unity.

Heidegger rejects not so much Hegel's attempt to conceive the history of philosophy as unity, but the idea of dialectical advance which, as a measure, allows Hegel to systematically order the phases of this history.[25] Heidegger considers this logical principle—grafted as it is onto the structure of the subject that is divided within itself—to be unsuitable for revealing the proper dynamic of history. His own concept of temporality should make it possible to distinguish the various essential moments in the course of history in a different way. We will see that Heidegger in his own approach to the history of philosophy does not give up the distinction between alienation and return, but rather achieves a modification thereof.

Hegel—to begin with him—understands the history of spirit as the return of the absolute idea to itself. The absolute idea can only actualize itself by externalizing itself in time and space, and gradually annulling that externalization. This movement proceeds according to the principle of dialectic: every difference that is brought about engenders of necessity a higher unity. The history of spirit reaches its highest possibility when the necessity of this process is comprehended. Then thinking realizes that it is part of the absolute movement of the concept and transcends the finitude to which all the preceding manifestations of spirit must remain bound.

I have shown how Hegel reveals the past and future of a metaphysics that gets stuck in oppositions. In the *Logic* he lets the philosophy that struggles with the relation between "being" and "essence" be preceded by a thinking that by means of sensible perception and the understanding attains knowledge of beings and in this is guided by the basic category "being." When the mode of philosophy which remains tied to the understanding fails to overcome that struggle and collapses, space opens up for a thinking that comprehends the true unity of "being" and "essence." Since the pure concept opens up a realm within which the greatest possible externalization of the concept, that is, empty "being," necessarily leads to the greatest possible sublation of that externality, Hegel can understand the history of thinking as a closed circle of which his own philosophy constitutes the final link.

Heidegger, however, considers this end of philosophy to be merely an illusory conclusion of the history of thinking. He emphasizes time and again that Hegel was neither able to realize the meaning of the realm within which his thinking accomplished itself nor to inquire into its origin.[26] The realm within which the concept can externalize itself without running the risk of not being able to return to itself can, according to Heidegger, only come about if being has already been understood as presence. Absolute knowing can only freely unfold itself because it has from the outset expelled an insurmountable "not" from being itself. This is the concept of being with which the *Logic* begins. From Heidegger's perspective, therefore, the movement of absolute knowing does not appear as the completion of the history of thinking, but as its ultimate self-alienation (cf. GA 55:227–28). In order to understand the history of metaphysics, including Hegel, as an improper modification of a primordial possibility, Heidegger will also have to cast light on the origin and future of that history. To my knowledge, nowhere does he mention the fact that Hegel also does this in the *Logic*.

In *Hegel and the Greeks* from 1958, Heidegger maintains that the absolute subject produces its subjectivity in a dialectical way (WM 258 / PM 325). This occurs in history. Hegel considers Greek philosophy to be the phase in which thinking still immediately relates to objectivity, and has not yet turned to itself (261–62/328). This "not yet" of Greek philosophy is understood by Hegel as poor in comparison with the speculative knowing which completes that history (266/331). Whereas Hegel understands the history of thinking as a process of increasing enrichment, for Heidegger this same history rather constitutes a movement that increasingly turns away from its origin. From that perspective, Greek philosophy also appears as a "not yet," but now as a possibility that the later thinkers increasingly fail to accomplish (272/336). This means, I add, that the presentification of being had not yet really gained the upper hand in Greek philosophy.

This presentification constitutes the measure that allows Heidegger in *his* way to bring forth a certain unity and necessity of the history of thinking. We know that Heidegger distinguishes between the first thinkers who were still aware of the insurmountable counterstriving of being, metaphysics from Plato to Hegel, which tried in one way or another to reconcile being with itself, and finally his own thinking that, following in the footsteps of Hölderlin, for the first time explicitly attempts to do justice to that counterstriving. In a course on Hölderlin he makes the following remarks on this. If from the Christian perspective the human not-at-home-ness (*Unheimlichkeit*) is embedded between paradise and redemption, then

> the "negative" of the not-at-home (*das Unheimliche*), supposing that it is a negative, [is] always already toned down and abolished, and it is precisely this that contradicts the beginning and primordial essential experience of the essence of man in the Greek world. Greek history reaches the height of its essence when it preserves the counterturning of being itself and allows it to appear; for only then is there the necessity of dwelling in the ground of this counterturning, instead of flying to either the one or the other side. (GA 53:95)

Heidegger considers that philosophy from Plato onward, contrary to Sophocles, was unable to face this tragic counterstriving and conceived the "not" as that which should not be there. He also understands Hegel and Schelling to have clung to this "downgrading of the negative" (95–96).

The history of being begins with the withdrawal of being in favor of the other of itself, that is, in favor of constant presence. If it is true that a more primordial understanding of being has left traces in the fragments of the first thinkers, then these traces intimate something which has always already begun to withdraw itself and thus has never been present. Since being can initially only be thematized by starting out from beings, it cannot but make itself understandable by means of the horizon of Praesens. This "detour" brings about the history of thinking:

> The de-tour (*Um-weg*) however is not a de-tour in the sense that it has missed an immediate and shorter way to Being. For the detour first leads to the need of refusal (*die Not der Verweigerung*)

> and to the necessity of bringing to a decision what in the first beginning was only the hint of a gift (*phusis, alētheia*), which then could not be grasped or preserved. (B 434)

Like Hegel, Heidegger considers the detour of metaphysics to be necessary. This does not, however, mean for Heidegger that the detour, as the only possible way home, also guarantees the actual homecoming. What occurs at the end of the history of metaphysics is solely the possibility of disclosing a temporal realm within which being might appear as essential counterstriving; this realm has always already been given but could never be truly received. The history in which being itself is increasingly forgotten does not exclude the possibility of such a turn for the better, but keeps this possibility open. Thus, Heidegger manages to preserve a precarious balance between optimism and pessimism. The decisive difference between Heidegger and Hegel is that the contrariety or counterstriving which Hegel embeds between a preceding and a subsequent unity, from Heidegger's perspective as it were outstretches itself *into* the beginning and end of the movement. Hegel's circular movement is thus modified into a movement that tries to return to its starting point, but either fails to achieve or only apparently achieves this return. It is precisely because of this failure, however, that thinking gains the opportunity to keep its own end open.[27] By means of this modification of Hegel's *logical* principle, Heidegger can also understand the movement of history as a returning:

> History does not, in its hidden course, progress from a beginning to an end, but it is a returning (*Rückkehr*) of what once has been (*des Einstigen*) to the beginning. (GA 55:288)

We know that Hegel also does not regard history as a linear advance, but as the return of the absolute idea to itself. This circular movement can actually accomplish itself by means and by mediation of linear time. When Heidegger's perspective lets the history of thinking appear as a movement that increasingly turns away from its origin, then this movement hides another one: that turning away constitutes the necessary, albeit not sufficient, condition for the turning to itself and hence first opens up the possibility of returning home.[28] This is also the case for Hegel. Heidegger, however, is not concerned with a return of thinking to itself, but with a return to something that precedes every thinking:

> Maybe the disaster of reflection (*das Unheil der Reflexion*) is not due to the bending-back (*Rückbiegung*) as such, but rather to the fact that this bending . . . is directed to the essence of the human being. It may be . . . that the essence of the human being is in itself reflection, a primordial turning-to (*Zu-kehr*) that is a re-turning (*Rück-kehr*), but which also implies that in it the perversion (*Verkehrung*) increasingly gains the upper hand. (GA 55:209)

The "disaster" of traditional reflection—which, although Heidegger does not say this here, culminates in the self-reflection of absolute knowing—is that it thinks it can accomplish the return as a closed circle, and does not understand that precisely in this way it excludes its true beginning from what it thinks. It is far from certain, however, that thinking will be able to give up its apparent independence and turn to its temporal origin. Since Hegel holds that freedom necessarily realizes itself, he can ultimately let necessity and freedom be identical. Heidegger, by contrast, suggests that the destining of being as constant presence is in a certain sense fatal, but does not necessarily have to prevail as the only tendency. From his perspective it not only becomes possible, but also necessary to resist the presentification of being.[29]

When Heidegger modifies Hegel's principle of the circular movement in such a way that it does not close itself but endures the counterstriving, this may remind us of Hegel's interpretation of the finite reflection that remains tied to discursive understanding and gets stuck halfway in its circular movement. Does this not mean, then, that Heidegger's emphasis on the radical finitude of thinking makes him fall back into a mode of philosophy that Hegel had managed to overcome? To answer this question it will be necessary to thematize once again the difference between Hegel's concept of time and Heidegger's understanding of temporality.

The concept lets the other of itself—that is, time and space—proliferate so as to let the absolute idea occur as nature. Only by overcoming that externality can the idea actualize itself as spirit: moral action, art, religion, and thinking increasingly overcome the externality brought about by the concept itself. When Heidegger tries to indicate that life and history are dominated by a more primordial dynamic, he does this to undermine this reassuring order. He would not deny that in Hegel's *Logic* the pure concept unfolds the totality of pure concepts and returns of its own accord to its starting point. The problem is only that Hegel starts out from this logical principle to understand the movement of history and human life as such. From this perspective, history can only appear as the process in which an infinite principle increasingly attains its completion in our finite world. That principle guarantees that history necessarily goes in the right direction, even when that often seems not to be the case. Viewed in the light of the absolute concept, the greatest suffering, the deepest conflict, and the most abhorrent death cannot but appear as meaningful.

From *Being and Time* onward Heidegger steers well clear of a superficial relativism that maintains that every perspective happens to have its limitations. Heidegger too considers that philosophy is capable of raising itself above *this* kind of finitude. To understand what occurs in our actual history and can hardly occur in it, if at all, Heidegger—like Hegel—seeks a principle that grounds that history. Although he would not say it in this way himself, I think that Heidegger understands the primal distinguishing of temporality and being as the origin of the history of thinking. Temporality constitutes the "means" whereby being can make itself understandable as presence.

Like Hegel, Heidegger comprehends that that by means of which something realizes itself must to a certain extent be set free. The means has to resist the end, so that the end can come toward itself in overcoming that resistance. The being that lets the other of itself go its own way must, like the absolute, engage in the strife with what it has distinguished from itself. Unlike the absolute, however, being does not necessarily have the power to then sublate that otherness and thus bring its own history to a good end. The horizon of Praesens that ultimately also grounds the movement of the absolute concept differs from the time that is engendered by the absolute concept in that it hardly lets itself be annulled, if at all.

Heidegger's concept of temporality makes it possible to understand history as a movement in which the essential tries to actualize itself, but increasingly threatens to lose itself. The counterforce may then no longer be conceived as the necessary evil that is engendered by the spatiotemporal externality and can subsequently be overcome by the force of the concept itself. Precisely when thinking thinks it has overcome every resistance, it affirms the power of Present, which Heidegger considers to be the true source of every inauthenticity. The history that through Hegel understands itself as the triumph of the spirit, appears from Heidegger's temporal perspective as merely a phase in the history of being, albeit a phase that incessantly tends to become the only possible one.

11.6 The Absolute as Semblance of Being

In *The Principle of Identity* Heidegger remarks that philosophy needed more than two thousand years to understand, as speculative idealism, identity as that which contains the mediation in itself (ID 11, 30 / 25, 41). We may then certainly not expect—is the suggestion—that the turn of thinking toward the origin of this internally divided identity will let itself be accomplished in the short term. When Hegel overcomes the power of ordinary time and thus completes the circular movement of the concept, this is, according to Heidegger, due to a *logos* that is grounded in an inauthentic modification of temporality. Heidegger claims that he, in contrast to Hegel, attempts to modify this *logos* in such a way that it accords with the primordial threefoldness of the temporal ecstases.

Since the absolute *seems* to leave room for the "not," but deprives it of its power by incorporating it as self-sublating negativity in its own movement, Heidegger regards the absolute as the greatest self-alienation of being. The question is, however, whether Heidegger does not thus necessarily take up a standpoint that is even more absolute than that of Hegel. For how can Heidegger see more than Hegel, without thereby denying the finitude of every insight? In the *Contributions* Heidegger does not hesitate to call the *Logic* a necessary semblance:

> With regard to the occurring of Being (*das Wesen des Seyns*), the "Logic" is maybe *the least* rigid and serious way of determining the essential (*Wesensbestimmung*) and merely a semblance (*Schein*); a semblance however that has a deeper essence than the "dialectical semblance." . . . With respect to the grounding of the essence (*Wesensgründung*) of the truth of Being, the "Logic" itself is a semblance, but the most necessary semblance that the history of Being has known hitherto. (B 461)

The *Logic* unduly pretends to serve as an ultimate foundation. Heidegger sees his own thinking, by contrast, as indeed able—for the first time—to admit within itself the temporality that determines every thinking:

> Only *this* thinking of Being is truly un-conditional, that is, not conditioned and determined by something outside of itself that is itself conditioned . . . but exclusively determined by that which it has to think, that is, by Being itself—which is, to be sure, not "the absolute." (462)

Those who conceive philosophy as one of the many cultural expressions, he continues, will consider it arrogant to assign philosophy its unconditional origin. But in his view this cannot be avoided:

> If, however, in the transition out of metaphysics to a thinking of Being, thinking has to decide in favor of the latter, then the danger of inescapable daring (*Vermessenheit*) essentially increases. (462)

It does indeed. When Heidegger—only in the hidden *Contributions*—designates his own thinking as the only thinking which no longer depends on what it does not itself have within itself, this certainly seems to be a sign of hubris. We might certainly, as Heidegger remarks elsewhere, be tempted to compare the occurrence of own-ing with the absolute of Hegel (SD 53 / TB 49).

But matters are more complicated. I have shown how the absolute concept can only, according to Heidegger, actualize itself because of a temporal horizon that Hegel himself cannot see. When Heidegger includes this temporality as a principle in his thinking, he does this precisely to acknowledge that every thinking depends on something that it has not brought about itself. Since he is aware of how his own thinking can scarcely—if at all—escape the primordial power of time, he is able to understand in a very fundamental way the essential incapacity not only of traditional philosophy, but also of his own thinking. This self-understanding is unprecedented, and out of the question for Hegel. The temporal principle that guides Heidegger's thinking makes every self-sufficiency impossible; it is a ground that continually threatens to fall apart. Only a thinking that is able to waver seems able to still maintain itself here.

Although Heidegger tries to make thinking aware of its radical finitude, it turns out that he can only do this by conceiving every thinking that turns away from that finitude as an inauthentic modification of a possibility that does not succeed in accomplishing itself in history, but meanwhile is nevertheless preserved as possibility. Whereas Hegel presents himself as an all-knowing storyteller, Heidegger tries to show that Hegel—unknowingly—is only one of the leading actors in a different, more encompassing history. Heidegger, however, then seems to inevitably become the all-knowing teller of this other history. I have tried to show that Heidegger's projective preconception is indeed greatly akin to that of Hegel, but that his retrieving repetition nevertheless offers the possibility of escaping, at least to a certain extent, from this position. Heidegger sees that being occurs in the history of thinking by turning away from itself, but he also sees that it is hardly possible to overcome this alienation.

The storyteller—blind perhaps to what is too close—surveys what is possible, though he knows that history might not be able to achieve its end. He sees that every story, however carefully told, tends to incorporate that which of itself withdraws from its reach. It may be, then, that his only concern is whether the essential could take place in language without being forced to a standstill or—which is just as dreadful—being forced to eternally circle within itself. As soon as it is in one way or another translated into an ultimate, stable ground, it has already begun to disappear from the scene—unnoticed. Vulnerable, and hardly capable, if at all, of finding shelter in language or taking place otherwise in the world—if it comes.

Afterword

During the course of the book it turned out that much of what could have been said was unable to find a place. Sometimes an endnote could provide that place, but more often it could not. In closing, I should like to mention one or two of these issues.

My investigation focused on the logical, formal aspects of Heidegger's work. Yet Heidegger's attempt to admit the "not" into the essential itself ultimately serves the purpose of a more appropriate understanding of human existence. As often happens, this detour threatens to become an end in itself; in many of Heidegger's later texts this does indeed seem to be the case. I am convinced, however, that insofar as thinking can gain access to life—bound as it is by the *logos*—it may bring us closer to its core when it distances itself from what is familiar than when it does not venture this detour.

Heidegger's insight that not only thinking, but every movement that enacts itself *meta logou* is essentially threatened by that which makes it possible, has become—and I hesitate to say this—precious to me. It is a principle that in all simplicity does justice to the finitude of what we think, do, long for, and fail to do, without this leading to despair. The possibility that the "other" may not be incorporated in the movement in which the "one" affirms itself entails an essential undecidability.

If with the best will in the world one cannot prevent the good from overturning into its opposite without being able to subsequently undo that overturning, we should be able to admit this counterstriving. Even when we are entirely convinced that we are right, have the greatest confidence in the steadfastness of our love, or the sincerity of the friend we are talking to, a certain kind of uncertainty should accompany these certainties. Such an underlying uncertainty would not so much change our acting, as—perhaps unnoticed—cast a different light on it. This might be considered the categorical imperative yielded by Heidegger's concept of temporality.

It will come as no surprise that my interpretation of Heidegger owes a great deal to Derrida. My interpretation of Hegel would also have been different without Heidegger and Derrida. I wanted to show, however, that Heidegger's work cannot be so easily deconstructed as Derrida sometimes suggests. As I see it, Derrida's critique therefore begins too soon. I regard Heidegger as a systematic thinker who on the one hand can compete with Hegel in terms of depth and rigor, but on the other comes very close to Derrida's deconstructive philosophy. Heidegger's thinking may perhaps be understood as a systematic form of deconstruction. Or even as speculative deconstruction, if this means the attempt to understand that which appears by means of a fundamental principle of movement. I think that Derrida also, in his own way, starts out from Heidegger's concept of radical finitude, but goes one step further. The proper possibility of the turn for the better seems in his work to be even less possible, without entirely vanishing.

It was not my intention to characterize Heidegger's position as the last possible or the most true. I rather wished to show that Heidegger went as far as was possible from within his historical situation without relating to Hegel in an antithetical way. I take Hegel, Heidegger, and Derrida to indicate positions which somehow delimit the domain—that is, the essential possibilities—of the philosophy of our time. If philosophy is to be given the space to move, then I think that it is necessary to be kindred, at least to a certain extent, to these three thinkers. In any case, that is what I have tried to achieve. Some readers may think that I have too much neglected the differences between Hegel's speculative idealism, Heidegger's phenomenology, and Derrida's deconstruction. Others will perhaps regret that my interpretation does not focus on the hermeneutical phenomenologist or the thinker of the miraculous unconcealedness of beings. Not everyone may consider that the speculative-deconstructive Heidegger whom I offer instead sufficiently recompenses this loss.

Even though we cannot identify ourselves with the metaphysical tradition, neither can we entirely break away from its bounds. But we might try, I think, to be less afraid of what binds us to this tradition. Not only Hegel, then, but also the fear of Hegel must be overcome. Only thus might metaphysics still offer us a chance to interpret the reality which is ours in a way that in its long history may not have been possible, and indeed may hardly be possible at all.

Notes

Introduction to Part I

1. "[B]ecause the intention of this exposition is precisely to lead us to the ontological enigma of the dynamic of occurrence as such" (BT 389, tr. m.).

2. "Every thought in *Being and Time* is exclusively directed toward that which is called 'understanding of being'" (GA 49:41). This course on Schelling from 1941 contains a section in which Heidegger defends himself against "the rating of *Being and Time* among the philosophy of existence" (35) and in which he very clearly presents the basic idea of *Being and Time*.

3. "However, the concreteness of the analysis of the phenomena concerning Dasein . . . easily misleads one, first, into taking the concrete phenomena of Dasein as standing by themselves and, second, into interpreting them uniquely with respect to their existentiell character, that is, not with respect to the extreme, fundamental-ontological structure that underlies them. The more radical the existentiell involvement . . . the easier it becomes to principally misunderstand this existentiell involvement as that which is as such essential and alone of importance, whereas it becomes manifest during the projective analysis itself that this involvement is not for a moment of personal importance" (GA 26:176–77, tr. m.).

4. GA 24:1. See Heidegger's marginal note at p. 41 of BT.

5. See the following passage from the recently published text *Besinnung* (GA 66): "But the first elaboration of the properly 'systematic' division on time and being remained insufficient, and external circumstances (the swelling of the volume of the yearbook) at the same time prevented the publication of this part, in which I, aware of its insufficiency, did not have much confidence" (GA 66:413).

6. Von Hermann chooses the same starting point in a short study from 1991. He argues here that one should not only read GA 24 as a sequel

of *Being and Time*, but that it is also necessary to reinvestigate the analytic of Dasein from the perspective of GA 24: "If one sets oneself this task, one has to inquire about the significance of the chapters of the first and second divisions of the analytic of Dasein for the issues that would have been elaborated in "Time and Being." . . . Only this way of reading prevents the analytic of Dasein . . . from fatally appearing as a mere ontology or even an anthropology of Dasein, a philosophy of existence." However, Von Hermann goes no further than this indication. F.-W. von Hermann, *Heideggers "Grundprobleme der Phänomenologie." Zur "zweiten Hälfte" von "Sein und Zeit,"* 55–56.

1. The Development of *Being and Time*

1. See "Anmerkungen zu Karl Jaspers 'Psychologie der Weltanschauungen'" (WM 14 / PM 12) from 1919–1921. In 1921/22: "Thus, our interpretation is concerned with *getting through* to *a movement which constitutes a proper dynamic of life* (*die eine eigentliche Bewegtheit des Lebens ausmacht*), *in* which and *through* which it *is*, and, therefore, on the basis of which the ontological meaning of life becomes determinable" (GA 61:117). In two courses from 1920–1921 Heidegger takes the religious life as an example of a nonobjectifying self-interpretation of life. On the basis of his interpretation of texts by Paul and Augustine, Heidegger attempts to reveal the proper dynamic of life that is concerned with itself (cf. GA 60:208). On the one hand, this life struggles with evil—the lapsing tendency of life itself (199)—and on the other it is involved with a possible salvation. Since it is essentially uncertain whether and when the day of *parousia* will dawn, the proper temporality (*Zeitlichkeit*) of the Christian life cannot be understood on the basis of some objective concept of time: "There is no way to objectively grasp the 'when.' The factic experience of life is also founded on this temporality" (104, cf. 105). The historicity which is proper to human life is thus more than the occurrence of events in time (32). Nothing can be counted upon in this life: "In the final, most decisive and most pure concern with oneself lurks the possibility of the most abysmal falling (*des abgründigsten Sturzes*)" (240). However, the fact that Heidegger not only concurs with the self-interpretation of the early Christian life, but also tries to radicalize the uncertainty which this life permits, is not really elaborated in the texts. Heidegger considers even Augustine to be incapable of a "radically critical questioning and consideration of what is primordial." A deconstruction of his self-interpretation, guided as it is by Greek thinking, is therefore necessary (292, see 261, 298). Although GA 60, like the other texts from this first Freiburg period, begins to prepare the analytic of Dasein, the significance of these courses should not be overestimated.

2. BT 50n, cf. GA 20:101–2.

3. A course from 1923 (GA 63) is entitled *Ontology (Hermeneutics of Facticity).*

4. Cf. BT 38 and: "The possibility of radical discovery at the same time entails the corresponding danger that phenomenology may become hardened in its own results. It is most difficult to bring genuine phenomenological work into a critical attitude . . . toward itself" (GA 20:119, tr. m.). An analysis then follows of the way in which Husserl's phenomenology falls short with regard to the question concerning the being of intentionality and of the human being as such.

5. GA 20:183–84, tr. m. Cf.: "*[Even] phenomenological research stands under the constraints of an old tradition, especially when it comes to the most primordial determination of the theme most proper to it, intentionality. . . . Not only is the being of the intentional . . . left undetermined, but beings are categorially distinguished* (consciousness and reality), *while the meaning of the guiding perspective* which allows such distinctions to be made, that is to say, *being, remains unclarified and even unquestioned*" (GA 20:178, tr. m.).

6. These developments are described in detail in T. Kisiel, *The Genesis of Heidegger's Being and Time*, 248f. This extremely informative and complete overview is especially important for its summaries of unpublished early courses and other manuscripts.

7. This text (further referred to by the initial A) appeared in F. Rodi (ed.), *Dilthey-Jahrbuch für Philosophie und Geschichte der Geisteswissenschaften*, Bd. 6, Göttingen 1989, 237–69. The courses are *Phänomenologische Interpretationen zu Aristoteles. Einführung in die phänomenologische Forschung* (GA 61), and *Phänomenologische Interpretation ausgewählter Abhandlungen des Aristoteles zur Ontologie und Logik* (GA 62). The latter has not yet been published.

8. "For this reason a first preliminary highlighting of the specific objective character of factic life becomes necessary. Not only because it is the *object* of philosophical research, however, but also because philosophical research itself constitutes a determinate 'how' of factic life" (A 5, tr. m.).

9. "Is the meaning of being which ultimately characterizes the being of human life drawn genuinely from a pure and fundamental experience of this object itself and its being, or is human life taken as a being which is part of a broader ontological realm, and is it thus subjected to an ontological meaning that is bestowed upon it as archontical? How does Aristotle understand being at all, how can one gain access to it, how can it be grasped and determined?" (A 25–26, tr. m.). These questions are immediately answered in the following way, anticipating the interpretation: "The realm of objects that provides the primordial meaning of being is the realm of the objects that are *produced* and brought into practical use. . . . The

ontological realm of the things we practically deal with . . . determines the preconception from which the ontological structures of the object 'human life,' and consequently also of the ways in which this object is addressed and determined, are developed" (26–27, tr. m.).

10. See Aristotle, *Metaph.* VII, 7, 1032b 6–30; *Eth. Nic.* VI, 11, 1143a 28—1143b 6. See also GA 19:45, 156, 157 (example of doctor)-64.

11. Already in the introductory part of the text on Aristotle from 1922, Heidegger suggests that the imminence of one's own death should serve as a basis for the explanation of "the specific 'temporality' (*Zeitlichkeit*) of human existence" (A 12–13, tr. m.). However, the nature of this temporality is not yet understood as radically as in *Being and Time.* By giving *phronēsis* an existential meaning, Heidegger can make this phenomenon correspond with a "conscience" that has also been deprived of its moral character (cf. GA 19:56).

12. "With respect to its fundamental character . . . the explanation of being in the proper sense . . . is not gained from the being of human life, but stems from . . . a specifically *accomplished ontological radicalization of the idea of being-in-movement.* The movement of producing thereby functions as the example that guides the preconception of this being-in-movement. Being means 'being-completed,' the being in which the movement has come to its end. The being of human life is understood as a movement which unrolls itself by itself" (A 37–38, tr. m.).

13. GA 17:1–3. Cf. Kisiel, *op. cit.*, on this passage: "Aristotle is pitted against Aristotle, for example, in Heidegger's opening remarks urging his students to adopt a more 'phronetic' attitude toward their chosen science, contrary to the traditional equation of scientific comportment with *theorein*" (277). Also with regard to the text from 1922, Kisiel refers to the "'phronetic' sense of philosophy" with which he considered Heidegger to be concerned, "since its object is no longer the eternal and necessary *archai*, but that which also can be otherwise, the situation of factic life itself" (270). I think, however, that Heidegger was not concerned with leaving behind the involvement with essential, unchangeable principles, but with the possibility of revealing the (unchangeable) basic structures of beings that are above all dynamic, and that cannot be understood on the basis of the principles grounding Aristotle's concept of movement.

14. This theme is also elaborated in GA 33 from 1931. See 7.2.

15. See "Mein Weg in der Phänomenologie" (SD 81 / TB 74) and Heidegger's letter published as the preface in W. Richardson, *Heidegger, Through Phenomenology to Thought*, VIII–X.

16. Another later text in which Heidegger returns to his early interpretation of Aristotle is *On the Essence and Concept of Phusis in Aristotle's*

Physics B, 1 from 1939 (WM/PM). Here he extends the line of which in 1922 he could only survey the first part. T. Sheehan in an article on this text also examines an unpublished seminar from 1928 concerning the concepts *dunamis*, *energeia*, and *entelecheia*. He shows that Heidegger here develops a concept of movement on the basis of *energeia* as uncompleted movement, which he calls *Eignung*: in this movement *dunamis* does not merge into its actualization, but remains (p)reserved *as* possibility. Sheehan sees in this (correctly, in my view) a precursor of Heidegger's later concept *Ereignis*. T. Sheehan, "Getting to the Topic: the New Edition of Wegmarken," in J. Sallis (ed.), *Radical Phenomenology. Essays in Honour of Martin Heidegger*, see esp. 309f. See also Kisiel, *op. cit.*, 458.

17. See, e.g., GA 61:92, GA 24:153, GA 26:183, GA 31:51–53 and Kisiel, *op. cit.*, 288 on GA 18.

18. See Kisiel, *op. cit.*, 286f, 464.

19. Kisiel (*op. cit.*, 230) claims that the term *Geistesblitz* can be traced back to Pöggeler's discussions with Heidegger. Although it is not, as far as I can see, explicitly mentioned in the texts of Pöggeler to which Kisiel refers, I take the liberty of putting the word into Heidegger's own mouth. See, e.g., O. Pöggeler, "Heideggers Neubestimmung des Phänomenbegriffs," in *Neuere Entwicklungen des Phänomenbegriffs,* 129–30.

20. To be precise, Heidegger's understanding of temporality as the source and horizon of every understanding of being only becomes more concrete through his reading of Kant's doctrine of schematism (from 1925 onward). See from 1927/28: "In the schematism Kant attempts to grasp the synthesis a priori of productive imagination in a unified and original manner. . . . From the perspective of our interpretation, schematism indicates the primordial sphere of the radical grounding of the possibility of ontological knowledge. When some years ago I studied the *Critique of Pure Reason* anew . . . the scales fell from my eyes, and Kant became an essential confirmation of the path which I took in my search" (GA 25:430–31, tr. m.). In 7.3 I will examine Heidegger's interpretation of Kant. Kisiel, *op. cit.*, 224, plays down, in my view incorrectly, the significance of Heidegger's discovery of temporality.

21. M. Heidegger, "Wilhelm Diltheys Forschungsarbeit und der gegenwärtige Kampf um eine historische Weltanschauung," 176. This idea is also elaborated in the article *The Concept of Time* from November 1924, which is already beginning to look very much like *Being and Time*. This can be inferred from the afterword by H. Tietjen for the lecture with the same title. See Kisiel, *op. cit.*, 321f. In his letter to Richardson from 1962 Heidegger writes: "The disquieting question concerning being as presence (present), which was always on my mind, developed into the question concerning the temporal character of being. Soon it became clear that the tra-

ditional concept of time was in no respect adequate even for correctly posing the question concerning the temporal character of presence, let alone answering it. Time became questionable in the same way as being." Richardson, *op. cit.*, XII, tr. m.

22. See from 1928: "We are not concerned, however, with the usual isolated speculation on time. . . . Time, as we have shown, is rather related to the understanding of being as such, albeit still in an obscure manner. . . . It is not easy to come closer to it. The pathway I took myself is not the only one; but all of them are long and full of obstacles. For our purposes I choose another procedure: we will try to indicate the essence of time in a more direct and dogmatic manner" (GA 26:254, tr. m.). Heidegger is referring here to the detour of the analytic of Dasein.

23. This can clearly be seen in the introductory part of *Plato's Sophist* (GA 19), which is mainly devoted to *Eth. Nic.* VI and may be regarded as an elaboration of a part of the text on Aristotle from 1922. See F. Volpi, "Dasein comme *praxis*: L'assimilation et la radicalisation heideggerienne de la philosophie pratique d'Aristote," in *Heidegger et l'idée de la phénomenologie.*

24. See BT 114–15. Recently published courses such as GA 17 confirm that Heidegger's critique of the Cartesian subject-philosophy was primarily directed against Husserl. This is also confirmed by a later marginal remark (cf. BT 98), in which Heidegger states that his entire critique of Descartes was only inserted in *Being and Time* in order to attack Husserl's "construction of 'ontologies.'" I would add, however, that although Heidegger in *Being and Time* may have been primarily concerned with Husserl, there is no doubt that he ultimately intended the entire metaphysical tradition, to which Husserl had remained faithful. One might say that Heidegger in one complicated movement used his analytic of Dasein to defend Aristotle against Husserl, but no less to subsequently overcome Aristotle.

25. For Heidegger "the thing itself" that must be brought to light thus becomes something different than for Husserl: it is no longer intentional consciousness, but being as such. See W. Richardson, *op. cit.*, XII–XIV. This "turn" to being does not mean a lapse into the dogmatic, scholastic ontology that Husserl opposed. Continuing to build on the principle of phenomenological reduction, Heidegger thematizes being only as and insofar as it is understood by Dasein: "[O]nly as long as Dasein *is*, that is, as long as there is the ontic possibility of an understanding of being, 'is there' (*gibt es*) being" (BT 212).

26. See Kisiel, *op. cit.*, 321f.

27. Ibid., 357, 479. Kisiel refers here to a letter from Heidegger to Löwith of March 1925.

28. "Dilthey considers human existence to be the genuinely historical being (*das eigentlich geschichtliche Sein*). . . . He does not . . . pose the following question however: what is the meaning of the being of our own existence? Because he does not pose this question, he can also not answer the question concerning historicity. Up to now, the phenomenological research has failed for the same reason. Phenomenology determines the human being as a gathering of perceptions, held together by the unity of an ego that functions as the centre of these acts. The question concerning the ontological character of these acts is not raised," *Lectures on Dilthey*, 161–62. At the end of the text Heidegger remarks: "Thus, the historical-philosophical way of questioning is conducted back to the fundamental question concerning being itself" (177).

29. "The fundamental ontological task of the interpretation of being as such thus includes the elaboration of the *Temporality of being (Temporalität des Seins)*. In the exposition of the problem of Temporality the concrete answer to the question of the meaning of being is first given" (BT 19). The term *Temporalität* only appears in *Being and Time* in the introduction, which was written at the end.

30. BT 25, tr. m. A few of the many comparable passages in other texts are GA 21:193–94; GA 24:448–49; GA 26:182–84. In 1941 nothing has changed on this point: "Being, as constant presencing (*beständige Anwesung*) is understood with respect to time, while the essence of time and its claim to become the opening realm for the understanding of being, remain obscure" (GA 49:46, cf. 52).

31. "*Meaning . . . is the toward-which of the projective movement which makes possible the understanding of something as something* (*Sinn ist das . . . Woraufhin des Entwurfs, aus dem her etwas als etwas verständlich wird*)" (BT 151, tr. m.). Heidegger reserves the word *significance* (*Bedeutsamkeit*) for the projective movement that makes it possible for innerworldly beings to become practically significant (cf. BT 87).

32. GA 24:400, cf. 397, 402. Heidegger here concurs—in a retrieving way—with Plato's idea of the Good as the light that makes possible every form of "seeing." See GA 31:114–15. I come back to this theme in chapter 7.

33. See BT 41 and: "The question concerning the 'meaning of being,' that is, concerning the opening realm (*Entwurfsbereich*) or the openness within which 'being' as such (not yet a being) uncovers itself for understanding, is the question concerning the 'truth of being.' Because 'time,' insofar as its essence is conceived as ecstatic, appears to be this opening realm of being, 'time' is the provisional aim of the questioning of 'Being and Time' from its first step onwards" (GA 49:56–57).

34. Heidegger considers the fact that time from Aristotle onward was interpreted as a succession of now-moments not to be coincidental, but to

be a sign of the unavoidable forgetting of being (cf. BT 420f; GA 24:362f). Heidegger's deconstruction of the traditional concept of time will be thematized in 9.3.

35. See for the radicalization of the guiding question (*Leitfrage*) of metaphysics to the fundamental question (*Grundfrage*) concerning the truth of being, e.g., KM 224f and GA 31:116.

36. EM 155 / IM 204, tr. m. See "Why is being as such initially and mostly understood against the background of the specific temporal character of the present (presence)?" (GA 31:116; cf. GA 49:52). The expression known from *Being and Time* "initially and mostly" (*zunächst und zumeist*), keeps open the possibility that it can also be otherwise. Ontology is thus not necessarily identical to *that* metaphysics which understands being as objective presence (cf. GA 25:200).

37. What determines the hammer "as this being, that is, in its what-being and its how-being, is constituted by this 'in-order-to'" (GA 24:415, tr. m.; cf. esp. BT 68–69, 83–84). I come back to the analysis of utensils (BT §14–18) in 4.5.

38. GA 26:192–93; cf. GA 24, §10–12. I return to this in 5.2.

39. GA 33:223/192, tr. m. Cf.: "The term for the being of beings, which is however just as often used with respect to beings themselves, is *ousia*, beingness. It is what constitutes beings as beings, the *on hei on*, being as such. . . . The Latin translation *essentia* . . . therefore does not adequately render the Greek *ousia*; the latter is richer and also means 'existence'" (GA 26:182–83, tr. m.; cf. "Brief über den Humanismus," WM 161 / PM 251). W. Marx in his study *Heidegger und die Tradition* dwells extensively on Heidegger's attempt to think of "essence" as different from *ousia* or substance (cf. 14).

40. Heidegger argues in GA 26 that *ousia* both in the sense of the "what" and in the sense of "existence" is characterized in Greek thinking as presence: both basic meanings are oriented toward time and refer to that which is constantly present (GA 26:183–84; cf. GA 22:172).

41. When Heidegger at the end of the lecture *On the Essence of Truth* remarks that the question concerning the essence of truth should be conducted back to the question concerning the truth of essence, he adds: "But in the concept of 'essence' philosophy thinks being" (WM 96 / PM 153). This means that the philosophical concept of "essence" conceives being inadequately, and not in its truth.

2. The Analytic of Dasein

1. Cf. "Brief über den Humanismus" (WM 164 / PM 213); "Vom Wesen der Wahrheit" (WM 97 / PM 154).

2. "If Dasein is distinguished by its understanding of being, and if the projective preconception of being (*Entwurf des Seins*) avails itself of time as openness, then Dasein has to be essentially related to time as well, that is, it has to be 'temporal.' The preliminary and all-forerunning insight into the relation between being and time, which still has to be elucidated, is therefore that which not only solely and permanently motivates the reflection on the 'temporality' of Dasein, but also gathers everything together" (GA 49:47; cf. GA 26:189; GA 31:120–22). This self-interpretation, however, is somewhat one-sided: after all, from as early as 1920 Heidegger tries to understand the dynamic of human life as a specific temporality. Nevertheless, it is true that in *Being and Time* this analysis is indeed more radical. The introduction of *Being and Time* itself contains only one reference to the relation between the understanding of being and temporality: "Time must be brought to light and be genuinely conceived as the horizon of every understanding and interpretation of being. For this to become clear we need an *original explication of the time which constitutes the horizon of every understanding of being from out of the temporality* (Zeitlichkeit) *that constitutes the being of Dasein, that understands being*" (BT 17, tr. m.). The "out of" (*aus*) in the last sentence (which is not translated adequately in either translation of *Being and Time*) expresses the relation between the second and third divisions of *Being and Time*. It is precisely this "out of" that seems to become increasingly problematic for Heidegger.

3. In order for beings to be encountered, they must already have "been 'known' with respect to their ontological structure. . . . Dwelling always already in such an open space (*Spielraum*), bringing it about, is nothing other than the movement of transcendence that characterizes all finite comportment to beings" (KM 70–71, tr. m.; cf. GA 26:203f).

4. The analytic of Dasein "cannot hope to provide a complete ontology of Dasein, which should however be supplied if something like a 'philosophical' anthropology is to rest on a sufficient philosophical basis" (BT 17, tr. m., cf. GA 49:35f).

5. "The analytic [of existence] proceeds solely with the purpose of a fundamental ontology; the point of departure, its elaboration, its limits and the way in which certain phenomena are concretized are governed by this purpose. . . . The issue is therefore neither one of anthropology nor of ethics, but of the being of this being as such, and thus one of a preparatory analytic; the metaphysics of Dasein itself is not yet the central focus" (GA 26:171, tr. m., cf. 199, 201; KM 232). Heidegger here still uses the term "metaphysics" in a broad sense, which leaves open the possibility of an investigation into the being of beings that is not guided by constant presence. The same applies for what the early Heidegger understands by "science.' As early as 1921/22, Heidegger says about this: "The expression 'scientific philosophy' should only be taken . . . as a provisional solution, which is to (negatively) fend off *Schwärmerei* . . . ; it is a 'transitional expression'"

(GA 61:46). But since these terms led to misunderstandings, they very soon become reserved for the presentifying mode of thinking from which Heidegger wishes to distance himself (see "Brief über den Humanismus," WM 187–88/PM 271). Even in the Hölderlin courses, however, we still find the term "other metaphysics" for an appropriate possibility of thinking (GA 39:196). This leads Janicaud, in my view incorrectly, to create a sharp distinction between the Hölderlin courses from 1934/35 and those from 1941–1942, where Heidegger uses the term metaphysics only in a negative sense: as if Heidegger had only definitively freed himself from metaphysics during the intervening period. See D. Janicaud, "The 'Overcoming' of Metaphysics in the Hölderlin-lectures," in *Reading Heidegger. Commemorations*, esp. 387f.

6. Cf. resp. BT 108, GA 26:173; BT 108, 193–96, 345–46. The theme of the relation between humans and animals is particularly elaborated in GA 29/30. See for the sexual difference: "As factical, Dasein is, among other things, always already dispersed in a body and thereby at the same time, among other things, always already divided into a specific gender" (GA 26:173, tr. m.). See for this also J. Derrida, "Différence sexuelle, différence ontologique," in *Psyché*: *Inventions de l'autre* / "*Geschlecht*: Sexual Difference, Ontological Difference" in *Research in Phenomenology* 13 (1983).

7. Heidegger's distinction between (1) a preliminary analysis of Dasein, (2) an ensuing thematization of the "logical" problems concerning time and the understanding of being and (3) a concrete metaphysics of human beings and nature, shows an unmistakable kinship to Hegel's division of philosophy into the *Phenomenology of Spirit,* the *Science of Logic*, and the philosophy of nature and spirit. I will come back to this in 10.5.

8. GA 26:201. In *Kant and the Problem of Metaphysics*—from the same period—Heidegger also speaks of a "metaphysics of Dasein." Less ambiguously than in GA 26, he states here that the analytic of Dasein itself already belongs to this metaphysics: "The metaphysics of Dasein, guided by the question of ground-laying, should unveil the ontological constitution of [Dasein] in such a way that it proves to be that which makes possible the understanding of being" (That is the analytic of Dasein). "Fundamental ontology, however, is only the first phase of the metaphysics of Dasein. What belongs to this [metaphysics] as a whole cannot be discussed here" (KM 232, tr. m.). It evidently could be in GA 26.

9. "[After] the meaning of being had been clarified, the whole analytic of Dasein was to be repeated in a more primordial and totally different way." "Protokoll zu einem Seminar über den Vortrag 'Zeit und Sein'" (SD 34/TB 32, tr. m.).

10. BT 140, italics mine, tr. m., cf. 16; GA 63:15. Concurring with Husserl, Heidegger also describes this "going along with" as a "putting one-

self in the position of" in, for example, involvement with utensils, although, strictly speaking, as human beings we do not need to put ourselves in that position (BT 67).

11. The *relation* between these two levels remains somewhat unclear and ambiguous. Although the possibility of phenomenology is ultimately a possibility of concretely existing Dasein, in my view a distinction must nevertheless be made between the Dasein that retrieves itself at the *existentiell* level from fallenness and the Dasein that "has seized upon its inherent possibility not only of elucidating its own existence, but also of provisionally inquiring into the meaning of existentiality itself, and thus into the meaning of being as such" (BT 20, tr. m.). In my view, the possibility should not be ruled out that the "authentic" phenomenologist could fall short as a human being, for instance in his social life, political choices, etcetera.

12. "At the beginning of the analysis, Dasein is precisely not to be interpreted with regard to one of its different, specific modes of existence, but should be revealed with regard to the indifferent way in which it exists 'initially and mostly.' The indifference of this everydayness is *not nothing*, but rather constitutes a positive phenomenal character of this being" (BT 43, tr. m.). Phenomena such as idle talk, curiosity, and ambiguity "reveal a basic mode of everydayness, which we call the *fallenness* of Dasein. . . . Dasein has always already lapsed from itself, that is, from the authentic possibility of existing as itself, and has always already fallen prey to the 'world'" (BT 175, tr. m.). A few pages later: "On the other hand, *authentic* existence is nothing that hovers above the falling tendency of everydayness, but is, existentially, only a modified way of taking it upon oneself" (BT 179, tr. m., cf. 298; GA 24:228).

13. BT 326–328. Cf.: "*Ecstatic temporality* . . . is the primary regulator of the possible unity of all the essential existential structures of Dasein" (351).

14. "Temporality has different possibilities and different ways of *accomplishing itself* (*Zeitlichkeit kann sich in verschiedenen Möglichkeiten und in verschiedener Weise zeitigen*). The fundamental possibilities of existence, the authenticity and inauthenticity of Dasein, are ontologically grounded in possible accomplishments of temporality" (BT 304, tr. m., cf. 350). *Zeitigen* in German means, among other things: (cause to) ripen, bring into being. Heidegger's use of this word mainly pertains to the time that brings into being the openness of Dasein and determines the different possible ways in which Dasein accomplishes this openness. *Sich zeitigen* means: become concrete, take shape. In the existing translations "sich zeitigen" is translated as "to temporalize."

15. "Understanding (*Verstehen*), which has the character of a projective preconception (*Entwurf*), constitutes existentially what we call the *see-*

ing (*Sicht*) of Dasein" (BT 146, tr. m.). Dasein is existentially constituted by primordial openness and hence by the seeing that each time accomplishes itself in accordance with the fundamental modes of its being. Having characterized these modes as the circumspection of taking care of things and as the considerateness of concern, Heidegger calls "the seeing which is primarily and on the whole directed toward existence *transparency* (*Durchsichtigkeit*)" (BT 146, cf. 12, 69). A little later: "By showing how all seeing is primarily grounded in understanding . . . we have taken away from pure intuition its priority. . . . Even the phenomenological 'intuition of essences' is grounded in existential understanding" (147). It may be added that this modification cannot do justice to the phronetic dynamic of this understanding.

16. Heidegger's analysis of primordial openness results directly from his reading of Aristotle in the early 1920s. In *Eth. Nic.* VI, 1139b 15–18, Aristotle distinguishes five ways in which beings can be revealed. He uses here the word *alētheuein* (cf. A 29). See also 1.2 and 5.4.

17. See for these three moments BT 134f, 142f, 160f respectively.

18. "Just as Future primarily makes understanding possible, and Past makes mood possible, the third constitutive moment of care, *fallenness*, has its existential meaning in *Present*" (BT 346). In §68 (*The Temporality of Primordial Openness as such*), Heidegger seems to identify primordial openness with care (cf. 334–35). In my view, it would be clearer to understand primordial openness as a certain way in which the formal dynamic of care ("being-ahead-of-oneself in-the-world as being-with" (192, 327)) accomplishes itself. Disposition (*Befindlichkeit*) as being affected by moods thus pertains more to the way in which Dasein relates to its own thrownness than to this facticity itself (cf. 135). See also GA 20:411. The confusion may be caused by the fact that Heidegger tried to combine various earlier analyses in a short time.

19. D. Franck states, for instance: "If discourse (that is to say *Rede*) does not primarily temporalize itself from out of one of the three ecstases, it cannot be an authentic existential, that is to say, a mode of temporalization. . . . Thus, discourse has no proper temporal meaning . . . and a phenomenon of which the temporal meaning is exclusively improper is excluded from any temporality." D. Franck, *Heidegger et le problème de l'espace*,111–12. Franck's attempt to criticize the hierarchy between time and space in *Being and Time* is, in my view, inadequate insofar as Heidegger's concept of time is of an entirely different order than traditional spatiality. Pöggeler also sees inconsistencies in Heidegger's representation of the relation between *Rede* and *Verfallenheit*. O. Pöggeler, *Neue Wege mit Heidegger*, 129–30.

20. "Understood formally, every Present makes present, but not every Present does that as 'momentary vision' (*Augenblick*). When we use

the expression 'making present' without further qualification, we always mean its inauthentic mode, which is not determined by resoluteness and momentary vision" (BT 338, tr. m., cf. 326).

21. "[O]ur analysis of the way in which discourse is temporally grounded . . . can be tackled only when the problem of the fundamental connection between being and truth has been unfolded from out of (*aus*) the problem of temporality" (BT 349, tr. m.).

22. "The objectifying relation to innerworldly present things has the character of *a distinguished making present*" (BT 363, tr. m.). Heidegger could have added that in sensory perception the temporal dynamic has not yet been entirely lost; he thus could have given a place to Husserl's analysis of the retention and anticipation that constitute every perception of objects. From GA 59 it is evident that around 1920 Heidegger already knew of Husserl's analyses of temporal consciousness (GA 59:150–51), whose publication he arranged in 1928. By analyzing the dynamic of anticipating and retaining starting from the way we handle utensils, Heidegger implicitly criticizes Husserl's epistemological preference for the temporal structure of sensory perception. In 1928 he says on this: "[E]xpecting, retaining, and making present are not merely the way we grasp the 'then,' 'before' and 'now,' that is, the way we are conscious of them; they themselves constitute the origin" (GA 26:263, tr. m.).

23. The same applies for the time with which Dasein is primordially familiar; it levels down to a homogeneous series of now-moments (BT 422).

24. BT 115, 118, 124–25; cf. GA 20:326.

25. "In our previous analysis, the scope of what is encountered in the world was initially narrowed down to utensils at hand and to objectively present nature. . . . This restriction was not only necessary for the purpose of simplifying the explanation; but, above all, because the ontological mode of the existence of others encountered within the surrounding world is distinct from handiness (*Zuhandenheit*) and objective presence (*Vorhandenheit*)" (BT 118, tr. m., cf. 125). However: "Dasein understands itself, initially and for the most part, against the background of its world (*aus seiner Welt*), and the being-there-together (*Mitdasein*) of other human beings is often encountered against the background of innerworldly things at hand" (120, tr. m.).

26. Heidegger here does not explicitly use the terms authentic and inauthentic, although he does elsewhere. Here he is referring to the two extreme possibilities of the positive modes of concern, of which one pertains to an (innerworldly) "what" and the other to the authentic care of the other—that is, to his or her own existence (BT 122). The word "positive" here means: clearly distinguishable, not indifferent. Cf. in GA 21: "We have characterized here two extreme modes of concern, the authentic and the inauthentic,

because its factic, concrete forms can only be elucidated on the basis of these extreme modes. . . . These concrete forms can be understood as mixtures (*Mischformen*)" (GA 21:224). The analysis of concern prepares the analysis of the "they," which tends to take away Dasein's responsibility (BT 126f). This tendency follows naturally from inauthentic concern, provided that it now refers to a public openness (*Öffentlichkeit*) where the distinction between an I and an other has become subordinated to an impersonal institution that regulates and levels down the possible modes of existence.

27. Notice that authentic concern is described in terms of the "possible": "The mode of concern that leaps in to replace the other . . . determines the being-with-one-another to a large extent. . . . In contrast to this, there is the possibility of a concern . . . which essentially pertains to . . . the other's own existence and not to a 'what' with which he is concerned" (BT 122, tr. m.).

28. See BT 44–45 for the distinction between the usual categories and the existentials (*Existentialien*) that pertain to the being of Dasein.

29. "However, one should not overlook the fact that we use the term 'being-there-together' (*Mitdasein*) to indicate the being of existing others *insofar* as they are disclosed from within the world" (BT 120).

30. In GA 24 a few passages can be found where Heidegger briefly refers to the I-thou relationship, but here again the starting point is still that the other is encountered insofar as it is the one with whom I share a world: "The condition which makes it possible for the self to be together with others as a possible thou is grounded in the fact that Dasein is a self that itself exists as being-in-the-world. For 'thou' means: 'you who are with me within a world'" (GA 24:422–23, tr. m.; cf. BT 123; "Vom Wesen des Grundes," WM 54 / PM 122). In contrast to Levinas, Heidegger does not start out from the other person who summons me to my own infinite responsibility: the conscience is an anonymous institution that summons Dasein from within to come toward itself. Although authentic, resolute Dasein can indeed start to function as a "conscience" for the other (298), Heidegger appears to regard this ontic summoning of someone's conscience as grounded in the transcendental structure of the call that comes from Dasein itself and yet is directed toward it (275). Another human being thus appears to only act as a substitute in summoning someone to come toward his proper possibilities.

31. See "Brief über den Humanismus" (WM 187 / PM 271). In *The Anaximander Saying* from 1946 (HW/EGT) Heidegger tries to show what he understands by a primordial ethics that cannot be reduced to interpersonal relations. I will interpret this text in 6.8.

32. "[That should] intimate that *making present*, in which the falling prey (*Verfallen*) to the beings at hand or objectively present that we take

care of is *primarily* grounded, remains, in the mode of primordial temporality, *enclosed* within Future and Past" (BT 328, tr. m., cf. 12, 175f). In 1941: "For us, everydayness very easily leads up to the in-authentic" (GA 52:65).

33. "The more inauthentic Present is . . . the more it flees from a definite possibility of existence (*ein bestimmtes Seinkönnen*) and closes it off. . . . The 'breaking away' of Present also implies an increasing forgetfulness" (BT 347, tr. m.).

34. I also here leave aside Heidegger's deconstruction of the traditional concept of time (§81–82). This deconstruction is one of the detours that Heidegger takes in order to elucidate his own concept of primordial temporality. This detour has, in my view, the disadvantage that Heidegger's own analysis of time can then easily be regarded as a contribution to the thinking about time that can be *experienced*, while Heidegger himself ultimately intends a transcendental structure that is not accessible to experience. I come back to this in 9.3.

3. The Initial Attempt to Elaborate *Time and Being*

1. The sequence of the following chapters will not adhere strictly to Heidegger's own indications about what was to follow the published part of *Being and Time*. Thus, he writes that only when the meaning of being and the reach of the understanding of being as such have been clarified can one also analyze "what belongs to the concept of a science *of being as such*, its possibilities and modifications" (BT 230, tr. m., cf. 147).

2. This "historical" part will be discussed in chapter 5.

3. Namely: (1) the ontological difference, (2) the distinction between essence and existence, (3) the possible modifications of being and the unity of that manifold, and (4) the truth-character of being (GA 24:22–25, cf. 321). It is not certain that Heidegger had already planned this order for *Time and Being*. However, this is the view taken by Von Hermann, "*Being and Time* and *The Basic Problems of Phenomenology*," in *Reading Heidegger: Commemorations*, 125.

4. GA 24:324, tr. m. Cf.: "*[B]eing is understood and conceptually comprehended against the background of time.* When temporality functions as such a condition we call it Temporality" (GA 24:389, tr. m.). In order to distinguish between *Zeitlichkeit* and *Temporalität*, the two modes of primordial time will be translated as temporality and Temporality respectively, in line with existing translations. I would stress, however, that Heidegger also uses the term *Zeitlichkeit* in a "technical" sense; it does not pertain to the fact that all beings will one day pass away.

5. "Temporality (*Temporalität*) is the most primordial way in which temporality accomplishes itself (*Temporalität ist die ursprünglichste Zeitigung der Zeitlichkeit als solcher*)" (GA 24:429, tr. m.). In the introduction of *Being and Time*: "In the exposition of the problem of Temporality the concrete answer to the question of the meaning of being is first given" (BT 19). *Being and Time* also points out that the temporality which underlies care only "prepares the understanding of a still more primordial way in which temporality accomplishes itself. This primordial mode of temporality grounds the understanding of being that constitutes the basic structure of Dasein" (235, tr. m.). See also Heidegger's preface in Richardson, *op. cit.*, XIII.

6. Cf. GA 24:426. See for transcendence as the being-in-the-world of Dasein GA 26:203f, esp. 213–16; "Vom Wesen des Grundes" (WM 33–35, 54f / PM 107–9, 122f).

7. "[T]he ecstases of temporality (Future, Past, Present) do not simply exceed themselves by reaching out to . . . they do not reach out as it were to the nothing. Rather . . . they each have a *horizon* which is prefigured by the mode of the self-exceeding reaching out *and belongs to the ecstasis itself*" (GA 24:428, tr. m.). In *Being and Time* the horizonal schemes of the three ecstases are described at the *existentiell* level of temporality as follows: "With factic Dasein, a possibility of existence has always been projectively preconceived within the horizon of Future, the 'being-always-already' is disclosed within the horizon of Past, and beings that we deal with are discovered within the horizon of Present" (BT 365, tr. m.). The relation between ecstasis and horizon can be understood as analogous to the relation between intentio and intentum, although Heidegger is referring to a phenomenon that is more original than every intentional relation. Likewise, the Kantian concept of schema, used here by Heidegger, relates to a category as the objective side of a subjective structure. What Heidegger takes from Kant is the meaning of the schema as that which always already has to guide our understanding if we are to thematize something as something. The horizonal scheme is that aspect of the ecstasis which we can "see" before us, while the ecstasis itself sheds its light as it were from behind the back of Dasein. The level of intentionality is thus for Heidegger an entirely secondary level (cf. e.g., GA 24:378–79, 444; GA 26:215).

8. "Present, by exceeding itself projectively, brings about Praesens. Praesens is not identical with Present, but *basically determines the horizonal scheme of this ecstasis* and therefore belongs to the full temporal structure of Present" (GA 24:435, tr. m.). Not without good reason does Heidegger use a Latin term to refer to this temporal horizon; in this way the primordial temporal dimension of the understanding of being is distinguished from the other modes of temporality (433). By analogy with the distinction between temporality and Temporality, I render *Praesenz* with

"Praesens" instead of "praesens." Heidegger does not suggest any Latin names for the horizons of the ecstases Future and Past. However, the term "Absence" (*Absenz*) (442) does seem to be related to them.

9. It is therefore misleading of A. Hofstadter to translate "Vergegenständlichung" as "objectification" (see 398, 456 of the German pagination), when it is crucial for Heidegger to distinguish between an objectifying and a nonobjectifying mode of explicit elucidation or thematization.

10. See F. Dastur, *Heidegger et la question du temps*: "Therefore, temporal ontology is not a 'theory' in the traditional sense . . . , for the objectification of being that it requires does not have the meaning of a making present" (108).

11. Thus, projective preconception "takes the direction toward thought, comprehension, soul, mind, spirit, subject, without understanding the necessity of a primordial and preliminary ontological preparation of especially these areas—that is, the necessity of being serious about this work" (GA 24:459, tr. m.).

12. In *Being and Time* Heidegger indicates the character of this freedom as follows: "Temporality (*Zeitlichkeit*) already holds itself ecstatically in the horizons of its ecstases and, accomplishing itself, comes back to the beings encountered in the 'there' (*das Da*). With the factical existence of Dasein, innerworldly beings are also already encountered. That such beings are discovered along with the 'there' of Dasein's own existence is not something that Dasein can choose. Only *what* it discovers and discloses at times, in *which* direction, *to what extent*, and *in what way*, is a matter of its freedom, although always within the limits of its thrownness" (BT 366, tr. m.). That certainly does not apply to the involvement with innerworldly beings alone.

13. "What it means to say that being 'is' . . . can only be asked in a concrete way when the meaning of being and the reach of the understanding of being have been clarified as such. Only then can one also analyze primordially what belongs to the concept of a science *of being as such*, its possibilities and modifications" (BT 230, tr. m.).

14. Later in *Being and Time* Heidegger does indeed apply his analysis of interpretation to his own work: "Ontological research is a possible way of interpretation, which we characterized as a development and appropriation of a certain understanding. Every interpretation has its preliminary having, view and grasping (*ihre Vorhabe, ihre Vorsicht und ihren Vorgriff*)" (BT 231–32, tr. m., cf. 156, 311). In order to appropriately interpret something, this whole of preliminary decisions which Heidegger calls the hermeneutical situation, must be clarified as such (232). That which the analysis always already "has before itself" is Dasein as a whole, while the perspective from which Dasein is interpreted is the idea of existence. This *Vorhabe* and *Vorsicht* "then prefigure at the same time the conceptuality

(preliminary grasping) to which all ontological structures are to be brought" (232, tr. m.). In a course from 1923/24 we find similar passages about the preliminary structure of understanding (GA 17:110, 116).

15. This leads Heidegger to distinguish between the primary constitution of meaning as such and the linguistic articulation of meanings (BT 87). He later drops this distinction: even if the phenomenon of language cannot be understood by starting out from the whole of spoken words, the articulation that brings about this primary meaning must itself be understood as "language." See Heidegger's later note at BT 87: "Language is not imposed, but *is* the primordial essence of the truth of the 'there' (*Da*)."

16. Cf. BT 167–68 and GA 17: "Language not only speaks whenever we perceive, but even *guides* our perceiving, we see *through* language. In so far as language has been appropriated in a traditional and nonoriginal way, it rather *covers over* things, while this very language has nonetheless the basic function of pointing out things" (GA 17:30). The language that belongs to facticity and from the outset structures the encounter of beings does not come sufficiently to the fore in *Being and Time*. This is probably because in §34 of *Being and Time* Heidegger is particularly concentrating on the ontological genesis of language. However, this analysis in no way rules out that the way Dasein *actually* relates to beings is determined from the outset by the spoken language in which it is thrown.

17. BT 168, italics mine, tr. m. Cf.: "Dasein is not only inclined to abandon itself to its world (*an seine Welt zu verfallen*) . . . at the same time Dasein also abandons itself to the tradition to which it belongs and which it has more or less explicitly assumed. This tradition deprives Dasein of the possibility of guiding itself, of asking, and of deciding for itself. This is *especially* true of *that* understanding—and of the way it is made explicit—which is rooted in the most proper being of Dasein, namely, its ontological understanding" (BT 21, first italics mine, tr. m.).

18. The fact that Heidegger was concerned from the outset about this metaphysical "idle talk" (and about the fallenness of ontology as such) is more evident in the courses from the early 1920s than in *Being and Time*. The analytic of Dasein here still plays a subordinate role compared with the question concerning philosophy itself. Thus, in 1923 Heidegger says that the philosophy of his time is characterized by not only curiosity (which refers to philosophy's tendency to be everywhere and nowhere at the same time) but also by public openness (*Öffentlichkeit*): "Insofar as philosophy is a way of interpretation, it takes part in public openness; it *is* there in the same way as everything that is public, that is . . . it makes sure that others talk about it so as to play an active part in idle talk and keep itself alive" (GA 63:62). In GA 61 Heidegger uses the terms "lapsing" (*Abfall*) and "ruining" (*Ruinanz*) to express this dynamic. However, philosophy does have the possibility of resisting this ruining dynamic and accomplishing a countering movement:

"The way in which *philosophical interpretation* accomplishes itself, and does this in the appropriated *way of gaining access which consists in questioning*, is a *movement which runs counter to the ruin (eine gegenruinante Bewegtheit)*" (GA 61:153). In contrast to the rigid academic philosophy at which Heidegger directs his criticism, this questioning thinking is characterized by the "resoluteness of its understanding, which occurs in a more certain way the less it exhibits itself, and is able to keep silent and wait" (71).

19. Cf. BT 190–91. In his discussion with Cassirer from 1929, Heidegger says on this: "The analysis of anxiety does not intend to make visible a central phenomenon in man, but is solely meant to prepare the following question: Which metaphysical meaning of Dasein itself allows human beings at all to find themselves face to face with the nothing? The analysis of anxiety aims at pointing out that the possibility of only conceiving the nothing as an idea, is partly grounded in anxiety as a specific determination of disposition (*Befindlichkeit*). Only when I understand the nothing, or anxiety, do I have the possibility of understanding being" (KM 283–84, tr. m.). Dasein always already understands being and is always already guided by the mood of anxiety, but both the understanding of being and the anxiety usually remain "latent" or implicit (BT 192).

20. B 21–22, cf.: "In astonishment (*Er-staunen*), the basic mood of the first beginning, beings for the first time receive the shape that brings them to a halt. Dread (*Erschrecken*), the basic mood of the other beginning, unveils the obscure emptiness of aimlessness and the flight for the first and last decisions that is hidden behind every progressivity and every domination of beings" (GA 45:197, tr. m.). Cf. also *Was ist das—die Philosophie?* (1956), esp. 24–28; GA 39:139–48. In 1920/21 Heidegger distinguishes, less radically still, between wonder and curiosity as authentic and inauthentic attitudes of phenomenology (GA 61:195). I was made aware of these themes by M. Haar, "*Stimmung*, époque et pensée," in *La fracture de l'Histoire. Douze essais sur Heidegger*: "The *Stimmung* every time translates the degree of negativity of the *Grundstimmung*, a degree that varies according to its historical modality" (230). However, Haar sees a problematic discrepancy between the analysis of anxiety in *Being and Time* and that of the disposition of thinking in the later texts (see esp. 224–25, 236), which—in my view—is eliminated in my interpretation.

21. "In the structures of both thrownness and projective preconceiving essentially lies a nothingness. . . . *Care itself is in its essence thoroughly permeated by nothingness (Nichtigkeit)*" (BT 285, tr. m.).

4. The Temporality of Thinking: Heidegger's Method

1. §7 of *Being and Time* gives a "preliminary concept of phenomenology" (BT 34), which would have been elaborated in *Time and Being*: "How-

ever, a completely adequate existential interpretation of science cannot be carried out until the *meaning of being and the 'connection' between being and truth have been clarified* from out of the temporality of existence. The following considerations are to prepare the understanding of *this central problem area*. Only within this area will it be possible to develop the idea of phenomenology, that is to be distinguished from the preliminary concept indicated in the introduction" (BT 357, tr. m.).

2. With regard to the early courses, reference can be made to Kisiel's aforementioned study.

3. This course from 1919 was published, together with the course *Phenomenology and Transcendental Philosophy of Value* and a short text on the essence of the university, under the title *Zur Bestimmung der Philosophie* (*Toward the Definition of Philosophy*) (GA 56/57). The first of these courses is the more important with regard to the question of method.

4. GA 56/57:29. The term *Destruktion* is not yet used here. In the first part Heidegger directs his criticism mainly at neo-Kantians such as Rickert and Windelband. He argues that phenomena like validity and value are not clarified in a sufficiently primordial way and that it is therefore incorrect to take them as a starting point (47, 50).

5. GA 56/57:59. See: "However, the fact that thinking has got so deeply stuck in the theoretical still seriously hinders us from really measuring the reach of the lived experience of the environing world (*das umweltliche Erleben*)" (88, cf. 87).

6. GA 56/57:98. Husserl is not named here. Evidently Heidegger here already wishes to no longer identify his thinking with that of his teacher, because Husserl uncritically conceives the intuitive beholding proper to phenomenology as analogous to sensory perception.

7. GA 56/57:101. See "Anmerkungen zu Karl Jaspers 'Psychologie der Weltanschauungen'" (WM 18–19 / PM 15–16); Heidegger on Natorp: GA 59:§12–16, GA 60:10–11.

8. GA 56/57:67–68. Heidegger says here: "Precisely because it is so simple . . . the mere 'there is' (*es gibt*) evokes many enigmas."

9. "When I experience a lectern by seeing it, something that belongs to an immediate, environing world is there for *me*. This environing character of the world . . . is primary, it is immediately given, without any thinking detour through the apprehension of things (*Sacherfassen*). While living in an environing world, significance occurs all the time and everywhere, everything is worldly (*welthaft*), 'it is worlding' (*es weltet*)" (GA 56/57:72–73). It is interesting to see how these formulations—like expressions such as *es gibt* and *Ereignis*—return in Heidegger's later work with a more radical meaning, no longer pertaining to concrete experiences.

Kisiel (*op. cit.*, 458), however, in his conclusion appears to be aware only of the return and not of the radical change that takes place along the way.

10. GA 56/57:73–74. Heidegger here plays on the word *Erlebnis*, which, in contrast to *Erfahrung*, is related to "life" and "living through." He chooses to create the terms *Ent-leben* and *Ent-lebnis* to indicate the—objectifying—experience in which this primordial character of being lived through has been repressed. This therefore concerns an (inauthentic) modification of the lived experience. To underline the distinction, I usually translate *Erlebnis* as "lived experience." Kisiel (*op. cit.*, 46) translates *Entleben* as "un-living."

11. GA 56/57:89. N.B.: "The experience of a thing (*Dingerfahrung*) is a lived experience (*Erlebnis*) indeed, and yet, when we understand it with regard to its origin in the lived experience of the environing world, it is already a de-living experience (*Ent-lebnis*)" (GA 56/57:90, cf. 89).

12. GA 56/57:114, cf. 115. Heidegger here makes use of Husserl's distinction between generalizing and formalizing in *Logische Untersuchungen* I, especially §67–68 and *Ideen* I, 32–34 / *Ideas* I, 26–27. According to Husserl, it is wrong to interpret "any object whatever (the empty Something) as the genus with respect to objects of all sorts and, therefore, naturally as simply the one and only summum genus . . ." (*Ideen* I, 32/26). This formal determination is not the result of a process that ascends from a given object to the more general. In GA 60 from 1921/22 Heidegger takes up this issue again (57–65). There it becomes clear that he also distinguishes his own method from Husserl's "formal ontology": "But precisely because the formal determination is totally indifferent to its content . . . [it] conceals that which has the character of an *enactment* (*das Vollzugsmäßige*) . . . and only directs itself to the *subject matter* (*Gehalt*)" (63). In that case a lived experience becomes an object in the same way as all other things to which consciousness can turn itself. I will come back to GA 60 in 4.2.

13. Heidegger argues that the "something" as such can sometimes also be experienced in life itself, for instance when we are at the border between two modes of experience, or at times when life is very intensive (GA 56/57:115). This possibility is indicated more concretely in *Being and Time* through (e.g.) the analysis of anxiety.

14. "One has to make a sharp distinction between the preworldly 'something' of life in itself, the de-living, formal thematization that springs from it, and the objectifying theorization." "Now it becomes clear how far there is a difference in quality between the motivation [that is, the source] of that which is formally thematized and of that which has the character of an object. What is formally thematized at the same time refers *back* to a basic stratum (*Grundschicht*) of life in and for itself" (GA 56/57:116). See Kisiel, *op. cit.*, 22 for the "KNS schema."

15. That Heidegger does not yet sharply delimit the difference between the positive sciences and philosophy is perhaps due to his attention to the sphere of experiences. The difference between ontic involvement and the thematization of experiences themselves is smaller than the difference between beings and being. Thus, Heidegger will first have to further free himself from Husserl's consciousness-oriented perspective.

16. This course mainly concerns the question as to how the primal or primordial science can gain access at all to its area of investigation, when the perspective of life itself does not disclose the structure of the experiences from within the flow of life itself. The only two passages in which Heidegger uses the term are a note for his own use, with the remark that the concept "life" is used initially in a formal-indicative way (GA 58:198), and the following passage: "[The concepts] only indicate certain phenomena, they point into a concrete area and therefore have a merely formal character (meaning of the 'formal indication')" (248). This passage comes from the lecture notes taken by O. Becker.

17. GA 59:85. The *Duden* dictionary gives as the first, yet rare meaning of *Antastung*: to touch with the hands. Only as the second meaning, but probably less rare: to damage, infringe. I think it is possible to understand all Heidegger's thinking on the basis of the ambivalence of the infringing or noninfringing touch.

18. The course is a part of *Phenomenology of Religious Life* (GA 60), which also includes a course on Augustine and the outline of a course on mediaeval mysticism.

19. GA 60:63; cf. GA 61:52–53.

20. In GA 63 from 1923 "being in a world" is understood as the formal indication of a structure that subsequently is to be concretized (*Erfüllung*) and confirmed (*Ausweisung*) by the interpretation of concrete phenomena (GA 63:80).

21. "We will apply the achieved results to the problem of the historical. When we take the historical as that which is formally indicated, we do *not* assert thereby that the most general determination of 'historical' as 'that which occurs in time' designates a final meaning" (GA 60:64). "The problem of time has rather to be conceived with respect to the way we experience temporality in the factic experience—setting aside all pure consciousness and all pure time" (65).

22. Kisiel has added the following commentary to what he calls the *cursus interruptus:* "This is most unfortunate for posterity, since Heidegger was in the middle of his one and only truly sustained treatment of the 'formal indication' at the time; he abruptly dropped this vital but somewhat advanced topic and never really returned to it again" (*op. cit.*, 150).

The formal indication, "perhaps the very heart and soul of the early Heidegger," will from now on mostly only be mentioned by name and, also in *Being and Time*, applied (172). This application can itself be thematized—which Kisiel does not do. It will then be found that the formal indication constitutes only one of the moments of the "heart" of Heidegger's thinking. It gives as it were merely a first indication of his methodical principle.

23. GA 61:152–53. The elimination of inadequate philosophical interpretations from (for example) what philosophy itself is, is itself a moment of the counter-ruining (*gegenruinante*) movement: "In this elimination . . . consists the *fight* of factic philosophical interpretation *against its own factic ruinance* (*Ruinanz*). This fight takes place whenever philosophy occurs" (153, cf. 178).

24. "We just have to realize that the formal characteristic does not give the essence, but . . . only indicates the decisive task of understanding the relation in terms of its own dimension" (GA 29/30:425). The brief, and last, discussion of the formal indication in this course from 1929/30 will not be considered here. I would like to point out, however, that Heidegger also refers again to the formal indication in the *Beiträge zur Philosophie* from 1936–38, namely in connection with the expression "ontological difference": "[W]hereas this formally understood . . . distinction can be nothing but an indication (*Anzeige*) of the fact that the relation to being is different from the relation to beings" (B 467).

25. However, in GA 61 Heidegger does remark that the categories which showed forth in the "dynamic of caring" "are deformalized in a certain direction" in the different "formally-indicating determinations of the ruinance," and this—I would add—with regard to one of the basic movements of life (GA 61:141, cf. BT 35). Heidegger also mentions the deformalization in "Anmerkungen zu Karl Jaspers 'Psychologie der Weltanschauungen'" (WM 24 / PM 21). In this text from 1919–21 Heidegger repeatedly refers to the importance of the method and the significance of the formal indication (cf. WM 9–11, 29 / 8–9, 25). Husserl also uses the term deformalization (cf. *Ideen* I, 32 / *Ideas* I, 26).

26. *Fortunately for posterity*, such a change of perspective is always possible. Because Heidegger's texts often break off at crucial moments, the reader who tries to follow the indications in the text, or tries to take the text as an indication, is more or less forced to leave the texts behind.

27. In his text on Aristotle from 1922, Heidegger says about fallenness: "This dynamic character is not a bad quality that turns up from time to time and could be cultivated away in more progressed and happier times of human culture. So little is it so, that interpretations of human existence which take their point of departure in a realizable perfection . . . are themselves only extensions (*Ausladungen*) of this very inclination toward falling prey to the world" (A 10).

28. Heidegger characterizes the "everyday being-in-the-world nearest to us" as "falling, circumspect taking care of things" (BT 335, tr. m.). The temporality that grounds this kind of care allows for its modification into pure sensory perception and into objectifying, theoretical knowledge. "The whole of these analyses reveals that Dasein's inauthenticity is ontologically grounded in a certain possibility of temporality to accomplish itself. These analyses lead to the question of how the temporal character of everydayness—the temporal meaning of the 'initially and mostly,' which we have continually been using—is to be understood" (BT 335, tr. m.).

29. Cf. for the threefold formal—inauthentic—authentic: P. Fürstenau, *Heidegger. Das Gefüge seines Denkens*, esp. 11–16. Counter to what he calls the traditional view, he tries to elucidate the unity of Heidegger's thinking—also with regard to the early and later work—on the basis of a "structural interpretation" (3). However, he scarcely thematizes the meaning of temporality. When discussing Heidegger's interpretation of Hegel, he does not take sufficient distance from Heidegger's texts to thematize the relation between the threefold of Heidegger's method and Hegel's dialectic. I will discuss this in chapter 10.

30. Thus, for example, Heidegger remarks: "But even so, the authentic being-toward-death which we have deduced existentially as an authentic possibility of being-a-whole, still remains a purely existential projective preconception *(ein rein existenzialer Entwurf)* that lacks an attestation of the order of Dasein itself" (BT 301, tr. m.). See 2.2. For his analyses of such experiences, Heidegger draws from the work of, for instance, Kierkegaard. He says in 1923: "The interpretation presented here received strong impulses from the work of Kierkegaard. However, preconceptions, point of departure . . . and goal are fundamentally different" (GA 63:30; cf. BT 190n, 235n).

31. See from 1941: "I believe that I know something about the failures of this book myself. It is the same as with climbing a never-climbed mountain. Because it is steep and unknown at the same time, the person who goes this way will sometimes happen to slide down. . . . Sometimes he also slides down without the reader noticing it; for the page numbers continue anyway. . . . The misinterpretations are supported by the inevitable fact that such an attempt can least of all break away from its time. It must consciously, yet also to a large extent against its will, speak the language of its time and think within the beaten tracks from which it frees itself" (GA 49:27–28).

32. "As a utensil, this indicating utensil (*Zeigzeug*) is constituted by reference (*Verweisung*). It has the character of in-order-to, its specific serviceability, it is there in order to indicate. The indicating of the sign can be taken as a kind of 'referring.'" However, this explicitly indicating character of the sign is to be distinguished from referring in the sense of an "onto-

logical-categorial determination of utensils *as* utensils." The indicating of the sign is an "ontic concretion" of the ontological referring. "But just as surely as indicating is fundamentally different from the kind of referring that constitutes every utensil, it is just as incontestable that signs have a peculiar and even distinguished relation to the kind of being that is proper to the whole of utensils at hand in the environing world and to the worldly character of this whole" (BT 78–79, tr. m.).

33. "The foregoing interpretation of signs should simply offer *phenomenal support* for our characterization of reference" (BT 82, italics mine). Thus, there is still a difference between "for Dasein" and "for us."

34. Heidegger himself reserves the terms inauthentic and authentic for the being of Dasein. I only wish to indicate that his analysis of the being of innerwordly beings is guided by the same scheme as the analytic of Dasein in the narrower sense. As far as I know, Heidegger never thematizes the temporal modification that grounds the sign.

35. Heidegger seems to give the peculiar example of the pointer of a motor car (BT 78) because of its similarity with the formal indication. Concerning the latter, he remarks in 1921: "[T]he content, the determinations of the object, are precisely *not to be thematized themselves*; but the grasping understanding has to follow the indicated direction of the meaning (*die angezeigte Sinnrichtung*)" (GA 61:32).

36. Support for this thesis comes from the fact that the analysis of the sign only appears in GA 20 from 1925 (278f)—that is, after the courses in which the formal indication is discussed.

37. See 1.4. These courses are GA 17 from 1923/24 and GA 20 from 1925. Even in 1923 (GA 63) Heidegger is already very critical of Husserl. He argues that because Husserl, influenced by neo-Kantianism, increasingly fixates the theme of phenomenology on the region of experiences, phenomenological investigation has "sunk into colorlessness, rashness and rapidity." The final note of Heidegger's unusually vehement tirade appears to be aimed at the superficial followers rather than at Husserl himself: "That is the way it is, instead of assuming the possibility that lies in phenomenology. Starting from this bustle, it is impossible to make out anything about phenomenology or gain a definition. The matter is hopeless! All such tendencies betray phenomenology and its possibility. The ruin cannot be resisted any longer!" (GA 63:73–74). The matter cannot, however, be so hopeless that there could be no possibility of going along in an authentic manner with the original impulse of phenomenology and thus of enacting a counter-ruining movement. This would be, according to Heidegger, the task of a hermeneutics of facticity (cf. 76).

38. See GA 24: "Being does not become accessible like beings, we do not simply come across it, but it must . . . each time be brought to view in a free,

projective preconception (*in einem freien Entwurf*). We call this projective preconception of the given beings with regard to their being and its structures *phenomenological construction*" (GA 24:29–30, tr. m., see 458–59; BT 375).

39. "The way of encountering being and the structures of being . . . must first be *wrested* from the objects of phenomenology. Thus the *point of departure* of the analysis, the *access* to the phenomenon and *passage* through the prevalent coverings, must secure their own method" (BT 36).

40. Heidegger formalizes the usual meaning of "guilt" in such a way that only the determination "being-the-ground of a nothingness" remains (BT 283, tr. m.). This formal indication can then be given another, second meaning and come to pertain to the being of Dasein as such: being thrown and radically finite, Dasein essentially falls short, and must take upon itself the responsibility for what it has not itself brought forth. This existential being-guilty then has an inauthentic and an authentic mode, insofar as Dasein itself initially and mostly turns away from the "not" which pervades its being, yet has the possibility of facing up to its essential finitude. The first interpretive movement (the formalization) serves as preparation for gaining access to the being of Dasein, that is to say, to an existential structure. The existential analysis proper subsequently understands this structure in relation to its inauthentic and its authentic modification.

41. In *Being and Time* Heidegger calls the formal, preceding structure an "a priori perfect" (BT 85). In a later note he adds to this: "It is not something ontically past, but rather what is always earlier, what we are referred *back* to in the question of beings as such."

42. Since there is a further distinction *within* the apriorical structure of Dasein between the formal "what" and its possible modifications, this formal structure is again, in comparison with those modifications, the "earlier," and as such disclosed by Past. Heidegger does not thematize this here. Cf. however: "The primordial structural whole of care (*Sorge*) is an existential a priori which as such lies 'before,' and therefore always already *in* every factic 'relation' and 'position' of Dasein" (BT 193, tr. m.). In the existential analysis these factic possibilities can be delimited on the basis of the inauthentic and authentic modifications of that formal structure. See for the a priori also BT 41, 65.

43. GA 24:26; cf. BT 11–13 and: "The *concept of philosophy*, as well as that of the *nonphilosophical sciences*, can be expounded only on the basis of a properly understood concept of Dasein" (GA 24:455, tr. m.).

44. GA 24:27, tr. m. The outline of the course indicates that this elaboration corresponds to the thematization of "the apriority of being and the possibility and structure of a priori knowledge" (33).

45. GA 24:29–30, tr. m. See for the term "phenomenological construction": KM 289; BT 375, 376. This construction is distinguished from arbitrary constructions (BT 303).

46. "It is for this reason that all philosophical explanation, even when it is most radical and beginning all over again, is pervaded by traditional concepts and thus by traditional horizons and perspectives. . . . It is for this reason that a *deconstruction*, that is, a critical dismantling of the traditional concepts—which initially must necessarily be employed—with regard to the sources from which they were drawn, necessarily belongs to the conceptual interpretation of being and its structures" (GA 24:31, tr. m.).

5. The Turn toward Being Itself in *The Basic Problems of Phenomenology*

1. GA 24:33. The first two themes correspond to the basic structures and basic modes of being that are named in the title of part II; this title is: *The Fundamental Ontological Question Concerning the Meaning of Being as Such. The Basic Structures and Basic Modes of Being* (32).

2. "The possibility of ontology, of philosophy as a science, stands and falls with the possibility of a sufficiently clear accomplishment of this differentiation between being and beings, and accordingly with the possibility of negotiating the passage from the ontic consideration of beings to the ontological thematization of being. The discussions in this chapter will therefore claim our preponderant interest" (GA 24:322). Heidegger evidently already foresaw that he would not be able to complete his program.

3. See GA 24:118 and "The indefinability of being does not dispense with the question of its meaning, but forces it upon us" (BT 4). (In)definability can only pertain to *beings*; not to being: "The assertion—being is indefinable—can have a real meaning . . . namely, when it says that being, because it is fundamentally different from beings, demands a different point of departure than the definition" (GA 21:77).

4. "This articulation (*Gliederung*) of being has been accepted since antiquity. One makes use of it as something obvious, without ever asking for its source—that is, for the intrinsic possibility of this articulation of the idea of being as such" (GA 26:192; tr. m., cf. "Brief über den Humanismus" (WM 159–60 / PM 250).

5. Heidegger seems to more or less disregard the distinction between the "that" and the "how." For instance, in GA 24 he proposes that every being is determined by a "what-it-is" (*Was-sein*) and a "way-of-being"

(*Weise-zu-sein*) (GA 24:24), while in GA 26—also in relation to essence and existence—he asks why every something is always determined by a what-it-is (*Wassein*) and a possible that-it-is (*Daßsein*) (GA 26:192).

6. I take the view that only GA 24 permits us to understand that a fundamental articulation of being precedes the different ontological regions. One may therefore expect that only texts written after 1976 will consider this theme. Von Hermann, however, in his essay on GA 24 states merely that the articulation of being in existence and essence shows forth in the different regions in different ways, without thematizing the traditional twofold as such: "For as far as the basic articulation of being as such is concerned, we are dealing with the division into *Existenz* and *Mitdasein*, on the one hand handiness, extantness, life and constants—while on the other hand we are dealing with whoness, *Bewandtnis*, thinghood, and the whatness of both living beings as well as of constancy." F.-W. von Hermann, "*Being and Time* and *The Basic Problems of Phenomenology*," in *Reading Heidegger: Commemorations*, 133. Von Hermann's interpretation fails above all, I think, in that he repeatedly equates being as such—distinguished from the being of Dasein—with the being of beings other than Dasein (that is, of innerworldly beings) (see esp. 125, 132).

7. BT 45. With regard to the distinction between innerworldly beings and Dasein, Heidegger says in his response to Dilthey and Yorck—using the terms of the latter: "The idea of being encompasses the 'ontic' *and* the 'historical.' *This idea* is what must be 'generically differentiated'" (BT 403 tr. m.; cf. GA 24:219).

8. In this Heidegger is repeating Hegel's critique of Kant, as this appears in, for instance, the famous statement in the preface of the *Phenomenology of Spirit.* "In my view . . . everything turns on grasping and expressing the true not only as *substance*, but equally as *subject.*" G.W.F. Hegel, *Phenomenology of Spirit*, 13–14/10. While Hegel regards being or substance as a moment of the absolute concept, Heidegger searches in his own way for a dynamic fundamental structure that in the being of innerworldly beings does not show forth as itself, and in the being of Dasein does. I will discuss this further in chapter 10.

9. "*Being is the transcendens as such*. The transcendence of the being of Dasein is a distinctive one, since in it lies the possibility and necessity of the most radical *individuation*" (BT 38, tr. m.). That Dasein itself can exist in an authentic or an inauthentic way, that is to say, can explicitly assume—or not—this openness or transcendence, only complicates the matter. We must keep in mind that there is a difference between the inauthentic and the authentic existence of Dasein itself on the one hand, and the inauthentic and the authentic thematization of the *being* of Dasein on the other.

10. See the following passages in the *Contributions*: "Essentia and existentia are not richer than what is unifold (*das Einfache*), and neither do they result from it, but they are, on the contrary, a certain impoverishment of an essence of being (*Seyn*) and its truth, which is richer in itself" (B 271). "The occurring of essence (*Wesung*), however, is not only a linking of a 'what' *and* a 'how-it-is' and thus a richer conception, but is rather the more primordial unity of both" (289).

11. "Being is given only if there is primordial openness—that is to say, if there is truth. But there is truth only if a being exists which opens up, which discloses. . . . We ourselves are such a being" (GA 24:25, tr. m.; cf. BT 230).

12. See for Heidegger's deconstruction of the traditional conception of truth as correspondence between a thing and a judgment also BT 33, 214f; GA 21:10–11, 128.

13. According to Heidegger, the analysis of the temporal constitution of discourse "can be tackled only when the problem of the fundamental connection between being and truth has been unfolded from out of (*aus*) the problem of temporality. Then the ontological meaning of the 'is' can be delimited. . . . Only by starting out from the temporality of discourse, that is, of Dasein as such, will it become possible to clarify the 'genesis' of 'significance' and to give an ontological explanation of the possibility of bringing about concepts" (BT 349, tr. m.). Kisiel remarks that in the first editions of *Being and Time* there is a note with this passage which refers to a second chapter of the third division, where this problem was to have been thematized. This note is still there in the third edition from 1931. Of the several notes in *Being and Time* that refer to the second half of *Being and Time* and have been omitted from the later editions, Kisiel considers this to be "the most tantalizing" (Kisiel, *op. cit.*, 456). Kisiel does not mention the comparable passages in *Being and Time* pertaining to the "is" and discourse where the reference to the third division (in the main text) still appears. Such as: "When assertions and the understanding of being constitute existential-ontological possibilities of Dasein itself, the 'is' and its interpretation are brought to belong to the interrelated problems of the existential analytic. The elaboration of the question of being (cf. part I, division 3) will then again come across this peculiar ontological phenomenon within the *logos*" (BT 160, tr. m., cf. 328, 360).

14. We find a first version in Heidegger's text on Aristotle from 1922 (A 29–33). See from 1924/25 GA 19:181–88, 196, 224. GA 17 and GA 20 also thematize this issue. In GA 29/30 from 1929/30 Heidegger again repeats this analysis in detail (GA 29/30:435f).

15. Heidegger particularly draws on *Metaph.* IX, 10 (1051a 34–1052a 11). See GA 21:170f.

16. The title of this part is: *The Radicalized Question: What is Truth? Retrieving Repetition of the Analysis of Falsity with Respect to its Temporality (Temporalität)* (GA 21:197).

17. BT 158; cf. GA 21:154–59, 207.

18. GA 21:187–91; cf. BT 220. In GA 21 Heidegger gives the examples of someone in a wood who mistakes a bush for a deer (187) and of involvement with a piece of chalk (217–19). In GA 29/30 Heidegger remarks that every 'as' springs from the "occurring of world (*das Walten von Welt*)," that is to say, from the unconcealment of the being of beings (GA 29/30:510, cf. 498, 526–31). We know that *Being and Time* is also working toward Praesens as the temporal condition of possibility of world and thus of every constitution of meaning. Heidegger implicitly allocates this theme to its third division: "[H]ow is something like world possible at all, in what sense *is* world, what and how does the world transcend . . . ? The *ontological exposition* of these questions does not already entail their answer" (BT 351).

19. The question as to whether *alētheia* was experienced by the Greeks themselves in the sense of unconcealment is not particularly relevant. This meaning can be read into the word, and Heidegger makes use of this. It is "in the end the business of philosophy to protect the *power of the most elementary words* in which Dasein expresses itself" from the misunderstanding of common sense (BT 220). Heidegger says that the word *alētheia* refers to a preontological understanding of being as unconcealment, which is still "alive" in Aristotle's thinking but is also already covered over by what Aristotle explicitly thematizes. This explicit interpretation is guided by "*The understanding of being of Dasein which was initially dominant, and has still not been overcome today in a fundamental and explicit way*," namely, objective presence (225). This "initially" refers to the fact that fallenness has always already begun. In 1969, Heidegger says it was misleading to call "truth" the primordial unconcealment which he read in the word *alētheia* and which grounds every truth and untruth (SD 76–77/BW 446–47; cf. BT 219).

20. GA 21:180. Heidegger bases this on *Metaph.* 1052a 1–4.

21. "[T]he way of relating (*Verhalten*) to something must have, insofar as it is a relating, in itself a presential meaning (*präsentischen Sinn*)." That is the case insofar as it "has the meaning of a presentification (*Präsentieren*) or . . . of a *making present* (*Gegenwärtigen*) of something. . . . This making present, *in which I constantly live* . . . allows for the possibility of encountering something at all, that is to say, for present beings to be discovered" (GA 21:192).

22. "[A]ristotle strives indeed, with the idea of *sophia*, to go beyond *logos* to a *noein* that is free of *legein*. But closer inspection shows that even his determination of the ultimate *archē*, the *adiaireton*, is acquired from an

orientation toward *logos*. . . . [W]hat, in speaking about something, in discussing an interrelated whole of beings, is there in advance, prior to all speech and for all speech—namely, that which is spoken about—is the *hupokeimenon*, the *on*, the *ousia*, in a formal sense." This means *"that even the alētheuein of sophia, uncovering in the purest sense, still remains in a way meta logou. . . . This intrusion of logos . . . is motivated by the fact that the on, the being of beings itself, is primarily interpreted as presence, and that logos is the primary way in which I make something present"* (GA 19:224–25, tr. m.).

23. This interpretation constitutes the basis of *Kant and the Problem of Metaphysics* from 1929, and would also have constituted the first division of the second, historical part of *Being and Time*.

24. See Kisiel, *op. cit.*, 456. Von Hermann writes in his epilogue to the edition of *Being and Time* in the *Gesamtausgabe* that Heidegger himself said he burned a first version of *Time and Being* shortly after writing it (GA 2:582).

25. "I count on few people to study it; as regards the proper intentions, you will be the only one to understand what I want. It is for me, on the whole, a transitional work." *Martin Heidegger—Karl Jaspers. Briefwechsel 1920—1963*, 64.

26. *Martin Heidegger—Elisabeth Blochmann. Briefwechsel 1918–1969*, 54.

27. WM 159/PM 249–50, tr. m. A remark added later to "On the Essence of Truth" (1930) shows that Heidegger had wanted to supplement this lecture with a second part about the "Truth of Essence," which also failed because of the inadequacy of language. He makes a clear connection with *Being and Time*: "The decisive question (in *Being and Time*, 1927) of the meaning, i.e., . . . of the truth of being and not merely of beings, remains intentionally undeveloped" (WM 97/PM 154). Thus, in "On the Essence of Truth" we encounter the same movement and the same incapacity to fully enact this movement as in *Being and Time*.

28. In Richardson, *op. cit.*, XVI–XX, tr. m.

29. "In the ensuing years it thus came to some publications, which were meant to steer the reader toward the proper question by means of different detours" (GA 49:40). The thematization of the understanding of being, Heidegger writes in the *Contributions*, is nothing but "a first and trying step on a very long springboard, during which one is hardly aware of what it requires, at the end of the springboard, to actually leap" (B 468) The work *Beiträge zur Philosophie. Vom Ereignis* was published in 1989 (GA 65), in accordance with Heidegger's own instructions, only after most of the courses. This text will be further discussed in part II.

30. "Whenever an essential questioning raises more primordial questions, it has to radically change itself. This is not a matter of gradual 'development.' And even less is there *that* relation between the later and the earlier according to which the later would already be implied in the earlier. . . . The 'alterations' are so essential that their extent can only be determined when time and again the *one and only* question is continuously raised from out of its own domain" (B 84–85). This means that the same question concerning the "meaning of Being (*Seyn*)" is constantly asked from essentially different perspectives (84).

31. Thus, Heidegger says in the *Contributions* that the thinking of being is not grounded in "mere human manoeuvres," without however "falling prey to the claim of 'absoluteness'" (B 439). See also W. Bröcker, *Auseinandersetzungen mit Hegel*, esp. 7, 22.

32. US 93 / OWL 7; cf. N II, 194–95 / N 4, 140–41.

6. The Gigantic Strife of Being for Itself

1. "[T]he nothing is at first and for the most part distorted with respect to its originary character" (WM 13 / PM 91). "No matter how much or in how many ways negation, expressed or implied, permeates all thought, it is by no means the sole authoritative witness of the revelation of the nothing belonging essentially to Dasein" (14/92).

2. "Throughout the present investigation, the Temporal (*temporale*) interpretation of transcendence is intentionally set aside" (WM 62n / PM 128n, tr. m.).

3. "Errancy (*Irre*) is the free space for that turning in which insistent ek-sistence adroitly forgets and mistakes itself constantly anew" (WM 92/PM 150). Cf.: "Errancy . . . is the essential space of history" (HW 310/EGT 26, tr. m.).

4. "Ein Entwurf der Wesung des Seyns als *das Ereignis* muß gewagt werden" (B 11). Cf.: "The question concerning the 'meaning' of being, that is to say—according to the elucidation in 'Being and Time'—the question concerning that which grounds the reach of the projective preconception (*Entwurfsbereich*), in short, concerning *the truth of being* is and remains *my* question and is my *only one*; for it pertains to what is most unique" (10). I have translated *Wesung* and *Wesen* as "occurrence" or as "occurring of essence" to underline the dynamic character of these terms; as I see it, Heidegger uses them to indicate the movement in which an essential possibility enacts itself and thus occurs in accordance with itself or not in accordance with itself. As I noted in the preface, I consider it crucial to maintain the difference between *Sein* and *Seyn*. I therefore reserve the capital B for

Seyn and render *Seyn* with "Being." I translate *Ereignis* as "the occurrence of own-ing," meaning the movement of turning toward one's innermost possibilities or of coming into one's own. I will try to show in this chapter that this movement primarily pertains to the dynamic of being itself. *Ereignis* necessarily entails its own countermovement; what Heidegger calls *Enteignis* is translated as "the occurrence of dis-owning."

5. "Time-space itself the conflictory battleground" (B 260, cf. 5, 371f).

6. B 436. I permit myself with regard to Heidegger's choice of the old spelling to think not only of the inaudible difference between *Seyn* and *Sein*, but also of the accidental shape of the Y, which in itself seems to express a differencing movement. The familiar "crosswise erasure" of the word "being" also has this function. Starting out from the concept "being," one should be able to intend that which exceeds that concept, but nevertheless is inherent to it. See "Zur Seinsfrage" (WM 238f / PM 310f).

7. B 465, 467. On page 424 Heidegger calls the ontological difference a "foreground-like concealment" of the space meted out to thinking. And "as necessary as it [the ontological difference] may be . . . to establish at all a first field of vision for the question concerning Being, this distinction remains nonetheless fatal. For this distinction precisely springs from a questioning concerning beings as such (concerning beingness). . . . In a transitional thinking, however, we have to endure this ambivalence (*dieses Zwiespältige*): *first*, to stake this distinction for the sake of a first elucidation, and *then* nevertheless to leap beyond precisely this distinction" (250–51). One could say that this "leap" is only really accomplished in the *Contributions*. Derrida also considers the ontological difference to be insufficiently radical. Yet he turns against Heidegger with the following remark: "For us, *différance* remains a metaphysical name, and all the names that it receives in our language are still, as names, metaphysical. . . . [A]bove all . . . when they state the determination of *différance* as the difference of being and beings. 'Older' than being itself, such a *différance* has no name in our language." J. Derrida, "La différance," in *Marges de la Philosophie*, 28 / "Différance," in *Margins of Philosophy*, 26.

8. "This truth of Being is not at all different from Being, but is its own and most proper occurring (*Diese Wahrheit des Seyns ist gar nichts vom Seyn Verschiedenes, sondern sein eigenstes Wesen*)" (B 93). "In *Being and Time*, being is not something other than time: 'time' is a preliminary name for the truth of being (*die Vorname für die Wahrheit des Seins*); this truth is the occurrence of being (*das Wesende des Seins*) and is thus being itself." "Einleitung zu 'Was ist Metaphysik?'" (WM 205 / PM 285, tr. m.; cf. GA 49:160).

9. "History is . . . the occurrence of Being itself (*das Wesen des Seyns selbst*)" (B 479). Also in language, art, and establishing a state a (more or

less explicit) occurrence of being or truth takes place: the flaring up of the strife between meaningfulness and that which resists this, between unconcealment and the concealment from which every unconcealment ensues. With regard to the way in which this strife enacts itself in art, Heidegger also speaks about the strife between world and earth. See B 477, 482, 484 and "Die Ursprung des Kunstwerkes" (HW 37f, 51 / PLT 49f, 62–63).

10. "Historicity (*Geschichtlichkeit*) means the ontological structure of the 'occurrence' of Dasein as such, on the basis of which something like 'world history' first becomes possible" (BT 20, tr. m., cf. 382f). This implies that the "dominant way we treat the history of ontology" must also be deconstructed (22–23).

11. "*Being as occurrence of own-ing is history (Das Seyn als Er-eignis ist die Geschichte); one must start out from here to determine the essence of this history, independent from the ideas of becoming and development, and independent from historiographical views and interpretations*" (B 494, cf. 32).

12. "Only within Being are beings, as beings, brought to safety (*geborgen*); this happens in such a way, however, that these beings are *forthwith* abandoned by Being (*so freilich, daß das Seiende alsogleich vom Seyn verlassen werde*) and can only persist as appearance (*Anschein*), *on* as *idea* and what followed from that" (B 323, italics mine). How, then, Heidegger asks, are we to surmise "*that the refusal (Verweigerung) is the first and highest gift of Being, and indeed is itself its primordial occurring (dessen anfängliche Wesung)*. This occurring occurs (*ereignet sich*) as withdrawal (*Entzug*)" (241). See: "The history of being begins with the forgetting of being, with being keeping itself and its essential occurring (*sein Wesen*)—its difference from beings—to itself." "Der Spruch des Anaximander" (HW 336/EGT 50, tr. m.).

13. Although the Greek *phusis* and Kant's concept of objectivity (*Gegenständigkeit*) seem to have nothing in common, Heidegger considers them to be different expressions of the same meaning of being: "Initially, as well as later on, being cleared and lit itself, though in different ways, as having the character . . . of presencing (*Anwesen*)." *Der Satz vom Grund* 154. The term *Anwesen* here seems to have the same meaning as *Anwesenheit* in other texts.

14. B 175, 177. Cf.: "Presence (*Anwesenheit*) can be conceived as gathering (*Sammlung*) and thus be understood as unity (*Einheit*). When the *logos* prevails, it even has to be understood this way. And yet, unity itself and as such is not a primordial essential determination of the being of beings. The first thinkers, however, had to come across this determination, because . . . the truth of being had to remain concealed from them and because, in order to grasp being at all, one has to retain presencing as the

first and initial way in which being opens up itself (*seines Aufgehens*). . . . When starting out from the other beginning . . . this never refuted or questioned determination of being (unity) has to become questionable itself; thus, 'unity' will turn out to refer back to 'time'" (459–60). The words "first and initial (*Erstes und Nächstes*)" refer to the *zunächst* of the indifferent modification.

15. "Besides, we have moved from the outset *within* one projective preconception of Being (*in einem Entwurf des Seyns*), whereas this preconception could never have been experienced *as* preconception. (The truth of Being was not a possible question.) The fact that this question failed to occur, continuously motivates the history of the basic metaphysical positions" (B 449).

16. "The occurring of essence (*Wesung*), however, is not only the coupling of the 'what' *and* the 'how' and thus a richer conception, but is the more primordial unity of both" (B 289). The obsolete verb *wesen* means "to be" or "to occur."

17. In *Time and Being* from 1962, Heidegger calls *Zuhandenheit* and *Vorhandenheit* modes of presencing (*Anwesen*) (SD 7 / TB 7). This suggests that the meaning of being as presence stems from the realm within which innerworldly beings appear and has been wrongfully extended to the realm of being as such.

18. B 504, cf.: "This 'thinking in a Greek fashion' is experienced and accomplished as the way in which beginning thinking can be encountered; this encountering dialogue has the sole purpose of leading us into the German thinking which is assigned to us" (GA 55:366; cf. GA 39:196; US 133 / OWL 38; HW 309–10 / EGT 25).

19. "The more I become immersed in my own work, the more I am, time and again, compelled to go back to the great beginning of the Greeks. And often I waver and doubt whether it would not be more essential to give up all my own attempts and only strive in order that we come to see again the greatness of this world . . . and take it as an example. . . . And then I realize again that this is impossible without my own work, just as much as this work is impossible without the dialogue with these great thinkers" (Correspondence with Blochmann, *op. cit.*, 55–56, Dec. 1932).

20. GA 45:221, tr. m. This course from 1937/38 is closely related to the *Contributions*.

21. B 416. In *The Anaximander Fragment* from 1946 Heidegger remarks that being itself is eschatological, that is to say, takes leave of its "hitherto occurring" and—I add—turns itself toward its most proper possibility. This means for the *thinking* of being: "If we think from within the eschatology of being, then we must someday expect what once took place

(*das Einstige der Frühe*) in what is yet to come (*im Einstigen des Kommenden*)" (HW 302 / EGT 18, tr. m.). In this expectation the "end" is left open and not encountered as completion. Derrida appears to radically criticize the distinction between the traditional theological eschatology and that of Heidegger (cf. J. Derrida, *D'un ton apocalyptique adopté naguère en philosophie*, 61 / "On a Newly Arisen Apocalyptic Tone in Philosophy," in *Raising the Tone of Philosophy*, 146). On the other hand, his distinction between the "absolutely undetermined messianic hope" and the concrete messianisms that are grounded in it is not entirely foreign to this distinction (*Spectres de Marx*, 111–12, cf. 124, 266 / *Specters of Marx*, 65–66, cf. 73, 167).

22. The meaning of these originary words constitutes the basis of the study by M. Zarader, *Heidegger et les paroles de l'origine*.

23. GA 54:198–99, cf. 129, 202, 214.

24. GA 54:207, cf. 145, 180, 185; GA 55:31, 100. These themes are discussed in many texts.

25. "The occurring of openness (*das Aufgehen*), that is, *phusis*, can be understood as the aforementioned juncture (*Fügung*) only if thinking . . . is also aware of the primordial out-of-joint" (GA 55:146).

26. "Because what matters is that which is . . . present (*das Anwesende*), that is, beings (*das Seiende*), therefore the occurring of openness (*das Aufgehen*) 'holds sway'" (GA 55:159).

27. "The occurring of openness (*das Aufgehen*) allows self-concealment (*das Sichverbergen*) to occur within its own occurring of openness; self-concealment can only occur, however, if it allows the occurring of openness to 'be' this openness" (GA 55:132). "*Phusis* itself . . . is the juncture (*Fügung*) within which the occurring of openness complies with self-concealment, and the latter with the occurring of openness" (141, cf. 160, 299).

28. "This is the enigma, however: on the one hand, *phusis* names the occurring of openness (*das Aufgehen*) as distinguished from the return to concealment (*das Untergehen*) . . . ; on the other, it names the one occurring of the juncture (*Fügung*) of the aforementioned *phusis* and *kruptestai*. . . . If we were able to immediately say what this enigma of the essential ambivalence of *phusis* conceals, then we would already have named the essence of the beginning" (GA 55:158–59). See on friendship 128f.

29. GA 55:33. See: "Greek history reaches the summit of its essential occurrence (*die Höhe seines Wesens*) when it preserves the counterturning dynamic of being itself (*die Gegenwendigkeit des Seins selbst*) and lets this appear; for only then is there the necessity to remain within the ground of the counterturning (*in dem Grund des Gegenwendigen*), instead of fleeing to either the one side or the other" (95, cf. 104).

30. The evolution of Heidegger's interpretation of Nietzsche will not be discussed here. See for this M. Haar, *La fracture de l'Histoire. Douze essais sur Heidegger*, Part II, 199f. My interpretation is based mainly on *Nietzsche* I and II, that is, not on the original versions of the courses which appeared in the *Gesamtausgabe.*

31. See "Nietzsches Wort 'Gott ist tot'" (HW 200 / QT 61); N I, 242 / N 1, 209–10; N II, 33 / N 3, 4.

32. "For that reason the need to destroy (*das Zerstörenmüssen*) belongs essentially to creation. In destruction, the contrary, the ugly, and the evil are posited; they are of necessity proper to creation, i.e., will to power, and thus to being itself" (N I, 73 / N 1, 61). "To overcome evil (*das Böse*) is not to eliminate it but to acknowledge its necessity. As long as evil is merely repudiated in disgust, as long as our contempt is determined merely by nausea, that contempt remains dependent upon the contemptible" (N I, 315 / N 2, 60, tr. m.).

33. "When we define the interconnection of this doctrine with the fundamental thought of the will to power, we bring Nietzsche's philosophy to the fore as the final distinctive position in the history of Western metaphysics" (N II, 8 / N 3, 162; HW 219 / QT 81–82). "Now, if the eternal return of the same is the fundamental thought of Nietzsche's philosophy proper, and if his philosophy is itself a countermovement, then the thought of thoughts is inherently a *counter-thought* (*Gegengedanke*)" (N I, 434 / N 2, 172).

34. "It is indeed true that Nietzsche's metaphysics turns 'being' into a mere value; but this 'being,' devaluated into a mere value, has . . . less 'value' than 'becoming,' that is, than the will to power. Because the being of beings, which had always remained the object of thought of metaphysics, is sent up in final smoke by Nietzsche's metaphysics, this metaphysics is the end of any metaphysics whatsoever" (GA 55:84). Because Nietzsche no longer accepts the ontological difference, he cuts off the possibility of understanding being itself as radically distinguished from beings.

35. N I, 654–55; cf. GA 54:205.

36. N II, 375–76, 379 / N 4, 231–32, 234–35.

37. "The thought of the will to power is to conceive the permanence proper to what is in the highest and most appropriate sense becoming and in movement—that is, to life itself. Certainly, Nietzsche wants the basic character of the whole of beings to be becoming and that which is becoming; but he wants this becoming to be *that which is permanently present* (*das Bleibende*)—that is, that which truly 'is' (*das eigentlich 'Seiende'*)" (N I, 656; cf. N II, 11 / N 3, 164–65).

38. N II, 335 / N 4, 199, tr. m. In GA 54 Heidegger suggests that Nietzsche interprets "truth" as justice (*Gerechtigkeit*) and thus completes the metaphysical concept of truth: "The circle of the history of the essence of truth, as metaphysically experienced, is now closed. Yet *alētheia* remains outside this circle" (GA 54:78; see N I, 469 / N 2, 205).

39. B 176; cf.: "Still, what remains decisive in all this is to hear Nietzsche himself, to inquire with him and through him *and therefore at the same time against him*, but *for the sake of* the one single innermost matter of Western philosophy" (N I, 33 / N 1, 24, tr. m.).

40. On Nietzsche and Hölderlin: "They are separated by an abyss" (GA 52:78; cf. 143; GA 39:293–94). On Hegel and Hölderlin: "Instead of interpreting Hölderlin against the background of Hegel's system, as one usually does . . . we have to learn to experience the great contrariety (*Widerstreit*) between them . . . ; only thus will it be possible to understand something of their true harmony (*wahre Einklang*)" (GA 39:129; cf. GA 4:85–86n; GA 52:99; GA 53:158; B 464).

41. GA 39:1, 164, 214.

42. Heidegger attempts to bring to the fore "the truth still veiled from the poet himself" (GA 52:79).

43. The texts concerned are: *Erläuterungen zu Hölderlins Dichtung* (GA 4); *Hölderlins Hymnen "Germanien" und "Der Rhein"* (GA 39); *Hölderlins Hymne "Andenken"* (GA 52) and *Hölderlins Hymne "Der Ister"* (GA 53). The theme of the gods is mainly discussed in GA 4 and part I of GA 39. Part II of GA 39 concentrates on source and river; GA 53 on returning home. The problem of language could be regarded as a fourth theme, but is here deferred to 6.7.

44. "Wherever theology arises, the god has already started to flee" (GA 52:133). "The long christianization of the god" has "undermined the preconditions by virtue of which something concerning the flight or arrival of the god remains in the distance of undecidability (*die Ferne der Unentscheidbarkeit*)" (B 24). In a letter to Jaspers from 1935 Heidegger mentions the necessity of a confrontation with the belief in which he was brought up (*op. cit.*, 157). The way in which he retrieves the meaning of the belief, however, deprives the belief of (almost) all specifically Christian content. What Heidegger tries to articulate by *means* of his interpretation of God or the gods may not, however, be conceived as a return to the Greek world of the gods.

45. "It is precisely because the river's own path unhesitantly tears loose everything, that it tears human beings out of the habitual midst of their lives, so that they may be in a center outside of themselves, that is, be eccentric" (GA 53:32, tr. m.; cf. GA 52:189). And: "A people is *only* a peo-

ple when it finds its god and thereby is given its history. . . . Only in that case does it escape the danger *of circling around itself* and of idolizing the preconditions of its existence by taking them as unconditional" (B 398).

46. GA 4:18, 57–58; cf. GA 53:173; WM 182 / BW 253–54.

47. See on the fourfold (*Geviert*): GA 4:163, 170f, 179; GA 52:100. Heidegger calls *Gestell* the "own-ing occurrence of the fourfold, which covers itself up (*das sich selbst verstellende Ereignis des Gevierts*)" (GA 4:153). The fourfold (*Geviert*) or *Verhältnis* refers to the authentic mode of world: "Since the rise of the great beginning . . . the whole of what holds together (*das ganze Verhältnis*) has prepared itself to come" (GA 4:179–80). See also "Das Ding" (VA 172/PLT 180).

48. GA 39:81, 87, 223.

49. The calling of the poet "is the unfolding (*das Austragen*) of a contrariety between a preparedness which opens itself and a fulfillment that fails to occur. Enduring such a contrariety is *pain* (*Schmerz*)" (GA 39:81; cf. B 400). In the *Contributions* Heidegger calls the coming God, which will be entirely different from the existing one, "the last God" (B 403). Just as death is our ultimate possibility, this God will come last (405). Not as an ending, however, but as an other beginning of our history (411). A proper comportment to God or the gods is only possible when the presentification of being itself is no longer allowed to take place. What Heidegger says on this in the *Letter on Humanism* (WM 181–82 / PM 266–68) ensues from the *Contributions*. At the end of *De l'esprit. Heidegger et la question*, 138–43 / *Of Spirit. Heidegger and the Question*, 107–13 and "Comment ne pas parler. Dénégations," in *Psyché. Inventions de l' autre* / "How to Avoid Speaking: Denials," in *Languages of the Unsayable*, 58–62, Derrida radically criticizes the relation between the openness (*Offenbarkeit*) that allows the appearance of God on the one hand, and the theological concept of holy revelation (*Offenbarung*) on the other. If the holy is understood as the temporal disclosedness that grounds the appearance of the essential either as constant principle or as dynamic divided against itself, it is in my view more difficult to criticize Heidegger's debt to theology (see "Vom Wesen des Grundes," WM 55n / PM 123n62). Hence, I consider Derrida's critique to start too soon. On the other hand, it is true that Heidegger's retrieving repetition of onto-theology attempts to modify in an authentic way—by means of a deconstruction—what has already been thought.

50. GA 39:107, 109. Heidegger is here referring to *Being and Time*. A little further on: "This authentic time is hard to know, however, and the knowledge of it can be easily . . . destroyed" (110; cf. GA 52:54).

51. Cf. GA 39:254; GA 52:40; GA 53:17, 20.

52. "The whole course of the river belongs itself to the origin. . . . It is this whole that the poet hears" (GA 39:202, cf. 275).

53. GA 39:241, cf. 275: "That which purely springs forth (*das Reinentsprungene*) . . . occurs as the contrariety between the springing and the having-sprung-from (*west als Widerstreit des Entspringens und Entsprungenseins*). To be a river means to unfold this contrariety into the highest enmity (*Feindseligkeit*) and to preserve this enmity as intimacy (*Innigkeit*)." In GA 53 (42f, 199f; cf. GA 52:185f) Heidegger quotes from Hölderlin's "Der Ister" about the upper reaches of the Danube, where the water sometimes appears to stand still or to want to flow backward: "It appears however almost / to go backwards (*Der scheinet aber fast / Rükwärts zu gehen*)." Heidegger seems to suggest that the stream appears to wish to go back to its origin, but is not as strong as the prevailing direction of the river and must (initially) go along with it.

54. "The intimacy (*Innigkeit*) is the primordial unity of the enmity between the powers of what has sprung forth from the pure source (*die Mächte des Reinentsprungenen*)" (GA 39:250). "Thus . . . the *strife* (*Streit*) is shifted to the ground of Being itself (*Seyn*). But this primordial enmity (*Feindseligkeit*) is the truest intimacy (*die wahrste Innigkeit*)" (273, cf. 117, 275, 283). These passages seem to be directed against Hegel's idea that any enmity can be sublated into a higher unity.

55. GA 53:51, cf. 203; GA 39:260.

56. "[D]as Gesetz des Unheimischseins und Heimischwerdens" (GA 53:155, tr. m.). Cf. F. Dastur, *Hölderlin. Tragédie et modernité*. She approaches this theme by means of theoretical fragments from Hölderlin about the relation between Germany and Greece, and the meaning of tragedy.

57. GA 53:144, 146–47, GA 4:88.

58. GA 53:144, see 39–46, 91. "What is most proper to someone (*das Eigenste*) is never one's property—it is most of all one's own only as that which is sought in the seeking" (GA 52:173).

59. Right at the start of the *Contributions* we read: "[H]ere, the act of saying is not opposed to what is to be said, but this saying—which is the occurring of being—is itself what is to be said" (B 4, cf. 86). And: "In thinking there is neither method nor theme, but rather the region (*Gegend*), so called because it brings within the region (*gegnet*) and releases what thinking is given to think. Here the way is part of the region itself and belongs to it" (US 178–79 / OWL 74, tr. m.).

60. "Being (*Seyn*) needs the human being to occur, and the human being belongs to Being, in order that it, as Da-sein, may accomplish its ultimate destiny" (B 251). "[B]eing the guardian of the truth of being . . . constitutes . . . the essence of the human being" (500, cf. 489).

61. This is a "task that has concealed itself from philosophy since its very beginning, even in virtue of that beginning, and thus has withdrawn

itself continually and increasingly in the times that followed." "Das Ende der Philosophie und die Aufgabe des Denkens" (SD 66 / BW 436).

62. B 384; cf. 246, 293, 383.

63. "There is much to be said for the fact that the essence of language precisely refuses to come to language, to that language, that is, in which we make statements about language. If language everywhere refuses to give its essence in this sense, then such refusal (*Verweigerung*) belongs to the very essence of language (US 186 / OWL 81, tr. m.; cf. WM 150 / PM 243).

64. "I only know one thing: because reflection on language and being has determined my path of thinking from early on, therefore their elucidation has stayed as far as possible in the background" (US 93 / OWL 7, tr. m.).

65. Heidegger remarks in *Being and Time* that if there is no Dasein, "it can neither be said that beings are, nor that they are not. It is possible, however, to say *now* that as long as there is understanding of being . . . beings will *then* still continue to be" (BT 212, cf. 227, tr. m.).

66. This seems to me to be the case with all modes of idealism, certainly with Hegel and Husserl.

67. *Logos* is called the "foreword" of language (GA 55:383). See concerning *Dichtung*: "With regard to its essence, however, language itself is the most primordial poetry" (GA 39:217).

68. "Only where language, there world occurs (*Nur wo Sprache, da waltet Welt*)" (GA 39:62). "Language occurs as the occurring difference for world and things (*Die Sprache west als der sich ereignende Unter-Schied für Welt und Dinge*)" (US 30 / PLT 207, tr. m.).

69. "What occurs (*west*) as being . . . can only be said in poetry or be thought in thinking" (GA 53:150). "For the word, when it names the essential, separates the essence from what is not essential" (GA 4:57).

70. "Poetry (*Dichtung*), as the primordial dialogue (*Gespräch*), is the origin of language. With this language, which belongs to human beings as that which is most dangerous, human beings venture into being as such. There, they either stand their ground or fall and thus—blowing up and destroying themselves—abandon themselves to idle talk" (GA 39:76). "Language is the most dangerous and as such more double-edged and ambivalent than anything else" (62, cf. 63–64).

71. "Brief über den Humanismus" (WM 192 / PM 274, tr. m.). This passage moderates the well-known phrase "language is the house of being" (145/239); what language possibly is will not always realize itself.

72. "Poetry opens the 'enmity of the powers of Being'" (GA 39:257).

73. For this Heidegger goes along with Hölderlin's words in the poem "Rousseau": "and hints are/of old the language of the gods (*und Winke sind / von Alters her die Sprache der Götter*)." He adds: "Poetry is the hinting further of these hints to the people . . . that is to say, it is indicating, showing, and in this showing the gods are revealed insofar as they hint, not as something that is meant and can be contemplated" (GA 39:32).

74. VA 184 / PLT 216, tr. m., see US 179–80 / OWL 75–76.

75. "Language needs human speaking, and yet it is not merely the making of our speech activity" (US 256 / OWL 125, tr. m.; see GA 55:379).

76. "Keeping silent (*Erschweigung*) is the 'logic' of philosophy, insofar as this philosophy poses the basic question (*Grundfrage*) from out of the other beginning" (B 78).

77. The motif of the secret (*Geheimnis*) appears in many texts. See, e.g., GA 4:24; GA 39:119, 251; GA 53:40, 132. Cf. J.-L. Chrétien, "La réserve de l' être," in *Martin Heidegger*, Cahiers de l'Herne.

78. See in *Being and Time*: "Authentic silence is possible only in genuine discourse. In order to be silent, Dasein must have something to say—that is, must be in command of a rich and authentic disclosedness of itself. Then reticence (*Verschwiegenheit*) becomes revealing and puts down 'idle talk'" (BT 165, tr. m.). Heidegger refers to this section in US 262 / OWL 131.

79. GA 55:179. "The showing (*das Zeigen*) brings closer what is shown and nevertheless keeps it at a distance" (GA 4:138). See also *Was heißt Denken?* 6/9; US 254 / OWL 123; GA 53:184; GA 54:46–47.

80. Up to now two texts on Anaximander have been published: part II of GA 51 from 1941 and the text in *Holzwege* from 1946. I base my interpretation mainly on the latter. A course on Anaximander and Parmenides from 1932 (GA 35) has not yet been published. It would have been interesting to have been able to compare this text from before the *Contributions* with the later ones.

81. "However, the distinction between being and beings can only be experienced as that which is forgotten if it has already unveiled itself with the presencing of what is present (*mit dem Anwesen des Anwesenden*) and thus has left a trace (*eine Spur*) which remains preserved in language. . . . Thinking along those lines, we may surmise that the distinction has come to light more in that early word of being than in later ones; yet at no time has the distinction been designated as such" (HW 336, cf. 340 / EGW, tr. m.). That which has never arrived—the truth of being—has thus left the traces of its withdrawal in language.

82. In 1923 Heidegger uses the word *Jeweiligkeit* to indicate the way in which Dasein exists factically—that is, is "there" for itself. Dasein's own

being is not given as an object, but is always that which is enacted in one way or another; it is transitive (GA 63:7, 29). In *The Anaximander Fragment* this transitional character has come to pertain to beings as such.

83. HW 326–27 / EGT 41. The word *Fug* actually occurs in German only in the expression "mit Fug und Recht," when it means something like "appropriately." The word which is used for "joint" or "coherence" is *Fuge*, which occurs, for example, in the expression "aus allen Fugen gehen." In the *Contributions* the time-space is called the *Gefüge* or the *Fügung* of the *Da* (B 371). In *An Introduction to Metaphysics* from 1935 Heidegger also briefly thematizes Anaximander's fragment and translates *dikē* as *Fug* instead of *Gerechtigkeit* (EM 123, 126 / IM 160, 163). As I said, (see 6.4) Heidegger in *Heraklit* makes a connection between *Fügung* and *phusis*. I take no account of Heidegger's nuanced use of and play with the German meanings of the terms *Fug*, *Fuge*, and *Unfug*, which cannot really be adequately rendered in English, but use various possible translations without distinction. Heidegger seems to use *Un-Fug* and *Un-Fuge* as synonyms (cf. HW 328–29 / EGT 42–43).

84. See with respect to Heidegger's idea of a primordial ethics: "Brief über den Humanismus" (WM 187 / BW 258), also written in 1946, and 2.5.

85. HW 327 / EGT 41, tr. m. In his course on Heraclitus from 1943 (GA 55:146), Heidegger calls the disjointedness of being itself primordial (*der anfängliche Un-Fug*).

86. "None heeds the lingering occurrence (*das weilige Wesen*) of the other. The lingering beings are inconsiderate toward one another, each driven by the craving for permanence which indwells . . . the whiling presencing itself" (331/45–46, tr. m.).

87. Heidegger makes use of the etymological affinity between *to chreōn* and *chrao* in order to understand *to chreoon* as handing over (cf. 337/52). I will not try here to follow Heidegger's problematic and difficult etymological elaborations.

88. HW 339–40 / EGT 54, tr. m. The translation of *Brauch* as "usage" may convey the normal meaning of *Brauch*, but not Heidegger's own, peculiar use of the word. As I understand it, he hears in *Brauch* primarily the verb *brauchen*: to need. In GA 51, *to chreōn* is translated as "die nötigende Not" (GA 51:94, 116). As the original giving gesture seems to be motivated by a kind of original lacking, *Brauch* could perhaps be understood as "that which needs and is needed."

89. "What if being in its occurrence (*Wesen*) needed the occurrence of man? If the essence (*Wesen*) of man consisted in thinking the truth of Being? (343/58, tr. m.).

90. "To think being itself, appropriately requires us to relinquish being as the ground of beings in favor of the giving which happens concealed in

unconcealment, that is, in favor of the 'it gives' ('*es gibt*'). As the gift of this 'it gives,' being belongs to this giving" (SD 6 / TB 6, tr. m.). In his later works Heidegger uses this expression to indicate the most primordial opening movement. See from the *Summary of a Seminar on the Lecture "Time and Being"*: "If the occurrence of own-ing (*Ereignis*) is not a new molding (*Prägung*) of being in the history of being, but if it is rather the case that being belongs to the occurrence of own-ing . . . then the history of being is at an end for that thinking which is part of the occurrence of own-ing, that is, for a thinking which itself enters into this occurrence (*Ereignis*). For this thinking, being insofar as it is destined to us (*das Sein, das im Geschick beruht*) is no longer what is properly to be thought" (SD 44 / TB 40–41, tr. m.).

91. BT 212, 230, cf. GA 56/57:67; GA 24:13–14. In the *Letter on Humanism* Heidegger seems to conceive of being as that which gives. Referring to *Being and Time*, he suggests here: "For the 'it' that here 'gives,' is being itself. The 'gives,' however, names the essence (*Wesen*) of being that is giving, granting its truth" (WM 165 / PM 254–55). The "however" (the *jedoch* is not translated in the PM translation) implicitly expresses the difference between being insofar as it gives—the essence or essential occurrence of being—and being insofar as it is given. This is expressed in the *Contributions* as the difference between *Seyn* and *Sein*. The *Seyn* or the "it" (*Es*) only lets itself be understood as being (cf. B 166).

92. SD 18 / TB 17. See: "Insofar as being such as it is destined to us (*das Geschick des Seins*) is grounded in the reaching (*das Reichen*) of time, and time, together with being, is grounded in the occurrence of own-ing (*Ereignis*)" (23/22, tr. m.).

93. "Being as it is destined to us (*Das Geschick des Seins*) is . . . not something fatalistic. . . . Why not? Because being, in destining itself to us, brings into play the free openness of the time-space (*das Freie des Zeit-Spiel-Raumes*) and, in so doing, first frees humans unto the openness of whatever essential possibilities they happen to have." *Der Satz vom Grund* 158, tr. m.

94. SD 7 / TB 7, tr. m. The many possible transformations of this presencing show forth in the history of thinking as, for instance, the One (which always remains identical to itself), as *logos*, idea, *ousia*, substance, being *posited,* and ultimately as the will that wants nothing but itself (7/7). With these concepts, thinking *responds* to what is given.

95. Heidegger here calls the unity that holds the three temporal dimensions both together and apart, the fourth dimension of time. This is the "nearing nearness (*nähernde Nähe*)": that which brings nearer. This first, primordial reaching (SD 16 / TB 15) "keeps open Past (*das Gewesen*) by denying its arrival as Present (*Gegenwart*)." And it "keeps open what arrives from Future by withholding Present from what is coming" (16/15, tr. m.).

96. Heidegger considers the movement of coming toward itself as such—or the occurrence of own-ing—to constitute the most essential moment of the counterstriving dynamic which determines both the being of human beings and being itself. Every actual turning away from oneself he considers to be grounded in a preceding involvement with one's own "future." This is why already in *Being and Time* he regards ecstatic Future, which opens up this movement, as the most important: "*The primary phenomenon of primordial and authentic temporality is Future*" (BT 329). "The primordial and authentic Future is the toward-oneself (*das Auf-sich-zu*)" (330).

97. "Insofar as being and time are only given in the occurrence of own-ing (*im Ereignen*), it belongs to this occurring to bring the human being—the being that is aware of being because it stands within authentic time—into its own (*in sein Eigenes*). The human being is such that it belongs to the occurrence of own-ing" (SD 24 / TB 23, tr. m.). The word *Ereignis*, however, primarily pertains to the occurrence of the essential as such—that is, to the way in which the essential comes into its own or comes toward itself, and only on this ground does it pertain to the relation between being and human beings. The meaning of *Ereignis* may not, in my view, be understood on the basis of this relation, as is done by, among others, M. Haar in *La fracture de l'Histoire*, 12, 217.

Introduction to Part III

1. "Philosophy . . . now faces the huge task of fundamentally confronting the system of a historical worldview which is most powerful with regard to its fullness, its depth, its conceptuality, and the richness of its experiences, and which as such has resumed and surpassed all preceding fundamental philosophical problems; that is, it has to confront Hegel" (GA 1:410–11).

2. "In spite of the superficial talk (*Gerede*) about the breakdown of Hegelian philosophy, one thing remains true: only this philosophy determined reality in the nineteenth century. . . . The countermovements to this metaphysics belong *to* it. Ever since Hegel's death (1831), everything is merely a countermovement." "Überwindung der Metaphysik" (VA 72 / EP 89; cf. GA 32:57).

3. This is already the case in the opening paragraph: the question concerning being "sustained the avid research of Plato and Aristotle but from then on ceased to be heard as a thematic question of true investigation. What these two thinkers achieved has been preserved in various distorted and 'camouflaged' forms down to Hegel's *Logic*" (BT 2, tr. m.).

4. GA 61:150, cf. GA 63:43–46. In another early course Heidegger notes in connection with the Marburg school (Natorp is mentioned): "*Incli-*

nation to dialectic. Thinking is the organ of the determination of objects. Absolute power of thinking . . . (relation to *Hegel*).—Dialectic is blind to the givenness. . . . (That indicates the necessary confrontation with *neo-Hegelianism*)" (GA 58:225–26). Cf. H.-G. Gadamer, *Hegels Dialektik. Fünf hermeneutische Studien*, esp. 49, and D. Schmidt, *The Ubiquity of the Finite. Hegel, Heidegger and the Entitlements of Philosophy*, 28n. In 10.1 I will come back to the meaning of dialectic in Heidegger's early courses.

5. Heidegger did actually give a seminar in 1925/26 on *The Doctrine of Being*, but in this he mainly thematized the concepts "being" and "nothing." See Kisiel, *op. cit.*, 465, and in the letters to Jaspers from December 1925: "I delight more than usual in the seminars on Hegel and Kant. . . . [I] understand . . . very well . . . that being and nothing are identical. For Hegel determines being—a peculiar beginning!—entirely negatively; as that which is *un*determined and *im*mediate. . . . [B]ut the best part of it is that I am beginning to *really love Kant*" (*op. cit.*, 57). In February 1926: "Concerning Hegel's *Logic* I have not gone beyond 'becoming,' that is to say, the second triad" (61).

6. Neither of them would appreciate being compared with the other. For instance, Hegel suggests in the *Logic*: "External reflection relates what is diverse to likeness and unlikeness. This relation, which is a *comparing*, passes to and fro between likeness and unlikeness. But this relating to likeness and unlikeness, back and forth, is external to these determinations themselves" (L II, 50/420). With regard to Heidegger, one may refer to the summary of a seminar on *Time and Being*. Here it is said (let us assume by Heidegger) that if his thinking were considered a deepening recapitulation of Hegel, similarities could undoubtedly be found between all aspects of the two thinkers: "[O]ne could, so to speak, set up a table of concordances and thus find out that Heidegger says pretty much the same as Hegel." This cannot be what is at stake: because Heidegger's thinking moves in a different dimension—I add—"every comparison would lose the basis of its comparability," although this does not mean that there may not be a *relation* (SD 51 / TB 48).

7. Hegel: "The genuine refutation must penetrate the opponent's stronghold and meet him on his own ground; no advantage is gained by attacking him somewhere else and defeating him where he is not" (L II, 250/581). Heidegger quotes and agrees with this passage in *Die ontologische Verfassung der Metaphysik*, but adds: "We, however, do not seek the force in what has already been thought: we seek it in something that has not been thought, and from which what has been thought receives its essential space" (ID 38/48, tr. m.). See: "If, however, the standpoint of a necessary confrontation with Hegel is to cope with this confrontation—that is to say, is to be essentially superior to it—although, on the other hand, this standpoint should not be introduced from the outside . . . then this standpoint . . . must lie hidden *in* Hegel's philosophy, albeit as the ground that is essentially inaccessible to this philosophy itself" (GA 68:4; cf. GA 32:44–45).

7. The Power of Time

1. Enc. II, §258 rem., tr. m.; cf. BT 435, where Heidegger quotes a part of this passage.

2. GA 32:92, tr. m., cf. 55–56. With respect to his relation to Hegel, Heidegger refers once to *Being and Time*: "The direction of our path, which is to cross that of Hegel, is indicated by 'Being and Time.' That means negatively: time—not *logos*" (143; my translation: this passage is missing in the translation of Emad and Maly).

3. "In Hegel, philosophy—that is—ancient philosophy—is in a certain sense thought through to its end. . . . But there exists just as much the legitimate demand to start anew—that is, to understand the finiteness of the Hegelian system and to see that Hegel himself has come to an end with philosophy because he moves in the circle of philosophical problems. This circling in the circle forbids him to move back to the center of the circle and to fundamentally revise it. It is not necessary to seek another circle beyond the circle. Hegel saw everything that is possible. But the question is whether he saw it from the radical center of philosophy, whether he exhausted all the possibilities of the beginning so as to say that he is at the end" (GA 24:400, tr. m.).

4. "Das Ende der Philosophie und die Aufgabe des Denkens" (SD 71 / BW 441, tr. m.).

5. "The understanding of being as constant presence . . . is clearly expressed again precisely when Occidental metaphysics has reached its true completion, that is to say . . . with Hegel" (GA 31:109).

6. "[T]hat which is true however, the idea, spirit, is *eternal*" (Enc. II, §258 rem.). "[T]he eternal [is] absolute presence" (§258 add., tr. m.).

7. "That is to say: if we philosophically understand the philosophical logic that was founded by Aristotle and completed by Hegel, then this logic will not be furthered by other sons and grandsons. To advance philosophically we need a new line (*Geschlecht*). It is indefinite when this line will come—we, the present generation, are definitely not this new line" (GA 21:14). Thus, Heidegger here implicitly acknowledges his kinship with Hegel.

8. GA 33:51, 54 / 41, 44–45. The entire course consists of a detailed interpretation of Aristotle, *Metaph.* VIII, 1–3.

9. "*eidos* is genuinely understood as *eidos* only when it appears within the horizon (*Gesichtskreis*) of one's immediate addressing of a being. . . . Therefore, in what follows when we speak simply of 'appearance,' we always have in mind the appearance as (and insofar as) it puts itself forth into a given thing that is 'there for a while' (*das Jeweilige*)" (WM 345–46 / PM 210–11).

10. WM 354 / PM 217.See: "*entelecheia* . . . fulfils what *ousia* is to a greater degree and more originally than *dunamis* does" (357).

11. Cf. GA 33:163/139, and Aristotle, *Metaph.* VIII, 1046b 29–1047b 2.

12. "How is this securing for its part connected . . . with the question concerning the being present (*Vorhandensein*) of *dunamis* qua *dunamis*, of capability as capability, prior to all actualization in enactment?" (GA 33:213/183).

13. "Higher than actuality stands *possibility*" (BT 38).

14. When a being, for instance, warms up another being, that movement or change is not *as* concerned with the possibility of its failure as the doctor who tries to cure a patient. In this process the doctor is concerned with the *eidos* "health," and in this is also always concerned with its opposite, which he tries to prevent or exclude. Heidegger takes this to mean that the doctor is given a *realm* of possibilities: "[T]he openness (*Geöffnetheit*) of the realm of force happens for this force in and through the *logos* which belongs to it" (GA 33:133–34/114). Anyone who acts or makes is thus also always concerned with the opposite of what he intends; this is the *sterēsis* that always "follows along" necessarily as that which is to be avoided (142–43/122). See *Metaph.* 1046a 37—1046b 29.

15. "*Dunamis is in a preeminent sense exposed and bound to sterēsis*" (GA 33:112/95).

16. GA 33:142–43/122; WM 365 / PM 225–26.

17. One may here recall the analysis of the phenomenon of guilt in §58 of *Being and Time*. Heidegger interprets "guilt" here as an insurmountable lack that from the outset underlies the being of Dasein. On the other hand, one's own death is a possibility that cannot be actualized and thus withdraws from the realm of presence.

18. BT 285, tr. m. This passage immediately precedes the passage from *Being and Time* with which this section began.

19. "It is essential to realize that there is something simple (*daß es ein ganz Einfaches gibt*), containing in itself a multiplicity that does not yet explicitly exist. . . . With Aristotle we may say that in the simple thing, in what is 'in itself,' in *dunamis* or *potentia*, in the capacity (*Anlage*), everything is contained which develops. In a development nothing emerges but what was there originally in germ or 'in itself.'" Hegel, *Einleitung in die Geschichte der Philosophie*, 102/72; cf. Enc. I, §142 add., and the study inspired by Heidegger of H. Marcuse, *Hegels Ontologie und die Theorie der Geschichtlichkeit*, 47, 116, 202.

20. KM XIV/XVII. See: "[I]n order to wring from what the words say, what it is they want to say, every interpretation must necessarily use violence" (202).

21. "The explicit characterization of the power of imagination as a basic faculty must have driven home the meaning of this faculty to Kant's contemporaries. . . . Whether in this way the essence of the power of imagination as seen by Kant was recognized . . . cannot be discussed here. The following interpretation . . . grows out of another way of questioning and moves, so to speak, in the opposite direction from that of German Idealism" (KM 137n196).

22. KM 108. Heidegger repeatedly refers to the movement that gives rise to this horizon as "transcendence." This movement is "the holding-open of the horizon within which the being of beings becomes discernible in a preliminary way" (123) and is itself grounded in primordial time: "Primordial time allows the pure formation of transcendence to occur" (197, tr. m.).

23. Kant's own transcendental philosophy might be regarded as a thinking in which reason stays within its limits. The transcendental "turn" means that on the basis of what is *given* we only inquire into the conditions of possibility of what is given, without however hypostatizing them. Hence that which must be thought as the "preceding" does not have the status of the first or most fundamental. The question remains, however, whether Kant can always live up to that claim.

24. My interpretation is mainly based on the texts "Differenz des Fichteschen und Schellingschen Systems der Philosophie" (D) and "Glauben und Wissen" (FK), both in *Jenaer Schriften* 1801–1807.

25. Hegel, *Vorlesungen über die Geschichte der Philosophie* III, 347–348/441. Heidegger quotes this passage in GA 21, with the remark: "Kant's understanding of the function of time, as expressed in the doctrine of schematism . . . is completely misjudged by the subsequent idealistic philosophy. Hegel is an extreme example in this respect" (GA 21:201–2). Heidegger proposes that Kant seeks a mediation through which the categories can pertain to objects: time. This did not concern Hegel, and he sought—though Heidegger does not name it in this context—the unity of pure sensibility and pure understanding in transcendental imagination (*Einbildungskraft*). Since Hegel does not understand this "temporally," Heidegger's rather short-sighted reaction is that Hegel has no understanding whatsoever of the "pivotal problematic that Kant encountered" (GA 21:202–4). But Heidegger also considers that Kant himself was not able to fathom that problematic, since he understands time as a way of schematically structuring the plurality given in sense-perception—that is to say, merely as nature-time (203).

26. D 45/112–13. See: "Therefore the usual practice of separating understanding and reason is, from every point of view, to be rejected. When

the concept is regarded as irrational, this should be interpreted rather as an incapacity of reason to recognize itself in the concept. The determinate and abstract concept is . . . an *essential moment of reason*" (L II, 287–88/612).

27. Hegel maintains that nothing can be understood of the totality of transcendental deduction "without distinguishing what Kant calls the faculty of the original synthetic unity of apperception from the ego which does the representing and is the subject, and recognizing *this imagination* . . . as that which is primary and original and as that out of which subjective ego and objective world first sunder themselves . . . and as the sole in-itself. " (FK 308/72–73, italics mine, tr. m.).

28. FK 328/92. See: "Whereas the understanding had previously been handled by reason, it is now, by contrast, reason that is handled by the understanding. This makes clear what a subordinate stage the identity of subject and object was grasped at" (D 10/80; cf. FK 303/68).

29. "[T]he necessary dichotomy (*Entzweiung*) is *one* factor in life. Life eternally forms itself by producing oppositions, and with respect to the greatest vitality, totality is only possible through its own reestablishment out of the deepest fission" (D 21–22/91, tr. m.).

30. D 24/93, tr. m.; cf. L II, 287/611. Hegel here states that understanding is the "infinite force" that determines the universal and thus, conversely, imparts a certain fixity and persistence to transient beings. If this goes no further than fixed determinations, this is not the fault of the understanding, but is due to a "subjective impotence" of reason itself, which then does not have the power to retrace these determinations to their unity. We may assume that Hegel regards this *subjective* impotence of reason as something which ultimately always overturns into power through the "dialectic force" (which is *not* a subjective faculty), that is opposed to the understanding (see also Enc. I, §11).

31. "[T]he pure positing of reason . . . would be . . . subjective infinity: the realm of freedom as opposed to the objective world. Because this realm is in this form itself opposed to and conditioned by something, reason, in order to absolutely sublate this opposition, must also annul the independence of this realm" (D 27/96, tr. m.). From this ensues the movement of the *Phenomenology of Spirit.*

32. "Nietzsches Wort 'Gott ist tot'" (HW 247 / QT 112, tr. m.).

8. Hegel's *Logic* as a Deconstruction of Metaphysics

1. "The indispensable foundation, the concept (*Begriff*), the universal which is the thought itself . . . cannot be regarded as *only* an indifferent

form attached to a content. . . . [T]he profounder basis is the soul itself, the pure concept which is the very heart of things, their simple life-pulse, even of the subjective thinking of them. To become conscious of . . . this *logical* nature, this is the task" (L I, 26–27/37, tr. m.). What is usually understood by "content" is not formless, but only has "soul and meaning" through form; it is form itself "which is transformed only into the semblance (*Schein*) of a content" (29/39).

2. "The essential point of view is that what is involved is an altogether new concept of scientific procedure. Philosophy . . . cannot . . . borrow its method from a subordinate science" (L I, 16, cf. 48/27, cf. 53). The concept of science itself belongs to the content of that science, namely as its ultimate result (30, cf. 49/40, cf. 53).

3. L I, 37/45. What rightly applies for the understanding is unduly also carried out into the sphere of reason, which precisely does not have the confinement of the understanding (37/45). If logical determinations are conceived as merely subjective principles, then philosophy is lifted above "this timid, incomplete standpoint" (45/51).

4. When Kant maintains that the understanding necessarily comes into contradiction with itself, he does not recognize "that the contradiction is precisely the rising of reason above the limitations of the understanding and the resolving of them" (L I, 39/46).

5. See esp. D 110–11/169–70. This text can be considered the germ of the *Logic* (see Phen. 14/9–10).

6. For Hegel this means: "The teleological process is the *translation* (*Übersetzung*) of the concept that has a distinct concrete existence as concept into objectivity. . . . The externality into which the end translates itself is itself . . . already posited as moment of the concept. The end possesses, therefore, in externality *its own moment*" (L II, 454/747–48).

7. Whereas Kant still understands the pure form as ego, Hegel states that this form has still to be relieved of its finite determinateness: "The form, when thus thought out in its purity, will have within itself the capacity to *determine* itself, that is, to give itself a content, and that a *necessarily* explicated content—in the form of a system of determinations of thought" (L I, 61/63, tr. m.).

8. *Vorlesungen über die Geschichte der Philosophie* I, 49/30, tr. m.; cf. Enc. I, §14.

9. Hegel does, however, often refer to the understanding (the representation or opinion) that is incapable of comprehending the unity of a determined opposition. We have seen that the strife between understanding and reason is indeed explicitly thematized in *The Difference between Fichte's and Schelling's System of Philosophy.*

10. The *criterion* is thus constituted by the concept and not by the historical time at which it was thought. Thus, Hegel in *The Doctrine of Being,* for example, thematizes the conceptions of the pre-Socratics, Aristotle, Kant, and the mathematicians of his own time.

11. The germ of the plant "is impelled toward development; it cannot bear to be merely in itself." *Vorlesungen über die Geschichte der Philosophie* I, 41/22, tr. m. See "Thus consciousness suffers this violence at its own hands: it spoils its own limited satisfaction" (Phen. 63/51).

12. L I, 69, 74–75/70, 74. Being, "this simple determination, which has no other meaning of any kind" (79) is identical to itself and cannot be distinguished from something inside or outside itself (75, 82/75, 81). Thus it is "abstract indifference" (I, 445, tr. m.). Being as the "indeterminate immediate " (82/81) is, however, itself "the result of complete abstraction" (104/99). Being must "be taken only in the one-sided character of pure immediacy, precisely because it is here as beginning" (72/72, tr. m.). This means that Hegel has already had to carry out a vast "reduction" in order to start with pure "being." Deliberately leaving out the totality of pure determinations that always already inhere in being, he thus creates a lack that consequently yields of itself the systematic unfolding of this totality. For this to happen, the *beings* which initially present themselves to consciousness must also be neglected right from the start. The beginning is not "an immediate of *sensuous intuition* or of *representation*, but of thinking, which on account of its immediacy may also be called a supersensuous *inner intuition*" (L II, 553/827–28).

13. "[R]eflection must resort to finding a fixed predicate for being. . . . Thus we find being identified with what persists amidst all change, with matter, susceptible of innumerable determinations. . . . But these additional and more concrete characterizations do not allow being to be as *pure being*, as it is here immediately in the beginning" (Enc. I, §87 rem., tr. m.).

14. All different forms of "not" inhere in this first "nothing" and are increasingly developed from out of it. Since the term "nothing" used by Hegel evokes associations with "not existing," I use the terms "not" and "nothing" here without distinction.

15. These pure categories also inhere in everyday language: "The forms of thought are, in the first instance, displayed and stored in human *language*." Everything expressed in language "contains a category—concealed, mixed with other forms or clearly determined as such" (L I, 20/31).

16. The term "philosophy" here pertains to that form of thinking which explicitly accomplishes the distinction between the essence and the totality of beings. Hegel maintains that this was not yet the case with the Greek philosophers of nature. The later philosophy, however, does also concern itself with the categories of being. On the other hand, modern nat-

ural sciences make use of distinctions which logically belong in *The Doctrine of Essence*. Thus, Hegel understands the distinction between cause and effect primarily as an *ontological* distinction, which we use in attempting to understand reality as such. Hegel thematizes the natural sciences only insofar as they make use of ontological categories. For the sake of clarity, I read *The Doctrine of Essence* as the part of the *Logic* where the concepts that constitute the proper domain of traditional metaphysics are developed.

17. "Since knowing wants to know the true . . . it does not stop at the immediate and its determinations, but penetrates it on the supposition that at the back of this being there is something else, something other than being itself" (L II, 13/389, tr. m.).

18. "[T]his semblance (*Schein*) is not something external to or other than essence; on the contrary, it is essence's own semblance. The showing of this semblance (*das Scheinen*) within essence itself is *reflection*" (L II, 17/394, tr. m., cf. 23–24/399).

19. From the historical point of view, we may here think of Plato's distinction between *eidos* and appearance.

20. "Reflection therefore is the movement of returning (*Rückkehr*) which, only in that it is returning, is that which starts or returns. . . . Immediacy merely manifests itself as the return and is . . . the semblance of a beginning (*der Schein des Anfangs*) . . . which is negated by the return" (L II, 26–27/401, tr. m.). However, external reflection presupposes a "being" as the beginning (28/403) and does not understand that what it finds is a result of the process of reflection (29/403–4). Unlike Kant, then, Hegel is not concerned with reflection as subjective capacity, but with the self-returning movement of essence as such, within which this external reflection is one of the moments (see 30). This movement of determining reflection brings about the essential distinctions that Kant calls concepts of reflection (see KRV, B 316; L II, 33f/406f).

21. In *The Doctrine of Essence* Hegel lets these and other oppositions systematically arise and perish. Each time, the basic category "essence" opens up a perspective wherein that which is distinguished in reflection becomes independent and obstructs the view of the unity of the determinations. If the essential and the nonessential are merely conceived as relation, then their true unity cannot manifest itself. From this perspective—that is to say, for the understanding—a concept such as "identity" will also appear as opposite to "distinction," and not as the *whole* of identity and distinction within which "identity" posits the other of itself over against itself, in order to thus confirm itself *as* the identical (L II, 40–41/412–13). The determinations that come about in reflection are one-sided and therefore only have truth in the movement in which that one-sidedness is sublated. They are, however, "stubbornly opposed to their movement" (31/405). Only

when the concept "relation" itself has been overcome will the absolute unity of the immediate and the universal that comes about in reflection be able to manifest itself (166/513).

22. The movement of essence "consists in positing within itself the negation or determination, thereby giving itself *existence* (Dasein) and becoming as infinite being-for-itself what it is in itself. It thus gives itself the existence that is *equal* to its being-in-itself and becomes the *concept*" (L II, 16/391, tr. m.). In the *concept* the distinction has become totally transparent (240): universality, particularity, and singularity are no longer allowed to become independent and thus to cover up their inner unity—that is, the one and only movement of the concept itself.

23. L II, 245/577. I have taken the expression "specular reflexivity" from R. Gasché, *Inventions of Difference*, 210.

24. "Being" and "essence" are the moments of the *becoming* of the concept: "They are contained in it because it [the concept] is their result, but no longer as *being* and *essence*. That determination they possess only in so far as they have not withdrawn into this their unity" (L II, 245/577). See "The concept is the *most concrete* and *richest* determination because it is the ground and the *totality* of the preceding determinations, of the categories of being and of the determinations of reflection; these, therefore, are also present in it" (L II, 295/617).

25. "The judgment (*Urteil*) is the self-diremption of the concept. . . . It is thus the original division (*die ursprüngliche Teilung*) of what is originally one." From the standpoint of ordinary thinking, however, "subject and predicate are considered to be complete, each on its own account, apart from the other" (L II, 304/625). "To restore this *identity* of the concept, or rather to *posit* it, is the goal of the *movement* of the judgment" (309/630).

26. L II, 461–62/754–55, cf. 258, 271/587, 597. See also: "Now the idea as such is nothing but the concept, the reality (*Realität*) of the concept, and the unity of both . . . in this unity the concept remains predominant (*das Herrschende*). For . . . it . . . generates reality out of itself as its own. . . ." This reality is nothing but the "self-development" of the concept (*Vorlesungen über die Ästhetik* I, 145/107, tr. m.).

27. L II, 549/824. See: "Reason, which is the sphere of the idea, is the *self-revealed truth* in which the concept possesses the realization that is wholly adequate to it, and is free, inasmuch as it cognizes this its objective world in its subjectivity and its subjectivity in its objective world" (271/597).

28. "Thus the logical idea has itself as the *infinite form* for its content." The general side of this form is the method; this is determined by the concept and is in this way "the soul of all objectivity." From the movement of the

"logical" so far, the method has emerged as "the *self-knowing concept that has itself*, as the absolute . . . *for its subject matter*" (L II, 550–51/824–26).

29. The concept is "the absolute reflection-into-itself out of the finite" (L II, 363/673). With *The Doctrine of the Concept* Hegel as it were breaks through the barrier erected by Kant's transcendental dialectic against the possibility of metaphysical knowing.

30. While dialectic is commonly regarded as "a subjective itch for unsettling and destroying what is fixed and substantial," Hegel considers Kant to understand at least the necessary character of the contradiction. But he clings to the abstract-negative aspect of the dialectical principle and denies reason the capacity to know the infinite. Hegel, by contrast, also shows that the dialectic has a positive side—namely, the "grasping of opposites in their unity." This he considers to be "the most important aspect of dialectic," yet also "the most difficult" (L I, 51–52/56; cf. L II, 558–59/832; Enc. I, §81, 82).

31. This negativity is "the innermost source of all activity, of all animate and spiritual self-movement, the dialectical soul that everything true possesses and through which alone it is true." For on this negativity rests "the sublation of the opposition between concept and reality, and the unity that is truth" (L II, 563/835). "That which enables the concept to advance itself is the already mentioned *negative* which it possesses within itself; it is this which constitutes the genuine dialectical element" (L I, 51/55).

32. "Thus all the oppositions that are assumed as fixed . . . are in and for themselves a transition. . . . If a consideration that ignores the concept stops short at their external relationship, isolates them . . . , it is the concept, on the contrary, that keeps them steadily in view, moves them as their soul, and brings out their dialectic" (L II, 560/833).

33. That a concept—which constitutes the totality of itself and its opposite—becomes a moment within that totality is considered by Hegel to be "*the specific, original ground of all activity and self-movement*" (L II, 47/417). This is so because the contradiction that always already inheres in the concept becomes explicit, which is a condition for sublating the contrariety.

34. The result "is a new concept . . . and is the unity of itself and its opposite. It is in this way that the system of concepts as such has to be formed—and has to complete itself in a purely continuous course in which nothing extraneous is introduced" (L I, 49/54).

35. Hegel has shown that in principle this is already the case with essence, but essence itself—that is to say, metaphysics—does not comprehend that. "Essence is being-in-and-for-itself, but in the determination of being-in-itself. . . . Its movement consists in . . . becoming as infinite being-for-itself what it is in itself" (L II, 16/391). But the unity between in-itself and for-itself does not yet here come to completion.

36. "Thus *form* in its realization has penetrated all its differences and made itself transparent. . . . The distinction of *content* and form itself has also vanished" (L II, 214/551). The method is thus "the absolute form, the concept that knows itself and everything as concept" and determines every content (568/839).

37. Enc. I, §240, cf. §161; L II, 307/627–28). Marcuse, *op. cit.*, 142–43, thematizes this issue. His clarifying interpretation of the *Logic* focuses repeatedly on the specific dynamic proper to life and history, which he considers to be grounded in "the absolute difference between being-in-itself and existence" that characterizes all beings (205). He argues that Hegel's concept of movement should be taken as a starting point when post-Hegelian theories of history such as Dilthey's are discussed (386). He claims that Hegel developed a concept of movement that allows the phenomenon of historicity to be adequately understood, but in the *Logic* subordinated this concept to the absolute knowledge that brings this movement of history to a halt (354). His interpretation does not, however, contain an elaborated critique of Hegel or Dilthey.

38. It is the "genuine nature of essential thinking to sublate the mediation in the very act of mediation" (Enc. I, §50 rem., p. 82, tr. m.). Whereas Kant considers the "mediation" of discursive understanding to be a necessary condition of knowledge, Hegel sees it as serving the purpose of a purely intuitive knowing. He repeatedly emphasizes that what is immediately given must still be brought about *as* the immediate. The understanding "mediates" the initially given immediacy with the immediacy which constitutes the *aim* of knowledge. Reason divides itself for this purpose into reason and understanding, and lets the understanding proceed. The danger with this, however, is that the understanding tends to revolt against its mediating, subordinate task, and to appear as the aim itself. Although this thwarts the movement in which the primordially given unity tries to actualize itself, from Hegel's perspective this necessary tendency will always be overcome—the true aim is not lost in this process (cf. L II, 453/747). The same principle underlies Hegel's conception of the relation between the individual and history.

9. Concept, Time, and History

1. "It is not only that in nature the play of forms has unbounded and unbridled contingency, but that each shape by itself is devoid of its concept (*entbehrt des Begriffs ihrer selbst*)" (Enc. II, §248 rem., cf. §250).

2. The philosophy of nature and spirit is elaborated in greatest detail in the *Encyclopaedia*, but already inheres in the *Logic* itself. The absolute idea has "various shapes, and the business of philosophy is to cognize it in

these. Nature and spirit are as such different modes of manifesting *its existence*. . . . Philosophy . . . is the highest mode of apprehending the absolute idea, because its mode is the highest mode, the concept. Hence it embraces those shapes . . . and comprehends them and itself. . . . The *logical* aspect of the absolute idea . . . [is] the universal mode in which all particular modes are sublated and enfolded" (L II, 549–50/824–25, tr. m.). In the *Logic*, however, the absolute idea is still "enclosed within pure thought." The idea is the "urge" to sublate this lack; the result of the *Logic* thus becomes "*the beginning of another sphere and science*" (572–73/842–43). Hegel understands this course of the idea as the scientific *repetition* (in retrospect) of what has actually accomplished itself as nature and spirit. The unity of reality now becomes accessible for the first time from the perspective of the pure concept. The many ways of conceiving this unity, which are still tied to representation, including that of a divine creation, are sublated in this perspective.

3. The absolute idea is absolute self-differentiation: "Now this other, that which it distinguishes from itself, is, on the one hand, precisely nature. . . . We therefore have to conceive nature as containing the absolute idea within itself," yet in the *form* of the other of spirit (*Vorlesungen über die Ästhethik* I, 128/92, tr. m.; cf. Enc. II, §247). On the other hand, the absolute idea or spirit distinguishes itself from itself as subjective, finite spirit, still opposed to nature as a "restricting otherness" that it has not yet overcome (129/93). This standpoint is sublated when spirit comprehends the absolute itself. In doing this, spirit raises itself to the standpoint of absolute spirit, and it becomes manifest that this spirit itself "posits the finitude of spirit, within which it becomes the absolute object of the knowledge of itself" (130/94, tr. m.).

4. "On the contrary, the pure idea in which the determinateness or reality of the concept has itself become concept, is an absolute *liberation*. . . . Because of this freedom, the *form of its determinateness* is also utterly free—the *externality of space and time* existing absolutely for itself without the moment of subjectivity" (L II, 573/843, tr. m.). "[T]herefore externality is the determination of [the idea] as nature" (Enc. II, §247, tr. m.). "The primary or immediate determination of nature is . . . *space*" (§254). My interpretation of space and time as the *form* of the determinateness of the idea—which can thus appear as nature, that is to say, as the realm of becoming—does not entail that form and content are here posited over against one another. Hegel always understands form as that which determines itself and thus gives content to itself. The idea that is first only determined by the pure forms space and time is increasingly determined with respect to its content by concepts such as movement and matter. In Hegel's view, these can be developed from the concepts time and space.

5. This distinction must even precede the point at which the *Logic* begins. The distinction between being on the one hand and space and time

on the other allows the *Logic* and the philosophy of nature and spirit—relating to one and the same reality—to be treated separately and in sequence. It could be that Hegel's presentation remains too tied to this sequence for him to thematize how the one pure concept from the outset distinguishes itself into being, essence, and concept on the one hand, and time and space on the other. It is therefore not clear that the logical development of the concept *actually* only occurs in the one, temporally determined reality. See I. Dubsky, "Über Hegels und Heideggers Begriff der Zeit," 78 and D. Wandschneider/V. Hösle, "Die Entäußerung der Idee zur Natur und ihre zeitliche Entfaltung als Geist bei Hegel." These authors follow Hegel in their thesis that the logical determinations of the concept must individualize themselves in nature (190), although nature also "thwarts" the unfolding of the idea (195). The authors, however, hold to the representation of a supratemporal divine idea, which realizes itself in time as "the becoming world of God" (198).

6. Phen. 524–25/487. Thus, time is the intuitable manifestation—or "explanation"—of the eternal movement of the pure concept. See: "Time is the same principle as the ego = ego of pure self-consciousness, but as time, this principle, or the simple concept (*der einfache Begriff*) is still completely external and abstract as mere intuited *becoming*" (Enc. II, §258 rem.).

7. Enc. II, §258 rem. See: "Time is the negative in what is sensible (*Die Zeit ist das Negative im Sinnlichen*); thought is the same negativity, but it is the deepest, the infinite form, in which therefore all beings are dissolved as such" (*Vorlesungen über die Philosophie der Geschichte* 103/77, tr. m.). This infinite negativity constitutes the principle of spirit, which "particularizes and negates itself, yet also sublates this self-particularization and self-negation . . . and thus . . . unites itself with itself in free universality (*sich in freier Allgemeinheit mit sich selbst zusammenschließt*)." Its "appearance is inadequate to its true essence" as long as *finite* spirit still has nature as the other over against itself (*Vorlesungen über die Ästhetik* 129/92–93, tr. m.). That is to say, this *appearance* of spirit accomplishes itself in time.

8. *Vorlesungen über die Geschichte der Philosophie* 51/32, tr. m., see D. Wandschneider/V. Hösle, *art. cit.*, 187n. See also: "The changes that take place in nature—how infinitely manifold soever they may be—exhibit only a perpetually self-repeating circle; in nature there happens 'nothing new under the sun.' . . . [O]nly in those changes which take place in the region of spirit does anything new arise" (*Vorlesungen über die Philosophie der Geschichte* 74/54). The way in which spirit actualizes itself in world history has no graduality: "Thus spirit . . . is for itself the truly hostile obstacle to its goal, that it has to overcome. That development which in the sphere of nature is a peaceful growth, is in the sphere of spirit a severe and infinite strife against itself (*ein harter unendlicher Kampf gegen sich selbst*). Spirit wishes to attain its own concept; but it hides this concept

from itself—it is proud and, in its self-alienation, thoroughly enjoys itself" (76/55, translation completely modified). We recognize here the strife between understanding and reason, which from Hegel's perspective is ultimately decided in favor of reason. See: "World history . . . is therefore the explication (*Auslegung*) of spirit in *time*, as nature is the explication of the idea in space" (96–97/72, tr. m.).

9. Cf. L I, 215; Enc. II, §258 rem. See also: "But the powerlessness (*Ohnmacht*) of life manifests itself in the fact that the commencement and the result are disjoined from each other (*auseinanderfallen*)."*Vorlesungen über die Philosophie der Geschichte* 104/78, tr. m. This powerlessness of finite spirit refers to the power of time, which lets everything that is become disjoined and compels linearity.

10. The actual history is thus approached by means of the basic category "concept," that is to say, by means of the principle of self-actualizing freedom: "To be directed at this category is to be directed at that which is truly essential" (*Vorlesungen über die Philosophie der Geschichte* 88/65, translation completely modified).

11. Although Hegel's philosophy still actually remains tied to externality, this is only—he would say—with respect to its "nonessential" side (cf. e.g. L I, 16, 30–31/27, 40). From his perspective the inadequacy of the presentation of the absolute does not have to crucially obstruct the view of the perfect and the infinite. The externality of something like linguistic articulation cannot, according to Hegel, infringe upon the absolute (cf. L II, 550/825). It is precisely this which makes the text so difficult and obscure for the reader, who "hears" the word with the ear of the outsider—or even with deaf ears—and is not immediately able to annul its externality.

12. Phen. 524–25/487, tr. m., cf. 34/27. When Hegel maintains that the power of time is annulled in absolute knowing, this does not mean that human life is no longer marked by finitude and conflict: "[T]he spiritual nature of man yields duality and inner conflict, and in their contradiction he is tossed about. . . . But where there is finitude, opposition and contradiction always break out again anew, and satisfaction does not get beyond being relative" (*Vorlesungen über die Ästhetik* I, 135–36/97–98, tr. m.). A philosophy that succeeds in raising itself above this finitude (137–138/100) can understand those finite manifestations for the first time *in the light of* the movement of absolute self-actualization—which entails (although Hegel does not say this here) that much of what is essential from the finite, human perspective vanishes into the background. Meanwhile, history itself also remains largely dominated by the manifestation of time, which lets everything rise and fall, but without this leading to essential progress. Thus, when there are transitions between wars and periods of peace without any evidence of progress, this indicates that the time which controls natural processes still has the upper hand here.

13. "To him who looks upon the world with reason, the world in its turn presents a reasonable aspect." *Vorlesungen über die Philosophie der Geschichte* 23/11, tr. m. True science of nature and spirit is only possible when these domains are understood with respect to their logical structure—that is to say, as yielded by the movement of the concept (cf. L II, 265/592). This investigation entails a certain risk, since here it is more difficult for Hegel to surpass the perspective of his historical situation. The more concrete the field of investigation, the more difficult it becomes to find the pure concept (on the basis of the distinction—not always easy to make—between what is essential and what is nonessential). I take the view, however, that a real critique of Hegel should focus on the logic that constitutes the background of his analyses. The *Phenomenology of Spirit*, which itself is already thought by means of that logical structure and constitutes an *example* of the scientific method (L I, 49/53), still starts out from consciousness as it appears (67/68). The science of appearing consciousness is hence not yet a true, pure science. The "logical" *is* implicitly present here, namely, as the movement in which something—here natural consciousness—is confronted with what it is not, sublates that lack, and becomes increasingly able to fully recognize as itself the otherness which time and again is posited over against it. The "development of this object . . . rests solely on the nature of the pure essentialities (*reine Wesenheiten*) which constitute the content of logic" (17/28). Although this movement of spirit culminates in absolute knowing, this does not mean that absolute knowing has already been understood with respect to its pure *logical* origin (cf. L II, 496/782; Phen. 60/49). Phenomenology has thus not yet attained the level of true science, and this "lack" is only sublated in the *Logic*. It is on the basis of the *Logic* that the philosophy of subjective spirit can be given its place *within* the system. Heidegger is somewhat preoccupied with this relation between the *Phenomenology* and the system of the *Encyclopaedia*. I will return to this issue in 10.2.

14. See L II, 573/843. Hegel writes on this in his *Differenzschrift*: "[T]he point of transition, the middle term through which identity constructing itself as nature passes over to identity constructing itself as intelligence, is the internalization of the light of nature, or the lightning stroke of the ideal upon the real, as Schelling calls it" (D 111/86).

15. This motivation is, however, evident from a letter to Jaspers from December 1925: "Hegel . . . did not see . . . that one has to question more radically not only becoming and movement, occurrence and *history*—but being itself" (*op. cit.*, 59).

16. *Die Vernunft in der Geschichte*, 153/127, tr. m.; cf. BT 428.

17. "In the vulgar interpretation of time as succession of nows, both datability and significance are *lacking*. . . . The nows are cut off from these

relations, so to speak, and, as thus cut off, they simply range themselves along after one another so as to constitute the succession" (BT 422, cf. 426–427, 431).

18. "Thus the concept is the conceivedness (*Begriffenheit*) of the self conceiving itself" (BT 433). Heidegger here quotes the following passage from the *Logic*: "[T]he I is the pure concept itself which, as concept, has come into existence" (L II, 253/583). That the pure concept manifests itself *as* self-consciousness does not mean for Hegel that the concept as such is identical to that manifestation. If that were the case, there would be no difference between the *Phenomenology of Spirit* and the *Logic*.

19. "Hegel conceives of the formal structure of self-differentiation as a relating back to itself (*Rückbeziehung zu sich selbst*) . . . and he can therefore intelligently state, yet without basis in the matter itself, that time is abstract subjectivity insofar as it is the negation of a negation" (GA 21:260–61, cf. 259). It seems better to me in this connection to characterize time as that which *remains identical* to itself than as that which is *related* to itself. In the *Encyclopaedia* Hegel does indeed call time abstract subjectivity: "Time is the same principle as the ego = ego of pure self-consciousness, but as time this principle, or the simple concept, is still completely external and abstract" (Enc. II, §258 rem.). This passage makes clear that Hegel understands time and self-consciousness on the basis of a principle that underlies both manifestations.

20. BT 434, see: "Thus spirit is in itself divided against itself; it is for itself the truly hostile obstacle to its goal, that it has to overcome" (*Vorlesungen über die Philosophie der Geschichte* 76/55, translation completely modified).

21. *Die Vernunft in der Geschichte* 153, 154 / 127, 128, tr. m. Apart from the first sentence, Heidegger does not quote these passages.

22. See *Die Vernunft in der Geschichte* 150/125. Heidegger refers to this passage (see BT 434).

23. BT 436, tr. m. The expression "In der Zeit fallen" used by Hegel just means "to take place in time." Heidegger emphasizes—clearly in an exaggerated way—the movement of "falling," omitting to say that only the *development* of history occurs in time.

24. "Present breaks away from (*entspringt*) its authentic Future and Past, so that it lets Dasein come to authentic existence only by taking a detour through that Present. The origin of this 'breaking away' of Present—that is, of falling into lostness (*des Verfallens in die Verlorenheit*)—is primordial, authentic temporality itself" (BT 348, tr. m., italics mine).

25. When Hegel regards time on the one hand as "the process of actual things" and on the other as abstract subjectivity (Enc. §258 add.,

resp. §258 rem.), Heidegger's reaction shows clearly his incomprehension or resistance: "Thus, time is the things themselves, time is pure self-consciousness and time is neither of them. Thus here again . . . something peculiar: Hegel can say anything about anything. And some people discover profundity in such a confusion" (GA 21:259–60).

26. Heidegger says rather petulantly in GA 21: "Hegel basically does not see the function of time in the interpretation of being, for if he did, he should have introduced time into the explanation of being as such. Traces thereof cannot be found in Hegel; quite the contrary." And that is because he "traditionally and dogmatically conceives of time as now-time" (GA 21:257). Heidegger here misunderstands the status that Hegel assigns to the concept. Heidegger understands *everything* on the basis of a dynamic which he calls "time" and which has very little to do with usual time. Hegel does the same on the basis of a dynamic, which he calls "concept" and which has equally little to do with usual time or with the usual "concept." And that has certainly left traces in his interpretation of being. I will let Heidegger add one of his rare qualifying remarks from GA 21: "[I] do not want to be absolutely dogmatic and contend that being can only be understood from out of time; perhaps someone will discover a new possibility tomorrow" (GA 21:267).

27. When Heidegger's relation to Hegel is approached by means of §82 of BT, the focus is generally on Heidegger's critique of Hegel's concept of time as now-time. I consider this critique to be of subordinate importance. I would here like to briefly thematize some of those interpretations. In "Heidegger's Critique of Hegel's Notion of Time" (1979), J. P. Surber rightly maintains that Heidegger is not aware of the position of Hegel's analysis of time within the entire system (367). His interpretation of Hegel is therefore not sufficiently fundamental (375). Surber sketches out that system, but then mainly focuses the confrontation on the question concerning the status of (finite) reflection—that is to say, he limits himself to the existentiell level of *Being and Time* on the one hand and the *Phenomenology of Spirit* on the other. He understands time primarily with respect to the activity of spirit, which pertains to time (374) and not with respect to the structure of the concept as such. Surber does not consider the question concerning the relation between time and history, which is actually what concerns Heidegger. D. Souche-Dagues in "Une exégèse heideggerienne: le temps chez Hegel d'après le §82 de *Sein und Zeit*" (1979) gives a clarifying interpretation of Hegel's concept of time in the *Encyclopaedia* and the *Logic* of Jena. She indicates the points on which Heidegger does not do justice to Hegel's concept of time, to conclude that Heidegger is wrong in considering Hegel to base his interpretation on the now-moment (119). The fact that Hegel understands the "now" as that which sublates its independence as soon as it has come about does not, however, diminish Heidegger's critique as much as Souche-Dagues suggests. She approaches the issue mainly from Hegel's perspective and does not show the proper dimension of Heidegger's concept of time. While Surber and Souche-

Dagues defend Hegel against Heidegger, P. Emad in "The Place of Hegel in Heidegger's *Being and Time*" (1983) takes Heidegger's side. Heidegger is perhaps better served by good opponents. Emad ignores the fact that Heidegger in §82 refers to Hegel only in order to distance himself from the latter's concept of time. When he quotes the passage where Heidegger says that the result of his analysis of time *seems* to agree with that of Hegel (see BT 405), he ignores the word "seems" and merely asserts: "Heidegger states that the result of the 'preceding' analysis of temporality agrees with Hegel" (170, see 171). He wrongly introduces an opposition between Heidegger's "indirect elucidation" of his own concept of time and the deconstruction of metaphysics, which Heidegger was to have made in part II of *Being and Time* (160, 169). He actually accuses Surber and Souche-Dagues of being unaware of what Heidegger understands by this "elucidation" (159n). Emad can ultimately do little more than conclude that it is impossible to throw light on meaningful time by starting out from Hegel's now-time, although the converse is indeed possible. He calls this a "central thesis" in *Being and Time* (171, 173). D. Schmidt in his study on Heidegger and Hegel thematizes the positions of Hegel and Heidegger in a more nuanced way. His thesis is that Heidegger in §82 does not succeed in really distancing himself from Hegel, with the consequence that Heidegger does not manage to complete the project of *Being and Time* (*op. cit.*, 59, 64). Schmidt focuses the discussion between Hegel and the early Heidegger on the temporality that grounds the being of Dasein. Basing his argument on Kojève's interpretation of the *Phenomenology of Spirit*, he maintains that finite spirit is grounded in a time that can indeed compete with Heidegger's ecstatic temporality (59, 61). He says that this time underlies the structure of the longing that entails that spirit, despite all its attempts, is not identical to itself (56). Heidegger should have taken account of this "human time" (59). In my own interpretation, I have conceived the specific movement of finite spirit as determined by the movements of time on the one hand, and of the concept as such on the other. The tension between these movements might perhaps indeed be understood as a separate mode of time, although I doubt whether that was Hegel's intention. This interesting issue would require further investigation. It is understandable that Kojève, inspired by Heidegger, has reasons to emphasize the agreement between Hegel and Heidegger (see 54); the *difference* between the dynamic of care and finite spirit is not, however, thematized by Schmidt either. He concludes that Heidegger has "more than apparent kinship with the Hegelian dialectic" and suggests that this unexpected result of §82 compelled him to take up a more nuanced position with regard to metaphysics (59–60). He takes Heidegger to realize that the difference between a primordial and a vulgar time is no longer adequate for this task (60–61). First, I do not think that Heidegger was capable of being surprised by the course of his own analysis; Schmidt overestimates his flexibility. Second, it is unfortunate that Schmidt, while describing time as that which makes it possible for being to appear (37), like the authors mentioned above overlooks the difference between *Zeitlichkeit* and *Temporalität*. In my view it is not enough with regard to the relation between time and negativity to focus attention on the temporality that grounds the being of Dasein. Schmidt creates an unnecessary difference between time on the one hand and the problem of negativity, as that shows forth in the texts after *Being and Time*, on the other (62).

28. GA 26:254. Heidegger fiercely defends himself against the evidently disappointing reactions to his recently published work: "Why does the metaphysical projection of Dasein move in the direction of time and the radical interpretation of time? Possibly . . . because Bergson and, following him, Spengler deal with time? Or because Husserl worked at the phenomenology of internal time consciousness? Or because Kierkegaard speaks, in the Christian sense, of temporality in contradistinction to eternity? . . . Was the analysis of Dasein then projected on the backdrop of time because it was believed the result would be good if the above-mentioned were fused together?" (177–78).

29. BT 354; GA 24:367. As I noted earlier, Heidegger's analysis at this level is in line with Husserl's conception of protention and retention as factors that underlie every perception. However, whereas Husserl in his *Texte zur Phänomenologie des inneren Zeitbewußtseins / The Phenomenology of Internal Time-Consciousness* starts out from (objectifying) perception, Heidegger focuses his attention mainly on the temporal dynamic of practical involvement with beings. This dynamic, like expecting, remembering, experiencing continuity, and all other modes of intentionality, is made possible by the temporality that grounds the primordial openness of Dasein. This temporal structure is of a different order than the time within which all events occur and which we experience by means of the distinction between past, present, and future (BT 326). Heidegger's distinction between a vulgar and a primordial time can in no way be reduced to the traditional distinction between a cosmic time and an experienced time. Whoever wishes to criticize this proposed dichotomy, as Ricoeur, for example, does, will in any case have to take seriously the transcendental status of temporality. See P. Ricoeur, *Temps et récit* III / *Time and Narrative*, vol. 3, esp. 133, 137–38/89, 91–92.

30. BT 325, cf. GA 24:392. When Heidegger gives priority to the temporal ecstasis Future (BT 329), this is because the proper character of the movement enacted by Dasein consists in the projective opening up of a realm of possibilities. The movement characterized by the *logos* is animated by an orientation upon how it should or could be. Although here we might think of the *eidos* that the Greek artisan intends or of the Hegelian urge that entails that something wishes to actualize that which it is in itself, Heidegger is concerned with a modification of that movement such that its future can never be reduced to a present. This constitutes the difference between the coming toward its proper possibilities and self-actualization.

31. Derrida is one of those who questions Heidegger's distinction between a primordial and a vulgar time. He considers that this distinction keeps Heidegger indebted to metaphysics. Derrida therefore tries in "Ousia et Grammè. Note sur une note de 'Sein und Zeit'" in *Marges de la philosophie* / "Ousia and Grammè: Note on a Note from *Being and Time*," in *Margins of Philosophy* to show that Aristotle in his analysis of time is indeed aware of the impossibility of giving priority to the "now." Derrida tries in this way to nuance Heidegger's thesis that metaphysics is not capable of adequately thinking time. It seems, however, that he does not relate Heidegger's critique of the metaphysical conception of time to the more fundamental level of Heidegger's comprehension of metaphysics. The two themes, Heidegger's distinction between a primordial and a vulgar time on the one hand and his thesis that metaphysics could only understand "being" as presence on the other, thus remain more or less separate from each other. This may be due to the fact that Derrida in 1972 did not have access to GA 24. He does, however, see that the theme of time as horizon for the understanding of being only emerges at the beginning and the end of *Being and Time* (35/32). He also takes over that aspect: he calls it "the closure of metaphysics" (58/51). But Derrida chooses to no longer give the name time to that which brings about, maintains, and threatens from within that *clôture:* "Time is that which is thought on the basis of being as presence, and if something—which bears a relation to time, but is not time—is to be thought beyond the determination of being as presence, it cannot be a question of something that still could be called *time*" (69/60). Something important happens here. Heidegger himself was aware that temporality—the time which is not thought *on the basis of* being, but which grounds every understanding of being—had only very little to do with usual time; I think he would have had no objection to Derrida's choice of different words, such as, in this text, the term *différance* (77–78/66–67). Derrida on the one hand proposes that Heidegger's quest for an ultimate *archē* or origin is still metaphysical (73–74/63–64), but on the other hand does not himself give up the attempt to speak in a nonmetaphysical way about "origin" and "end" (78/67). Like Heidegger, he knows that such a different way cannot move beyond the closure of metaphysics, but at most can try from within to admit the other of what is present (41, 58–59/38, 51–52). Derrida seems not to see that Heidegger's idea of temporality is precisely intended to articulate the possibility of a thinking that does not reduce origin and future to modes of presence. When Derrida, as evidenced by the motto drawn from *Time and Being,* agrees with Heidegger's thesis that *Abwesen* remains very much determined by *Anwesen* (SD 7 / TB 7), he does not see that this thesis ensues directly from Heidegger's early conception of a primordial time (74/64). That a concept such as *différance* in my view has more to do with what Heidegger understands by primordial time than Derrida admits, does not mean that I would wish to deny the distinction between the two thinkers. I am surprised that D. Wood in *The Deconstruction of Time* merely takes over Derrida's critique of Heidegger's concept of

time and entirely ignores the distinction between temporality and Temporality which he could have observed in the English translation of GA 24.

32. "Brief über den Humanismus" (WM 190 / PM 273; cf. BT 286).

33. In 1931: "[S]everal repeated attempts have recently been made to prove that the problematic of "being and time" already exists in Hegel. This exercise is perfectly acceptable so long as the aim is energetically to find fault with my presumed originality. . . . By contrast, to see the positive aspect here, one must have already put in the effort of actual work. . . . If reading the problematic of *Being and Time* into some other text is ever nonsensical, then this is the case with Hegel" (GA 32:208–9).

10. The Threefold of Thinking: Heidegger's and Hegel's Conception of Method

1. "In the process . . . of the 'articulation' the phenomenological method already proceeds by means of a critical deconstruction of the objectifications, which are always prepared to cling to the phenomena. Herewith the intuitive comportment seems to have been abandoned in favor of a discursive thinking. For I say first of all that a certain phenomenon is *not* such and such. This can only be done in the manner of an *argumentation*—that is to say, in a manner which is somehow *dialectical*" (GA 58:255). One may here recognize the problem of the relation between *nous* and *logos*. The *logos* is indispensable for the accomplishment in human thinking of the *nous*, but constantly threatens to thwart its proper character. See also GA 19:560–61.

2. "But the meaning of the eidetic has been isolated far too much, and has been tied to the idea of a generalization. 'Essence' is identified with 'genus.' Starting out from understanding (*Verstehen*), the concept of essence gains another meaning" (GA 58:241, cf. GA 33:223).

3. See from the previously cited letter to Jaspers of December 1925: "Hegel . . . did not see . . . that one has to question more radically not only becoming and movement, occurrence and *history*—but being itself. . . . It seems to me—it is neither a species nor something formal-universal—but something that Hegel could not possibly characterize and that he also does not ask about" (*op. cit.*, 59).

4. GA 68:65–66. Here I follow part II of GA 68 from 1942, where Heidegger thematizes this question in greatest detail. See similar passages in GA 32: especially 1–6, 10–13 and "Hegels Begriff der Erfahrung" (HW 105 / HCE 7).

5. Human knowledge must "accomplish the self-manifestation of appearing knowledge." In order to accord with the absolute, this accom-

plishment itself has to be absolute. "If the 'Phenomenology of Spirit' is this accomplishment, then the work with this title has undertaken a metaphysical task that had previously never needed to be set and later could no longer be set" (GA 68:73, cf. 97).

6. "If we wish to confront Hegel, then we are required to be 'kindred' with him. . . . To be kindred means to be *committed* to the first and last necessities of philosophical inquiry *arising from the matter*" (GA 32:44–45, cf. 55). Heidegger here draws on a passage in Hegel's *Differenzschrift* (D 16/6).

7. GA 32:107. See: "[W]e will call the freeing accomplishment ('absolving') of the appearance of the absolute its absolvence. The absolute 'is' solely as absolvence. The knowledge of the absolute . . . is . . . itself absolute—that is, absolvent—that is, a course and path of the absolute toward itself" (GA 68:83, cf. "Hegels Begriff der Erfahrung," HW 124–25 / HCE 38–39).

8. "What takes place in the first part is the coming of spirit to itself on the path that is appropriate to the character of its own possibility of movement (experience, phenomenology). The *reach* of its domain (*der Bereich seines Reiches*) unfolds out of and in this kind of movement" (GA 32:39, tr. m.). This domain is the actuality of absolute knowing itself. It is striking that Heidegger usually does not consider the philosophy of nature and spirit, and takes the first system to consist of only two parts (cf. 145).

9. GA 32:22–23, see 63, 195.

10. GA 32:140, tr. m., cf. 144; GA 68:88–89. There Heidegger says that it is inadequate to understand this threefold as the sequence of thesis, antithesis, and synthesis, since the analysis is guided from the outset by the synthesis (which still has to come about). At the end of the *Logic* Hegel suggests that his method could perhaps also be divided into four moments, namely (1) the beginning, (2) the coming about of an opposition, (3) the self-sublation of the opposition, and (4) the immediacy that is the result of that sublation. In his view, however, the fact that two aspects may be distinguished in the moment of negativity does not change the threefold principle (L II, 563–64/836).

11. "But this turning back (*Rückwendung*) of the other into the one, whereby the difference becomes a nondifference and wherein what is differentiated remains preserved and sublated, this reflection (*Reflexion*) that marks the essence of infinity is genuinely actual in the I. . . . Herein is manifest the inner connection between the logical and the subjective I-like (*ichliche*) grounding of infinity. What is truly and really infinite in the declared logical sense is the subject and, what is more, the absolute subject as spirit—as is to be shown in the *Phenomenology*."(GA 32:111, cf. 108–9).

12. I will here briefly recall how Hegel regards the three moments in which the concept articulates itself as moments of a circular movement that has fully overcome the power of time (Enc. II, §258 add.). The "infinitely important form of triplicity" (L I, 388/327; see II, 565/837; Phen. 37/29) is the principle of the absolute method and hence does not occur in time—not in the time which entails that all beings are transient. While the beings that are subjected to time are unable to hold fast their identity in the process of becoming, the concept always remains identical to itself in its infinite movement. Nevertheless, it is possible to distinguish a "before" and an "after" in that movement. Thus, Hegel remarks that science (that is to say, true philosophy) constitutes a circle, within which every separate science is a fragment circling within itself that "has a 'before' and an 'after'—or, expressed more accurately, only has the 'before' and *indicates* its 'after' in its conclusion" (L II, 572/842, tr. m.). Elsewhere he affirms that "essence is past—but timelessly past—being (*das vergangene, aber zeitlos vergangene Sein*)" (13/389): Essence precedes being, but thinking only "recollects" this after the passage of time. Ultimately thinking will realize that essence itself is a moment within the movement of the concept, and thus is equally not the "first" (245/577). From the perspective of the absolute concept, it thus turns out that the different moments may only provisionally be conceived as beginning, middle, and end: "The method, which thus winds itself into a circle, cannot anticipate in a *development in time* that the beginning is, as such, already something derived. . . . [T]here is no need to deprecate the fact that it may only be accepted *provisionally* and *hypothetically*" (570, first italics mine). It is not only in order to meet the confined understanding of common, representing thinking that Hegel presents the movement of the concept as he does. This presentation rather indicates a certain confinement of articulation as such. Hegel is forced to use the distinction between a "before" and an "after" which usually only applies to movements that are determined by time. The pure movement of the concept has to bring about a semblance of linearity while it expresses itself because linguistic interpretation, no matter how transparent Hegel claims this can become, still has to occur in time. Hegel would maintain, however, that this interpretation itself is able to subsequently annul the semblance that it has produced.

13. "However, what moves Hegel and us in the same way (*zum Gang drängt*), is the *question* concerning the essence (*Wesen*) of being. . . . Hegel . . . responds with the fundamental thesis that the essence of beings is infinity. . . . This infinity means . . . the return of something into itself" (GA 32:113, tr. m.).

14. "But not only is a contribution (*Zutat*) by us superfluous, since concept and object, the criterion and that which is to be tested, are present in consciousness itself, but we are also spared the trouble of comparing the two and really *testing* them, so that, since what consciousness examines is

its own self, all that is left for us to do is simply to look on (*das reine Zusehen*). For consciousness is, on the one hand, consciousness of the object, and on the other, consciousness of itself" (Phen. 65/54).

15. Phen. 67/55; see: "[K]nowing is this *seeming inactivity* which merely contemplates how what is differentiated spontaneously moves in its own self and returns into its unity" (528/490, italics mine).

16. GA 68:128–29, cf. 118, 149; HW 174–77/HCE 127–31.

17. "[T]he distinction between what and how (or *essentia* and *existentia*) has basically no place in the absolute" (GA 32:71). Although Hegel treats "the essential" in the *Logic* as a category that is part of the logic of essence, I use this concept here as the common denominator for what Heidegger calls "being" and Hegel calls "concept."

18. "In contrast with Hegel's usage we use the term 'being' both for what Hegel, following Kant, calls objectivity, and also for what he presents as the truly real and calls the reality of spirit. We do not interpret *einai*, being as the Greeks understood it, from Hegel's point of view, as the objectivity of an immediately representing subjectivity that has not yet found itself, but . . . as presencing (*Anwesen*)." "Hegels Begriff der Erfahrung" (HW 142 / HCE 69, tr. m.). The being which as presence grounds Hegel's thinking thus even precedes the distinction between being and concept in the narrower sense.

19. "Fundamental ontology is always only a repetition (*Wiederholung*) of what is ancient, early. But what is ancient gets transmitted to us by repetition only if we grant it the possibility to transform itself" (GA 26:197, tr. m.).

20. "As we know, already at the beginning of the *Phenomenology* Hegel says that 'we' have to take our place in immediate knowledge, in consciousness, since otherwise the relative for itself would not move from the spot; for it is peculiar to the relative to stick to its own place." When knowing ultimately knows itself in an absolute way, the difference "between a knowledge which does not yet know itself absolutely . . . and one which knows absolvently vanishes" (GA 32:161, tr. m.). Heidegger is here referring to the following passage, among others: "To begin with, therefore, we must step into its place and be the concept that develops and fills out what is contained in the result" (Phen. 94/80). See 2.2.

21. GA 26:199. See: "[T]o conceive the problem of being radically and universally means, at the same time, to thematize beings in their totality in the light of ontology" (GA 26:200, tr. m.). See 2.1.

22. "Being determines itself logically, but such that the logical proves to be egological. We see this egological determination of being gradually

unfolding since its beginning in Descartes, until via Kant and Fichte it receives its comprehensive and explicitly absolvent justification in Hegel's *Phenomenology*" (GA 32:182–83, see HW 122 / HCE 34–35).

23. I. Görland in her interpretation of GA 32 in *Transzendenz und Selbst. Eine Phase in Heideggers Denken* restricts herself to the *Phenomenology of Spirit*. This brings her to the question: "What in the development of spirit in the *Phenomenology* could be seen as corresponding to the ontological difference between being and beings? To what extent can we here speak of something that makes it possible for beings to be grasped?" (65, cf. 71). She does not answer this question; in my view, that can only be done on the basis of the *Logic*, which in fact begins with this difference.

24. As mentioned earlier, *Hegel's Concept of Experience* (HW / HCE) shows considerable similarities to part II of GA 68. My interpretation is based mainly on the former.

25. "[N]atural consciousness . . . cannot avoid including in its representation the being of beings in general, because without the light of being it could not even lose itself *to* beings." "Hegels Begriff der Erfahrung" (HW 136 / HCE 61).

26. See Phen. 58/47; HW 120, 148 / HCE 30, 80; GA 68:80, 98.

27. GA 68:72; cf. HW 120, 126–27 / HCE 30–31, 43–44.

28. G. Gray and F. D. Wieck translate *verborgene Zeit* as "concealed area."

29. See from 1925/26: "Every philosophical problematic has something behind its back that it cannot reach itself, notwithstanding its highest transparency. For it owes this transparency precisely to the fact that it does not know of this presupposition" (GA 21:280). This theme recurs in later texts on Hegel.

30. "In spite of all our fundamental critical reservations regarding the manner of the absolvent overcoming of the finitude of transcendence, we must admire in a positive sense the unprecedented power, confidence, and fullness with which philosophizing here moves within transcendence itself" (GA 32:195, tr. m.).

11. Bound by the *Logos*: Heidegger's Later Texts on Hegel

1. GA 55:191. See: "The direction of our path, which is to cross that of Hegel, is indicated by 'Being and Time.' That means negatively: time—not *logos*" (GA 32:143; my translation).

2. "Because Hegel with *this* foundation of the 'idea' as reality of the real gathered the whole of the . . . history of philosophy hitherto in one belonging-together, and because this knowing conceived itself as absolute self-knowing in its phases and in the order of its phases, he got hold of a necessity that springs from the essence of beingness (idea) and according to which the phases of the history of ideas had to elevate itself" (B 214; cf. e.g. ID 33/43–44; "Hegel und die Griechen" (WM 256 / PM 324); "Brief über den Humanismus" (WM 166 / PM 255–56).

3. In the lecture *Time and Being* from 1962 Heidegger says on this: "Epoch . . . [means here] the fundamental characteristic of sending (*Schicken*), the . . . holding-back of itself in favor of the discernability of the gift, that is, of being with regard to the grounding of beings. The sequence of epochs in the destining of being (*Geschick von Sein*) is not accidental, nor can it be calculated as necessary. Still, what has the character of sending (*das Schickliche*) announces itself in what is destined to us (*im Geschick*), and what has the character of belonging (*das Gehörige*) announces itself in the belonging together of the epochs. The epochs overlap each other in their sequence so that the original sending of being as presence is more and more obscured" (SD 9 / TB 9, tr. m.). With regard to its history, thinking can observe "something like necessity in the sequence, something like an order and a consistency. Thus one can say that the history of being is the history of the oblivion of being escalating itself" (SD 56 / TB 52).

4. ID 40/50, tr. m. Thinking that understands the "most radical withdrawal of being" *as* the way in which being manifests itself in metaphysics, can "glance back upon the whole of Western thinking" and "recollectively preserve it as being insofar as it has been destined to us in the past (*das gewesene Geschick des Seins*)" (*Der Satz vom Grund* 150, tr. m.).

5. B 200, cf. 199; GA 68:19–21.

6. B 427, italics mine. See: "Besides, we have moved from the outset *within* one projective preconception of Being (*in einem Entwurf des Seyns*), whereas this preconception could never have been experienced *as* preconception. . . . The fact that the subjectivity of the subject finally unfolds itself into absolute subjectivity merely indicates obscurely how, since the beginning of the history of being, this projection has continuously occurred" (449). Only when this projection has been brought to light *as* projection does the possibility arise of modifying it from within.

7. In *The End of Philosophy and the Task of Thinking* from 1969 Heidegger actually heaps Hegel and Husserl together: he claims that their common "matter" is "the subjectivity of consciousness" (SD 68–69 / BW 439). See further (in addition to the mentioned texts on the *Phenomenology*) GA 68:12, 37, 51; "Hegel und die Griechen" (WM 269 / PM 333) and ID 32/42. Peperzak, who rightly regards such characterizations as problem-

atic, points out that Heidegger relies too much on the *Phenomenology of Spirit* for his conception of Hegel's philosophy. See A. Peperzak, "Einige Fragen zum Thema 'Hegel und Heidegger,'" in M.-F. Fresco et al. (eds.), *Heideggers These vom Ende der Philosophie*, Bonn 1989, see 65–66. Whereas Peperzak concludes that Heidegger's portrait of Hegel was unsuccessful (68), I would offer the defense that although some of Heidegger's assertions are careless or wrong, this should not be the final or only criterion in assessing the *intention* of his interpretation of Hegel.

8. I showed in 6.2 that the ontological difference is not Heidegger's last word. This is confirmed by GA 68: "This 'difference' . . . is foreground, is *still* metaphysical,—the ultimate clarification of the ground of metaphysics from within metaphysics itself" (GA 68:43; cf. B 465, 467). When Heidegger in *Identity and Difference* uses words like *Unter-Schied* or *Differenz* (cf. 56–57/64–65), it is difficult to decide whether these still pertain to the difference between being and beings, or rather to the movement in which being distinguishes itself from itself. But perhaps these two differences are nothing but scarcely distinguishable moments of one and the same movement.

9. "However, it is by no means thinking that, as it were, first plunges into the strife of what is at strife. The matter of thinking is that which, of a strife, is at strife with itself (*das in sich Strittige eines Streites*)" (ID 31, my translation; this passage is omitted in Stambaugh's translation, cf. 42). See concerning the strife that being itself is: "Brief über den Humanismus" (WM 167, 189 / PM 256, 272). In PM (p. 256) "die 'liebende Streit' *der* Sache selbst" is wrongly translated as "the strife *concerning* the matter itself" (italics mine).

10. See ID 58/66 and also: "However, if there is some truth in saying that being always destines itself to us (*sich uns zuschickt*) . . . then it follows that 'being' means something different from 'being' as it occurs in the different epochs of its destining (*Geschick*). Yet there reigns in the whole of what is destined to us by being something that is the same, although it cannot be represented by means of a general concept or be extracted as a guideline from the manifold course of history." *Der Satz vom Grund*, 110, tr. m.

11. ID 35, 38–39/45, 48–49. See: "Nonetheless, Hegel's definition of history as the development of 'spirit' is not untrue. . . . Absolute metaphysics, with its Marxian and Nietzschean inversions, belongs to the history of the truth of being." "Brief über den Humanismus" (WM 166 / PM 255–56).

12. ID 44/53. Heidegger here refers to the passage in which Hegel remarks in parentheses that God, if anything, would have the most undisputed right to serve as the beginning of science (see L I, 79/78). He does not

seem to notice, however, that this remark is conditional (neither, incidentally, did the translator of the *Logic*). Hegel states not far from this passage that science should begin with being as "simple immediacy" (78/77). Insofar as the absolute, the eternal or God is more than this pure being, this "more"—which indeed has to be enclosed in that beginning from the outset—can only gradually be revealed.

13. See GA 32:141f. In GA 19 from 1924/25 Heidegger states that Aristotle's first philosophy is both ontological and theological: "Theology considers beings according to what they already are in advance, i.e., according to what constitutes, in the most proper and highest sense, the presence of the world. . . . The theme of ontology is beings insofar as they are present in all their determinations. . . . Thus the theme of *theology* is *the highest and most proper presence*, and the theme of *ontology* is *that which constitutes presence as such in general*" (GA 19:222–23). Near the end of GA 32 Heidegger even calls Hegel's concept of being "onto-ego-theological" (GA 32:209; cf. KM 220–21; WM 207–8 / PM 287).

14. However, in the *Contributions* Heidegger notes concerning the difference between infinity and finitude: "Ultimately, the question concerning the occurring of Being stays outside of the strife between these sentences; and the sentence 'Being is finite' was solely meant to transitionally keep off any kind of 'idealism'" (B 268; see GA 68:15).

15. BT 286, 435. Cf. 7.2.

16. GA 68:32, cf. 14, 20, 33.

17. Herein lies the difference between Hegel's *Aufhebung* and Heidegger's *Schritt zurück*. See ID 39/49. In the *Contributions* Heidegger explicitly regards his deconstruction as a sustained "no." He considers that the current conceptions concerning the negation could never admit of the idea that the "no" might perhaps be more primordial than any "yes" (B 178–79).

18. GA 68:47; see "Brief über den Humanismus" (WM 190 / PM 273).

19. GA 68:47. We recognize here the dynamic which Heidegger in *Being and Time* describes by starting out from the phenomenon of anxiety. This analysis is also concerned with the possibility of facing up to the "not" that arises in anxiety and entails that beings no longer offer security.

20. GA 68:21–22, 26.

21. GA 68:19; see GA 32:85; B 483. In several texts Heidegger alludes to Hegel's distinction between being and nothing, although he is in fact concerned with a difference that exceeds the limits of Hegel's perspective. See KM 226; GA 24:18, 443; "Was ist Metaphysik?" (WM 17 / PM 94).

22. B 267. See: "Being occurs irradiated (*durchstrahlt*) through and through by the nothing" (B 483; cf. GA 68:29). Passages like this are very difficult to understand. We do not know what they refer to. But the same can also be said of the beginning of Hegel's *Logic*. Basic concepts such as "being" and "nothing" do, however, ground the concepts whose meaning we *can* understand. By radicalizing Hegel's concept of negativity, Heidegger tries to develop a different concept of the essential. Against this background, Dasein and history may also be understood as characterized by an insurmountable lack; we must not lose sight of the fact that this was Heidegger's initial concern.

23. "This self-externalization merely in order to appropriately obtain oneself and to have oneself *in* this obtaining and 'to be' oneself in this having" (GA 68:16).

24. GA 68:24. See Phen. 134/117. Concerning the catastrophe that turns human beings away from their own essence, see also GA 53:94.

25. "Hegel's relation to the history of philosophy is the speculative, and only as such a historical relation. The character of the movement of history is an occurrence in the sense of the dialectical process" (ID 33/44).

26. "Only this openness grants to the movement of speculative thinking the passage through what it thinks." "Das Ende der Philosophie und die Aufgabe des Denkens" (SD 71 / BW 441). See "Hegel und die Griechen" (WM 268–69, 272 / PM 332–33, 335–36).

27. As mentioned earlier, Heidegger indicates in the *Contributions* that the distinction between infinite and finite is not suitable for characterizing the movement of being. While idealism comprehends the infinite as a "closed circle," Being as occurrence of own-ing endures its counter-striving: "The occurrence of own-ing, on the other hand, stands in its "turning'! (at strife)" (B 268–69; cf. GA 68:15).

28. "Being releases itself into this nonessence (*Unwesen*) and can only allow this release to happen because it meanwhile . . . has already begun to return into its truth" (GA 55:386–87).

29. M. Haar, on the other hand, in "Structures hégéliennes dans la pensée heideggérienne de l'Histoire" regards Heidegger's "quasi fatalistic resignation to the progress of errancy" (59) merely as a reversal of Hegel's philosophy: "The Hegelian becoming of truth becomes the progressive establishment of the realm of errancy—that is, the development of nihilism" (55). This seems to me an oversimplified representation of matters. Precisely because he regards his own thinking as an authentic modification of a possibility that inauthentically modifies itself in history, Heidegger manages to avoid an antithetical position in relation to Hegel.

Bibliography

Works by Heidegger

Cited texts which are not (or not only) part of the *Gesamtausgabe*:

	–*Der Begriff der Zeit* (1924) (Tübingen: Max Niemeyer Verlag, 1989)/*The Concept of Time*, trans. W. McNeill (Cambridge: Blackwell, 1992).
BT	–*Sein und Zeit* (1927) (Tübingen: Max Niemeyer Verlag, 1927, 1986[16]) / *Being and Time*, trans. J. Stambaugh (Albany: State University of New York Press, 1996).
KM	–*Kant und das Problem der Metaphysik* (1929) (Frankfurt a. M.: Vittorio Klostermann, 1973, 1991[5] / *Kant and the Problem of Metaphysics*, trans. R. Taft (Bloomington: Indiana University Press, 5th enlarged ed., 1997).
HW	–*Holzwege* (1935–1946) (Frankfurt a. M.: Vittorio Klostermann, 1950, 1980[6]).
WM/PM	–*Wegmarken* (1919–1961) (Frankfurt a. M.: Vittorio Klostermann, 1967, 1978) / *Pathmarks*, ed. W. McNeill (Cambridge: Cambridge University Press, 1998).
EM/IM	–*Einführung in die Metaphysik* (1935) (Tübingen: Max Niemeyer Verlag, 1953, 1987[5]) / *An Introduction to Metaphysics*, trans. R. Manheim (New Haven and London: Yale University Press, 1987).
VA	–*Vorträge und Aufsätze* (Pfullingen: Neske, 1954, 1985[5]).
N I, II/N 1–4	–*Nietzsche*, 2 Bände (1936–1946) (Pfullingen: Neske, 1961) / *Nietzsche*, 4 vols., reprinted in 2 paperback vols., ed. and trans. D. F. Krell (San Francisco: Harper Collins, 1991).

US/OWL –*Unterwegs zur Sprache* (1950–1959) (Pfullingen: Neske, 1959, 1960[2]) / *On the Way to Language*, trans. P. Hertz (San Francisco: Harper Collins, 1971).

–*Was heißt Denken?* (1951/52) (Tübingen: Max Niemeyer Verlag, 1954) / *What is Called Thinking?*, trans. J. Glenn Gray (New York: Harper & Row, 1968).

–*Der Satz vom Grund* (1955/56) (Pfullingen: Neske, 1957, 1958[2]) / *The Principle of Reason*, trans. R. Lilly (Bloomington: Indiana University Press, 1991).

ID –*Identität und Differenz* (1956–1957) (Pfullingen: Neske, 1957, 1990[9]) / *Identity and Difference*, trans. J. Stambaugh (New York: Harper and Row, 1969).

SD –*Zur Sache des Denkens* (1962–1964) (Tübingen: Max Niemeyer Verlag, 1969) (partly translated as *On Time and Being*; see below).

A –"Phänomenologische Interpretationen zu Aristoteles" (1922), in F. Rodi (ed.), *Dilthey-Jahrbuch für Philosophie und Geschichte*, Bd. 6, 1989 / "Phenomenological Interpretations with Respect to Aristotle," trans. M. Baur, in *Man and World* , vol. 25, 1992.

–"Wilhelm Diltheys Forschungsarbeit und der gegenwärtige Kampf um eine historische Weltanschauung," in F. Rodi (ed.), *Dilthey-Jahrbuch für Philosophie und Geschichte*, Bd. 8, 1992/93.

–"Vorwort" / "Preface," in W. Richardson, *Heidegger: Through Phenomenology to Thought* (The Hague: Martinus Nijhoff, 1963).

Cited texts which are part of: Martin Heidegger, Gesamtausgabe (Frankfurt a. M.: Vittorio Klostermann 1975—):

GA 1 –*Frühe Schriften* (1912–1917) 1978.

GA 4 –*Erläuterungen zu Hölderlins Dichtung* (1936–1968) 1981.

GA 12 (US) –*Unterwegs zur Sprache* (1950–1959).

GA 15 –*Seminare* (1951–1973) 1986.

GA 17 –*Einführung in die phänomenologische Forschung* (1923/24) 1994.

GA 19 –*Platon: Sophistes* (1924/25) 1992 / *Plato's Sophist*, trans. R. Rojcewicz and A. Schuwer (Bloomington: Indiana University Press, 1997).

GA 20 –*Prolegomena zur Geschichte des Zeitbegriffs* (1925) 1979 / *History of the Concept of Time. Prolegomena*, trans. Th. Kisiel (Bloomington: Indiana University Press, 1985).

GA 21 –*Logik. Die Frage nach der Wahrheit* (1925/26) 1976.

GA 24 –*Die Grundprobleme der Phänomenologie* (1927) 1975 / *The Basic Problems of Phenomenology*, trans. A. Hofstadter (Bloomington: Indiana University Press, 1982).

GA 25 –*Phänomenologische Interpretation von Kant's Kritik der reinen Vernunft* (1927/28) 1977 / *Phenomenological Interpretations of Kant's Critique of Pure Reason*, trans. P. Emad and K. Maly (Bloomington: Indiana University Press, 1997).

GA 26 –*Metaphysische Anfangsgründe der Logik im Ausgang von Leibniz* (1928) 1978 / *The Metaphysical Foundations of Logic*, trans. M. Heim (Bloomington: Indiana University Press, 1984).

GA 29/30 –*Die Grundbegriffe der Metaphysik. Welt—Endlichkeit—Einsamkeit* (1929/30) 1983 / *The Fundamental Concepts of Metaphysics*, trans. W. McNeill and N. Walker (Bloomington: Indiana University Press, 1994).

GA 31 –*Vom Wesen der menschlichen Freiheit. Einleitung in die Philosophie* (1930) 1982.

GA 32 –*Hegels Phänomenologie des Geistes* (1930/31) 1980 / *Hegel's Phenomenology of Spirit*, trans. P. Emad and K. Maly (Bloomington: Indiana University Press, 1988).

GA 33 –*Aristoteles, Metaphysik IX 1–3. Von Wesen und Wirklichkeit der Kraft* (1931) 1981 / *Aristotle's Metaphysics Theta 1–3. On the Essence and Actuality of Force*, trans. W. Brogan and P. Warnek (Bloomington: Indiana University Press, 1995).

GA 39 –*Hölderlins Hymnen "Germanien" und "Der Rhein"* (1934/35) 1980, 1989[2].

GA 49 –*Die Metaphysik des Deutschen Idealismus. Zur erneuten Auslegung von Schelling.* (1941) 1991.

GA 51 –*Grundbegriffe* (1941) 1981 / *Basic Concepts*, trans. E. Aylesworth (Bloomington: Indiana University Press, 1993).

GA 52 –*Hölderlins Hymne "Andenken"* (1941/42) 1982.

GA 53 –*Hölderlins Hymne "Der Ister"* (1942) 1984 / *Hölderlin's Hymn "The Ister,"* trans. W. McNeill and J. Davis (Bloomington: Indiana University Press, 1996).

GA 54 –*Parmenides* (1942/43) 1982 / *Parmenides*, trans. A. Schuwer and R. Rojcewicz (Bloomington: Indiana University Press, 1996).

GA 55 –*Heraklit.* [1. Der Anfang des abendländischen Denkens (1943) 2. Logik. Heraklits Lehre vom Logos] (1944) 1979, 1987[2].

GA 56/57 –*Zur Bestimmung der Philosophie* [1. Die Idee der Philosophie und das Weltanschauungsproblem. 2. Phänomenologie und transzendentale Wertphilosophie. 3. Über das Wesen der Universität und des akademischen Studiums] (1919) 1987.

GA 58 –*Grundprobleme der Phänomenologie* (1919/20) 1993.

GA 59 –*Phänomenologie der Anschauung und des Ausdrucks* (1920) 1993.

GA 60 –*Phänomenologie des religiösen Lebens* [1. Einleitung in die Phänomenologie der Religion (1920/21). 2. Augustinus und der Neuplatonismus (1921). 3. Die philosophischen Grundlagen der mittelalterlichen Mystik] (1918/19) 1995.

GA 61 –*Phänomenologische Interpretationen zu Aristoteles. Einführung in die phänomenologische Forschung* (1921/22) 1985.

GA 63 –*Ontologie (Hermeneutik der Faktizität)* (1923) 1988.

GA 65 (B) –*Beiträge zur Philosophie (Vom Ereignis)* (1936–1938) 1989.

GA 66 –*Besinnung* (1938/39) 1997.

GA 68 –*Hegel* [1. Die Negativität (1938/39,1941). 2. Erläuterung der "Einleitung" zu Hegel's "Phänomenologie des Geistes"] (1942) 1993.

Letters:

–Martin Heidegger / Elisabeth Blochmann. *Briefwechsel 1918–1969*, J. W. Storck (ed.) (Marbach am Neckar: Marbacher Schriften, 1989).

–Martin Heidegger / Karl Jaspers. *Briefwechsel 1920—1963*, W. Biemel/H. Saner (eds.) (Frankfurt. a. M./München: Vittorio Klostermann/ Piper, 1990).

English translations not mentioned above:

BW –*Basic Writings*, ed. D. F. Krell (New York: Harper and Row, 1977).

EP –*The End of Philosophy*, trans. J. Stambaugh (New York: Harper and Row, 1975).

EGT –*Early Greek Thinking*, trans. D. F. Krell and F. Capuzzi (New York: Harper and Row, 1975).

HCE –*Hegel's Concept of Experience*, trans. J. G. Glay and F. D. Wieck (New York: Harper and Row, 1970).

PLT –*Poetry, Language, Thought*, trans. A. Hofstadter (New York: Harper and Row, 1971).

QCT –*The Question Concerning Technology and Other Essays*, trans. W. Lovitt (New York: Harper and Row, 1977).

TB –*On Time and Being*, trans. J. Stambaugh (New York: Harper and Row, 1972).

Works by Hegel

In most cases I refer to the following edition of Hegel's works:

G. W. F. Hegel. *Werke* (in zwanzig Bänden). Auf der Grundlage der Werke von 1832–1845 neu edierte Ausgabe, Redaktion E. Moldauer und K. M. Michel (Frankfurt a. M: Suhrkamp, 1986).

D –"Differenz des Fichteschen und Schellingschen Systems der Philosophie" (1801), in *Jenaer Schrifte 1801–1807 / The Difference between Fichte's and Schelling's Systems of Philosophy*, trans. H. S. Harris and W. Cerf (Albany: State University of New York Press, 1977).

FK –"Glauben und Wissen oder Reflexionsphilosophie der Subjektivität in der Volständigkeit ihrer Formen als Kantische, Jacobische und Fichtesche Philosophie" (1802), in *Jenaer Schrifte 1801–1807 / Faith and Knowledge*, trans. W. Cerf and H. S. Harris (Albany: State University of New York Press, 1977).

L –*Wissenschaft der Logik* (2 Bände) (1812–16) / *Hegel's Science of Logic*, trans. A. V. Miller (Amherst, NY: Prometheus Books, 1997).

Enc. I –*Enzyklopädie der philosophischen Wissenschaften im Grundrisse I* (1830) / *Hegel's Logic*, trans. W. Wallace (Oxford: Clarendon Press, 1975).

Enc. II –*Enzyklopädie der philosophischen Wissenschaften im Grundrisse II* (1830) / *Hegel's Philosophy of Nature*, ed. and trans. M. J. Petry (London/New York: Humanities Press, 1970).

Enc. III –*Enzyklopädie der philosophischen Wissenschaften im Grundrisse III* (1830) / *Hegel's Philosophy of Mind*, trans. W. Wallace (Oxford: Clarendon Press, 1975).

–*Vorlesungen über die Philosophie der Geschichte* (1822–1831) / *The Philosophy of History*, trans. J. Sibree (Buffalo: Prometheus Books, 1991).

–*Vorlesungen über die Ästhetik I* (1820–1829) / *Aesthetics, Lectures on Fine Art*, vol. I, trans. T. M. Knox (Oxford: Oxford University Press 1975).

–*Vorlesungen über die Geschichte der Philosophie I* (1805–1831) / *Lectures on the History of Philosophy*, vol. 1, trans. E. S. Haldane (Lincoln/London: University of Nebraska Press, 1995).

–*Vorlesungen über die Geschichte der Philosophie III* (1805–1831) / *Lectures on the History of Philosophy*, vol. 3, trans. E. S. Haldane and H. Simson (Lincoln/London: University of Nebraska Press, 1995).

Other cited editions:

Phen. –*Phänomenologie des Geistes* (1806), H.-F. Wessels und H. Clairmont (eds.) (Hamburg: Felix Meiner Verlag, 1988) / *Phenomenology of Spirit*, trans. A. V. Miller (Oxford: Oxford University Press, 1977).

–*Einleitung in die Geschichte der Philosophie* (1823–1827/28), Hrsg. J. Hoffmeister (Hamburg: Felix Meiner Verlag, 1966[3]) / *Introduction to the History of Philosophy*, trans. T. M. Knox and A. V. Miller (Oxford: Oxford University Press, 1985).

–*Vorlesungen über die Philosophie der Weltgeschichte Band I: Die Vernunft in der Geschichte* (1830), J. Hoffmeister (ed.) (Hamburg: Felix Meiner Verlag, 1955[5]) / *Lectures on the Philosophy of World History. Introduction: Reason in History*, trans. H. B. Nisbet (Cambridge: Cambridge University Press, 1975).

Primary texts other than those of Heidegger and Hegel are not included in the bibliography.

Works on Heidegger

Bernet, R., "Origine du temps et temps originaire chez Husserl et Heidegger," in *Revue Philosophique de Louvain*, tome 85, 1987.

———. "Die Frage nach der Ursprung der Zeit bei Husserl und Heidegger," in *Heidegger Studies*, vol. 3/4, 1987/88.

Boer, K. de, "Heidegger's *Zeit und Sein*. Een schets van de contouren," in *Tijdschrift voor Filosofie*, jrg. 56, nr. 3, 1994.

Chrétien, J.-L., "La réserve de l" être," in M. Haar (ed.), *Martin Heidegger* (Paris: Cahiers de l'Herne, 1983).

Courtine, J. F., "Les traces et le passage du Dieu dans les *Beiträge zur Philosophie* de Martin Heidegger," in *Archivio di Filosofia*, LXII, 1–3, 1994.

Dastur, F., *Heidegger et la question du temps* (Paris: PUF, 1990).

———. *Hölderlin. Tragédie et modernité* (la Versanne: Encre marine, 1992).

———. *Dire le temps. Esquisse d'une chrono-logie phénomenologique* (la Versanne: Encre marine, 1994).

———. "Heidegger et la théologie," in *Revue philosophique de Louvain*, no. 2–3, 1994.

———. "Heidegger and Derrida: On Play and Difference," in *Epoché*, vol. 3, no. 1–2, 1995.

Derrida, J., *Marges de la Philosophie* (Paris: Les éditions de minuit, 1972)/*Margins of Philosophy*, trans. A. Bass (Chicago: Chicago University Press, 1982).

———. *De l'esprit. Heidegger et la question* (Paris: Galilée, 1987) / *Of Spirit. Heidegger and the Question*, trans. G. Bennington and R. Bowlby (Chicago: University of Chicago Press, 1989).

———. "Comment ne pas parler. Dénégations," *Psyché. Inventions de l'autre* (Paris: Galilée, 1987) / "How to Avoid Speaking: Denials," trans. K. Frieden, in S. Budick and W. Iser (eds.), *Languages of the Unsayable: The Play of Negativity in Literature and Literary Theory* (New York: Columbia University Press, 1989).

———. "Différence sexuelle, différence ontologique," *Psyché. Inventions de l'autre* (Paris: Galilée, 1987) / "*Geschlecht*: Sexual Difference, Ontological Difference," trans. R. Berezdivinin, in *Research in Phenomenology* 13 (1983).

———. *Spectres de Marx* (Paris: Galilée, 1993) / *Specters of Marx*, trans. P. Kamuff (New York/London: Routledge, 1994).

Diemer, A., "Grundzüge Heidegger'schen Philosophierens," in *Zeitschrift für Philosophische Forschung* V, Meisenheim/Glan 1950.

Franck, D., *Heidegger et le problème de l'espace* (Paris: Les éditions de minuit, 1986).

Fürstenau, P., *Heidegger. Das Gefüge seines Denkens* (Frankfurt a. M.: W. Kohlhammer Verlag, 1958).

Haar, M., "*Stimmung*, époque et pensée," *La fracture de l'Histoire. Douze essais sur Heidegger* (Grenoble: Millon, 1994).

Hermann, F.-W. von, *Heidegger's "Grundprobleme der Phänomenologie." Zur "zweiten Hälfte" von "Being and Time"* (Frankfurt a. M.: Vittorio Klostermann, 1991).

———. "*Being and Time* and *The Basic Problems of Phenommenology*," in J. Sallis (ed.), *Reading Heidegger: Commemorations* (Bloomington: Indiana University Press, 1993).

IJsseling, S., Heidegger: Denken en danken, geven en zijn (Antwerpen: De Nederlandsche Boekhandel, 1964).

———. "Das Ende der Philosophie als Anfang des Denkens," in F. Volpi (ed.), *Heidegger et l'idée de la phénomenologie* (Dordrecht: Kluwer Academic Publishers, 1988).

Janicaud, D., "The 'Overcoming' of Metaphysics in the Hölderlin-lectures," in J. Sallis (ed.), *Reading Heidegger. Commemorations* (Bloomington: Indiana University Press, 1993).

Kisiel, Th., *The Genesis of Heidegger's Being and Time* (Berkeley: University of California Press, 1993).

Marx, W., *Heidegger und die Tradition. Eine problemgeschichtliche Einführung in die Grundbestimmungen des Seins* (Stuttgart: W. Kohlhammer Verlag, 1961).

McNeill, W., "Metaphysics, Fundamental Ontology, Metontology 1925–1935," in *Heidegger Studies* vol. VIII, 1992.

Müller, M., *Existenzphilosophie. Von der Metaphysik zu Metahistorik* (Freiburg/München: Verlag Karl Alber, 1949).

Oudemans, Th., "Heideggers 'logische Untersuchungen,'" in *Heidegger Studies* vol. VI, 1990.

Pöggeler, O., *Der Denkweg Martin Heideggers* (Pfullingen: Neske, 1963).

———. "Heidegger's Neubestimmung des Phänomenbegriffs," in E. W. Orth (ed.), *Neuere Entwicklungen des Phänomenbegriffs* (Freiburg/München: Verlag Karl Alber, 1980).

———. "Zeit und Sein bei Heidegger," in E. W. Orth (ed.), *Zeit und Zeitlichkeit bei Husserl und Heidegger* (Freiburg/München: Verlag Karl Alber, 1983).

———. *Neue Wege mit Heidegger* (Freiburg/München: Verlag Karl Alber, 1992).

Ricoeur, P., *Temps et récit* III (Paris: Ed. du Seuil, 1985) / *Time and Narrative*, Vol. 3, trans. K. Blamey and D. Pellauer (Chicago: Chicago University Press, 1988).

Safranski, R., *Ein Meister aus Deutschland. Heidegger und seine Zeit* (München/Wien: Hanser, 1994).

Sallis, J., *Echoes: after Heidegger* (Bloomington: Indiana University Press, 1990).

Schulz, W., "Über den philosophiegeschichtlichen Ort Martin Heidegger's," in *Philosophischen Rundschau,* 1. Heft 2/3 und 4, Tübingen 1953/1954.

Sheehan, T., "Getting to the Topic: the New Edition of Wegmarken," in J. Sallis (ed.), *Radical Phenomenology. Essays in Honor of Martin Heidegger* (Atlantic Highlands, N.J.: Humanities Press, 1978).

Taminiaux, J., "*Poiesis* et *Praxis* dans l'articulation de l'ontology fondamentale," in Volpi, F. (ed.), *Heidegger et l'idée de la phénomenologie* (Dordrecht: Kluwer Academic Publishers, 1988).

Visker, R., "Dropping: The 'Subject' of Authenticity. *Being and Time* on Disappearing Existentials and True Friendship with Being," in *Research in Phenomenology*, vol. XXIV, 1994.

Volpi, F., "Dasein comme *praxis*: L'assimilation et la radicalisation heideggerienne de la philosophie pratique d'Aristote," in Volpi, F. (ed.), *Heidegger et l'idée de la phénomenologie* (Dordrecht: Kluwer Academic Publishers, 1988).

Wood, D., *The Deconstruction of Time* (Atlantic Highlands: Humanities Press, 1989).

Zarader, M., *Heidegger et les paroles de l'origine* (Paris: Vrin, 1986).

Works on Hegel

Flay, J.C., "Hegel's *Science of Logic*: Ironies of the Understanding," in G. di Giovanni (ed.), *Essays on Hegel's Logic* (Albany: State University of New York Press, 1990).

Gadamer, H.-G., *Hegels Dialektik. Fünf hermeneutische Studien* (Tübingen: J.C.B. Mohr, 1971).

Gasché, R., *Inventions of Difference. On Jaques Derrida* (Cambridge: Harvard University Press, 1994).

Hartmann, K., "Hegel: a Non-Metaphysical View," in A. MacIntyre (ed.), *Hegel. A Collection of Critical Essays* (Notre Dame/London: University of Notre Dame Press, 1976).

Marcuse, H., *Hegels Ontologie und die Theorie der Geschichtlichkeit* (Frankfurt a. M.: Vittorio Klostermann, 1968 (1932)).

Peperzak, A., "Logic and History in Hegel's Philosophy of Spirit," in G. Movia (ed.), *La logic di Hegel e la storia della filosofia* (Rome: Cagliari 1996).

Wandschneider, D./Hösle, V., "Die Entäußerung der Idee zur Natur und ihre zeitliche Entfaltung als Geist bei Hegel," in *Hegel-Studien*, Bnd. 18, Bonn 1983.

Works on Heidegger and Hegel

Bröcker, W., *Auseinandersetzungen mit Hegel* (Frankfurt a. M.: Vittorio Klostermann, 1965).

Coreth, E., "Das fundamentalontological Problem bei Hegel und Heidegger," in *Scholastik*, vol. 29, Freiburg 1954.

Derrida, J., "Ousia et Grammè. Note sur une note de *Sein und Zeit*," *Marges de la Philosophie* (Paris: Les éditions de minuit, 1972) / "Ousia and Grammè: Note on a Note from *Being and Time*," in *Margins of Philosophy*, trans. A. Bass (Chicago: Chicago University Press, 1982).

Dubsky, I., "Über Hegels und Heideggers Begriff der Zeit," in *Hegel-Jahrbuch*, 1. Halbband, Munich, 1961.

Emad, P., "The Place of Hegel in Heidegger's Being and Time," in *Research in Phenomenology*, Vol. XIII, 1983.

Flay, J.C., "Hegel, Heidegger, Derrida: Retrieval as Reconstruction, Destruction, Deconstruction," in E. Dallery and C. Scott (eds.), *Ethics and Danger. Essays on Heidegger and Continental Thought* (Albany: State University of New York Press, 1992).

Görland, I., *Transzendenz und Selbst. Eine Phase in Heidegger's Denken*, Frankfurt a. M.: Vittorio Klostermann, 1981) (ch. IV: Transzendenz und Dialektik).

Haar, M., "Structures hégéliennes dans la pensée heideggerienne de l'Histoire," in *Revue de Métaphysique et de Morale*, 85, no. 1, 1980.

Janicaud, D., "Heidegger–Hegel: un 'dialogue' impossible?," in F. Volpi, (ed.), *Heidegger et l'idée de la phénomenologie* (Dordrecht: Kluwer Academic Press, 1988).

Kolb, D. *The Critique of Pure Modernity. Hegel, Heidegger and After* (Chicago: Chicago University Press, 1986).

Meulen, J. van der, *Heidegger und Hegel oder Widerstreit und Widerspruch* (Meisenheim/Glan: Westkulturverlag, 1953).

Peperzak, A., "Einige Fragen zum Thema Hegel und Heidegger," in M.-F. Fresco (ed.), *Heideggers These vom Ende der Philosophie* (Bonn: Bouvier, 1989).

Pöggeler, O., "Hegel und Heidegger über Negativität," in *Hegel-Studien*, Bnd. 30, Bonn 1995.

Schmidt, D., *The Ubiquity of the Finite. Hegel, Heidegger, and the Entitlements of Philosophy* (Cambridge/Massachusetts: MIT Press, 1988).

Souche-Dagues, D., "Une exégèse heideggerienne: le temps chez Hegel d'apres le §82 de *Being and Time*," in *Revue de Métaphysique et de Morale*, tome 84, no. 1, 1979.

Stambaugh, J., "Time and Dialectic in Hegel and Heidegger," in *Research in Phenomenology*, vol. 4, 1974.

Surber, J.P., "Heidegger's Critique of Hegel's Notion of Time," in *Philosophy and Phenomenological Research*, vol. 39, 1978/79.

Taminiaux, J., "D'une ontologie fondamentale à l'autre: la double lecture de Hegel," in *Lectures de l'ontologie fondamentale. Essais sur Heidegger* (Grenoble: Millon, 1989).

———. "Dialectique et différence," in *Durchblicke. Martin Heidegger zum 80. Geburtstag* (Frankfurt a. M.: Vittorio Klostermann, 1970).

———. "Finitude et Absolu. Remarques sur Hegel et Heidegger, interprètes de Kant," in *Revue philosophique de Louvain*, tome 69, 1971.

Waelhens, A. de, "Identité et différence: Heidegger et Hegel," in *Revue internationale de philosophie*, vol. 14, no. 52, 1960.

Author Index

Subject Index